Palgrave Studies in Class

CW00815809

Series Editor
David Hardwick
Vancouver, BC, Canada

Leslie Marsh
University of British Columbia
Department of Pathology and Laboratory
Medicine, Faculty of Medicine
Vancouver, BC, Canada

This series offers a forum to writers concerned that the central presuppositions of the liberal tradition have been severely corroded, neglected, or misappropriated by overly rationalistic and constructivist approaches.

The hardest-won achievement of the liberal tradition has been the wrestling of epistemic independence from overwhelming concentrations of power, monopolies and capricious zealotries. The very precondition of knowledge is the exploitation of the epistemic virtues accorded by society's *situated and distributed* manifold of spontaneous orders, the DNA of the modern civil condition.

With the confluence of interest in situated and distributed liberalism emanating from the Scottish tradition, Austrian and behavioral economics, non-Cartesian philosophy and moral psychology, the editors are soliciting proposals that speak to this multidisciplinary constituency. Sole or joint authorship submissions are welcome as are edited collections (conference proceedings excluded), broadly theoretical or topical in nature.

More information about this series at
http://www.palgrave.com/gp/series/15722

Peter Lothian Nelson • Walter E. Block

Space Capitalism

How Humans will Colonize Planets, Moons, and Asteroids

Peter Lothian Nelson
PL Nelson Engineering Inc.
Lakewood, CO, USA

Walter E. Block
Loyola University
New Orleans, LA, USA

Palgrave Studies in Classical Liberalism
ISBN 978-3-319-74650-0   ISBN 978-3-319-74651-7   (eBook)
https://doi.org/10.1007/978-3-319-74651-7

Library of Congress Control Number: 2018942893

Cover illustration: Mark Garlick/Science Photo Library/Getty Images

Printed on acid-free paper

This Palgrave Macmillan imprint is published by the registered company Springer Nature Switzerland AG
The registered company address is: Gewerbestrasse 11, 6330 Cham, Switzerland

"In *Space Capitalism: How Explorers Will Set the Pace*, my friend Walter E. Block and his colleague Peter Lothian Nelson have written a *tour de force* on why government cannot be trusted to explore space. The reason? It will steal from and oppress all those who attempt to exercise personal liberty within it—just as government has done on earth. But this research rich book is not only about space. Its subtext is an advanced lesson in the history and future of freedom; and it is a joy to read."
   —Hon. Andrew P. Napolitano, *Senior Judicial Analyst, Fox News Channel*

"Nelson and Block demonstrate, definitively, that the best way—both ethically and economically—to obtain liftoff from our planet is the free enterprise system, not government central planning. There are many writers who focus on the space race; this is the only book that makes the case for *laissez-faire* capitalism in this regard."
   —Hans Hermann Hoppe, *Senior Fellow, Ludwig von Mises Institute*

"Walter Block is known for pushing libertarian theory into uncharted territory. To say this book continues in this tradition would be an understatement. Nelson and Block show that there is no good reason to believe that even major undertakings like space exploration require government backing, and very good reason to believe they would be more successful and efficient if handled voluntarily."
   —Tom Woods, *Senior Fellow, Ludwig von Mises Institute*

"This book must be described with superlatives. It addresses everything you'll want and need to know about the conquest and colonization of space and the planets. It's well written and fascinating. I give it five stars."
   —Doug Casey, *President, Casey Research*

"Oliver Wendell Holmes, the famous Supreme Court justice, famously said that 'One's mind, once stretched by a new idea, never regains its original dimensions.' Given Holmes' equally famous bias in favor of state control of all things, I find myself wishing most fervently that Holmes himself had been stretched by *Space Capitalism*. Occasionally approaching science fiction in their ability to imagine the future, Nelson and Block nonetheless keep their analysis firmly grounded in sound economic principles. The range of the analysis is inspiring, and the quality of the insights presented here is likely to attract a big following. Fifty years from now, scholars and pundits alike may look back at this book and say, 'That was the work that showed the way.'"

—Michael C. Munger, *Professor of Economics, Duke University*

"A United States senator once said that if the government were put in charge of the Mojave desert there would soon be a sand shortage. Or as Ringo Starr once observed, 'everything government touches turns to crap.' These are not merely the impressions of a few politicians and rock stars; they are validated by generations of experience and reams of economic research. There is no reason to believe that anything is exempt from the poison of bureaucratic government interventionism, including space travel. Walter Block and Peter Nelson make a solid case for why capitalism and free markets, not government bureaucracy, should guide the future of space travel and exploration. Their book should be made into a feature film, or even a television series, as a sort of libertarian Star Trek for the next generation of 'trekkies.'"

—Thomas DiLorenzo, *Professor of Economics, Loyola University Maryland and Senior Fellow, Ludwig von Mises Institute*

"Dr. Walter Block, famous for his dictum to 'privatize everything,' is back with a typically thought-provoking look at the economics and ethics of space exploration. Starting with the premise that governments have a terrible track record of threatening human survival, Block and his co-author Peter Nelson argue for keeping them well apart from a purely private system of space travel. Extraterrestrial human activity, while technologically innovative, requires no new systems of law, economics, or ethics. In fact, Block and Nelson tell us, there really is nothing new under the sun: 'Earthbound precedents' grounded in private property and free markets provide the best way to deal with space commons and supposed public goods. This book is perfect for this era of burgeoning private space travel, and provides [Block's] most trenchant analysis of this most libertarian issue."

—Jeff Deist, *President of the Mises Institute*

Foreword

How does one become a libertarian? There are as many paths as there are advocates of the freedom philosophy. Following are two personal stories related to how your authors were able to write this book. As personal stories, they are written in the first person. The first explains how the first author (Nelson) became a libertarian while the second is illustrative of his observations that keep him there.

Here is Nelson's Story

First incident: One day in school, I became aware that my sixth-grade teacher was lying to us students. It was not just him, it was the administrative staff as well. I doubt that he understood his actions as deceitful. In hindsight, I believe he was ignorant. There was a way of doing things, and he just did them. It was his job.

That day I observed a fellow student break the rules by passing a note behind the teacher's back to another student. This pupil, Frank Adams, and this was the lie perpetuated by the teacher and staff, was regarded as not smart; he was always in trouble and received poor grades. It occurred to me that, in reality, he was quite smart. Despite my only being a sixth grader and though I did not know it at the time, subsequent events proved my assessment correct. He became a successful entrepreneur founding a business (florist) that lasted his entire career. No fool does that. After my observation, I looked around the class room and saw several others. Rick Carlos, for example, was in the same camp. In high school, he became a star football player and in adult life a restaurateur. In a town known for short-lived, failed restaurants, his Casa Carlos, outlived his career. Again, that deserves respect.

As for me, from that school day I always took what my teachers said with a pinch of salt. No authority was taken at face value; I was on my way to becoming a libertarian. When I was in high school, I concluded that the Supreme Court had erred in the case of *Engel v. Vitale*, 370 U.S. 421 (1962), commonly known as school prayer. Why? The error was in the failure to look at the entire clause which reads "Congress shall make no law respecting an establishment of religion, or prohibiting the free exercise thereof…." Okay, granted that by this clause it seems fairly obvious that a state-run school cannot compose a mandatory prayer for the students, except for a few little, bitty details. First, neither the school board nor the administrators are Congress. So, it is not so obvious after all. Further, if it is the student's belief that out-loud common prayer is essential before embarking on a serious endeavor such as an education, then the ruling inhibits the "free exercise thereof." It appeared that no ruling was possible except one: Public education is unconstitutional at least in so far as the Central government can speak to the issue.

Well—if the SCOTUS got it wrong, anybody can fall short. ALL authorities can fail. One must become his own authority. While I had not by that time reasoned out all the implications, I was even then effectively a libertarian. In a six-year period, I had intellectually moved there from believing whatever I was told. Since that time, stories that tended to challenge broadly held authority would catch my attention. It is in this spirit that the next story is worth telling.

Second incident: This story is one of many that confirms my freedom philosophy. My brother-in-law is an incredibly nice black man. He is extremely dark complexioned. The following tale dates from decades before my sister-in-law introduced him to the family. His account reinforces my commitment to libertarianism; though, I suspect he would be surprised by that. It amazes me how two people can provide such opposite meanings to the exact same sequence of events. While I cannot say that I recall his exact words from the first time he told me this, he has reviewed this passage for accuracy; so, I repeat it in first person with quotes.

I worked as a deliveryman. My route serviced an auto-parts store. Usually, I had a truck that was boldly painted with the artwork and logo of the company. One night, it was in the shop for servicing, and I had an unmarked box van. I pulled up to the loading dock of this one store and proceeded to make up the order. I had a clipboard with all the various orders. So, according to the form, I would drop off cases of merchandise. I had a key to the back door and would put the order inside. At the same time, I would pick up any returns and load them in the truck.

At this store, a neighbor lady became suspicious and called the police. Think of how it must have looked: It was a dark alley where hardly anything was visible—pitch black. I had a shiny metallic clipboard that could have looked like a gun in the dark. My back was to the alley. I had the door open, and I was loading boxes from inside the store into my van. Suddenly I heard "FREEZE!" I slowly raised my hands straight up[1] and froze. The policeman was a young guy, may have been a rookie. He looked scared and probably thought he might get shot by me at any minute. He had his gun drawn and aimed right at me. Fortunately for me, though seeing only my silhouette and the flash of my clipboard, in the split second he felt he had to act, he did not shoot.

After he had verified my identity and determined that I was on legitimate business, he explained that the neighbor had reported me to him. He said it was a good thing that I raised my hands the way that I did because "if you had turned around with your clipboard or swung your arms up, I probably would have shot you."

I love my brother-in-law and am grateful he survived this incident. The thought that my sister-in-law might never have met him is deeply disturbing. But what does this have to do with my confirmation in libertarian thinking?

The policeman, whether a rookie or not, is an "authority." We are told: "If we see something, say something." The neighbor, without knowing all or any of the facts, did just that. One must be careful because way too

---

[1] He physically demonstrated how he raised his hands over his head in a manner resembling a pantograph on an electric train.

often the police will become afraid and shoot first and ask questions later. Then they will get off scot-free because they were just acting according to their training. Knowing that the death of an innocent may occur, my mantra is never call constabulary forces until you know the facts, and even then, be careful.

This policeman ended up not shooting my now brother-in-law, but was ready to pull the trigger nevertheless. If an innocent suspect raises his hands one way (straight up) he will live. If he raises them in any other way, he gets killed. I find these options unacceptable. Even though this particular case happened to turn out alright, once again, I find abhorrent the authorities acting outside the range of tolerable conduct in this way.

Here Is Block's Story

How I became a libertarian by Walter E. Block

Born in New York City of Jewish parents, and living in a half-Jewish neighborhood, I became a left liberal pretty much through osmosis. My views were just about the same as those of Bernie Sanders (who was a fellow track team member of mine at Madison High School; we ran in the same events (half mile and up); we lived in the same quadrant away from school, so would sometimes walk back and forth together from one place to the other; he was one of the best runners in the entire city; I was mediocre; we overlapped for four years at Madison, and one year at Brooklyn College).

I was not very political, but when Ayn Rand came to lecture at Brooklyn College, I was among many undergraduates who met her there to boo and hiss at her, since she favored free enterprise, and all rational and moral people knew this would be the death knell for the poor (these were before the days when free market speakers were physically prevented from lecturing at institutions of "higher learning"). I hadn't spewed enough venom during her lecture; I wanted to further demonstrate my hatred of her and her teachings. So, at the conclusion of her talk when the Ayn Rand study group that had invited her to campus announced there would now a luncheon in her honor, and all audience members were invited to attend even if they did not agree with her, I took them up on their offer.

When I arrived at the lunch room, I saw a long table, with maybe 50 people on each side. Miss Rand was sitting at the head of it, surrounded by such luminaries as Nathaniel Brandon, Leonard Piekoff, Alan Greenspan, and other members of her "senior collective." I was relegated to the foot of the table, whereupon I turned to my neighbor and averred that socialism was the way to go, or something to that effect, and capitalism must be replaced with this system. He replied that he didn't know all that much about the subject, but that the people who did were located at the other end of the table. So, chutspanick (assertive fellow) that I was (still am), I marched over there, stuck my head between Ayn's and Nathan's, and challenged either or both of them to a debate on socialism versus capitalism. (I was then a senior at Brooklyn College, 22 years old; Brandon maybe 30–35, and Rand some 25 years older than that). Brandon was exceedingly polite to me. He said he would come to the other end of the table to discuss this matter with me, there being no more room for anyone else at this end, if I agreed to two provisos. First, I had to promise to keep our debate going until we "settled matters" and not allow the conversation to lapse after this one session. And second, I would read two books (*Atlas Shrugged* by Ayn Rand and *Economics in One Lesson* by Henry Hazlitt). I promised, and we moved to the other end of the table to begin our first interaction.

I duly read the two books. I simply could not put down *Atlas*. Although some 1100 pages, I read it in one weekend. I was equally blown over by the Hazlitt book. I visited Branden and Rand several times in their apartments in Manhattan in the coming weeks, and, viola, I became a libertarian of the Objectivist variety (I was pretty much interested, only, in their views on economics and liberty; all else, epistemology, metaphysics, aesthetics, etc., left me cold). Subsequently, I attended Nathaniel Brandon Institute (NBI) lectures over the next few months. During the question and answer period after the lectures, Ayn Rand was very welcoming to "soft ball" queries such as: "Miss Rand, on page 436 of Atlas you said this… Could you please elaborate." But, if you asked anything more challenging such as "Miss Rand, on page 436 of Atlas you said this… and on page 759 you said that… and I see a contradiction between your two statements," she would fly into a rage. She would literally kick you out of the lecture hall, and announce she was deleting you from her mailing list.

Needless to say, I was more than just a bit put off by such goings on. I was a supporter of *laissez-faire* capitalism by then, but not a member of what I was now regarding as her cult. So, for months I would stay away. But these were the only people I then knew who supported economic freedom, so I would later return, only to be again perturbed by her cultish behavior, and leave once again. Like a schizophrenic, I adopted an approach-retreat pattern with the Randroids.

When I was a second year student in the Ph.D. program at Columbia University, Larry Moss, a year behind me, approached me based on my comments in a class we were both taking, and said I had to meet this Murray Rothbard, who was an anarchist. "An anarchist," I said? "He's a maniac. I don't want to meet him." (I was still a Randian limited government supporter, or a minarchist, and like her, adamantly favored a very limited state.) I resisted Larry's repeated invitations for several months. But, finally, he and his then room-mate, Jerry Woloz, "ganged up" on me and I agreed to meet the ogre.

Before doing so, I read a bit of his work. I pictured a 6'4" muscle-bound boxer-athlete, holding a gun in one hand and a machete in the other, with a snarl on his face. What I got, instead, was pretty much the very opposite. He was a short rotund man with a wild sense of humor who kept me in stiches for hours on end; a real "sweetie pie," his term of endearment for those he liked. It took him about 10 minutes to rescue me from my minarchist ways. He used Henry Hazlitt type arguments on me, with which I had become very familiar. Why wouldn't competition and the profit and loss system work not only for pedestrian goods and services such as post offices, shoes, and cars, but also for courts, police, and armies? He knocked my socks off with these challenges, and for the first time in my life, I became a full libertarian, anarcho-capitalist variety. I hope and trust that Murray will be proud of my contribution to this book which, like pretty much all of my intellectual output, I owe to his tutelage, his mentoring and his love of liberty and sound economics.

Loyola University   Walter E. Block
New Orleans, LA, USA

Contents

About the Authors

Walter E. Block is Harold E. Wirth Endowed Chair and Professor of Economics, College of Business, Loyola University New Orleans, and senior fellow at the Mises Institute. He earned his PhD in economics at Columbia University in 1972. He has taught at Rutgers, SUNY Stony Brook, Baruch CUNY, Holy Cross, and the University of Central Arkansas. He is the author of more than 500 refereed articles in professional journals, two dozen books, and thousands of op eds. He lectures widely on college campuses, delivers seminars around the world, and appears regularly on television and radio shows. He is the Schlarbaum Laureate, Mises Institute (2011), has won the Loyola University Research Award (2005, 2008), the Mises Institute's Rothbard Medal of Freedom (2005), and the Dux Academicus award, Loyola University (2007).

Peter Lothian Nelson has master's degrees in engineering and divinity. He has over 40 years of experience in civil engineering and is the retired president of PL Nelson Engineering Inc. He is, along with Walter Block, the co-author of *Water Capitalism: The Case for Privatizing Oceans, Rivers, Lakes, and Aquifers.* He has served as an expert witness and has written reports regarding the standard of care for professional engineering on two dozen cases including depositions by dozens of attorneys and responding to rebuttal reports. He has presented several papers at engineering symposia and was granted the outstanding project awards for his work on the Florida

Interceptor Storm Sewer by the American Public Works Association and Willow Farm Park by the Colorado chapter of the American Society of Landscape Architects. He frequently offers presentations regarding theology to groups ranging in size from half a dozen to several hundred.

List of Tables

1

Privatize Space Travel!

We argue two things in this book. One, space travel is vital and beneficial to human well-being. Two, it should be done privately; the state should be kept as far from this initiative as possible, ideally, totally.[1] These two principles inspire this book. We believe that an overwhelming majority of citizens will wonder if we have gone completely bonkers. Our critics will tend to dismiss both propositions out of hand. So, what persuades us to favor these themes? Our main motivation for the first is love for human beings.[2]

---

[1] This aphorism applies to all initiatives. The conflict is private vs. bureaucratic management. For a detailed account of the shortcomings of the latter refer to von Mises (1944). While all endeavors (even such as caring for the disabled) benefit from private administration this becomes ever more important where great opportunities and challenges are at stake.

[2] Statists will think us "Out of touch" and even call us sickos and weirdos. We do not care. Our love for humanity is so great that we are willing to bear the "slings and arrows" (Hamlet, Act III, Scene 1) of critiques of this variety. No matter what the opposition, we cleave to our desire to leave the human race in as good a position as we can, after our departure from it. Most of our best friends are human beings. All of our family members are of this species. We generalize our love for them to the entire human race. We would hate to see them or it disappear. That would be the worst possible disaster imaginable in our view. Space colonization is an insurance policy against that horrid scenario.

© The Author(s) 2018
P. L. Nelson, W. E. Block, *Space Capitalism*, Palgrave Studies in Classical Liberalism,
https://doi.org/10.1007/978-3-319-74651-7_1

Why space—it is so … well, "OUT THERE." As *Star Trek* would have it, explorers are driven "to go where no man[3] has gone before." That, alone, suffices. Then, there are the more practical considerations. Moving into space will be profitable. We will learn new technologies which will endow the remaining earthlings with electrifying spillover advantages. For example, will near or actual weightlessness cure diseases? Will resources be discovered in the heavenly bodies (apart from the Moon's green cheese) that will open new horizons?

We find our second theme, that efforts in this regard be undertaken by market participants, not crony capitalists supported via compulsory tax payments, similarly compelling. Real entrepreneurs throw the dice with their own funds, or those voluntarily entrusted to them. They coerce no one. Why this limitation? Would not our first goal, space exploration, be better served by government itself, given its taxing power or, at the very least, via a partnership between the state and private interests? Absolutely not! Says Rothbard (2015):

> The myth has arisen that government research is made necessary by our technological age, because only planned, directed, large-scale 'team' research can produce important inventions or develop them properly. The day of the individual or small-scale inventor is supposedly over and done with. And the strong inference is that government, as potentially the 'largest-scale' operator, must play a leading role in even non-military

---

[3] Note the use of this word, "man." It is politically incorrect, but we do not buy into the cultural Marxist requirement that "inclusive" language be used, such as "person." This word, too, would fall victim to this crazed desire to alter the language, since its last syllable is "son," which would never do in that realm. Must we resort, instead, to "perdaughter?" This inanity has spread far and wide. Many of the newer biblical translations use "inclusive terminology." Little or no notice is given to the fact that the original 2000 plus year-old manuscripts use masculine forms. Yet the words are taken to be "inclusive" while similar English is not. "When Paul wrote that 'a man (*anthrôpos*) is justified by faith' (Rom. 3:28), the Greek word *anthrôpos* does not mean 'a man'; it means 'a person.'" So say Strauss and Wegener (2000). That may be, yet, "Ανθρωποσ" in Greek is a first person, *masculine*, singular form. As that very same article demonstrates, the English word "man" also has a "generic" meaning. To illustrate what they are saying, when Jefferson wrote that "All men are created equal," he did not refer to only males. No, he meant to include all human beings. The point is not to make a more accurate or even a more "inclusive" translation. No, politically correct versions are intended solely to score political points and to improperly, *ex post facto*, impose them on writers from two millennia in the past. We have here yet another reason to escape from this "third rock from the sun" of ours: to leave this particular insanity behind. Throughout, this book uses Jeffersonian not Dalyian (after Mary Daly) style inclusiveness.

scientific research. This common myth has been completely exploded by the researches of John Jewkes, David Sawers, and Richard Stillerman in their highly important recent work.[4]

Pretty much anything touched by government comes with fatal flaws starting with corruption and compulsion. Eliminating state involvement in space frees people rather than limits them. Besides, the ruling powers notoriously mismanage all enterprises.[5] It becomes a self-fulfilling prophecy, because that very incompetence makes the venture appear far more expensive than it really needs to be.

The record of "picking winners" on the part of governing establishments[6] does not engender much confidence in government's capacity to promote this goal. Nor is "contracting out" to private interests likely to provide efficiency in this context. If government cannot do the job itself, there is no reason to believe it will be effective in choosing and funding collaborators. In addition, we believe that even if the state could be effective in promoting such tasks, it would still be improper for it to do so, since its funds are mulcted, unwillingly, from their rightful owners, the long-suffering taxpayers (Rothbard, M. 1998).

In addition to the two primary themes, in a third we note that our species, while admirable in many ways such as the need to explore, is also often quite silly and even more destructive. We have developed weapons of mass destruction, and one despicable government apparatus, venerated by many worldwide, even used them, twice, in 1945.[7] But we do not

---

[4] Rothbard is referring to *The Sources of Invention*, St. Martin's Press, 1959. It discusses such wild inventions as the helicopter and polyethylene. In it Jewkes et al. discuss the influence and relationships of research organizations on and to recent inventions.

[5] This applies even to such mundane activities as collecting refuse (Savas, E. 1979), delivering mail (Adie, D. 1988) and fighting fires (Ahlbrandt, R. 1973).

[6] A recent case in point is Solyndra. But the record is replete with numerous failures; for a long list of such unrequited bailouts, see Bailout Tracker 2015; Kiel, P. 2012; Sprague, I. 2000.

[7] For the view that this had little or nothing to do with ending World War II, but rather was the opening salvo in the Cold War, see Alperovitz, G. (1994, 1996). For the opinion that U.S. entry into World War II in Europe was unnecessary in the first place because prior to December 7, 1941 Germany was already guaranteed to lose the war, see Maybury, R. and Williams, J. (2003). For the perspective that had the United States not entered World War I, there would not have been any World War II, see Barnes, H. 1982, 2004; Buchanan, P. 2014; Fay, S. 1967; Ferguson, N. 2000; Fleming, T. 2004; Keynes, J. 1920; Nock, A. 2011; Radosh, R. and Rothbard 1972; Rothbard, M. 1972, 1980, 1989; Stockman, D. 2014; Tooley, T. 2014.

need to resort to such high technology to murder our fellow creatures. We are fully capable of doing so on a massive scale, without such sophistication. Estimates are that governments have done away with almost 200 million of their citizens in the twentieth century, and this is apart from wars[8] and traffic fatalities on public highways.[9]

In support of this contention, much in the following pages details the violent nature and destructive results of states. The same applies to would-be governments like ISIS and others that go around shooting police officers. In recent days and months, the evening news (of whichever source the reader consults) has been filled with graphical depictions of bombings and shootings.[10] These are being done by those who do not so much disapprove of government per-se but who do not like *this* state and wish to substitute their own. In addition to being anarchists, we do not approve of would-be states either. As Shaw (1903) said: "He who slays a king and he who dies for him are alike idolaters." We concur completely that one who ambushes or kills or purposely injures policemen simply lowers himself to the level of these idolaters. To be libertarian requires adoption of the Non-Aggression Principle. That in turn does not admit of murder, assault, or aggression in any way whatsoever against even those of whom we most strongly disapprove.

How will space travel help alleviate mankind's tendency to kill us? Simple. If we can establish colonies starting with the Moon, Venus, and Mars, and then later, as improved technology will permit, on other planets and moons,[11] the odds will improve that if people blow up any one home of the human race, there will still be others, so that our species will still "live long and prosper."

---

[8] Block, W. 2006; Branfman, F. 2013; Conquest, R. 1986, 1990; Courtois, S. et al. 1999; DiLorenzo, T. 2006; Rummel, R. 1992, 1994, 1997.

[9] For which we also hold responsible statists acting through governments (Block, W. 2009).

[10] Recent examples include such sickening happenings as the mass shooting of police officers in Dallas, TX, the shooting up of Istanbul Airport in Turkey, the Paris attacks in France, and the riots in Milwaukee, WI.

[11] And then, in other solar systems. While time-consuming, expensive, and risky, travel to the binary (possibly trinary) Alpha Centauri (Proper name: Rigel Kentaurius) system (NASA n.d.-a), Barnard's Star (Dolan, C. 1989), or Wolf 359 (Dolan, C. 1989) would probably be possible with existing or readily anticipated technology. The spaceship would have to be, in effect, a self-sustaining world that could keep people alive for the duration. Of particular interest is Proxima Centauri, a red dwarf which appears to orbit the central Alpha Centauri couple. At 4.22 light years, it is now near our side of the solar system and approaching. Round trips would be in the order of a century, maybe less.

There are of course other ways of raising the odds that our fellow creatures will survive their base instincts. There is psychology; perhaps we can eradicate our malevolent impulses through talk therapy. There is biology; maybe human beings can be engineered so that we are not so given to mass murder. Who knows? Maybe we can hypnotize ourselves so that we are more likely to continue to live. But those are topics for other books. The present one assumes away these elegant possibilities for changing the human element.[12]

We probe, instead, the inelegant scenario of leaving members of our species exactly as they are in terms of viciousness, and instead keeping us apart from each other,[13] so that at least some branch of *homo sapiens* can continue forever.[14] This is but one result that could naturally follow from space exploration. The point is, we desperately want to save (remnants?) of the human race, but, we impose upon ourselves one essential constraint: we obligate ourselves to the non-aggression principle (NAP).[15] Why? Because in our view, violations of the rights of men constitute a significant danger justifying departure from Earth in the first place.[16]

Challenges

As long as we limit travel to the inner planets of the solar system, technical challenges are not too severe. However, when we go beyond them, especially past Pluto and Neptune, they become categorically daunting. The story of space is one of ever-expanding orbits. On Earth a person, the

---

[12] To recreate mankind, as each of the forgoing programs would do, in one's own image is the unfortunate first impulse of tyrants.

[13] Far apart: fences (or the great distances of space) make good neighbors.

[14] This may sound like the pessimism that leads to statism. In fact, we are optimistic regarding the prognosis of the race. Humans are resilient. No matter how destructive governments act, individuals overcome and prosper. Hiroshima, a shining example and the first city to be nuked back to the stone age, is now a prosperous and vibrant community after only 72 years and has been for some time.

[15] See on this Bergland, D. 1986; Block, W. 2008; Hoppe, H. 1993; Huebert, J. 2010; Narveson, J. 1988; Nozick, R. 1974; Rockwell, L. 2014; Rothbard, M. 1973, 1978; Woods, T. 2013; Woolridge, W. 1970.

[16] Here, we are talking about the salutary effects of exploration. Perhaps more important are the adventurous motivations discussed elsewhere in our book.

experiencer, is faced with a floor, or ground, walls, or edges, and a ceiling or forest canopy. This book attempts to break through those limits. But then immediately we arrive at a further one: gravity.

Actual physical restrictions abound. Out there, air does not exist, nor does pressure, nor atmosphere, nor reflections, nor, even if one is far enough away from the Sun, light. In the event, even though gravity pulls a would-be traveler towards Earth, in the outer limits, this force is much less powerful than that to which we are accustomed. Wherever one is in outer space, he would feel like he was falling, unless there was artificial gravity. Until he developed his "space legs," he would feel constantly sick to his stomach and disoriented.

Thus, the initial impression of the extreme freedom away from planetary or solar gravitation may be somewhat less liberating than it appears at first glance. On Earth, should one wish to go to a particular place, he looks out over the plain and starts walking in that direction. No problem. When flying through the air or diving under the water, one again moves in the direction he desires. Piece of cake.

In space, gravity and colossal distances change all that. Because of gravitational effects, to get where one wants to visit, one first must travel an orbital trajectory. Is the object of travel a long distance away? Then speed is of the essence: that is to say hyper-speed. The speed of light, or even approaching that rapidity, is an unavoidable limitation due to physical principles stemming from relativity theory.[17] For all practical purposes, these limits are severe. Even the speed of light itself is nowhere near fast enough if one wants to travel to distant stars in a lifetime. Therefore, contemplation of life on board ships built for multi-generational voyages is a given.

This book advocates private exploration and ownership of planets and moons and spaceships as well as development. First things first, the book starts with things with which people have familiarity. The concept of first in use, first in right is the mantra. Homesteading is the name for it. But how does this process apply to space?

---

[17] For more on this see Hawking, S. 1996. His book is written for the layman and is easy to follow.

We would not want our readers, at this point, to throw up their arms and give up the possibility of extra-terrestrial settlement. All this talk of light speed is certainly beyond human ability for the foreseeable future. We may well have to wait for the next Einstein, or a few of them in each generation, to overcome these problems,[18] if, that is, it is even physically possible to do so. On pragmatic grounds, we need to walk before we can run. Setting up colonies on the Moon or Mars is not beyond present abilities, or at least those that can be employed in the next decade or two. And, as for reaching the stars, this, too, can be accomplished even in the absence of such astronomical speeds. All we would need is large space-ships and a lot of patience. In two or three generations,[19] at far less than "warp speed" other solar systems can be attained.[20] And, in the meantime, these spaceships will constitute a refuge for human beings, if governments blow up the Earth as the tyrants of this Earth seem intent to do.

In succeeding chapters, man's inhumanity, the advantages of private launches, privatization, and ownership concepts will be discussed in more detail. The scientific limitations implied in the physics of orbits, the properties of extra-terrestrial objects, speed and acceleration limitations, etc. will be taken seriously. In other words, nothing herein will rely on science fiction concepts such as "warp speed"[21]; rather, market support of basic research will be discussed.

Then the human, economic, and physical principles will be applied to the Moon, Mars, the inner planets of the Solar System, the gaseous planets and their moons, asteroids, comets, and other non-planetary objects.

---

[18] But already implications suggest themselves. We will be more likely to save mankind in this manner if charitable and other discretionary money is directed less towards addressing knowledge gaps between various ethnic groups, and helping mentally handicapped people, and more on the intellectually gifted. As advocates of the free enterprise system we urge no such policy on the part of government. Our recommendation here is a complete separation of the state and education. But, still, as a purely cause and effect relationship, more emphasis on child geniuses and less on others, would be logically implied.

[19] Well, maybe, several hundred generations for distant stars.

[20] On the issue of earth-like planets in other solar systems see Jet Propulsion Laboratory 2015; Mother Nature Network 2015; Zolfagharifard, E. 2015; Knapp, A. 2014; Kavli Foundation n.d.

[21] While impossible in terms of our current knowledge, we do not mean to say that trans-light speed is forever beyond the possible. However, before it can become possible, it will take a revolutionary scientific breakthrough in the order of a new theory, like relativity was.

Interstellar travel and extra-terrestrial life including the "prime directive" or the rights of intelligent beings will be discussed under Space Law. All exploration is fraught with risks, many of which seem insuperable prior to travel.[22] The entrepreneurs of our planet have the imagination and ingenuity to figure out what the real risks are and how to mitigate them. Certainly, no book such as this one can pass up the chance to have fun with NASA and other government boondoggles.

References

Adie, Douglas K. 1988. *Monopoly Mail: Privatizing the United States Postal Service*. New Brunswick, NJ: Transaction.

Ahlbrandt, Roger. 1973. Efficiency in the Provision of Fire Services. *Public Choice* 16 (Fall): 1–15.

Alperovitz, Gar. 1994. *Atomic Diplomacy: Hiroshima and Potsdam*. Pluto Press.

———. 1996. *The Decision to Use the Atomic Bomb*. Vintage.

Bailout Tracker. 2015. Bailout Recipients. July 13. https://projects.propublica.org/bailout/list.

Barnes, Harry Elmer, ed. 1982. *Perpetual War for Perpetual Peace*. Institute for Historical Review.

———. 2004. *The Genesis of the World War an Introduction to the Problem of War Guilt*. Kessinger Publishing.

Bergland, David. 1986. *Libertarianism in One Lesson*. Costa Mesa, CA: Orpheus Publications.

Block, Walter E. 2006. Deaths by Government: Another Missing Chapter. November 27. https://www.lewrockwell.com/2006/11/walter-e-block/deaths-by-governmentanothermissingchapter/. Accessed 29 June 2015.

———. 2008. Homesteading, Ad Coelum, Owning Views and Forestalling. *The Social Sciences* 3 (2): 96–103. http://www.medwelljournals.com/fulltext/TSS/2008/96-103.pdf; http://medwelljournals.com/new/5/archivedetails.php?id=5&jid=TSS&theme=5&issueno=12. Accessed 20 Apr 2016.

---

[22] *Ex-ante*, risks can only be surmised. One probable peril is the collision with natural space debris such as asteroids too small to be detected yet large enough to destroy a spaceship. For interstellar travel, such an obstacle could be an earth-sized object which would be invisible when the nearest light source is, say, 2 light years (1×10^{13}, or 10 trillion miles) away. That is almost beginning to sound like the size of the national debt.

————. 2009. *The Privatization of Roads and Highways: Human and Economic Factors*. Auburn, AL: The Mises Institute. http://www.amazon.com/Privatization-Roads-And-Highways-Factors/dp/1279887303/; http://mises.org/books/roads_web.pdf; http://mises.org/daily/3416. Accessed 23 Aug 2016.

Branfman, Fred. 2013. World's Most Evil and Lawless Institution? The Executive Branch of the U.S. Government. *Alternet*. June 26. http://www.alternet.org/investigations/executive-branch-evil-and-lawless?paging=off.

Buchanan, Patrick J. 2014. Behind the Sinking of the Lusitania. September 3. http://www.lewrockwell.com/2014/09/patrick-j-buchanan/wilson-lied-us-into-wwi/.

Conquest, Robert. 1986. *The Harvest of Sorrow*. New York: Oxford University Press.

————. 1990. *The Great Terror*. Edmonton, Alberta: Edmonton University Press.

Courtois, Stephane, Nicolas Werth, Jean-Louis Panne, Andrzej Paczkowski, Karel Bartosek, and Jean Louis Margolin. 1999. *The Black Book of Communism: Crimes, Terror, Repression*. Trans. from French by Jonathan Murphy, and Mark Kramer. Cambridge, MA: Harvard University Press.

DiLorenzo, Thomas. 2006. Death by Government: The Missing Chapter. November 22. http://www.lewrockwell.com/dilorenzo/dilorenzo114.html. Accessed 11 July 2015.

Dolan, Chris. 1989. The Closest Star to the Earth, The Nearest Stars, as Seen from the Earth. http://www.astro.wisc.edu/~dolan/constellations/extra/nearest.html. Accessed 8 July 2015.

Fay, Sidney Bradshaw. 1967. *The Origins of the World War*. The Free Press.

Ferguson, Niall. 2000. *The Pity of War: Explaining World War I*. New York: Basic Books.

Fleming, Thomas. 2004. *The Illusion Of Victory: Americans in World War I*. New York: Basic Books.

Hawking, Stephen. 1996. *A Brief History of Time*. New York: Bantam Books Trade Paperbacks.

Hoppe, Hans-Hermann. 1993. *The Economics and Thics of Private Property. Studies in Political Economy and Philosophy*. Boston: Kluwer Academic Publishers.

Huebert, Jacob. 2010. *Libertarianism Today*. Santa Barbara, CA: Praeger.

Jet Propulsion Laboratory, California Institute of Technology. 2015. Finding Another Earth. http://planetquest.jpl.nasa.gov/news/207.

Kavli Foundation. n.d. Coming Soon—Earth-Like Planets in Other Solar Systems. http://www.kavlifoundation.org/science-spotlights/coming-soon-earth-planets-other-solar-systems#.VcbenbnbKic.

Keynes, John Maynard. 1920. *The Economic Consequences of the Peace*. New York: Harcourt Brace. http://www.gutenberg.org/ebooks/15776.

Kiel, Paul. 2012. Biggest Financial Crisis Bailout Fails. September 6. http://www.huffingtonpost.com/2012/09/06/financial-bailout-wallstreet_n_1861853.html.

Knapp, Alex. 2014. NASA Has Discovered the First Potentially Habitable Earth-Sized Planet. April 17. http://www.forbes.com/sites/alexknapp/2014/04/17/nasa-has-discovered-the-first-potentially-habitable-earth-sized-planet/.

Maybury, Richard, and Jane A. Williams. 2003. *World War II: The Rest of the Story and How It Affects You Today* (Revised). October 1. Bluestocking Press.

Mother Nature Network. 2015. 10 NASA Images of Planets Like Earth. http://www.mnn.com/earth-matters/space/photos/10-nasa-images-of-planets-like-earth/a-new-earth.

Narveson, Jan. 1988. *The Libertarian Idea*. Philadelphia: Temple University Press.

NASA. n.d.-a. National Space and Aeronautics Administration. The Nearest Star. https://heasarc.gsfc.nasa.gov/docs/cosmic/nearest_star_info.html. Accessed 8 July 2015.

Nock, Albert Jay. 2011. *The Myth of a Guilty Nation*. Auburn, AL: The Mises Institute.

Nozick, Robert. 1974. *Anarchy, State and Utopia*. New York: Basic Books.

Radosh, Ronald, and Murray N. Rothbard, eds. 1972. *A New History of Leviathan*. New York: E. P. Dutton.

Rockwell, Jr., Llewellyn H. 2014. What Libertarianism Is, and Isn't. March 31. http://www.lewrockwell.com/2014/03/lew-rockwell/what-libertarianism-is-and-isnt/. Accessed 29 June 2016.

Rothbard, Murray. 2015. *Science Technology, & Government*. Ludwig von Mises Institute. July 9.

Rothbard, Murray N. 1972. War Collectivism in World War I. In *A New History of Leviathan*, ed. R. Radosh and M.N. Rothbard, 66–110. New York: E. P. Dutton.

———. 1973. *For a New Liberty*. New York: Macmillan. http://mises.org/rothbard/newlibertywhole.asp. Accessed 23 Aug 2016.

———. 1980. Review of *World War I and the Origins of Civil Liberties in the United States*, by P. Murphy. *Inquiry* 9: 22–24.

———. 1989. World War I as Fulfillment: Power and the Intellectuals. *The Journal of Libertarian Studies* 9 (1): 81–125. http://mises.org/journals/

jls/9_1/9_1_5.pdf. Reprinted in *The Costs of War*, by J.V. Denson (ed.). New Brunswick, NJ: Transaction Publishers, 1998, pp. 203–254. Also Appears in 2nd Edition, 1999.

———. 1998 [1982]. Isaiah Berlin on Negative Freedom. In *The Ethics of Liberty*, chapter 27, 215–218. New York: New York University Press. http://www.mises.org/rothbard/ethics/ethics.asp. Accessed 20 Apr 2016.

Rummel, R.J. 1992. *Democide: Nazi Genocide and Mass Murder*. Rutgers, NJ: Transaction Publisher.

———. 1994. *Death by Government*. New Brunswick, NJ: Transaction.

———. 1997. *Statistics on Democide. Center on National Security and Law*. Charlottesville, VA: University of Virginia.

Savas, E.S. 1979. Refuse Collection: A Critical Review of the Evidence. *Journal of Urban Analysis*. 6: 1–13.

Shaw, George Bernard. 1903. *Man and Superman*. "The Revolutionist's Handbook"—Maxims for Revolutionists—Idolatry.

Sprague, Irving H. 2000. Bailout: An Insider's Account of Bank Failures and Rescues. Beard Books. http://www.amazon.com/Bailout-Insiders-Account-Failures-Rescues/dp/1587980177.

Stockman, David, 2014. If the U.S. Had Stayed Out of WWI, There Would Have Been No Hitler or Stalin. July 13. http://libertycrier.com/u-s-stayed-wwi-hitler-stalin-david-stockman/#SgprliBV9jCVSFcb.99; http://libertycrier.com/u-s-stayed-wwi-hitler-stalin-david-stockman/?utm_source=feedburner&utm_medium=feed&utm_campaign=Feed%3A+LibertyCrier+%28Liberty+Crier%29.

Strauss, Mark L., and David Wegener. 2000. The Inclusive Language Debate, How Should The Bible Be Translated Today? Statement DI401. *Christian Research Journal* 22 (4).

Tooley, T. Hunt. 2014. World War I in Our Minds: A Historical View. October 23. https://www.lewrockwell.com/2014/10/t-hunt-tooley/the-evil-of-wwi/.

Von Mises, Ludwig. 1944. *Bureaucracy*. New Haven: Yale University Press.

Woods, Tom. 2013. The Question Libertarians Just Can't Answer. June 5. http://lewrockwell.com/woods/woods237.html. Accessed 29 June 2016.

Woolridge, William C. 1970. *Uncle Sam the Monopoly Man*. New Rochelle, NY: Arlington House.

Zolfagharifard, Ellie. 2015. Two Earth-like Planets Could Be Hiding Close to Our Solar System—And Scientists Say There May Be Watery Worlds Nearby. March 27. http://www.dailymail.co.uk/sciencetech/article-3015308/Two-Earth-like-planets-hiding-close-solar-scientists-say-watery-worlds-nearby.html.

2

Man's Inhumanity to Man

A primary reason for proposing space exploration stems from man's inhumanity to man and our love for human beings.[1] We greatly fear nuclear, chemical, or biological warfare, where all people on the planet are wiped out.[2] If some of our fellow creatures can locate to other planets, such as Mars, or the Moon, then at least a few of our relations will

---

[1] We contend that the reason the state should not be involved in space exploration is because it has demonstrated a tendency toward oppression and needs to be restrained, not granted a wider field of action. In this chapter, we explore that dispute in detail with many real-world examples.

[2] We exaggerate, but only slightly; we are more optimistic than we sound here. Humans are resilient. As evil as states are, it is unlikely, nay impossible, for them to wipe out humanity. During World War II, Dresden and Hamburg suffered urban fire storms which left those towns devastated. People experienced a return to Paleolithic conditions. Earlier, London too found itself subjected to intense damage. Today, all of those communities are vibrant, prosperous cities. Additionally, the German government adopted a policy of extermination intended "wipe out" the entire Jewish population of Europe. It did much damage and killed millions. It did not, however, succeed in its aim. More likely is a worst-case scenario of unlimited modern war as depicted in such dystopian novels as Veronica Roth's *Divergent* series. These describe a landscape of utter and "complete" devastation but one where people survive. Notice too that in both fiction and reality, these types of tragedies only arise from the deprivations of government activity. Is it any wonder that we decry the involvement of would be overseers in space ventures?

© The Author(s) 2018
P. L. Nelson, W. E. Block, *Space Capitalism*, Palgrave Studies in Classical Liberalism,
https://doi.org/10.1007/978-3-319-74651-7_2

survive.[3] We also advocate that this initiative be undertaken entirely by private enterprise.

Why not leave such matters to the government? Why, at least, not call for the state along with the private sector, whether in tandem or separately, to engage in this process? Why, insist, not only that this be done, but, also, under the auspices of individual initiative? The answer is simple. The state apparatus is responsible for the plight in which it has placed the human race in the first place. If this conflagration, God forbid, occurs, it will be due to the acts of those with a monopoly on the use of power. Asking them for help is thus like inviting the fox to guard the proverbial chicken coop. It is the state, not the private individual, that is most likely to create a nuclear Armageddon.[4] It is armed regimes that inflicted the chemical nightmare of trench warfare (Taylor, A. 2014). Throughout history the worst atrocities have always come from coercive governments (Rothbard, M. 1973, pp. 56–57):

> For centuries, the State (or more strictly, individuals acting in their roles as 'members of the government') has cloaked its criminal activity in high-sounding rhetoric. For centuries the State has committed mass murder and called it 'war'; then ennobled the mass slaughter that 'war' involves. For centuries the State has enslaved people into its armed battalions and called it 'conscription' in the 'national service.' For centuries the State has robbed people at bayonet point and called it 'taxation.' In fact, if you wish to know how libertarians regard the State and any of its acts, simply think of the State as a criminal band, and all of the libertarian attitudes will logically fall into place.

---

[3] Note: we do not favor space exploration and colonization on the ground that the Earth will soon be over-populated, and we will need room for far more people than now exist. For a critique of this Malthusian over-population thesis, see Bauer 1981; Boudreaux 2008; Friedman 1972, 1977; Robbins 1928, 1966; Rothbard 2011; Simon 1981, 1990, 1996; Sowell 1983; Williams 1999; Wittman 2000. According to Sowell (1983): "Every human being on the face of the Earth could be housed in the state of Texas in one-story, single-family homes, each with a front and a back yard. A family of four would thus have 6800 square feet- about the size of the typical middle-class American home with front and backyards." However, we appreciate all initiatives for colonies on other planets, and welcome that from all quarters, including those who favor our goals even if for reasons we regard as fallacious.

[4] We regard ISIL, or ISIS, as a government entity, not a private one. But they are not the ones that employed a nuclear device, twice.

This is not to say that private individuals cannot inflict grave injury on their neighbors; they can and do. But bullying people into a desired behavior is the preeminent *modus operandi* of governments. To initiate brute force against the citizens and experience the exhilaration of imposing one's will on others is *the* motivation for the despotically inclined to enter governmental employment.

The school bully beats his classmates and all too often enjoys the feelings he derives from his action. Perhaps his victim suffers some bruises or at worst a broken bone. Most people grow up and eschew playground brawls. Tyrants, never do. Sociopaths relish the hurts they inflict so much that they make schoolyard whacking their career. That is to say they become bureaucrats, politicians,[5] presidents, etc. Genocide only comes from the state. That a human being might be free to act according to his own will grates on the thugs' nerves. By their way of thinking, the biggest problem with space travel and colonization is that the astronaut cannot be oppressed: he is too far away and unreachable.

Mass killings from the nineteenth century to the recent murders in Darfur have been all too common. Table 2.1 presents but a partial list[6] of such atrocities.[7]

Aside from those mass murders, states also indulge in day-to-day inhumanity which, while relatively minor on a per incident basis when compared to the above sorry episodes, add up to major abuse when taken in aggregate. Even those governments which are supposed to be relatively free cannot escape condemnation for the wholesale cruelty they inflict on people. The United States has less than 5% of the world's population while somewhat short of 25% of the world's prisoners[8] are oppressed

---

[5] Even though while in office he made a few compromises with liberty (supported 10% residual income tax for those who "opt-out," took the pro-life position, and backed many restrictions on immigrants, for example) we make an exception for Ron Paul in this regard. On the case on behalf of Congressman Paul see Block (2012b). For criticisms from the libertarian point of view of his position on immigration, see note 10, below. For a libertarian analysis of abortion sharply different from his, see Block 2014.

[6] The present authors are not historians. We are very far from experts in this field. We cite what we regard as standard or traditional literature on this subject. We do not vouch for its veracity.

[7] For a supplemental list, see Pinker (2011). For a critique of that book, Block (2014).

[8] A closer investigation will reveal that not all of the prisoners of the world are counted. In particular, data is limited for certain closed countries such as China or missing altogether for hellacious places like North Korea (Ye He Lee 2015); but the fact remains that the United States has far more

Table 2.1 Genocides

Date(s)	Location	Issue	Number of Dead
1810–1828	Zulu Kingdom	Zulu armies targeted enemies for total annihilation.	1 to 2 million[a]
1890s	Congo/Belgian Empire	Forced labor first for ivory then rubber.	10 to 15 million[b]
1899–1902	Philippine Islands	Subjugation of Filipinos under the U.S. rule.	200,000 to <1 million[c]
1915–1923	Armenia/ Ottoman Empire	State initiative to unify: one empire, one religion, one language.	>1 million[d]
1932–1933	Ukraine	Persecution of Ukrainians by starvation: the Holodomor.	4 million[e]
1933–1945	Germany	Eliminate Jewish people and other "undesirables" in Europe.	>6 million Jews and 5 million others[f]
1966–1976	China	The Great Proletarian Cultural Revolution.	1.5 million plus many millions persecuted[g]
1975	Cambodia	Re-education of political dissidents.	1.7 to 2.0 million[h]
1994	Rwanda	Persecution of Tutsi and moderate Hutu.	800,000[i]
1995	Bosnia	Persecution of Bosniak and Croat people.	100,000[j]
2005– present	Darfur	Territorial dispute over Abyei, South Kordofan, and Blue Nile.	300,000 plus 2 million refugees[k]

[a]Walter 1969; [b]Osborn 2002; [c]Frontline 2003; [d]United to End Genocide 2015; [e]Holodomor n.d.; [f]History.com 2015; [g]Ibid; [h]Ibid; [i]Ibid; [j]Ibid; [k]Ibid

therein (ACLU 2015; Ye He Lee 2015). The question is: Why are these prisoners being held? What is to be accomplished by this outrage, and whom does it serve?

According to the Federal Bureau of Prisons (2015), 48.7% of the inmates in the United States are there for drug offences. These victimless crimes do not constitute misconduct at all.[9] Almost half the prisoners

---

than its proportionate share of oppressed people and at best is comparable to the most beleaguered populations. See on this Liptak, A. 2008; Walmsley, R. 2010; Statista 2016.

[9]That is unless the perpetrator was using drugs to assault an innocent victim. Otherwise, this is victimless and therefore no real crime.

have been locked up for non-crimes, or mere political "crimes" that did not violate anyone's rights. That of course is what makes an act criminal: the perpetrator has *mens rea*; he deliberately injures his victim for gain. But it gets worse than that. The next most common "offences" of inmates are, in order: weapons, explosives, arson (16.2%); immigration (9.3%); sex offences (7.1%); and extortion, fraud, and bribery (6.3%) (Federal Bureau of Prisons 2015). Many of these are not crimes either. With few exceptions, weapons and explosives at worse can be called political "crimes" but are not wrongdoings in and of themselves.[10] In like manner, immigration is non-criminal under libertarian law.[11] There are of course criminals (sometimes called "coyotes") who take money from poor people contracting to transport them across a national border only to abandon them in the desert.[12] They are guilty of kidnapping; but they are not the immigrants. And so it goes with many non-offenders being lumped together with a few real criminals.

The objective of these assaults on humanity is akin to that of the primary school bully: to feel superior to one's neighbors and to assuage one's fears. By defining vast numbers of people as criminals the tyrannically inclined can control them. As Rand (1957) observed:

'Did you really think we want those laws observed?' said Dr. Ferris. 'We want them to be broken… There's no way to rule innocent men. The only power any government has is the power to crack down on criminals. Well, when there aren't enough criminals one makes them. One declares so many things to be a crime that it becomes impossible for men to live without breaking laws. Who wants a nation of law-abiding citizens? What's there in that for anyone? But just pass the kind of laws that can neither be observed nor enforced or objectively interpreted—and you create a nation of

---

[10] It might be thought that arson is *per se* a real crime. Perhaps in most cases in these statistics it is. But suppose a man burns down his own factory to get rid of it for a non-fraudulent reason; for example, the government will not allow him to close his establishment since his workers will be dis-accommodated, and he wishes to retire. In this case, it would not be considered a crime from the libertarian perspective. See Rand (1943) for a somewhat similar fictional case in point.

[11] For support of this contention see Block 1998, 2004, 2011a, b, 2013c; Block and Callahan 2003; Gregory and Block 2007.

[12] Coyotes represent the all too common situation where the state enables or at least encourages real crime. Without prohibition, in this case the prevention of immigration, such crimes could not exist.

law-breakers—and then you cash in on guilt. Now that's the system, Mr. Reardon, that's the game, and once you understand it, you'll be much easier to deal with.'

"Much easier to deal with," that is to say, much easier to *control*. The perpetrators of ordinances defining non-criminal offenses desire the kind of power Dr. Ferris sought in the preceding passage. Who gains from having so many people in prison? Legislators, state employees, lawyers, "law" enforcement agents, border guards, and generally anyone able to adopt superior airs and compel those around him to bow, scrape, and do as he commands. To sum up, the overwhelming majority of inmates have violated no one's rights but are innocent victims of state malfeasance.

On top of that, there is enforcement. The outrage that is civil asset forfeiture (Rothschild and Block 2016) corrupts police departments across the United States and other common law countries. This misguided policy encourages outright theft on the part of uniformed people who are charged with *preventing* theft. Small store owners are at particular risk. They sell many inexpensive items and end up with cash. When they deposit these funds on a regular basis in a bank, the hoodlums acting in an official capacity call it illegal structuring and steal the contents of the bank account (Hoover 2015; WND 2014). Motorists are at risk. Corrupt police officers encourage other men in blue to engage in this type of theft and brag about it (Brandon 2014).

Brutes often burst into the wrong house to inflict harm on innocent residents. One example is the case of a baby seriously injured by a flash-bang grenade during a no-knock raid. A SWAT[13] team tried to break down a door without notice and, without first looking, tossed the explosive into the face of a 19-month-old sleeping toddler. These geniuses, who are "well trained" in how to handle weapons, will not be charged with assault or with child abuse, at least not locally (McLaughlin 2014). And what was the supposed warrant for this premeditated attack? There was a drug deal made earlier, although no drugs were found on the premises. Even if there were, it would still be a victimless act as far as libertarianism is concerned. In other words, there was no real offence

---

[13] SWAT = Senseless Whackers Administering Tyranny; well, we suppose we ought to also share the official meaning that the statists prefer us to use: Special Weapons And Tactics.

and the officer in question and his comrades were conducting an unprovoked mugging of the residents. In Denver, Colorado, a SWAT team
dashed into the house of an innocent man named Ismael Mena and shot
him to death (ACLU 1999). Once again, non-existent drugs were offered
as justification—i.e. not genuine misconduct. Officers even like to shoot
pets as in the case in Whitehall, Ohio (McCormack 2015). Oh wait—
that is man's inhumanity to animals not man. That is unless you count
the fact that while in his rush to kill a dog, one of the policemen shot a
four-year old child in the leg.[14]

The supposedly acceptable reason why the foregoing perps have not
been locked in prison with long sentences is that they made understand-
able mistakes. They were only doing their jobs. They were trained[15] to act
so. They were in fear of their lives. We are sure all those reasons are true.
So, why do we decry their behavior? Their conduct was criminally blame-
worthy because they were enforcing unjust laws.[16] They had no business
being in the locations and situation where these "mistakes" could occur.
Let us consider an analogy. A gang goes into a jewelry store to conduct a
robbery. During the implementation, one of their members is confronted
with a guard who draws his weapon. Fearing for his life, he shoots and
kills that sentinel. Is he therefore justified because he is scared? No, he
should not have been in that position in the first place. He is guilty
because he was already in the process of committing a crime. The same
applies to the preceding wrongdoers.

Who does this cruelty serve? The innumerable and appalling barba-
risms perpetrated by governments benefit the control freaks and sociopaths who man the reins of power. Such savage behavior inflicts a deep

---

[14] Here again we present an example of "well trained." By the way, we cannot avoid asking what is
the most likely attitude concerning the police and people in general to be adopted by that girl when
she reaches adulthood?

[15] Regarding "training", one ought to note some of the aspects of this process that are often over-
looked. Target practice frequently involves using human-shaped targets. It may include active
shooter mazes wherein realistic human-like targets suddenly come into view. These and others have
the effect of desensitizing the trainee about shooting at people. These constitute a contributing
factor to the unprovoked assaults by officials.

[16] "Woe to those who make unjust laws, to those who issue oppressive decrees, to deprive the poor
of their rights and withhold justice from the oppressed of my people, making widows their prey
and robbing the fatherless." (Isaiah 10:1–2).

and lasting depression[17] on victims extending far beyond their immediate injuries. When people do not know they are in violation of some obscure ordinance and live in constant fear of attack by those who are charged to provide protection, they tend to become passive and sedentary. Why risk starting a new enterprise just to have it despoiled by the savages? Alas, because of surveillance by government agents and their NIMBY[18] friends, many a would-be innovator, entrepreneur, or adventurer never develops his full potential. Regarding space exploration, this despair is potentially fatal. It serves as a reason for us to offer an insurance policy against the very disappearance of the human race and to disdain state participation.

We eschew state power in space because we want to restrict governmental inhumanity to the narrowest sphere possible if not eliminate this scourge altogether. We hope free adventurers will lead the way into the deep. On the other hand, we do not advocate state subsidies of space exploration. Bureaucratic meddling inevitably results in mal-investment.[19] Furthermore, in exchange for the "aid," the tyrants demand free benefits and, more seriously, cooperation in achieving political goals. Far from being a boon to the enterprise,[20] the recipients are often saddled with heavy moral and financial burdens. The worst part of this is that poor folks who cannot afford it, as well as people with no interest in the project, are forced to pay.

---

[17] Man's inhumanity to man is depressing to most men of good will. One way to grapple with this melancholy mental state is to conjecture the following: suppose that there were but two choices for the prehistoric human race, when we faced the saber-toothed tiger, the giant bear, and their ilk, and all we had was brains, opposable thumbs, rocks, sticks, and *viciousness*. Without the latter, we would have perished. Which would we rather have, a human race that lacked brutality, and perished, or one that had more than just a few traces of it and survived, but at the cost of engendering many Hitlers, Stalins, Maos. We know not how others may answer this question but for us we will accept, be grateful for, the present situation hands down. Better a very flawed human race than none. Yes, we are humanists, fervently biased in favor of human beings, and make no apology for it. Despite that, we yearn for the day when the brutes of this race grow up and join with those who have learned what civilization means.

[18] NIMBY = Not In My Back Yard.

[19] Solyndra (Chap. 1, note 6) is the perfect case in point. To encourage alternative sources of energy, the state subsidized manufacturers of solar voltaic equipment. After pouring millions of loan guarantees into this outfit, it went bankrupt. See on this Stephens and Leonning 2011; Welch 2011.

[20] In the case of crony capitalism, this of course is not true in the short term. In the long term, even the cronies suffer loss. Look at how the railroads which built extra miles of track have suffered after the initially enthusiastic political support faltered.

Space exploration funded by the private sector is self-financing and does not involve oppression. The concerned individual does it for one of three reasons.[21] Either he is, one, curious and explores out of personal enjoyment; two, expects to make a profit; or three, is a humanitarian and agrees with the thesis of this book (or all three). If the state stays away, far away, he is free to pursue his dreams as he sees fit. If he is mistaken about the efficacy of the project, he alone, along with his voluntary partners, suffers the loss. No one is shot either. No one is oppressed under *laissez-faire* capitalism since it necessarily involves volitional commercial acts between consenting adults.

A further advantage follows when governments keep out. Historically, private exploration initiatives tend to encourage liberty in the old world as well as in the new. From the seventeenth through the nineteenth centuries, based on the private settlements on the frontier in North America, a new commitment to freedom spread worldwide. At first it consisted of small gradual steps. Settlers, on their own far away from their place of birth, figured out how to live in their new environments. Lacking the ready resources of their homeland, they could not afford misguided political theories. As a result, they quickly learned the advantages of liberty; or they perished (Rothbard 1975a, b). With this liberty, and without their former rulers micro-managing their every act, they prospered and became the envy of the world.[22] In a kind of symbiotic relationship with the pioneers, others in the old world emulated these freedom-loving people. Observing these realities, philosophers wrote treatises explaining how freedom works. Liberty spread into many lands wherein previously the people had been terribly oppressed.

---

[21] We list three reasons. However, the entrepreneurs who pursue space exploration likely have a variety of motivations beyond these three.

[22] "The colony of a civilized nation which takes possession either of a waste country, or of one so thinly inhabited that the natives easily give place to the new settlers, advances more rapidly to wealth and greatness than any other human society." (Smith 1776, IV.7.23). "The progress of many of the ancient Greek colonies towards wealth and greatness seems accordingly to have been very rapid. In the course of a century or two, several of them appear to have rivalled, and even to have surpassed their mother cities. Syracuse and Agrigentum in Sicily, Tarentum and Locri in Italy, Ephesus and Miletus in Lesser Asia, appear by all accounts to have been at least equal to any of the cities of ancient Greece." (Smith 1776, IV.7.26).

That is in stark contrast to state exploration initiatives.[23] Starting with Columbus (financed by Queen Isabella), Spanish and Portuguese conquistadores despoiled native lands, killed inhabitants,[24] and stole their valuables.[25]

The writers of this book hope that the tyrants will stay at home,[26] that the free spirits will explore the planets and the stars as they see fit, and that the new-found freedom will spread back throughout the Earth. We look forward to the day when the space initiative will mightily reduce man's inhumanity to man by limiting governments and inspiring liberty. If not, then with colonization of other heavenly bodies, at least some people will escape. In the following chapters, we explore how this ingenuity might unfold.

References

ACLU. 1999. 'No-Knock' Warrant Resulting in Denver Man's Death Should Not Have Been Issued. The American Civil Liberties Union. https://www.aclu.org/news/no-knock-warrant-resulting-denver-mans-death-should-not-have-been-issued-aclu-says. Accessed 25 June 2015.
———. 2015. The Prison Crisis. The American Civil Liberties Union. https://www.aclu.org/prison-crisis. Accessed 24 June 2015.
Bauer, Peter. 1981. The Population Explosion: Myths and Realities. In *Equality, the Third World, and Economic Delusion*. Cambridge, MA: Harvard University Press.
Block, Walter E. 1998. A Libertarian Case for Free Immigration. Journal of Libertarian Studies: An Interdisciplinary Review 13 (2): 167–186.
———. 2004. The State Was a Mistake. Book Review of Hoppe, Hans-Hermann, *Democracy, The God that Failed: The Economics and Politics of*

---

[23] "The Spanish colonies, therefore, from the moment of their first establishment, attracted very much the attention of their mother country, while those of the other European nations were for a long time in a great measure neglected. The former did not, perhaps, thrive the better in consequence of this attention; nor the latter the worse in consequence of this neglect." (Smith 1776, IV.7.29).

[24] Many atrocities related to this era could, if we had space, be added to the forgoing list. For a defense of imperialism, on the ground that it benefitted the recipients of it see Ferguson (2011).

[25] This is in contrast to the liberty seekers who tended to purchase land or negotiate treaties with native people.

[26] Better to disappear altogether.

Monarchy, Democracy and Natural Order, May 25, 2001. http://www.mises. org/fullstory.asp?control=1522. Accessed 11 July 2015.

———. 2011a. Hoppe, Kinsella and Rothbard II on Immigration: A Critique. *Journal of Libertarian Studies* 22: 593–623.

———. 2011b. Rejoinder to Hoppe on Immigration. *Journal of Libertarian Studies* 22: 771–792.

———. 2013c. Rejoinder to Todea on the 'Open' Contract of Immigration. *The Scientific Journal of Humanistic Studies* 8 (5): 52–55.

———. 2014. Book Review Essay of Steven Pinker's: *The Better Angels of Our Nature: Why Violence Has Declined*. New York, N.Y. Penguin; Part II. *Management Education Science Technology Journal MEST* 2 (1): 141–160.

Block, Walter E., and Gene Callahan. 2003. Is There a Right to Immigration? A Libertarian Perspective. *Human Rights Review* 5 (1): 46–71.

Boudreaux, Donald. 2008. Optimal Population? April 8. http://cafehayek. com/2008/04/optimal-populat.html. Accessed 10 Aug 2016.

Brandon, Russell. 2014. Cops Are Seizing Hundreds of Millions of Dollars from Drivers and Bragging About It in Chat Rooms. *The Verge*. September 8. http://www.theverge.com/2014/9/8/6120971/cops-are-seizing-hundreds-of-millions-of-dollars-from-drivers-and. Accessed 25 June 2015.

Federal Bureau of Prisons. 2015. Statistics, Offences. May 30. http://www.bop. gov/about/statistics/statistics_inmate_offenses.jsp. Accessed 24 June 2015.

Ferguson, Niall. 2011. *Civilization: The West and the Rest*. Penguin Books.

Friedman, David. 1972. *Laissez Faire in Population: The Least Bad Solution*. New York: Population Council.

———. 1977. A Theory of the Size and Shape of Nations. *Journal of Political Economy* 85: 59–77.

Frontline World. 2003. Philippines, Islands Under Siege, 1898–1933 America's Colony. PBS. June. http://www.pbs.org/frontlineworld/stories/philippines/ tl01.html. Accessed 23 June 2015.

Gregory, Anthony, and Walter E. Block. 2007. On Immigration: Reply to Hoppe. *Journal of Libertarian Studies* 21 (3): 25–42.

History.com. 2015. Cultural Revolution. http://www.history.com/topics/cultural-revolution. Accessed 23 June 2015.

Holodomor 1932-33. n.d. Holodomor Facts and History. http://www.holodomorct.org/history.html. Accessed 23 June 2015.

Hoover, Kent. 2015. IRS Seizes Millions from Law-Abiding Businesses; 3 Live to Tell House About It. *The Business Journals*. February 11. http://www.bizjournals.com/bizjournals/washingtonbureau/2015/02/irs-seizes-millions-from-law-abiding-businesses-3.html. Accessed 25 June 2015.

Liptak, Adam. 2008. U.S. Prison Population Dwarfs that of Other Nations. April 23. http://www.nytimes.com/2008/04/23/world/americas/23iht-23prison.12253738.html?pagewanted=all. Accessed 21 Nov 2015.

McCormack, Simon 2015. Ohio Cop Trying to Shoot Dog Shoots 4-Year-Old Girl Instead. *The Huffington Post* 6–22. http://www.huffingtonpost.com/2015/06/22/cop-shoots-girl-dog_n_7637456.html. Accessed 26 June 2015.

McLaughlin, Elliot C. 2014. No Indictments for Georgia SWAT Team that Burned Baby with Stun Grenade. CNN. October 7. http://www.cnn.com/2014/10/07/us/georgia-toddler-stun-grenade-no-indictment/. Accessed 25 June 2015.

Osborn, Andrew. 2002. Democratic Republic of the Congo, Belgium Confronts Its Colonial Demons. *The Guardian* (US Edition). July 18.

Pinker, Steven. 2011. *The Better Angels of Our Nature: Why Violence Has Declined.* New York: Viking.

Rand, Ayn. 1943. *The Fountainhead.* New York: Signet.

———. 1957. *Atlas Shrugged.* New York: Random House.

Robbins, Lionel. 1928. The Optimum Theory of Population. In *London Essays in Economics: in Honour of Edwin Cannan,* ed. T. Gregory and H. Dalton. Abingdon: Routledge.

———. 1966. *The Theory of Economic Development in the History of Economic Thought.* Lecture Two: Population and Returns, 22–33. London: Macmillan, St Martin's. http://library.mises.org/books/Lionel%20Robbins/The%20Theory%20of%20Economic%20Development.pdf. Accessed 10 Aug 2016.

Rothbard, Murray N. 1975a. *Conceived in Liberty, Volumes I & II—A New Land, A New People, The American Colonies in the Seventeenth Century.* New Rochelle, NY: Arlington House Publishers. With the Assistance of Leonard P. Liggio.

———. 1975b. Society Without a State. *The Libertarian Forum* 7 (1), January. http://www.lewrockwell.com/rothbard/rothbard133.html. Accessed 23 Aug 2016.

———. 2011. Malthus and the Assault on Population. August 2. http://mises.org/daily/5501/. Accessed 10 Aug 2016.

Rothschild, Daniel Y., and Walet E. Block. 2016. Don't Steal; The Government Hates Competition: The Problem with Civil Asset Forfeiture. *The Journal of Private Enterprise* 31 (1): 45–56. http://journal.apee.org/index.php/2016_Journal_of_Private_Enterprise_vol_31_no_1_parte4.pdf. Accessed 10 Aug 2016.

Simon, Julian. 1981. *The Ultimate Resource*. Princeton: Princeton University Press.

———. 1990. The Unreported Revolution in Population Economics. *The Public Interest* Fall: 89–100.

———. 1996. *The Ultimate Resource II*. Princeton University Press.

Smith, Adam. 1979 [1776]. *An Inquiry into the Nature and Causes of the Wealth of Nations*. Indianapolis, IN: Liberty Fund.

Sowell, Thomas. 1983. *The Economics and Politics of Race: An International Perspective*. New York: Morrow.

Statista. 2016. Countries with the Largest Number of Prisoners per 100,000 of the National Population, as of April 2016. http://www.statista.com/statistics/262962/countries-with-the-most-prisoners-per-100-000-inhabitants/. Accessed 10 Aug 2016.

Stephens, Joe, and Carol D. Leonnig. 2011. Solyndra: Politics Infused Obama Energy Programs. December 25. http://www.washingtonpost.com/solyndra-politics-infused-obama-energy-programs/2011/12/14/gIQA4HllHP_story.html. Accessed 11 July 2015.

Taylor, Allen. 2014. World War I in Photos: Technology. *The Atlantic*. http://www.theatlantic.com/static/infocus/wwi/wwitech/. Regarding Gas see Photos: 9, 13, 22, 28, 37, 38, and 39. Accessed 21 Oct 2015.

United to End Genocide. 2015. Past Genocides and Mass Atrocities. http://endgenocide.org/learn/past-genocides/. Accessed 23 June 2015.

Walmsley, Roy. 2010. World Prison Population List. 9th ed. http://www.idcr.org.uk/wp-content/uploads/2010/09/WPPL-9-22.pdf. Accessed 21 Nov 2015.

Walter, Eugene. 1969. *Terror and Resistance, A Study of Political Violence*. New York: Oxford University Press.

Welch, Matt. 2011. Creation Myth: Governments Are Worse than No Good at 'Creating Jobs.' November. http://reason.com/archives/2011/10/10/creation-myth?utm_source=feedburner&utm_medium=feed&utm_campaign=Feed%3A+reason%2FArticles+%28Reason+Online+-+All+Articles+%28except+Hit+%26+Run+blog%29%29. Accessed 11 July 2015.

Williams, Walter E. 1999. Population Control Nonsense. *Jewish World Review*; February 24. http://www.jewishworldreview.com/cols/williams022499.asp. Accessed 10 Aug 2016.

Wittman, Donald. 2000. The Wealth and Size of Nations. *Journal of Conflict Resolution*. 44 (6): 868–884.

WND. 2014. IRS Seizes Life Savings for Deposits Under $10,000, Money Confiscated Even Though No Crime Committed. *WND Weekly*. 10/27. http://www.wnd.com/2014/10/irs-seizes-life-savings-for-deposits-under-10000/. Accessed 25 June 2015.

Ye He Lee, Michelle. 2015. Does the United States Really Have 5 Percent of the World's Population and One Quarter of the World's Prisoners? *Fact Checker, The Washington Post*. April 30. http://www.washingtonpost.com/blogs/fact-checker/wp/2015/04/30/does-the-united-states-really-have-five-percent-of-worlds-population-and-one-quarter-of-the-worlds-prisoners/. Accessed 24 June 2015.

3

Why Privatize Anything?

Introduction

There are three and only three formats that goods can take in terms of ownership. First, the state can claim to own the items in question.[1] Second, land, machines, final products, etc. can remain in a condition of non-ownership, or commons. Third, they can exist under the control of individuals or partnerships as private property. This chapter in particular and the book in general is dedicated to making the case for the third option. It does so by focusing on the disadvantages of the former two categories, and the benefits of the latter, both from an ethical and economic point of view.

---

[1] Since everything that the state claims involves the use of violence, nothing "owned" by this institution is legitimate proprietorship but is more akin to stolen goods. In the view of Rothbard (1998): "The State is nothing more nor less than a bandit gang writ large."

© The Author(s) 2018
P. L. Nelson, W. E. Block, *Space Capitalism*, Palgrave Studies in Classical Liberalism,
https://doi.org/10.1007/978-3-319-74651-7_3

Ethics

The State

What, then, is the problem with state ownership? On moral grounds, this stems from the fact that the government is a coercive institution. For one thing, it taxes people without their consent. Were any private individual to engage in a forced transfer of income from innocent people who have not agreed, contractually, to pay, we would have no difficulty labeling this, and accurately so: "categorical theft." It is only clever apologists who hide this. They will say, "But, but, splutter, splutter, we have the Constitution, and it justifies taxation." True enough. But is a constitution akin to a contract, in which several consenting parties agreed to a commercial interaction? It is not. No one ever signed it (Spooner 1870).[2]

Another argument put forth by shills of the state is that taxes are akin to club dues. If you want to be in club USA, pay your dues, and stop grousing. If you don't like it here, then leave. Unlike in some countries, you are free to depart,[3] and good riddance to you too. After all, no one stays in the golf or tennis club without paying their dues. Why should remaining in this nation's territory be any different?[4]

This sounds reasonable, but a bit of peering beneath the rug will show the fallacy in this line of thought. First, this is a circular argument. It assumes as true the very point under debate: that the government has the right to determine who may be a resident and who not. Secondly, at one time, this institution did not exist. It had to come into being. Was its birth unanimous? Of course not. Some people who had been in the territory long before the creation of the state did not agree to its formation. They, at least, were coerced into joining.[5] As for the others, there is no

---

[2] No one that is other than those who wrote it, James Madison, Jr. et al.
[3] At least for now. Refer to Casey, D. 2015.
[4] For an opposing view refer to Thoreau, H. 1849. Paragraph 202.
[5] Additionally, in the case of conquered and/or "purchased" territory, people were forced into the state against their will. "We didn't cross the border, the border crossed us." (Castro III, P. 2014). Also see Charlotte Lloyd's speech in court on this subject in James Michener's *Centennial*, Chapter 11.

record, no contract, no evidence, no signatures, that they ever voluntarily supported any such institution.[6]

Then there is the claim that taxes are really voluntary: we fill them out ourselves for the IRS (Internal Revenue Service) or HM Revenue and Customs. This view is even less rational than the previous ones in that this is done under duress. There is the credible threat that if a citizen does not do so, or does so erroneously, he will be subject to fines and/or jail.[7]

Private

In sharp contrast, each and every transaction that occurs under *laissez-faire* capitalism can boast volunteerism. When A purchases a pen from B for $1, they *both* agreed to the transaction. It was unanimous. And the same goes for all other commercial interactions, whether buying or selling, trading or bartering, lending or borrowing, or saving and investing. Thus, if property remains in the private sector, there is no violation of any just law as there is with public property.

How can property rights be established? From the libertarian perspective, this is accomplished through homesteading. How does this work? The general rule is simple.[8] One mixes his labor with the land, by planting a field or harvesting trees; a man captures and domesticates an animal, or kills one for food. Then, he becomes the owner of the resource

---

[6] If someone claims that someone else owes him as little as $100, the just court will insist the plaintiff supply some sort of *evidence*. Without it, the case would summarily be dismissed by the judge. Schumpeter, J. (1942, 198) states: "The theory which construes taxes on the analogy of club dues or of the purchase of the services of, say, a doctor only proves how far removed this part of the social science is from scientific habits of mind."

[7] There is another closely related idea that is frequently confused with consent. Spending effort to resist taxes may be regarded as not worth the effort or deleterious to one's moral compass. On this refer to the Book of Luke 20; 23–25. The resisting of taxes can be compared to not paying a thief in that it causes one to focus attention on a superfluous object. Refer to Matthew 5; 39–41. These are not consensual actions; they are decisions to not make war even as approval is not offered.

[8] For some complexities, see Block 1990, 2002a, b; Block and Edelstein 2012; Nelson, P. 2015; Block and Yeatts 1999–2000; Block vs. Epstein 2005; Bylund 2005, 2012; Grotius 1625; Hoppe 1993, 2011; Kinsella 2003, 2006, 2009; Locke 1948; Paul 1987; Pufendorf 1673; Rothbard 1973, p. 32; Rozeff 2005; Watner 1982.

in question. After that, any voluntary interaction between property owners establishes just title. So, if one man grows corn, and another milks a cow, and then they barter, the farmer owns the milk, even though he did not produce it, as does the rancher the corn, ditto. But, both can trace titles to what they now own to initial homesteading and voluntary interaction.

The problem with so-called government ownership is that no politician, no bureaucrat, ever homesteaded or freely traded anything.[9] Instead, the king, or the congress, simply declared control over certain territories. But this is on a par with everything else done by this institution. There is no justification, merely the fraudulent claim: "Might makes right."

We therefore conclude that private property, the very basis of the free enterprise system, is justified.

Commons

What of unowned property not controlled by either government or private individuals? The ethical status of the commons depends upon exactly how and why this occurs. The short answer is, if property is unowned because it is sub-marginal, then all is well. If, on the other hand, this status arises because the state refuses to allow private parties to homestead virgin territory and take ownership over it, then this is contrary to the libertarian ethos. The unowned property itself, of course, is not to blame; it is inanimate. The fault lies with the institution that refuses to allow homesteading and settlement on it.

Why is some land sub-marginal? This is because it does not pay to settle on it. The terrain is too rough, or too far away from civilization to be economical, or too dangerous, or for any other reason unsuitable for habitation by any but the heartiest and most adventurous persons and even then, only temporarily. For example, land near a volcano, or in

---

[9] Another argument by statists is singularly offensive. The idea is that a baron who has taken control of a region has thereby "homesteaded" it and the people in it are a sort of livestock. This claim is nothing short of slavery. Libertarians find involuntary servitude, and the claim of baronial rights, repulsive in the extreme.

Antarctica,[10] or in the middle of Alaska or Siberia, or in the midst of the Sahara. Few would want to live or work in these places.[11] Most of the oceans may also fall into this category.[12]

Economics

Let us now consider the three forms of ownership not through a normative lens, but via economic efficiency.

The State

Statism is inefficient in terms of serving the needs of the citizenry. Governments have several disadvantages *vis-à-vis* the private sector, which renders them less than effective in dealing with social problems, including the ones we are likely to run into during the eventual conquest of space. Referring to Table 3.1, the dollar vote occurs every day, indeed many times daily, while the political vote typically takes place every two or four years. Political voters must accept a package deal; consumers need not. For example, Jones might like policies 1, 3, 5, 7…, of candidate A, and policies 2, 4, 6, 8…, of candidate B, but he cannot pick and

Table 3.1 Comparing the dollar and the political vote

	$ vote	Political vote
Time	All times	Two or more years
Focus	Narrow	Package deal
Intensity	Counts	Irrelevant
Winners	All participants	Winners and losers
Rational ignorance	No	Yes
Encourages wealth	Yes	No

[10] But see Krasnozhon, Benitez, and Block (2015) on this.

[11] Barring the discovery of valuable assets such as mineral deposits, that is. And these would have to be very valuable indeed to justify the extra expense necessary to bring them to market. Further, these conditions are very likely temporary. As innovative technology becomes available, all of the listed challenging conditions will without much doubt be overcome.

[12] Block and Nelson (2015) argue this point regarding oceans, rivers, and lakes.

choose. He is limited in his choice at the ballot box to supporting *all* of A's, or B's, plans. In the market, in contrast, there are no such necessary limitations. Jones may care intensely about these issues, and Green not at all, and yet their votes count equally. In the market, *all* dollar votes win. If Green has minority tastes in food, music, clothes, his desires can almost always be met. In the political sphere, losers are disappointed. There is rational ignorance (Caplan 2007) in the ballot box, not in the market. In the former case, the most knowledgeable voter has an equal say with the one who has not studied the issues at all. In the latter context, if a consumer does not seek out information from friends, consumer magazines, etc., he will bear the costs of his ignorance. For all these reasons, consumers have more "control" over businessmen than do citizens over politicians. The market, not the political system, is the best way to increase wealth. This has been proven over and over again, in examples ranging from East and West Germany to North and South Korea. These are almost laboratory experiments; there were peoples with the same culture, language, history, abilities, cut off from each other by accidents of war. They followed very different economic systems, with greatly divergent results.

Under pure socialism, the state owns all of the means of production.[13] This means there can be no market prices for land, machines, labor, etc. But, prices are to the economy as street signs are to the urban environment and as notes are to music. Without terms of trade as determined by buyers and sellers, rational planning is impossible (Mises 1922). From 1917 to 1922 the Soviet Union tried a system very much akin to this one. It was such a disaster, even in the eyes of the planners themselves, that they inaugurated the New Economic Policy, which considered market prices for factors of production—generated in the West—which they had previously ignored. This is why their system lasted as long as it did; no credit should be given to government ownership.[14]

---

[13] There never has been a society in which government, in addition, owned all private goods such as pens, underwear, umbrellas. But, this is the logic of statism, its ultimate end-point. If private property is exploitative, why should *any* of it be suffered?

[14] Boettke 2001; Ebeling 1993; Hayek 1948; Hoff 1981; Hoppe 1989; Mises 1922, 1977.

Free Enterprise

The system of *laissez-faire* capitalism depends upon a market test of profit and loss (Hazlitt 1946). If a firm can satisfy customers, suppliers, laborers, it can endure. If it does this well, its base of operations expands. If it does its tasks poorly, it loses money. If it does the latter once too often, it falls into bankruptcy, and the resources under its control pass to other, more successful, entrepreneurs. In sharp contrast, if the government post office does a poor job, or the Army Corp of Engineers presides over levees that fail, or the Federal Emergency Management Agency prevents aid from reaching New Orleans,[15] or government highways kill tens of thousands of people annually (Block 2009), or the Food and Drug Administration approves of a dangerous product, or the Federal Reserve System creates the business cycle, they remain in power. Shortfalls will be made up through increased taxes extracted from the very victims of these involuntary oppressions. In fact, for those bureaucrats anything less than stellar performance is good because they can use failure to demonstrate that they must have more funds with which to enrich themselves. There is no mechanism whatsoever that guarantees the disappearance of such agencies. In contrast, were private enterprise in charge of any of these initiatives, and failed so spectacularly, they would long ago have gone the way of Trans-World Airlines, Kodak, Lehman Brothers, and Enron (all heavily subsidized or encouraged in their activities by the U.S. government).

The Commons

The well-known concept "the tragedy of the commons" says it all. When no one owns a given resource, it is to no one's advantage to care for it. One startling example of this is the relative fates of the *bos taurus*, collectively cattle, and the American bison, commonly buffalo. These are very similar animals. Both are bovines of about the same size, have similar temperaments, are grass eaters, come equipped with horns and a tail, are

---

[15] Anderson 2005; Block 2006; Block and Rockwell 2007; Chamlee-Wright and Rothschild 2007; Cowen 2006; Culpepper and Block 2008; Lora 2006; Murphy 2005; Thornton 1999; Vuk 2006a, b.

edible, and can serve men in comparable ways. Yet one came within a whisker of extinction, the other never treaded within a million years of such a fate. What could account for such disparate destinies? The answer is that cattle were privately owned from before written history, while the buffalo suffered from the tragedy of the commons. The farmer who slaughtered his beef did so at great cost: he would not have this creature any more. So, he was expeditious in choices of this sort. In contrast, the hunter who killed a bison did so at a far lower cost; if he refrained, he would not benefit from this option in the next time period. Instead, tatonka would be miles away.[16] It paid the hunter to butcher the buffalo even if he only wanted the liver, as long as this was more valuable to him than the cost of a bullet. People thus treated the one animal like the precious resource it was, while the other was dealt with as an almost free good. Only after the law allowed people to own bison was salvation from extinction assured.[17]

One rather famous Nobel Laureate critic of the foregoing must be mentioned. According to Ostrom (1990), there is no such thing as the tragedy of the commons. She offers some half dozen cases where, presumably, this mode of ownership worked out just fine, with no tragedy attached. Her mistake is that she does not understand what a commons is. It is a tract of land, or indeed any resource, which anyone may partake of at will. In the heyday of the slaughter of the buffalo, and nowadays with the elephant, rhinoceros, whales, and fish, there are no effective barriers to entry: all and sundry hunters may access the resource. None of the examples she offers fit this bill. All, instead, were large *partnerships*. They were owned by numerous people, but strangers were not allowed property rights in them. For example, the meadows she discusses in

---

[16] "Tatonka" is a term in the Lakota tongue typically translated as "buffalo." Lakota is a council within the Great Sioux Nation located in the general area of Montana, North and South Dakota, Nebraska, and Wyoming. Sioux is pronounced like "Sue."

[17] From an economic point of view, the elephant is merely a buffalo with funny looking ears and nose; ditto for the rhino in the latter regard. The reason these two are endangered, again rests with non-ownership. See on this Anderson and Hill 1995; French 2012; Lora 2007; Kreuter and Platts 1996; Simmons and Kreuter 1989. Regarding the nose, see also Rudyard Kipling's *Just So Stories*, "The Elephant's Child."

Switzerland were accessed by numerous farmers, but ownership rights were limited to a few cattlemen, the effective owners of the fields in question. Outsiders were considered trespassers and were barred by the proprietors from partaking.[18]

References

Anderson, William. 2005. Katrina and the Never-Ending Scandal of State Management. September 13. http://www.mises.org/story/1909.

Anderson, Terry L., and Peter J. Hill, eds. 1995. *Wildlife in the Marketplace.* Lanham, MD: Rowman & Littlefield.

Block, Walter. 1990. Earning Happiness Through Homesteading Unowned Land: A Comment on 'Buying Misery with Federal Land' by Richard Stroup. *Journal of Social Political and Economic Studies* 15 (2): 237–253.

———. 2002a. Homesteading City Streets; An Exercise in Managerial Theory. *Planning and Markets* 5 (1): 18–23. http://www-pam.usc.edu/Volume5/v5i1a2s1.html; http://www-pam.usc.edu/. Accessed 23 Apr 2016.

———. 2002b. On Reparations to Blacks for Slavery. *Human Rights Review* 3 (4): 53–73.

———. 2006. Katrina: Private Enterprise, the Dead Hand of the Past, and Weather Socialism; An Analysis in Economic Geography. *Ethics, Place and Environment: A Journal of Philosophy & Geography* 9 (2): 231–241. Reprinted in 'Post-Katrina: Risk Assessment, Economic Analysis and Social Implications'—edited by Harry Richardson, Peter Gordon and James Moore. Edward Elgar Publishing.

Block, Walter E. 2009. *The Privatization of Roads and Highways: Human and Economic Factors.* Auburn, AL: The Mises Institute. http://www.amazon.com/Privatization-Roads-And-Highways-Factors/dp/1279887303/; http://mises.org/books/roads_web.pdf; http://mises.org/daily/3416. Accessed 23 Aug 2016.

———. 2011a. Rejoinder to Bertrand on Lighthouses. *Romanian Economic and Business Review* 6 (3): 49–67. http://www.rebe.rau.ro/REBE%206%203.pdf; http://www.economist.com/blogs/freeexchange/2012/07/economic-fables. Accessed 23 Apr 2016.

[18] For a critique of Ostrom on these grounds, see Block 2011a, b; Jankovic and Block 2016.

————. 2011b. Review Essay of Ostrom, Elinor. 1990. *Governing the Commons: The Evolution of Institutions for Collective Action.* Cambridge and New York: Cambridge University Press. In *Libertarian Papers*, Vol. 3, Art. 21. http://libertarianpapers.org/2011/21-block-review-of-ostroms-governing-the-commons/.

————. 2015. When Is It OK to Shoot Down a Drone? August 8. http://www.targetliberty.com/2015/08/when-is-it-ok-to-shoot-down-drone.html?utm_source=feedburner&utm_medium=email&utm_campaign=Feed%3A+TargetLiberty+%28Target+Liberty%29. Accessed 23 Aug 2016.

Block, Walter E., and Michael R. Edelstein. 2012. Popsicle Sticks and Homesteading Land for Nature Preserves. *Romanian Economic and Business Review* 7 (1): 7–13. http://www.rebe.rau.ro/REBE%207%201.pdf. Accessed 29 Sep 2016.

Block, Walter, and Richard Epstein. 2005. Debate on Eminent Domain. *NYU Journal of Law & Liberty* 1 (3): 1144–1169.

Block, Walter E., and Peter Lothian Nelson. 2015. *Water Capitalism: The Case for Privatizing Oceans, Rivers, Lakes, and Aquifers.* New York: Lexington Books; Rowman and Littlefield. https://rowman.com/ISBN/9781498518802/Water-Capitalism-The-Case-for-Privatizing-Oceans-Rivers-Lakes-and-Aquifers. Accessed 14 Dec 2015.

Block, Walter, and Llewellyn H. Rockwell Jr. 2007. Katrina and the Future of New Orleans. *Telos* 139: 170–185. http://tinyurl.com/2wv8lc; http://journal.telospress.com; http://journal.telospress.com/cgi/reprint/2007/139/170.

Block, Walter and Guillermo Yeatts. 1999–2000. The Economics and Ethics of Land Reform: A Critique of the Pontifical Council for Justice and Peace's 'Toward a Better Distribution of Land: The Challenge of Agrarian Reform'. *Journal of Natural Resources and Environmental Law* 15 (1): 37–69

Boettke, Peter J. 2001. *Calculation and Coordination: Essays on Socialism and Transitional Political Economy.* London: Routledge. http://www.mises.org/etexts/cc.pdf. Accessed 23 May 2016.

Bylund, Per. 2005. Man and Matter: A Philosophical Inquiry into the Justification of Ownership in Land from the Basis of Self-Ownership. Master thesis, Lund University, Spring Semester (June). http://www.uppsatser.se/uppsats/a7eb17de8f/; http://perbylund.com/academics_polsci_msc.pdf; http://www.essays.se/essay/a7eb17de8f/; http://www.lunduniversity.lu.se/o.o.i.s?id=24965&postid=1330482. Accessed 23 Apr 2016

———. 2012. Man and Matter: How the Former Gains Ownership of the Latter. *Libertarian Papers* 4 (1). http://libertarianpapers.org/articles/2012/lp-4-1-5.pdf. Accessed 23 Apr 2016.

Caplan, Bryan. 2007. *The Myth of the Rational Voter: Why Democracies Choose Bad Policies*. Princeton, NJ: Princeton University Press.

Casey, Christopher P. 2015. How GDP Metrics Distort Our View of the Economy. May 15. http://www.thedailybell.com/editorials/36294/Mises-Institute-How-GDP-Metrics-Distort-Our-View-of-the-Economy/. Accessed 23 Apr 2016.

Castro III, Pablo. 2014. We Didn't Cross the Border, the Border Crossed Us. https://www.youtube.com/watch?v=DYsJzzPcVT0. Accessed 21 Oct 2015.

Chamlee-Wright, Emily, and Daniel Rothschild. 2007. Disastrous Uncertainty: How Government Disaster Policy Undermines Community Rebound. Mercatus Center. http://www.mercatus.org/Publications/pubID.3579/pub_detail.asp; http://www.mercatus.org/repository/docLib/20070111_Disastrous_Uncertainty_complete.pdf.

Cowen, Tyler. 2006. An Economist Visits New Orleans: Bienvenido, Nuevo Orleans. April 19. http://www.mercatus.org/publications/pubID.2272/pub_detail.asp.

Culpepper, Dreda, and Walter E. Block. 2008. Price Gouging in the Katrina Aftermath. *International Journal of Social Economics* 35 (7): 512–520. http://www.emeraldinsight.com/Insight/viewContentItem.do;jsessionid=D99C6D908AEA5910439BB07AF99D0F48?contentType=Article&contentId=1729159.

Ebeling, Richard M. 1993. Economic Calculation Under Socialism: Ludwig von Mises and His Predecessors. In *The Meaning of Ludwig von Mises*, ed. Jeffrey Herbener, 56–101. Norwell, MA: Kluwer Academic Press.

French, Doug. 2012. Property Means Preservation. May 31. http://mises.org/daily/5960/. Accessed 11 June 2016.

Grotius, Hugo. 1625. *Law of War and Peace (De Jure Belli ac Pacis)*, 3 volumes. Trans. A.C. Campbell, London, 1814.

Hayek, F.A. 1948. Socialist Calculation I, II, & III. In *Individualism and Economic Order*. Chicago: University of Chicago Press.

Hazlitt, Henry. 2008 [1946]. *Economics in One Lesson*. Auburn, AL: Mises Institute. http://mises.org/books/economics_in_one_lesson_hazlitt.pdf. Accessed 29 June 2016.

Hoff, Trygve J.B. 1981. *Economic Calculation in a Socialist Society*. Indianapolis: Liberty Press.

Hoppe, Hans-Hermann. 1989. Fallacies of the Public Goods Theory and the Production of Security. *The Journal of Libertarian Studies* IX (1): 27–46. http://www.mises.org/journals/jls/9_1/9_1_2.pdf. Accessed 23 Apr 2016.

———. 1993. *The Economics and Thics of Private Property. Studies in Political Economy and Philosophy*. Boston: Kluwer Academic Publishers.

———. 2011. Of Private, Common, and Public Property and the Rationale for Total Privatization. *Libertarian Papers* 3 (1). http://libertarianpapers. org/2011/1-hoppe-private-common-and-public-property/. Accessed 23 Aug 2016.

Jankovic, Ivan, and Walter E. Block. 2016. Tragedy of the Partnership: A Critique of Elinor Ostrom. *American Journal of Economics and Sociology.* 75 (2): 289–318.

Kinsella, Stephan N. 2003. A Libertarian Theory of Contract: Title Transfer, Binding Promises, and Inalienability. *Journal of Libertarian Studies* 17 (2): 11–37. http://www.mises.org/journals/jls/17_2/17_2_2.pdf. Accessed 23 Apr 2016.

———. 2006. How We Come to Own Ourselves. September 7. http://www. mises.org/story/2291. Accessed 23 Apr 2016.

———. 2009. Homesteading, Abandonment, and Unowned Land in the Civil Law. May 22. http://blog.mises.org/10004/homesteading-abandonment-and-unowned-land-in-the-civil-law/. Accessed 23 Apr 2016.

Kreuter, Urs P., and Linda E. Platts. 1996. Why the Ivory Ban Is Failing. *Christian Science Monitor*. March 20. http://perc.org/articles/why-ivory-ban-failing. Accessed 11 June 2016.

Locke, John. 1948. *An Essay Concerning the True Origin, Extent and End of Civil Government*. In *Social Contract*, ed. E. Barker, 17–19. New York: Oxford University Press.

Lora, Manuel. 2006. What Happened to Katrina Aid? March 3. http://www. mises.org/story/2064.

———. 2007. If You Love Nature, Desocialize It. May 10. http://mises.org/ daily/2539. Accessed 11 June 2016.

Murrphy, Robert P. 2005. How the Market Might Have Handled Katrina. November 17. http://www.mises.org/story/1968.

Nelson, Peter Lothian. 2015. To Homestead a Nature Preserve. Liberty.me. July 14. https://peterlothiannelson.liberty.me/to-homestead-a-nature-preserve/. Accessed 29 Aug 2015.

Ostrom, Elinor. 1990. *Governing the Commons*. Cambridge Press.

Paul, Ellen Frankel. 1987. *Property Rights and Eminent Domain*. Livingston, NJ: Transaction Publishers.

Pufendorf, Samuel. 1673. Natural Law and the Law of Nations (De officio hominis et civis prout ipsi praescribuntur lege naturali).

Rothbard, Murray N. 1973. For a New Liberty. New York: Macmillan. http://mises.org/rothbard/newlibertywhole.asp. Accessed 23 Aug 2016.

———. 1998 [1982]. Isaiah Berlin on Negative Freedom. In *The Ethics of Liberty*, chapter 27, 215–218. New York: New York University Press. http://www.mises.org/rothbard/ethics/ethics.asp. Accessed 20 Apr 2016.

Rozeff, Michael S. 2005. Original Appropriation and Its Critics. September 1. http://www.lewrockwell.com/rozeff/rozeff18.html. Accessed 23 Apr 2016.

Schumpeter, Joseph A. 1942. *Capitalism, Socialism and Democracy*. New York: Harper.

Simmons, Randy, and Kreuter, Urs P. 1989. Herd Mentality: Banning Ivory Sales Is No Way to Save the Elephant. *Policy Review* (50): 46–49. http://agrilifecdn.tamu.edu/kreuter/files/2013/01/Simmons-Kreuter-1989_3.pdf. Accessed 11 June 2016.

Spooner, Lysander. 1966 [1870]. *No Treason: The Constitution of No Authority and a Letter to Thomas F. Bayard*. Larkspur, CO: Rampart College. http://jim.com/treason.htm. Accessed 23 Aug 2016.

Thoreau, Henry David. 1849. *Civil Disobedience*. https://en.wikisource.org/wiki/Aesthetic_Papers/Resistance_to_Civil_Government. Accessed 21 Oct 2015.

Thornton, Mark. 1999. The Government's Great Flood. September, 17 (9). http://www.mises.org/freemarket_detail.asp?control=8&sortorder=articledate.

Von Mises, Ludwig. 1981 [1922]. *Socialism: An Economic and Sociological Analysis*. Trans. J. Kahane. Indianapolis: Liberty Fund. http://mises.org/books/socialism/contents.aspx.

———. 1977. *A Critique of Interventionism*. New Rochelle, NY: Arlington House http://www.mises.org/etexts/mises/interventionism/contents.asp.

Vuk, Vedran. 2006a. Journalism and Underwater Basket Weaving. June 21. http://www.lewrockwell.com/orig6/vuk5.html.

———. 2006b. Socialist Man in the Big Easy. September 25. http://www.lewrockwell.com/vuk/socialist-man-no.html; http://www.mises.org/story/2319.

Watner, Carl. 1982. The Proprietary Theory of Justice in the Libertarian Tradition. *Journal of Libertarian Studies* 6 (3–4): 289–316. http://mises.org/journals/jls/6_3/6_3_6.pdf. Accessed 23 Apr 2016.

4

Why Privatize Space Travel and Colonization?

Advantages of Private Launches

Brief History of State-Run Programs

Space launches have traditionally been performed by states. While earlier pre-WWII rockets were developed by private individuals,[1] during the war the German government developed a large, liquid fueled, vertical-lift ballistic missile under the leadership of Wernher von Braun that was capable of delivering a warhead to England.[2] After the war, he and his crew escaped to the United States where they continued to lead research in this field.[3]

---

[1] Robert H. Goddard (American), Wernher von Braun (German), Sergei Korolev (Russian) to name a few. Granted that each of these people had government-paid employment, mostly in state-run academic institutions; still, their rocket work was largely on their own initiatives in association with other experimenters. Korolev was even committed to labor camp for pursuing his research on his own (Zak 2007). That changed fast when Stalin figured out he needed his knowledge.

[2] For more on von Braun and the early research on rocketry refer to Marshall Space Flight Center (n.d.).

[3] One might ask why the interest in rockets. They contain all of the components necessary for combustion including both the fuel and the oxidizer. For flight in the upper atmosphere where oxygen is sparse or outer space where it is non-existent, an aircraft or spaceship cannot rely on the air to continue to burn fuel.

© The Author(s) 2018   **41**
P. L. Nelson, W. E. Block, *Space Capitalism*, Palgrave Studies in Classical Liberalism,
https://doi.org/10.1007/978-3-319-74651-7_4

While the Deutsch personnel themselves immigrated to the United States, Russians occupied the rocketry research campus of Peenemünde. Sergei Korolev, the father of the Soviet space program, was sent by Joseph Stalin to Germany on September 8, 1945 where he obtained plans to reconstruct von Braun's V-2[4] (Zak, A. 2007). Korolev then led the effort to develop intercontinental ballistic missiles and space-launch vehicles based on liquid-fueled boosters. Hence, both major state-run space agendas (at the time all such schemes) derived from the Nazi[5] A-4 (or V-2) rocket with chemical propellants.

Once in the United States, von Braun became the chief researcher for the U.S. space program. As might be expected, he continued experimenting with booster rockets using liquid fuel and oxidizer. His team developed a series of ballistic missiles and launch vehicles including the Jupiter, Redstone, Titan, Atlas, and their derivatives. Eventually, the Saturn was used to send U.S. astronauts to the moon. These vehicles were enlargements and refinements of the German rocket. They were exceedingly expensive[6] ventures which contributed to the misconception that only governments had the resources to embark upon such efforts.

This entire history of space launches illustrates the problem with all government programs. A letter from von Braun to Lyndon Johnson (Von Braun, W. 1961) marvelously demonstrates the ossified[7] thinking that afflicted the plans for space travel of both Russia and the United States. In a missive intended to answer questions put forward by John F. Kennedy and forwarded by Johnson, von Braun spelled out the capabilities and needs of the space program as compared to the Soviet Union. In this letter, there are

---

[4] "V-2" Stands for Vergeltungswaffe-2 which may be translated Retribution Weapon-2.

[5] People use the name "Nazi" which is shorthand for "National Socialist," or more properly the NSDAP (*Nationalsozialistische Deutsche Arbeiterpartei*) or National Socialist German Workers' Party. See on this Nazi Party, 2015. When this book uses the word "Nazi" it is intended to refer to a historical German political party or its economic and political precepts.

[6] "… well over $1 Billion for FY 62, and that the required increases for subsequent fiscal years may run twice as high or more." (Von Braun, W. 1961).

[7] "Ossified?" Were not von Braun and other rocket scientists widely regarded as forward-thinking innovators of the first class? Yes, they were. And certainly, at least in the early years, they can be seen that way even today. We dare to call their thinking ossified because they essentially had one idea, innovative though it was, and never saw any need to seriously consider alternatives. So, they produced bigger, and chunkier, versions of the once highly progressive V-2. (We hesitate to use this "p" word, "progressive," given its exact opposite meaning in political discourse as we write in 2016, but have the effrontery to do this as well.)

alternatives suggested: multi-stage super-rockets with liquid fuel, rendez-vous in Earth's orbit to enable the use of smaller launch vehicles, strapping together several small rockets, nuclear fuel, and solid chemical propellants. This document goes on to discuss work hours, shifts, and whether "we are making a maximum effort? Are we achieving necessary results?"

The "ossified" response dismisses these alternatives to a large, multi-stage, liquid-fueled super-rocket, though it would be fair to say that some previous investigations might have looked more extensively at those approaches. In other words, the dismissals might not have been totally cavalier. More to the point, there is no mention at all of achieving space travel using any method other than vertical take-off rocketry. However, as history amply demonstrates, other methods are not only conceivable, but eminently viable.

But are not the present authors guilty of foisting on our readers a sort of self-contradiction with our previous comments? A critic might say of us that on the one hand we maintain that private rocketry is good, the governmental version thereof bad. And, that we use von Braun as an example of the former. On the other hand, we also maintain that his thinking was "ossified," and this phenomenon must of course be placed not in the asset column, but in the debit one. No, we reject this possible criticism. We want to have our cake and eat it too; we stick to both sides of this story. Yes, this rocket scientist initially worked mostly on his own separated from government, and we welcomed this occurrence. On the other hand, when he later worked for *government*, he became fossilized, and there was little or nothing that backward-looking institution could or did do to counteract this difficulty.[8]

Market Competition

Adolf Hitler had it all wrong. He was a power junky.[9] As such, he had to control everything in which he was involved, using a top-down approach. He needed to win the war. To accomplish that task, he collected brilliant

---

[8] We detail both practical and ethical reasons for this in Chap. 3.
[9] He was a chemical junky as well. In his later life, he relied on a mixture of drugs prescribed by Dr. Theodor Morell including crystal meth and cocaine among the 74 such substances he regularly imbibed (Colgrass, N. 2014).

people to perform the necessary tasks. One such person was Wernher von Braun who had made noteworthy progress based on his own prior interests in rocketry. Rockets had enormous potential in military applications. If anyone could bomb enemies of Germany from the sky without warning, using methods that at the time were the stuff of science fiction, von Braun would be the man. He was that brilliant and creative.[10] So the Chancellor appointed him to pursue that goal. The mistake is the classical assumption shared by all central planners that their system of command, control, and regulate can better accomplish an arduous task than can the free-enterprise system. Both the United States and the U.S.S.R. fell right into that very same trap, demanding their own V-2's and continued manufacturing bigger, vertical-launch, liquid-fueled launch platforms well past the time when they made sense.

The better way, and one of the main reasons your authors advocate private space exploration, is market competition. Rather than search for "the one best" creative innovator, let anyone interested develop his own solution to the problem. Of course, the statists of the world will misinterpret that statement. Their half-way response will be to host a contest wherein people will submit ideas to accomplish a given goal. Why is that half-way? The authorities will still leave themselves in charge of selecting "the best" alternative. One could argue that at least it would open more potential designs to consideration; that may be, but in the end only one program is executed, or attempted. Inevitably using cronyism, the supposed best theory is that presented either by the finest salesman or the most well-known, good old boy—not the most efficient concept.

Real market competition, not a crony capitalist approach, means that the individuals set the agenda. A Howard Roark (Rand, A. 1943) may conceive of a new product. He can, if he wishes, research the market to find whether anyone is interested and proceed by implementing this idea. If not self-financed, he would seek venture capitalists who for their own protection vet his creation and determine its practicality.

The mistake made by the statists in this regard is to fail to realize that the free-enterprise system constitutes an ongoing *process*. Government bureaucrats may choose an entrepreneur who has succeeded in the past.

---

[10] At least before he began working for the state, see above.

But this is no guarantee of *future* attainment. In the marketplace, the businessman must prove himself every moment. Previous profitability is no guarantee of a good bottom line even the very next day. The Fortune 500 changes, drastically, every decade. Where are the Packards or Trans World Airlines and their ilk nowadays? This brutal market test of profit and loss is ongoing. A businessman selected by the state apparatus no longer must please customers, employees, suppliers. He is himself now a bureaucrat, no longer a part of the marketplace.

Rather than focus the entire space effort on a rather silly adolescent goal such as beating Russia to the Moon, this book affirms that the private entrepreneur should set up shop there for no other reason than that he thinks it has exciting potential. In his view, numerous people would want to go there and harvest all that green cheese. More seriously, there are many legitimate reasons that potential customers may wish to travel to that brilliant orb; and entrepreneurs able to do so will step up to provide that service. Given economic freedom, many programs will operate in parallel. As time passes, some of those will fall by the wayside. The most efficient and resilient will remain. Some may even be found to address profitable goals other than space travel. It is impossible to know before-hand[11] what inventions might come to the fore, but two speculative launch platforms, which we shall now discuss, are aircraft and elevators.

Rocket Launches from an Aircraft

The idea of launching a rocket from an aircraft is more than speculative. From December 1945, it has been used by states in research for military applications. Researchers tested very fast rocket planes such as the Bell X-1, the North American X-15[12], through the X-51 using this method. More recently, a private launch firm, Virgin Galactic, has used this technology for commercial purposes. It utilizes an aircraft consisting of two planes joined together to fly a reusable spaceship to a high altitude. From there the spaceship is dropped and it uses a rocket engine to power itself into space.

---

[11] The opinion of tyrannical bureaucrats notwithstanding.

[12] These craft were carried aloft by heavy bombers such as the B-29 and the B-52 (Gibbs, Y. 2015a, b).

The goal is to enable a great many people to travel to space. One aim is to give numerous customers the "astronaut effect." That is a mental attitude that derives from having experienced the physical view of the Earth from space. While your authors have not yet done this, one of them (Nelson) can testify to something akin to it based on flying in small planes. This experience shrinks the world. Aloft, one sees vast stretches of the world. Borders disappear even as cities are readily visible. In the plane, highways can be seen; but high enough in the atmosphere, even those vanish. It has a uniting effect.[13] It makes one wonder whether national boundaries are really necessary or if they are merely devices used by power freaks to control people. The effect must be that much greater from 100 miles up, to say nothing of from the Moon or Mars.

Technically speaking, this concept can save a lot of energy, fuel, and money. With it, we no longer need a gigantic amount of brute force to lift and accelerate a massive vehicle straight up into the air. That approach includes the oxidizer and the first stage, which is spent within a few seconds and only about 40 miles from the launch point. This approach uses much more energy-efficient flight up to a level of about 9.5 miles. After that, the space craft continues to use aerodynamic lift while it is still available to continue upwards to a sub-orbital flight.[14]

Elevator to the Sky

The idea of a space elevator has been kicked around for decades. It would include a very high tower with an elevator. Much energy could be saved in two ways. First the engine running the elevator would remain on the ground so there would be no need to lift it and the fuel as a first stage to

---

[13] The effect is not the same for a passenger on a commercial airliner looking out of a small, book-sized window where the view is obscured by the wing. It is even less, if one is sitting in an aisle seat.

[14] Sub-orbital flight means that the craft does not have the speed to remain in space but will fall back to Earth. It also need not endure the hellacious heat of re-entry experienced by orbital space vehicles. These vehicles are useful in their own way. However, for the technique of aircraft-launched reusable spacecraft to be serious contenders, a system to attain Earth orbit and/or escape velocity (the velocity required to escape Earth's gravity), and to withstand re-entry from those speeds, will need to be devised.

a great height. Second, as with most elevators, it would include counter weights[15] to balance the effective burden of the vehicle and cargo.

There are at least two ways to look at this technique. First, the tower could extend to such an elevation that the traditional first stage of a rocket could be eliminated. Then what is now the second stage would become the first stage and a much smaller booster could lift the payload to perform any of the functions currently done or imagined (Gajanan, M. 2015).[16] The second is a tethered counter weight wherein the center of gravity of the structure is at the geosynchronous orbit elevation (Hirschfeld, B. 2002; Fleming, N. 2015). This approach eliminates all rocketry in attaining earth orbit as well as re-entry challenges. The cost of travel to 22,000 miles[17] above the surface of the planet could be cut to a small fraction of the current cost; it might well fall to an amount similar to intercontinental travel by commercial aircraft. Imagine passenger tourist travel to that level for under, say, $1000 (2017 dollars). The actual price would be determined by supply and demand, of course.

The space elevator is even more intriguing than it first appears.[18] The easiest way to build one is from a synchronous orbit. In other words, a lot of old-fashioned rocket launches would be required to move the initial cable and counter weight into place. Once there, though, building up its capability would be much simplified by a gradual process using the device itself to lift necessary materials. Additional elevators could be built for a small fraction of the original cost. Furthermore, the cost to build

---

[15] A counter weight refers to a mass of dense material suspended over a pulley so that the unloaded elevator room does not need to be lifted. If desired, efficiency can be improved further so part of the load is balanced as well. That means that effort would be needed to lift the counter weight when there is no load, but the force needed to lift a load would be reduced. In the same way, braking, slowing down, or stopping, is also simplified.

[16] U.S. and U.K. patents have already been granted for just such a structure to a Canadian company, Thoth Technology Inc.

[17] 22,000 miles is the height of a geosynchronous orbit (one wherein the satellite continuously maintains the same location over the Earth's surface).

[18] The elevator also presents major challenges for which existing technology does not have the answers, at least not yet. The biggest problem is the cable. It must be stronger than any known material and also very thin and lightweight (10 feet in diameter is suggested though thicker would not seem to be fatal to the concept). However, carbon nanotubes with an epoxy binder seem to offer considerable promise that a solution can be found within the next few years (Hirschfeld, B. 2002). More information can be found browsing for the "National Nanotechnology Initiative."

them on other planets would be less than the first one on Earth. They could easily be built on Mars at a location about 17,000 kilometers above the surface.[19]

Interplanetary Travel, Is It Always an Orbit, Implications for Property Rights?

An orbit is the most efficient way to move in terms of energy consumption,[20] though not necessarily on the basis of time.[21,22] As such, certain orbits and trajectories could be quite valuable. For example, Earth and Mars revolve around the Sun at differing rates. During certain limited time slots, there is a trajectory which would use the least amount of energy and time to make the trip. There would eventually be competition for the use of this slot.[23] Given this, it would become a perfect candidate for private ownership. A shipping firm could establish regularly scheduled flights to and from Mars. It is also possible that multiple companies could establish a time share for such assets. Who should have ownership of this limited

---

[19] The height of a Martian synchronous orbit is 17,000 kilometers. Because of the dynamics of orbiting bodies, this concept does not apply for some planets. If the heavenly body is in tidal lock (its period of rotation [one day] equals one revolution [one year] around the object it is orbiting) or if its angular velocity (the rate an object is spinning or rotating often expressed in degrees per minute) is too slow, the theoretical distance to a synchronous orbit would be so far that it would be beyond the gravitational influence of the planet. Venus is one such planet.

[20] An explanation of the physics of orbits and why they are efficient can be found in the Appendix.

[21] If one had unlimited resources, one could save a lot of time by powering straight out from the Sun in order to get to the outer solar system or from the Earth to the Moon. However, that would be energy intensive in the extreme.

[22] Think in terms of a bolo (bola), a weapon first used in South America, which is a rock tied to a string. In order to garner great power, the stone, before being released, is first turned in a circle, repeatedly faster and faster. Or, contemplate the field sports of discus and hammer throw. These implements are catapulted by first spinning them in a circle. In a way the armament's tether and the athlete's arm in these examples are analogous to gravity except that, as explained in the Appendix, the particles for imparting the gravitational field cannot be detected. (This is in sharp contrast to the shot put, which is released in a straight line, although as in the other two cases, the athlete is confined to a small circular area in which he may operate.)

[23] An analogous situation pertains on Earth. Great circle routes are the most efficient for transportation, whether in the air or on the oceans. These trajectories, too, will one day become scarce. Then, if the tragedy of the commons or of government ownership is to be avoided, private property rights, based in our view on homesteading, will have to be inaugurated. For a libertarian analysis of these earthly but analogous challenges, see Block and Nelson 2015.

resource? Based on the libertarian principles underpinning this book, that would be the first to homestead this path by being the first to use and maintain it.[24] The same principles apply for travel to Venus, the Moon, and other celestial objects. For little-used routes, there will be no need to establish ownership due to lack of scarcity. However, when a route becomes well-traveled and usable space in great demand, when debris and clutter choke the trail, these problems can best be solved with private owners who will have direct personal interests in maintaining and upgrading the path by removing the trash and limiting over-use by interlopers. Late-arriving users would then rent a time slot or establish an alternative route. The first user would be the first in right: the basic principle of homesteading.

The discussion of the two preceding methods, of getting to space while reducing the use of rockets, in no way suggests that other techniques, never before imagined, will not be forthcoming. Neither is it intended to suggest that we know that missiles will not remain the most economically efficient space transportation system. They might. The beauty of human ingenuity is that any person may come out of nowhere with any new idea, at any time, and blow away the competition. Such serendipitous moments occur with greatest frequency where liberty is maximized. Here again, we see why private for-profit exploration exceeds all others.

References

Block, Walter E., and Peter Lothian Nelson. 2015. *Water Capitalism: The Case for Privatizing Oceans, Rivers, Lakes, and Aquifers*. New York: Lexington Books; Rowman and Littlefield. https://rowman.com/ISBN/9781498518802/Water-Capitalism-The-Case-for-Privatizing-Oceans-Rivers-Lakes-and-Aquifers. Accessed 14 Dec 2015.
Colgrass, Neal. 2014. Report: Hitler Was on Crystal Meth. *USA Today*. October 14. http://www.usatoday.com/story/news/world/2014/10/14/hitler-drugs-crystal-meth/17242185/. Accessed 8 Nov 2015.

---

[24] At first glance, it seems preposterous to even discuss "maintaining" a path in space. However, this is explained immediately following in the main text.

Fleming, Nic. 2015. Should We Give Up on the Dream of Space Elevators? BBC. February 19. http://www.bbc.com/future/story/20150211-space-elevators-a-lift-too-far. Accessed 10 Nov 2015.

Gajanan, Mahita. 2015. Going Up? Space Elevator Could Zoom Astronauts into Earth's Stratosphere. *The Guardian*. August 17. http://www.theguardian.com/science/2015/aug/17/space-elevator-thothx-tower. Accessed 10 Nov 2015.

Gibbs, Yvonne. 2015a. NASA Armstrong Fact Sheet: First Generation X-1. NASA. August 12. http://www.nasa.gov/centers/armstrong/news/FactSheets/FS-085-DFRC.html. Accessed 9 Nov 2015.

———. 2015b. NASA Armstrong Fact Sheet: X-15 Hypersonic Research Program. NASA. August 13. http://www.nasa.gov/centers/armstrong/news/FactSheets/FS-052-DFRC.html. Accessed 9 Nov 2015.

Hirschfeld, Bob. 2002. Space Elevator Gets Lift. *G4 Media—TechTV Vault*. January 31. http://web.archive.org/web/20050608080057/http://www.g4tv.com/techvvault/features/35657/Space_Elevator_Gets_Lift.html. Accessed 10 Nov 2015.

Marshall Space Flight Center. n.d. Dr. Wernher von Braun First Center Director, July 1, 1960–Jan. 27, 1970. History Department. http://history.msfc.nasa.gov/vonbraun/bio.html. Accessed 5 Nov 2015.

Rand, Ayn. 1943. *The Fountainhead*. New York: Signet.

Von Braun, Wernher. 1961. Letter to Vice President Lyndon Baines Johnson. April 29. http://history.msfc.nasa.gov/vonbraun/documents/vp_ljohnson.pdf. Accessed 6 Nov 2015.

Zak, Anatoly. 2007. People: Korolev. *RussianSpaceWeb.com*. January 12. http://www.russianspaceweb.com/korolev.html. Accessed 1 Dec 2015.

5

Ownership Concepts

Ownership of Space Itself

While extra-terrestrial ownership presents challenges, it is the ability to actually own parcels of bodies in space[1] that will free the cosmos from the current fits and starts of tentative forays into the unknown. There is the rub; the definition of "parcels" in space is not easy. This chapter suggests several techniques that should work, but in the end, only the market can show us what functions well and what does not. In the tradition of libertarian thought, all the following are based on homesteading: first in use, first in right. The Lockean (1955, chapter 5) concept applies as well in space as on earth:

---

[1] It will be a long, long time before actual volumes of space can be owned, since private property can only apply to scarce entities. This is not likely to occur any time soon and will never take place if statists, as is their wont, forestall all efforts in that direction.

© The Author(s) 2018
P. L. Nelson, W. E. Block, *Space Capitalism*, Palgrave Studies in Classical Liberalism,
https://doi.org/10.1007/978-3-319-74651-7_5

[E]very man has a property in his own person. This nobody has any right to but himself. The labour of his body and the work of his hands, we may say, are properly his. Whatsoever, then, he removes out of the state that nature hath provided, and left it in, he hath mixed his labour with it, and joined to it something that is his own, and thereby makes it his property.[2]

Orbits

We start with orbits.[3] The establishment of, say, a weather satellite in geosynchronous orbit[4] should be sufficient to establish a homestead over a specific location at 22,236 miles above the Earth's equator.[5] Furthermore, operators have learned from both theory and experience that enough of the arc must be included to preclude gravitational attraction of a nearby artificial object pulling it out of position. We advocate that such specific volumes of space located strategically to meet the needs of their owners should come to be privately owned through the homesteading process. That is, a proprietor discovers a need, in this case a weather survey, and expends labor to place a machine in that space similar to how a resident might locate a house on a plot of land on *terra firma*. This process might more closely resemble a billboard or cell-phone tower in that it is definitely a useful and profitable device even though no one lives there.

---

[2] For other writings in this Lockean tradition, see Block 1990, 2002a, b; Block and Edelstein 2012; Nelson 2015; Block and Yeatts 1999–2000; Block vs Epstein 2005; Bylund 2005, 2012; Grotius 1625; Hoppe 1993, 2011; Kinsella 2003, 2006, 2009; Locke 1948 (pp. 17–19), 1955 (chapter 5); Paul 1987; Pufendorf 1673; Rothbard 1973, p. 32; Rozeff 2005; Watner 1982.

[3] Orbits are gravitationally induced elliptical or curved paths through space around an object with a gravitational field. While in three dimensions the orbit appears curved, in four-dimensional space it may be a straight line. For more on this see Hawking (1996). (Circles are a sub-category within the set of all ellipses wherein the radius is the same throughout the path.)

[4] Geosynchronous refers to a circular path wherein a satellite maintains its location over a given spot on the Earth's surface. The distance of such a circle above the planet's equator is 22,236 miles (Howell 2025). Similar synchronous orbits for other celestial bodies vary according to the object's properties. In other words, it takes 24 hours to complete one circuit even as the planet rotates the same angular amount.

[5] We can also infer this claim from the oceans and lakes. If a group of firms has been using a certain path on or in the Earth's waterways, we maintain they have a right to continue to do so, and to prevent others from trespassing once this route becomes scarce (e.g. crowded). For more on this see Block and Nelson 2015.

What about non-geosynchronous orbits? Comparable properties could be established for an object moving in this manner. Take a polar orbit for example. The probe would cross over the Arctic and Antarctic. However, as the Earth rotated, it would follow a different course over the surface with each pass. In effect, a shell shape around the Earth would be traced out, and then homesteaded. Conceivably, more than one satellite could occupy such a sphere, but the first occupant would have priority and all others would have to design their tracks to avoid the first. It might be simpler to pick a different altitude. The maintained orbit could be defined by including time as an essential characteristic. In other words, not only does the probe cross the poles at a given elevation but the implied frequency of artic crossings as well as the time it would pass over, say, Greenwich, England, would be included in the property's definition.

But why should anyone be interested in precise definitions and proprietorships of space volumes? Quite simply, the owner may legally exclude interlopers. As the first occupant and homesteader, he can protect his investment by intercepting and removing a wayward trespasser such as an unowned piece of junk or a valuable object launched by a scofflaw. He would back charge the trespasser who sent it his way and intruded on his space, and obtain an order from professional adjudication firms to cease and desist; were such an injunction ignored, there would be heavy penalties imposed by said firms (Rothbard 1982). Any unowned stuff intruding onto his property, whether a natural object or leftovers from previous government incompetence, could properly be swept from the sky. In the event the article of said trespasser should damage his property or distort his orbit, the offending party would be fully liable for repairs or replacement as well as returning it to its proper homesteaded orbit.

Lagrange Points

Lagrange points are actually orbits (Fig. 5.1). They involve two large objects which influence the movement of a third located at one of five specific orbiting points. That is to say, locations with respect to the two celestial bodies, i.e. paths. They revolve around the larger object, such as the Sun; but remain stationary with respect to the smaller one, like the

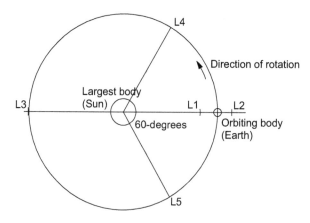

Fig. 5.1 Lagrange points

Earth. They are labeled L-1, L-2, etc. The Sun-Earth L-1 is between the two bodies. An object at L-1 moves about the Sun at a diameter that is smaller than the orbit of the Earth. Normally, such a satellite would pull ahead and complete one full circle in less time. However, due to the influence of the planet's gravity, it completes its orbit in the same time. Its year is identical. The other Lagrange locations are as follows: L-2 is aligned with the two objects (Sun/Earth in the case being described) but farther from the Sun than the planet; L-3 is slightly outside of the satellite's path but on the opposite side of the Sun; L-4 is on the same trail but 60 degrees ahead; while L-5 is 60 degrees behind. Points 1, 2, and 3 are meta-stable, like a ball on top of a hill (European Space Agency 2013). If it is moved even slightly from the summit, it rolls down the slope with no further effort. Points 4 and 5 are more stable as they are at the bottom of a depression. This means that to maintain an object at L-3 would require small artificial adjustments to compensate for perturbations that would tend to cause the satellite to move away from its position whereas a device at L-5 would not require such.

The stability of L-4 and L-5 implies two key facts about these points. First, an object can orbit[6] these positions even if they are unoccupied by massive heavenly bodies. Thus, one could homestead not only the point

---

[6] These orbits are not circular but are a sort of banana shape: elliptical but curved along a circle around the Sun.

itself but a path around it.[7] Second, these points tend to accumulate space junk. These spaces are "dirty." To use them, one might have to clean them up. On the other hand, some of this "dirt" is in the form of asteroids that could be used as foundations for structures.

Of what use are Lagrange points? One can think of many options. For example, L-2 which lies outside of the Earth's orbit around the Sun is always in the planet's shadow. What better place to locate a deep space telescope without any light interference or heat-induced deformations? L-3 would enable continuous observation of the far side of the sun. L-4 and L-5 could host factories that benefit from almost non-existent gravitational effects.

Trajectories

Trajectories constitute another type of special definition for travel paths to other planets. Like orbits, they are curved, but they do not close on themselves like an ellipse. They are handy because once a spaceship is on such a path to a specific destination, it will arrive at a particular time without the expenditure of additional energy.[8] Of course effort is required to enter the trajectory.

A Mars settler who regularly travels from our planet would use such a trail regularly. Thus, he will establish a homestead to that path. As with polar orbits described above, a time element would be required to establish the limits. Why? Both the destination and the home are in orbital motion around the Sun. The trajectory moves with them. The path homesteaded only occurs at regular chronological intervals.

Nor need we go too far afield to find analogies to these phenomena back here on Earth. Airline routes serve as a precedent for these deeper

---

[7] This bears no similarity to national claims to territorial waters surrounding sovereign land. Why? Because rather than illegitimately claiming an asset with which the nation did not mix its labor, homesteading a Lagrangian orbit would stem from the actual usage of the path and the work required to do so. On the subject of 12-mile limits, whether and to what extent any nation is justified in those territorial claims is discussed in Block and Nelson 2015.

[8] The statement that no further energy is required to maintain the trajectory assumes that it is accurate. Since such accuracy is unlikely, small amounts will usually be necessary for course corrections.

space claims. For example, planes flying according to visual flight rules (VFR) in an easterly direction (compass heading between 0 and 179) should cruise at an odd thousand feet plus 500 (e.g. 7500 feet) and in a westerly direction at an even thousand feet plus 500 (e.g. 8500 feet). On instrument flight rules (IFR) the cruising flight level should be on an ordinal thousand feet (e.g. 7000 or 8000 feet respectively) (FAR/AIM 2016). The obvious reason for this is to minimize the chances of collisions. But if the ABC, the DEF, and the XYZ airlines have been long travelling on any of these specific routes, at least according to the libertarian notion of homesteading, they come to own the right to continue to do so, and may, properly, exclude newcomers from occupying these spaces,[9] at least when they become crowded past a certain point.[10]

Land

Any celestial body with a hard surface[11] can be homesteaded in whole or in part. The larger the planet, planetoid, asteroid, whatever, the more likely it would be owned in parcels. A settler could do any of the things we discuss elsewhere in this work to obtain ownership: agriculture, mining, tourist colonies, etc. The possibilities are limited only by human imagination. These uses are necessarily limited in extent to the footprint of the operation. Therefore, as the number of developers increases to an extent where crowding becomes an issue, surveying of property boundaries as on Earth will become essential. The parcels can of course be three dimensional. A mine as opposed to a farm, for example, may have not only lateral extent but also depth. It is the use of one's labor in the form of discovery of a mother lode, digging, extracting, stockpiling, and selling the minerals that forms the basis of proprietorship.

---

[9] Or allow them to do so for a rental fee.

[10] Just how crowded must these paths become before it is justified for old-timers to prevent the entrance of would-be newcomers? That is difficult to say. It depends upon the culture, the danger, the historical practices. Who would make these determinations? The courts, of course; hopefully, private ones. For an analysis of the continuum problem the judges would face, see Block and Barnett (2008).

[11] If the covering is all or in major part water or another liquid, the challenge would be greater. However, it, too, could be overcome. See on this Block and Nelson 2015.

For smaller objects such as asteroids and comets, the same process applies. However, the limited extent may imply a technological unit[12] that does not admit of multiple owners.

A body with a liquid surface may also be amenable to homesteading. If a solid surface happens to exist below the fluid, it may be treated as described above. As for the liquid itself, that may be owned in a manner that accounts for the properties of the material. For example (Block and Nelson 2015), water can be extracted, used, traversed, converted, etc. If there are swimming creatures, these maybe husbanded. The wet surface may provide a medium for transportation. These and other uses may be compatible with one another and thus come into the possession of a multitude of entrepreneurs. Of course, gas is yet another kind of fluid. If a planet has an atmosphere that is sufficiently rare to justify ownership, it too can be homesteaded and put to beneficial use according to the wishes of its proprietor. As with liquid, vapor my also admit of multiple owners all using the atmosphere for mutually compatible purposes.

Space Probes

Space probes, as opposed to spaceships, permit unmanned missions. Without the constraint of human limitations and life-support systems, they allow for much more exciting missions than would otherwise be possible, given technological limitations. Current uses already include operations too numerous to fully include here: weather satellites; communications; deep space exploration; landings on the Moon, Mars, Venus, Mercury, Jupiter, Martian moon Phobos (unsuccessful as of 2015), and Titan (a moon of Saturn). They are used for mapping, locating, spying, and probably military weapons platforms (though this last one violates widely accepted international law). Some are even turned outward to observe distant space all the way back to near the Big Bang. Such observations are hyper accurate because they avoid peering through the thick soup of the Earth's atmosphere.

---

[12] This very important concept is explored by Rothbard 1982.

In the foreseeable future, these probes could be used to sweep near Earth orbits of space junk, detect the approach of asteroids and comets, and intercept and divert them from their collision courses. They could provide landings on planets in distant solar systems. Orbiting other stars and surveying planets is within the realm of possible accomplishments in the near future. The problems related to hyper speeds and acceleration would be much easier to solve without living beings aboard.

Probe Ownership

Ownership is relatively easy to determine, at least for the probe itself. If a company built it,[13] the probe is theirs. If they successfully launch it, they own a going concern.[14] This attractive feature of unmanned vehicles will be a compelling driver for these devices. Ownership of the orbit or trajectory they follow might be a little more challenging in a soon to be, more-crowed area.[15] While current space probes are not exactly "free market," the importance of congestion has already come into play.

The question is why a private company would undertake the expense of launching and owning such a device. Unmanned vehicles would provide initial reconnaissance at a small fraction of the cost of a manned spaceship. Acceleration[16] could take place at a much higher rate, which in turn could significantly reduce travel time and cost. Already one has been

---

[13] Of course, President Obama would say that no company ever built anything. He claims credit in behalf of government for all such initiatives. In our view, almost the exact opposite is the case. Private enterprise has created pretty much everything of value, and the state has been there all along preventing, slowing down, often forbidding, progress in this regard. In addition, it must rip off private resources to sustain itself.

[14] If they fail to get it off the earth, they are still the proprietors of it, but this machinery is likely to be only of value as scrap.

[15] The same issue confronts the air transportation industry. There is room for only so many passenger aircraft at 35,000 feet between large cities. In our view, the firms that own the right to travel on these paths should belong to those who have homesteaded them, by using them for this purpose.

[16] Imagine the time it would take to accelerate to a reasonable speed for interstellar travel without crushing everyone on board. It would take a month or more of constantly speeding up. The effortless acceleration seen in *Star Trek* and other fictional space odysseys where people remain standing is not possible without some sort of theory-busting revolution of scientific law: a conceptual innovation on the scale of Relativistic vs. Newtonian physics.

sent to Pluto, and is beaming back fascinating pictures and information, at the time of this writing (2015). Other celestial bodies have been or are planned to be explored with probes. They have landed and sampled the ground, tested rocks, searched for oxygen, water, etc. Such information could be used to develop a program of occupation and/or settlement.

Probes could be used for reconnaissance of distant stars. One could easily be sent to Proxima Centauri.[17] However, whereas a communication cycle, or latency,[18] would be in the order of nine years, the probe would necessarily be required to react to conditions found at its destination without communications from Earth. For all practical purposes, communications would be one-way transmission of data that is detected. It would have to be programed in such a way that after entering an alien solar system, it would slow to an orbit, survey the vicinity, and travel to any discovered planets on its own without input or commands from Earth. Such information would be invaluable for informing the decision as to whether to finance and proceed with manned travel. This, most likely, will occur; only a long way in the future. For the next few decades, man's off-Earth travel will undoubtedly be limited to the Moon and Mars and other destinations within the inner solar system.

Precedents

We have moved from branding cattle to barbed wire fences, and the law had to catch up to remain relevant. We are now in the process of transiting from boundaries on the Earth, to those in the air, and to barriers in space. In a like manner, the legal system will have to keep pace, lest confusion overcomes these gains. Happily, however, there are precedents for these developments. For example, air rights over buildings in large cities,

---

[17] PC is a red dwarf type of star somewhat more than four light years from Earth and the closest one outside the solar system. It orbits the binary Alpha Centauri system at a radius much greater than that of Pluto around the Sun.

[18] Latency is the time delay for communications and is limited by the speed of light. For the New Horizons fly-by of Pluto, by comparison, it is about nine hours.

and the blockading of views[19] on mountains or high-rise buildings. We can at least to some degree extrapolate to space from these earthly precedents.

References

Block, Walter. 1990. Earning Happiness Through Homesteading Unowned Land: A Comment on 'Buying Misery with Federal Land' by Richard Stroup. *Journal of Social Political and Economic Studies* 15 (2): 237–253.

———. 2002a. Homesteading City Streets; An Exercise in Managerial Theory. *Planning and Markets* 5 (1): 18–23. http://www-pam.usc.edu/volume5/v5i1a2s1.html; http://www-pam.usc.edu/. Accessed 23 Apr 2016.

———. 2002b. On Reparations to Blacks for Slavery. *Human Rights Review* 3 (4): 53–73.

Block, Walter E. 1998. Roads, Bridges, Sunlight and Private Property: Reply to Gordon Tullock. *Journal des Economistes et des Etudes Humaines* 8 (2/3): 315–326. http://141.164.133.3/faculty/Block/Blockarticles/roads2_vol8.htm; http://www.walterblock.com/wp-content/uploads/publications/block_roadsbridges-sunlight-reply-tullock-1998.pdf. Accessed 20 Apr 2016.

———. 2008. Homesteading, Ad Coelum, Owning Views and Forestalling. *The Social Sciences* 3 (2): 96–103. http://www.medwelljournals.com/fulltext/TSS/2008/96-103.pdf; http://medwelljournals.com/new/5/archivedetails.php?id=5&jid=TSS&theme=5&issueno=12. Accessed 20 Apr 2016.

———. 2014. Book Review Essay of Steven Pinker's: *The Better Angels of Our Nature: Why Violence Has Declined*. New York, N.Y. Penguin; Part II. *Management Education Science Technology Journal MEST* 2 (1): 141–160.

Block, Walter E., and Matthew Block. 1996. Roads, Bridges, Sunlight and Private Property Rights. *Journal Des Economistes Et Des Etudes Humaines* VII (2/3): 351–362.

Block, Walter E., and Michael R. Edelstein. 2012. Popsicle Sticks and Homesteading Land for Nature Preserves. *Romanian Economic and Business Review* 7 (1): 7–13. http://www.rebe.rau.ro/REBE%207%201.pdf. Accessed 29 Sep 2016.

Block, Walter, and Richard Epstein. 2005. Debate on Eminent Domain. *NYU Journal of Law & Liberty* 1 (3): 1144–1169.

[19] See on this Block 1998, 2008, 2014; Block and Block 1996; Tullock 1996.

Block, Walter E., and Peter Lothian Nelson. 2015. *Water Capitalism: The Case for Privatizing Oceans, Rivers, Lakes, and Aquifers.* New York: Lexington Books; Rowman and Littlefield. https://rowman.com/ISBN/97814985 18802/Water-Capitalism-The-Case-for-Privatizing-Oceans-Rivers-Lakes-and-Aquifers. Accessed 14 Dec 2015.

Block, Walter, and William Barnett II. 2008. Continuums. *Journal Etica e Politica/Ethics & Politics* 1: 151–166. http://www2.units.it/~etica/; http://www2.units.it/~etica/2008_1/BLOCKBARNETT.pdf. Accessed 23 Apr 2016.

Block, Walter and Guillermo Yeatts. 1999–2000. The Economics and Ethics of Land Reform: A Critique of the Pontifical Council for Justice and Peace's 'Toward a Better Distribution of Land: The Challenge of Agrarian Reform'. *Journal of Natural Resources and Environmental Law* 15 (1): 37–69

Bylund, Per. 2005. Man and Matter: A Philosophical Inquiry into the Justification of Ownership in Land from the Basis of Self-Ownership. Master thesis, Lund University, Spring Semester (June). http://www.uppsatser.se/uppsats/a7eb17de8f/; http://perbylund.com/academics_polsci_msc.pdf; http://www.essays.se/essay/a7eb17de8f/; http://www.lunduniversity.lu.se/o.o.i.s?id=2496 5&postid=1330482. Accessed 23 Apr 2016

———. 2012. Man and Matter: How the Former Gains Ownership of the Latter. *Libertarian Papers* 4 (1). http://libertarianpapers.org/articles/2012/lp-4-1-5.pdf. Accessed 23 Apr 2016.

European Space Agency. 2013. What Are Lagrange Points? June 21. http://www.esa.int/Our_Activities/Operations/What_are_Lagrange_points. Accessed 23 Oct 2015.

FAR/AIM. 2016. *Federal Aviation Rules/Aeronautical Information Manual.* Aviation Supplies and Academics, Inc.; 2016 Edition (July 1, 2015). http://www.amazon.com/FAR-AIM-2016-Regulations-Aeronautical/dp/1619542501. Accessed 30 Nov 2015.

Grotius, Hugo. 1625. *Law of War and Peace (De Jure Belli ac Pacis),* 3 volumes. Trans. A.C. Campbell, London, 1814.

Hawking, Stephen. 1996. *A Brief History of Time.* New York: Bantam Books Trade Paperbacks.

Hoppe, Hans-Hermann. 1993. *The Economics and Thics of Private Property. Studies in Political Economy and Philosophy.* Boston: Kluwer Academic Publishers.

———. 2011. Of Private, Common, and Public Property and the Rationale for Total Privatization. *Libertarian Papers* 3 (1). http://libertarianpapers.

org/2011/1-hoppe-private-common-and-public-property/. Accessed 23 Aug 2016.

Kinsella, Stephan N. 2003. A Libertarian Theory of Contract: Title Transfer, Binding Promises, and Inalienability. *Journal of Libertarian Studies* 17 (2): 11–37. http://www.mises.org/journals/jls/17_2/17_2_2.pdf. Accessed 23 Apr 2016.

———. 2006. How We Come to Own Ourselves. September 7. http://www.mises.org/story/2291. Accessed 23 Apr 2016.

———. 2009. Homesteading, Abandonment, and Unowned Land in the Civil Law. May 22. http://blog.mises.org/10004/homesteading-abandonment-and-unowned-land-in-the-civil-law/. Accessed 23 Apr 2016.

Locke, John. 1948. *An Essay Concerning the True Origin, Extent and End of Civil Government.* In *Social Contract*, ed. E. Barker, 17–19. New York: Oxford University Press.

Locke, John. 1955 [1690]. *Second Treatise on Government.* Chicago: Henry Regnery.

Nelson, Peter Lothian. 2015. To Homestead a Nature Preserve. Liberty.me. July 14. https://peterlothiannelson.liberty.me/to-homestead-a-nature-preserve/. Accessed 29 Aug 2015.

Paul, Ellen Frankel. 1987. *Property Rights and Eminent Domain.* Livingston, NJ: Transaction Publishers.

Pufendorf, Samuel. 1673. Natural Law and the Law of Nations (De officio hominis et civis prout ipsi praescribuntur lege naturali).

Rothbard, Murray N. 1973. *For a New Liberty.* New York: Macmillan. http://mises.org/rothbard/newlibertywhole.asp. Accessed 23 Aug 2016.

———. 1982. Law, Property Rights, and Air Pollution. *Cato Journal* 2 (1). Reprinted in *Economics and the Environment: A Reconciliation*, Walter E. Block, ed., Vancouver: The Fraser Institute, 1990, pp. 233–279. http://mises.org/story/2120; http://www.mises.org/rothbard/lawproperty.pdf. Accessed 20 Apr 2016.

Rozeff, Michael S. 2005. Original Appropriation and Its Critics. September 1. http://www.lewrockwell.com/rozeff/rozeff18.html. Accessed 23 Apr 2016.

Tullock, Gordon. 1996. Comment on 'Roads, Bridges, Sunlight and Private Property', by Walter E. Block and Matthew Block. *Journal des Economistes et des Etudes Humaines* 7 (4): 589–592.

Watner, Carl. 1982. The Proprietary Theory of Justice in the Libertarian Tradition. *Journal of Libertarian Studies* 6 (3–4): 289–316. http://mises.org/journals/jls/6_3/6_3_6.pdf. Accessed 23 Apr 2016.

6

The Moon

Man has landed on the Moon. Some people will give credit to the U.S. government for such an accomplishment with the conviction that freely acting individuals could not have done it; but this is too hasty. The market process would have been guided by profit potential, the interest rate, and other economic and fiscal facts; in other words—sound investment sense. The state ignores all that and using violence gets away with its economic illiteracy. Why do we now see that the space landing was premature? No follow-up has occurred in the past 45 years.[1] A better strategy might well have been for interested private parties to get their ducks lined up first in terms of better transportation vehicles, fuel, general technology, etc. and only then visit our nearest neighbor.[2] We could have done so with the

---

[1] There is talk from other countries, such as China launching its own lunar exploration program, but this is only another adolescent attempt to show up their predecessor. In any case, should it happen, it would not be a follow-up. Rather, it would be the piling up of yet more statism.

[2] This statement sounds wrong. Is it not a maxim for successful businessmen to "strike when the iron is hot"? It is indeed. The difference lies not so much in speed as in motivation. Sure, it takes time to develop "better transportation vehicles, fuel, general technology"; and one might lose the race by taking too much time to prepare. However, the goal of the state is to get to the Moon for no other sake than political. The businessman will have a very different goal in mind. The follow-up is built into his plan. As discussed below, he may want to open a moon-based holiday venue. Upon arriving, he has merely shown a proof of concept and immediately proceeds to the next step. But prior even to that, he will have realized a procedure for making his destination a reality. Without

© The Author(s) 2018
P. L. Nelson, W. E. Block, *Space Capitalism*, Palgrave Studies in Classical Liberalism,
https://doi.org/10.1007/978-3-319-74651-7_6

momentum necessary to quickly follow this up with more ambitious attempts (e.g., Mars, asteroids). This would have been the result had we left the entire matter to entrepreneurs. Their approach to the problem of extra-terrestrial exploration would have been based on their personal assessment of return on investment. In contrast, the actual impetus for this foray was John F. Kennedy's political ambition, a weak reed upon which to hang such an important undertaking. As it was, the moon landings were not much different from a U.S.S.R. vs. U.S. high school soccer game, but much more expensive. After the West had completely and thoroughly defeated the second world,[3] interest died; for no one had any compelling reason to continue this process.

In any case, what the U.S. astronauts found was a desolate place. Alas for casein lovers, we discovered no green cheese. It is rocky and dusty and dry! The Moon has no practical atmosphere. Daytime has unmitigated direct Sun for a bit less than 14 earth days followed by some two weeks of virtual total darkness. Certain of those nights will be partially bathed in earthlight. It is far from the most pleasant environment for man. Nevertheless, it is our closest celestial neighbor.[4]

This defeat and the defeatist attitude of NASA[5] need not deter space adventurers. One can imagine many exceedingly profitable ventures on the Moon. Those who are guided by a desire to serve their fellow man through the satisfaction of wants will find a way.[6] And that is the attraction

---

the possibility of both success and profit, he would not even start the venture. He would work on a more promising business and leave this one to others. The state, in contrast, will fixate on an impressive monument (a flag on the Moon, a pyramid) and admit of no spending limits to achieve what really amounts to nothing more than a circus act. As for "striking when the iron is hot" the question remains, precisely when is "it" hot? There is such a thing as prematurity, as well as tardiness. The market veers in the direction of neither one.

[3] Our moon landing supposedly outdid their Sputnik.

[4] Some people believe the Moon is a distraction (for example Zubrin 2011). It may be so if the only object is travel to another potentially habitable planet. We agree that if the sole purpose of reaching the Moon is a one-dimensional narrow goal to be used as a stepping stone to Mars, he may very well be correct. However, as shown herein, there are many potential uses for the Moon, even including permanent settlement. Once such permanent bases are set up for their own projects, the calculus that Zubrin considers changes completely. It is the economic calculations of the entrepreneur that will then govern.

[5] NASA = National Aeronautics and Space Administration. For critiques of this bureaucratic institution see Chap. 10, for more NASA boondoggles.

[6] To paraphrase Dr. Ian in *Jurassic Park*: "The free market—uh—finds a way." Those who believe the free market needs to be controlled would do well to consider this aphorism.

for honest men seeking financial or personal reward. After all, the Moon has low but useful gravity. It is about half the diameter of Mars or Mercury, both of which are much smaller than Earth and, more to the point, have much less mass. Once an efficient method is developed for leaving our planet (see Chap. 4), landings and departures would be easy to or from this, our natural satellite and launching pad. Herein is its potentially greatest value. Additionally, the likelihood of valuable minerals provides further enticement. The most common resource might well be a large amount of oxygen on the surface in the form of metallic oxides. But first things first.

Space Tourism

A likely early and profitable venture may be space tourism. One could build a spaceport and hotel on the Moon. Picture a selenology (the scientific study of the Moon) museum of local materials untarnished by the ravages of weather and atmosphere. Imagine the fun of using a trampoline where a man's weight is but a small fraction of what it is on Earth. In fact, a science exhibit could afford a mind-boggling understanding and appreciation based on an experience of the same inertia as on our home planet but with much less gravitational attraction. The difference between mass and weight would soon become apparent to these paying and delighted customers.

Of course, such a resort would necessarily include a vast bank of telescopes for tourists to view the Earth in a variety of magnifications.[7] During the extended 14-day night, these telescopes would offer visitors a view of the starry sky unavailable on Earth. There could be a truly unique exhibition of not only the Earth but also our celestial neighborhood from such a location.

It would be quite interesting to serve food grown on the Moon. Greenhouses could provide all sorts of grains and vegetables. Electricity through the night could be generated by solar power stations in the polar regions. Low gravity, long sunlight, vegetables grown in an artificial, CO_2

---

[7] Refer to Chap. 4 for a discussion of viewing Earth from a high altitude.

rich atmosphere could have some interesting characteristics such as over-sized vegetables resembling those grown on Earth in the land of the midnight Sun. Those could be sufficiently exotic to ship back to earthlings. Separate greenhouses could be used to raise llamas, alpacas, and other such animals in an oxygen-rich, low-pressure, and low-gravity environment. These greenhouses could very well provide their own science exhibit for the vacationers.

Agriculture

As discussed above, agricultural opportunities abound. While greenhouses, water, and power would be required, the extent of land could enable a vast supply of products both mundane and mysterious for shipment back to Earth.[8] Water can be manufactured by chemically processing natural lunar minerals and collecting oxygen and hydrogen,[9] possibly from the purification of metallic ores. The enclosures could be designed to forestall another major challenge, namely radioactivity from the Sun, the Van Allen radiation belts, cosmic rays from distant bodies in space, and secondary particle emission from the lunar surface.[10] If the "greenhouse" is made with the right plastic, the solar emissions can be reduced to safe levels (Wall 2013). Artificial magnetic fields could also help reduce radiation (Barry 2005).

A variety of atmospheres could be designed to provide the best habitat for the growth of each type of farm or dairy product. High CO_2 could be used for leafy green plants and dense O_2 for farm animals. Low pressure of, say, 15,000 feet of earth-equivalent elevation could be used for llamas and alpacas. Could lakes be used for fish farms? Yes, if the entrepreneurs found the opportunities worthwhile to manufacture enough water. In short, if left to private developers, a veritable Garden of Eden inspires the

---

[8] Or to Mars, or to wherever their owners can obtain the best terms of trade for them.

[9] Hydrogen in more simple forms than metallic ore has been discovered on the Moon (Steigerwald 2015).

[10] Cosmic rays from deep space striking the Moon blast protons from the Moon's surface (Barry 2005).

imagination. This is in stark contrast to the know-it-all apparatchiks who want complete control to forbid their nemeses: independent persons.

Agriculture could tie into the tourist trade by first providing sustenance for the vacationers and second by providing one of the more captivating exhibits complete with storyboards elucidating the processes.

Mining

The potential for mineral extraction is an added draw. Once underground, the mine could be shut off and the air inside made much like Earth's. The extreme temperature swings on the surface would be of little concern. But the main advantage is that there would be no influences to attract the deprecating attention of those Luddites who oppose technological innovation for the sake of limiting freedom.

A wide variety of lunar minerals are readily available (Prado 2013). Oxides of aluminum, iron, calcium, titanium, magnesium are present on or near the surface as well as phosphates. Energy from a source such as solar power stations located at the Moon's poles[11] can be used to refine Al_2O_3 into elemental aluminum and oxygen. Powdered aluminum (Al) is an intense fuel usable in rocket motors. In addition, manufacturers fashion it into lightweight structural bars and plates used to erect buildings or capsules for utilization in a vacuum environment.

Due to its high density, iron would not seem to be very useful until one considers that on a zero-free-oxygen, no-water celestial body, it would be immune to rust. Its main value would be for the building of structures and surface-bound vehicles or any structural purpose large or small.

What all these minerals provide are opportunities[12] for adventurous creators to profitably develop the Moon. That will only happen if they can do so without the constant impositions from statists.[13]

---

[11] Because of the slow month-long period of rotation, solar power stations located at the poles are more effective than at other locations because they are always exposed to sunlight. All other placements would be in the shade for 14 straight days every month.

[12] Only a few of which are listed herein.

[13] Presumably, on a free-enterprise Moon, there would be no building codes, no zoning laws, no rent control legislation, no public streets (Block 2009), no density requirements, etc.

Transportation/Communication Hub

The orb provides a nearly unparalleled opportunity for transportation. The energy required for landing and lift-off is a small fraction of such actions on Earth. The moon lies within a shallow gravity well; no doubt entrepreneurs, freed of government restrictions, will take full advantage of this happy circumstance, at least for transportation from the Moon toward the second and fourth rocks from the Sun and, eventually, beyond. It could host a major, easy-to-access, space port complete with local fuel and building resources. For decades, Great Britain used the land that is now South Africa for purposes like these: as a way station to properties further afield. The moon could become the twenty-first century equivalent.

Wireless communications would also be relatively easy because of the lack of atmospheric interference and the slow, month-long period of rotation. The Earth's air can and does distort radio and light waves. The moon will not suffer that constraint. The slow period of rotation (it is in tidal lock)[14] means that no complex tracking equipment is required for Earth/Moon communications, though the equipment on the home planet would need it.

Manufacturing

Opportunities for manufacturing beyond local uses for buildings and space vehicles discussed above are speculative. However, anything that could benefit from low gravity and/or a lack of atmosphere, especially oxygen, would be a candidate for creation on the Moon followed by transportation to Earth, or elsewhere.

---

[14] "Tidal lock" is a condition of an orbiting body that has experienced energy losses or breaking forces (such as the conversion of ocean water movement to heat) and has slowed rotation so that it matches the period of revolution about the larger object. The result is that the side of the Moon facing the Earth is always the same. Over many eons, the spin of rotating orbiters tend to slow down to this state.

Isolation

Isolation has been touched on earlier, but one of the primary benefits available on the Moon would be the lack of interference by busybodies and bureaucrats. Virtually anything could be performed with zero environmental damage and no one to complain or indulge in politically motivated meddling. With such associated expenses on Earth running up costs to three, four, or more times those of normal manufacturing inputs, the savings could easily offset the apparent excessive outlay for transportation and greenhouses.

References

Barry, Patrick L. 2005. Radioactive Moon. *NASA Science—Science News*. September 8. National Aeronautics and Space Administration. http://science. nasa.gov/science-news/science-at-nasa/2005/08sep_radioactivemoon/. Accessed 23 Nov 2015.

Block, Walter E. 2009. *The Privatization of Roads and Highways: Human and Economic Factors*. Auburn, AL: The Mises Institute. http://www.amazon. com/Privatization-Roads-And-Highways-Factors/dp/1279887303/; http:// mises.org/books/roads_web.pdf; http://mises.org/daily/3416. Accessed 23 Aug 2016.

Prado, Mark. 2013. Major Lunar Minerals. *Permanent*. http://www.permanent. com/lunar-geology-minerals.html. Accessed 1 Dec 2015.

Steigerwald, Bill. 2015. NASA's LRO Discovers Lunar Hydrogen More Abundant on Moon's Pole-Facing Slopes. July 30. http://www.nasa.gov/content/goddard/lro-lunar-hydrogen. Accessed 26 Apr 2016.

Wall, Mike. 2013. Plastic Could Protect Astronauts from Deep-Space Radiation. *Space.com*. June 14. http://www.space.com/21561-space-exploration-radiation-protection-plastic.html. Accessed 23 Nov 2015.

Zubrin, Robert. 2011. *The Case for Mars, The Plan to Settle the Red Planet and Why We Must*. New York: Free Press, Simon & Schuster.

7

The Inner Planets and Extra-Terrestrial Moons

Mars

It Can't Be Done, so They Say

An article by Regis (2015) suggests that travel to Mars borders on the preposterous. It is important to our thesis,[1] is relatively short, and appears in the *New York Times*, the supposed American newspaper of record. It is thus worth reacting to it thoroughly. Accordingly, we begin this chapter in that manner, by quoting from this article, and interspersing our criticisms of it:

> In the early years of the 20th century, zeppelins [sic] filled with flammable and explosive hydrogen were all the rage in Germany, a reckless infatuation that ended with the eruption and crash of the Hindenburg in 1937. Sometimes, technology is a triumph of wild-eyed enthusiasm over the unpleasant facts of the real world.

> Today we are witnessing a similar outburst of enthusiasm over the literally outlandish notion that in the relatively near future, some of us are going to be living, working, thriving and dying on Mars. A Dutch nonprofit ven-

---

[1] In a negative manner, of course, since it counsels against colonizing Mars.

© The Author(s) 2018
P. L. Nelson, W. E. Block, *Space Capitalism*, Palgrave Studies in Classical Liberalism,
https://doi.org/10.1007/978-3-319-74651-7_7

ture called Mars One aspires to send four people to Mars by 2026 as the beginning of a permanent human settlement. In the United States, the nonprofit Inspiration One has plans for a two-person team to fly within 100 miles of the planet, launching from Earth in January 2018. And the entrepreneur Elon Musk, who runs a rocket company called SpaceX, has said he hopes to send the first people to Mars in 11 to 12 years.

Unfortunately, this Mars mania reflects an excessively optimistic view of what it actually takes to travel to and live on Mars, papering over many of the harsh realities and bitter truths that underlie the dream.

Regis is indeed correct that "Sometimes, technology is a triumph of wild-eyed enthusiasm over the unpleasant facts of the real world" and the Zeppelin is a supposedly reasonable example of this phenomenon. Another might be Icarus' attempt to fly. However, the exact opposite mistake also occurs, and is probably much more prevalent. For example, tens of thousands of commentators thought the "horseless carriage" would never move (Glasscock 2011).[2] Or, man will never be able to fly. Or we could never reach the Moon. Or the iPhone would never capture any significant market share. Or no one would ever want a computer at home.[3]

First, there is the tedious business of getting there. Using current technology and conventional chemical rockets, a trip to Mars would be a grueling, eight- to nine-month-long nightmare for the crew. Nine months is a long time for any group of people to be traveling in a small, closed, packed spacecraft. (We're not talking about the relatively comfy confines of a hab-

---

[2] According to one published poem: "A horseless carriage they used to say: 'Surely it will never move, If not fueled with oats and hay'" (Abramson 2004).

[3] For valuable sources of such incorrect predictions, to the effect that this or that technology would never occur, consider the following ill-advised examples of wild-eyed claims of impossible dreams that are nearly endless. Here are some pithy examples: "What can be more palpably absurd than the prospect held out of locomotives traveling twice as fast as stagecoaches?"; "Well-informed people know that it is impossible to transmit the human voice over wires as may be done with dots and dashes of Morse code, and that, were it possible to do so, the thing would be of no practical value."; and "To place a man in a multi-stage rocket and project him into the controlling gravitational field of the Moon where the passengers can make scientific observations, perhaps land alive, and then return to Earth—all that constitutes a wild dream worthy of Jules Verne. I am bold enough to say that such a man-made voyage will never occur regardless of all future advances." One would think that with examples such as these under our belt, technological skeptics such as Regis would show a bit more modesty. For other inaccurate predictions, under-estimating technological progress see Pegg 2014; for yet more erroneous predictions by famous futurists, see Chappell 2014.

itable satellite like the International Space Station.) Tears, sweat, urine and perhaps even solid waste will be recycled, your personal space is reduced to the size of an S.U.V., and you and your crewmates are floating around sideways, upside down and at other nauseating angles.

Crew members are in microgravity for the entire trip, with consequent health problems: Your bone mass wastes away, your teeth become more susceptible to cavities, your body's muscles, including your heart, and even the small muscles that control your eye movements, atrophy and lose mass, and your immune, digestive, vascular and pulmonary systems function at impaired levels.

This author avers that a trip to Mars would require a "grueling, eight- to nine-month-long nightmare for the crew." Even if so, a voyage of this duration is hardly unprecedented. For example, Magellan's journey from Spain to the Spice Islands took three long, arduous years.[4] The fact is that the necessary technology to send a community of humans to the Red Planet is already within our grasp. All it would take is a bit of entrepreneurial imagination and the will to develop solutions to the challenges that will inevitably occur. For example, a dumbbell-shaped spacecraft (that does not even need to be very massive) could be set in rotation such that artificial gravity will negate all of Regis' supposed impenetrable complications, presumably preventing continuing health. Oh, and the two, or more, bulbous ends of the craft would provide get-away areas to provide relief and privacy[5] for the intrepid travelers.

---

[4] History.com n.d.; Marco Polo's trips are legendary; WNET. 2008. Roald Amundsen, a Norwegian explorer, was the first to successfully reach the South Pole on December 14, 1911; see Czech 2006. "The journey to the pole and back had taken 99 days—10 fewer than scheduled—and they had covered about 1860 nautical miles (3440 km)." Source: Amundsen et al. 1912. Magellan's Voyage began from Spain on September 20, 1519 and ended in the Philippines on March 16, 1521 (he was killed by natives on April 27). Source: Ferdinand Magellan Timeline 2015. Regarding HMS Bounty: "In December 1787, the Bounty left England for Tahiti in the South Pacific... After a 10-month journey, the Bounty arrived in Tahiti in October 1788..." Source: History.com 2016. We owe these citations to Richard Fast.

[5] Privacy is very important in this context, but it is not a (negative) right. Rather, it is a positive "right." That is to say, no right at all but rather an aspect of wealth. On negative versus positive rights in general see Block 1986; Gordon 2004; Katz n.d.; Long 1993; Mercer 2001; Rothbard 1982b; Selick 2014; Williams 2016. On the case for privacy not being a legitimate right, see, Block 1991, 2012, 2013a, b, ch. 18; Block, Kinsella and Whitehead 2006. Finally, we must ask, how much privacy did the crew members of *Nao Victoria* and Magellan's other vessels have during their voyages?

In addition, there will be persistent mechanical noise and vibration, sleep disturbances, unbearable tedium, trance states, depression, monotonous repetition of meals, clothing, routines, conversations and so on. Every source of interpersonal conflict, and emotional and psychological stress that we experience in ordinary, day-to-day life on Earth will be magnified exponentially by restriction to a tiny, hermetically sealed, pressure-cooker capsule hurtling through deep space.

To top it all off, despite these constraints, the crew must operate within an exceptionally slim margin of error. As with any cutting-edge technology, there will be continuous threats of equipment failures, computer malfunctions, power interruptions and software glitches.

Regis mentions health problems which would arise on a trip to Mars. But those who explored the Earth in sailing ships, and were away from land and civilization for long periods of times in cramped quarters, were subject to diseases such as scurvy, before the discovery that lemons and limes could safeguard sailors. Who is to say that similar breakthroughs will not occur regarding space travel? Regis bewails "persistent mechanical noise and vibration, sleep disturbances, unbearable tedium...." Of course, this just as aptly describes long-distance travel via sailing ships, or on elephant, camel or horseback. How do all his "horrific" trials differ in terms of physical or psychological effect on men's health from being in a covered wagon in the middle of the Utah/Nevada desert or in a sailing vessel smaller than that of an America's cup challenger 2000 miles from the nearest land?

And getting there is the easy part. Mars is a dead, cold, barren planet on which no living thing is known to have evolved, and which harbors no breathable air or oxygen, no liquid water and no sources of food, nor conditions favorable for producing any. For these and other reasons it would be accurate to call Mars a veritable hell for living things, were it not for the fact that the planet's average surface temperature is minus 81 degrees Fahrenheit.

Given the hostile conditions on the Martian surface, human inhabitants would have to produce all of the necessities of life for themselves. Consider the challenge of producing something as basic as an air supply. Since the atmosphere of Mars is 95 percent carbon dioxide, and since indefinitely large stocks of air cannot be brought from Earth, air must be synthesized from a collection of separate ingredients, as in a chemistry lab or factory.

This skeptic maintains there will be "no liquid water" on Mars.[6] But recent discoveries and even not so current ones have already dispelled any such notion (Chang 2015; Pearson 2015; Sample 2015; Whiteway et al. 2009). In any case, what is wrong with ice? There was "no liquid water" in Antarctica when the South Pole was reached by snow shoe and ski in 1911 either (Mason 2010; Schlenoff 2011). Surely, then, this lacuna cannot be dispositive. Furthermore, as long as the fourth rock from the Sun has oxygen and hydrogen, though they be tied up in chemical compounds such as metallic oxides and hydroxides, O_2 and H_2O can be manufactured, as even Regis admits.

As for the claim that "the planet's average surface temperature is minus 81 degrees Fahrenheit," it sometimes reaches that level of coldness, and worse, in Canada[7] and Russian Siberia. No, these places are not like Miami Beach, but people do live in these Northern climes, and, even, prosper. If they can do this at inhospitable parts of the Earth, there is no reason to expect this cannot be replicated on Mars.

Oxygen on Mars exists as a constituent of water—the O in H_2O. Thus, one way to get this essential component of air is to first obtain an adequate store of water. However, there being no proven liquid water reserves on Mars, water, too, must be produced from raw material sources, specifically from the soil. One plan calls for digging up the soil and placing it into a heater that will evaporate off any water within it. The water vapor is then condensed into a liquid.

Oxygen, in turn, can be separated from the hydrogen in the water by means of electrolysis, and then stockpiled. The nitrogen component of air could be "mined" from the thin Martian atmosphere. With these two constituents in hand, and then combined, we finally have a breath of air (although not 'fresh' air).

---

[6] We remind the reader that for all practical purposes, a sailor, except for the stale water which he brought along in a 90-foot vessel in the middle of the Atlantic Ocean would find no potable H_2O.

[7] https://www.theweathernetwork.com/news/articles/mars-officially-colder-than-canada-thursday/43251; http://www.cbc.ca/news/technology/mars-warmer-than-parts-of-canada-u-s-1.2895092; and temperature in the Canadian Yukon sometimes is on a par with the Asteroid Belt: http://nationalpost.com/news/canada/a-scientific-analysis-of-just-how-damned-cold-it-is-in-canada.

Moreover, during the early stage before human arrival on the planet, water-rich asteroids could be redirected to collide with the planet. If done with enough of these heavenly bodies, the process would tend to increase the planet's rotation,[8] warm it, and increase the available H_2O.[9]

> These are only a few of the many serious challenges that must be overcome before anyone can put human beings on Mars and expect them to live for more than five minutes. The notion that we can start colonizing Mars within the next 10 years or so is an overoptimistic, delusory idea that falls just short of being a joke.

Yes, air will have to be produced, water too if in insufficient supply, and recycling will have to become the order of the day. And, it cannot be denied, this will be rather difficult. Granted it will be lonely to live on Mars, at least at the outset, and trips back and forth will be costly.[10] Will swimming pools be available? Unlikely. But to claim that therefore a trip to Mars, and settlement thereof, "falls just short of being a joke" merely reveals petrified thinking and a strong lack of imagination.

This author makes a more valid point regarding the unlikelihood of such a trip being made "within the next 10 years or so." What is the optimal time horizon for such an adventure? The answer emanating from the present authors is: whenever the free-market system deems it worthwhile. Does this mean that such an enterprise will have to wait until it can be organized on a profitable basis? Yes, if we include not only monetary

---

[8] The increased rotation stems from the effect of angular momentum. It is like an ice skater entering a spin. At first, he starts to curve, as an object entering an orbit. Then he tightens his curvature and places his limbs close to his body. The conservation of momentum requires that the speed of rotation increases as the diameter decreases.

[9] We admit that any system of producing water on the planet's surface would be temporary and would need to be repeated unless a viable magnetosphere could be created. The latter effort would involve the Herculean effort of creating and maintaining a liquid core. Alternatively, a superconducting cable in orbit around the planet could produce a magnetic field (also Herculean). Without one to protect the new atmosphere, the solar wind would gradually blow it out to space. Hence the need to constantly replace it. We admit that goals such as creating liquid water on the surface and an atmosphere is difficult. Our point here is that it is not impossible, except perhaps for naysayers and bureaucrats.

[10] Rader (2014) advocates, at least initially, a one-way trip to Mars.

returns, but also psychic profits.[11] The prestige of being the first to land on Mars would be inestimable. The esteem derived from being among the earliest involved in any aspect of the colonization of Mars would be likewise beyond measure no matter whether one was an explorer, an initial resident, or the discoverer of a vast aquifer. Besides all of that, remember, one of our main motivations for supporting such a goal is to preserve the human race. There may be those who are more fearful of a nuclear war than others. Such people would have lower alternative costs than many other people for being amongst the first Martian colonists. Then, too, there might be very wealthy men who would achieve great satisfaction from under-writing the costs of such an initiative, and having, in return, sites named after them (e.g. Buffett City, or Gatesville).

Finally, the concept of the airship or Zeppelin was and is a successful one despite the experience of the *Hindenburg*. These craft represented a cutting-edge technology used to transport people in rapid time and in comfort across vast distances with efficiency. In addition, they were used for observation and patrol purposes. With any new skill or equipment mistakes will be made. Since it is *avant-garde*, no one knows how to do it. Accidents will be common initially. While Zeppelin used hydrogen, other airships employed helium. Today, the Goodyear blimp is well-known as an advertising vehicle. Not so well-known is the E-Green Technologies Bullet, a massive inflatable using helium for lift (Bates, C. 2012). Even a return to the use of hydrogen is conceivable with the use of improved fire prevention, isolation, and suppression methods.[12]

---

[11] It is important here to note that the necessity for profitability refers to the *ex-ante* viewpoint. After the accomplishment of the feat, should it be found to have been unprofitable is not the issue at this time, though it may be relevant to follow-up trips.

[12] While initially hydrogen appears much more efficient than helium for lift, in fact the advantage is not as great as it seems. The former comes in the form of H2 (atomic weight of 2 for the molecule as opposed to 1 for the atom). Thus, the density of helium (atomic weigh of 4) is only twice as great. Furthermore, lifting capacity is more related to the amount of displaced air. It is directly proportional to the difference between the weight of air (1.2 grams per liter) minus that of the gas filling the balloon (0.18 g/l for helium and 0.09 g/l for hydrogen), not that of the filling gas. If certain operational limitations could be overcome, hydrogen would be more efficient by only 0.09%. Incidentally, Luftschiffbau Zeppelin, GmbH was forced to use hydrogen in its airships because the U.S. government was hording helium for military reasons. For more on hydrogen vs. helium see UOH (2002). In other words, improving the purity of the He and the effectiveness of the membrane could make the former nearly as good as H2. Joke: The economist was asked: "How

Mars is perhaps the most important extra-terrestrial body to discuss because it is within our grasp in the short term compared to any other, except possibly the Moon. A far more interesting discussion than that of Regis comes from Robert Zubrin in *The Case for Mars* (Zubrin 2011). In this book, he lays out a practical plan to explore and permanently occupy the Red Planet. Key to Zubrin's optimism is that he worked for a private for-profit company. As a member of such an organization, his interest is to achieve his goal at a viable cost. He points out in detail how NASA (the National Aeronautics and Space Administration), an agency of the state, runs up the expense with objectives superfluous to the agenda of putting people on an extra-terrestrial planet. To illustrate how governments go astray, the diversions that Zubrin lists share the desire for extra projects to provide employment for favored cronies. As a result, NASA developed a plan that includes a massive orbiting space station in low Earth orbit and a manufacturing dock to build large-scale spaceships for interplanetary travel.[13] Zubrin insightfully mentions that the cost estimate for this program, called the Space Exploration Initiative (SEI), is $450 billion in order to put "flags and footprints" on Mars.[14]

By comparison this author introduces and explains what he calls the "Mars Direct" plan. Without going into all the details here, this involves the use of a couple of heavy lift boosters, similar to the Saturn V of the Apollo program, to launch a mission directly to Mars. It would not include as part of the mission building a base on the Moon nor an orbiting spaceship factory. Instead, the plan calls for the use of resources derived from the Red Planet itself. Zubrin points out how the Moon landings failed to lead to any permanent results because the goals were too limited. Mars Direct would have explorers spending months at a time for each mission on the Martian surface to explore for resources and over time to set up villages for permanent settlement. His estimate for a direct throw mission is $55 billion (p. 81), somewhat more than a tenth of the

---

is your wife?" Came the answer: "Compared to what?" The same response is apposite here. Yes, the Zeppelin was problematic compared to a modern jet plane, but not to a horse and buggy.

[13] Zubrin refers to them as "*Battlestar Galactica*," a massive fictional spaceship from the future (p. 2).

[14] Page 59. This by the way is what the authors of this present book mean when we suggest that much of what the state tries to accomplish in space resembles a highschool sports match.

SEI. In short, landing humans on Mars could be done in the near future for a much lower cost and would actually accomplish goals of genuine value for resources, exploration, and scientific knowledge.

However, even Zubrin does not go far enough in the direction of free enterprise and *laissez-faire* capitalism. Even though he complains bitterly about bureaucratic empire building, his plan was presented to NASA, not to a private entrepreneur. That is to say, it remains a government plan. The powers that be want to know how it furthers their political careers. Resources and knowledge of a distant planet are of no value to them unless they can be translated into political capital. Our book, in sharp contrast, is intended to overcome such obstacles by recommending that private organizations pursue the project; for they do have goals of real value. If they see a way to earn more than $55 billion,[15] they will undertake the task. Private entrepreneurs will find the investors to finance it. They will not need congressional approval.

Venus

Conventional wisdom tells us of the impossibility of colonizing Venus. All the same, the supposedly intractable transportation problems that apply to Mars remain in effect for this planet. If we cannot access the former sphere, we cannot do so regarding the latter. There is also the poisonous Venusian atmosphere which is many times the density of Earth's. The pressure on the surface is about 1300 pounds per square inch, 90 times that of the third rock from the Sun.[16] To find the same pressure on our planet would require diving under water to a depth of approximately 3000 feet.

Furthermore, there is intense heat. The temperature at the surface exceeds 460° C, or 870° F. That is the hottest planet in the solar system.[17] An additional challenge to surface settlement is the slow rotation in

---

[15] If it were really a private operation, it would undoubtedly be even cheaper than $55 billion. By comparison, this amount would buy about 163 F22 Rapters.

[16] The Venusian facts listed herein are taken or derived from Choi, C. 2014a.

[17] Mercury is much closer to the sun than Venus; so, it should be hotter should it not? Since the former has no significant atmosphere with which to retain its heat, it is actually cooler: about 450o C or 840o F on the day side and −170o C or −275o F on the night side (Choi 2014b). For more on this, see the discussion in this chapter below.

which one day lasts 243 Earth days. Any housing capable of sustaining men on the surface would need massive insulation plus one humongous air conditioner. The Venusian gas is unbearable. Consisting of 96.5% carbon dioxide, the atmosphere is unbreathable. Chemicals noxious to man fill out the remainder. This includes clouds of sulfuric acid. This is not where anyone wants to be, so the orthodox tell us.

In fact, entrepreneurs would find ways should the opportunity for profit present itself, and in the case of Venus, such opportunities appear to abound. First, it is an Earth-sized rocky planet. It can be expected to have all the mineral resources of Earth: iron, silicon, uranium, etc.

The existence of petroleum is unknown, but energy sources are plentiful. For one, because of its proximity to the Sun, solar energy would be far easier to access. But would not those acidic clouds reduce this possibility? The overcast would have a trivial effect when we consider one of the most promising methods of living on Venus. The place for humans to thrive is in balloons at a high elevation. Since the ambient atmosphere of Earth is much less dense, the balloons filled with air at Earth-like pressure would float.[18] The equivalent of Earth's atmospheric pressure occurs over 30 miles above the surface. At that elevation, the temperature is much less than at the surface.[19] The larger the container, the less structural matter would be required for the respective volume. The amount of resources required would be quite small compared to a similar occupied enclosure on Mars.

The biggest problems would be making the structure acid-resistant and finding ways to access the hard, rocky surface under so much pressure. The first issue is easily solved with a material such as Teflon-coated Mylar. It is of light weight. It could be manufactured on Earth and transported to its new location and then inflated with air. Where would the air come from? It would be filtered and derived from the Venusian atmosphere. While such compounds as sulfuric acid and carbon dioxide are prevalent,

---

[18]To keep the air from compressing and sinking to an elevation too low for human health, the colony would most likely need either a rigid structure like a Zeppelin or a second balloon compartment filled with helium, methane, or ammonia. While the molecular weights of the latter are much greater and less efficient than the first, they may be much easier to obtain.

[19]The same effect is observed here on Earth. When one drives to a higher elevation in the mountains, the temperature is found to be much cooler.

nitrogen, argon, and water are still present. These can be separated and pumped into the inflating sphere. Some of those compounds (carbon dioxide and water) of course contain oxygen. The planting of gardens in the proposed balloons would generate the breathable gas. In the interim, prior to the development of a self-sustaining local system, oxygen could be imported in liquid form or derived artificially from the environment with the use of solar power.

Other more rigid compounds would be used for access ports and doors. The vehicle would be of such a light weight that houses and factories could be built cheaply and thus be quite abundant. The entire structure could be organized like a condominium wherein the interior spaces are privately owned even while the exterior structural elements are owned by all in the form of joint stock shares.

Access to the surface could be made using pressure vessels. Humans already have most of the required technology for this type of vehicle. Existing submarines are capable of descending to the depth described above, 3000 feet of water, and more. Such a device might need different control surfaces that would more closely resemble an airplane, but there again, we already have that technology. It is just a matter of ascertaining the correct surfaces and shapes necessary to navigate the Venusian atmosphere. The same principles of physics would apply. The Reynolds[20] and Mach[21] numbers would come into play just as at home. Only the magnitudes would be adjusted to the actual density and viscosity found on the foreign body.

Once such aerial "submarines" were developed, travel to other balloon colonies and/or the surface might well be easier than on Earth. Similarly, Venus-bound surface vehicles could be developed for travel, and/or digging purposes.

---

[20] The Reynolds number is a dimensionless ratio of momentum forces to viscous forces. The number relates to whether gaseous flow over a wing will be laminar or turbulent. For more on this refer to Warhaft 1997.

[21] The Mach number is a dimensionless ratio between the velocity of an object moving through a fluid medium and the speed of a compression wave of which the speed of sound in air on Earth is an example. The number relates to whether the flow can be understood as incompressible or not. Generally, at speeds above Mach 1, the gas is effectively incompressible. For further reading on this see Jessa 2010.

Since none of the preceding has been accomplished, it is all speculative of course. This is presented merely to show that occupation of Venus is not as farfetched as the naysayers would have us believe. While new challenges to overcome will present themselves, there is nothing in either the Martian or Venusian environment that cannot be overcome. The key to space exploration is the freedom of explorers to try even at risk of life and limb for the sake of "going where no one has gone before" for the fun of it. The same applies to Mercury and the extra-terrestrial moons.

Mercury

This planet appears particularly inhospitable because it is the closest to the Sun, rotates very slowly,[22] and has little atmosphere. Nevertheless, "where there is a will, there is a way." Of course, much more than willingness would be required to colonize this innermost planet, at present. But that is just the point. Nowadays, except by using heat- and cold-tolerant robots, we lack the technology to even consider accessing Mercury. It will likely be a long way down our list, long after our Moon and Mars. But it is never too early to consider a trip there, and, eventually, a permanent settlement. When should this occur? In our opinion, not until in the view of an entrepreneur, the possible gains outweigh the costs. When and if such an expedition is undertaken, it will be solely with the "dime" of such a businessman. It would not violate the rights of anyone else. Thus, it would be no one else's concern as to whether and when it occurred. Hey, we all root for our sports teams; why not, also, for successful businessmen in general and colonizers?

Why is Mercury so inhospitable? Its elliptical orbit lies between 29 and 43 million miles from the Sun, by far the closest in the solar system.[23] It has a day equivalent to 59 Earth days or about two-thirds of a Mercurian year of 88 days. On this planet, many days will include an exposure at the

---

[22] It might be better if it were in tidal lock (that is where the orbiter has slowed rotation to match the period of revolution about the Sun because of the breaking forces induced by the spin). Then the entire terminator (the line at the edge of sunlight and darkness) would be relatively easy to colonize as the properties described below at the poles would exist for the entire belt.

[23] The data in this section is based on Choi 2014b.

perihelion.[24] In short there is no spot on the planet other than the poles that does not experience full exposure to Sol at a short range accompanied by extreme heat and deadly radiation. Due to the near perfect alignment of the axis of rotation perpendicular to the plane of orbit, there is no long-term or seasonal blockage of daylight. This coverage is in no way tempered by the negligible atmosphere.[25] During this time, heat and radiation would be devastating to all who ventured out into the open.

Another negative is the apparent energy requirements for travel to and from. While the escape velocity from this hellish planet is not too bad compared to Earth or Venus, one must consider that it is far down in the solar gravity cone. In other words, escape from the Sun would be a challenge. Apparent energy requirements could exceed those required to reach celestial objects much farther away. The required effort may necessitate the development of innovative technologies such as a solar sail[26] for both braking and acceleration.

In terms of colonization, the poles would be easiest. At or near these two places, the surface temperature would be quite reasonable. Water ice has been discovered in the floors of craters in those zones. Even so, should one stand up and be thus exposed, radiation protection would be mandatory. In fact, such depressions are the most likely places for habitation in that buildings could not be melted. Unfortunately, these "habitable" zones are small. The other possibility is movable vehicles that remain near the dark side of the terminator shortly after sunset.[27] There the ground would radiate heat from its recent exposure to 1400 hours of direct sunlight but would be shielded.

---

[24] In an elliptical orbit the perihelion is the phase closest to the Sun. At this point, Mercury moves faster than it rotates; so in a typical day, the Sun appears to rise in the East, proceeds Westerly across the sky, stops and backtracks towards the East, and then after about 90-some hours resumes its Westerly movement. If the Sun rises where one is standing when passing the perihelion, it would then fully set on the same horizon only to soon rise again. Its antonym, aphelion, refers to the point farthest away (Rao 2015).

[25] The "atmosphere" is constantly blown away by the solar wind but is replenished by material from that very same wind, radioactive decay of its crust, and bombardment of micro-meteors. It consists mostly of oxygen, sodium, and hydrogen with some helium and other elements (Choi 2014b).

[26] A solar sail is a large sheet-like structure resembling an airfoil but reacting to the solar wind. The size means that the force required to retain its form would necessitate a substantial structure (Light Sail n.d.).

[27] Here we refer not to a killer from the future but to the dividing line on a planet between night and day.

But why colonize Mercury of all places? As with many of the other potential targets, minerals seem to supply some interest. Mercury has a large metallic core which could be beneficial to exploit. Should entrepreneurs find this or any other assets profitable on net balance, the planet would be colonized.[28] Shortly after sunset, one could tunnel into the surface. Once there the temperature would be more even and moderate. The trick then would be to discover a likely place to drill.

Extra-terrestrial Moons (Europa, Ganymede, Titan, Etc.)

These moons exhibit wide variety.[29] One common element is that they are all very cold compared to the inner planets.[30] They vary in size with the larger ones falling within a range between Mars and Pluto. The smaller ones more closely resemble the objects discussed in Chap. 9. It is important not to conflate size with the strength of gravitational attraction. Density is the primary concern. Even though Jovian moons Ganymede, Callisto, and Io as well as Saturn's Titan are larger than Earth's Moon, all but Ganymede have less gravity. All are less dense because they tend to consist of materials of lower mass per volume, i.e. less iron, uranium, etc. but more silicon, carbon, oxygen, etc. Nevertheless, they are potentially attractive targets for exploration.

At 8% larger than Mercury but with only 45% of its mass, Ganymede obviously consists of much lighter materials. It appears to have massive oceans beneath a thick crust of ice (Zimmerman 2014; Kramer 2015). This layer of water could run about 60 miles thick. Though probably very salty (sodium and chlorine rich, though other salts such as lithium carbonate or potassium chloride would most likely exist as well), it could

---

[28] Most likely this would occur many years in the future, with a vastly improved technology.

[29] For a scaled chart of visual images of the known moons of the solar system refer to Dark Government n.d. For a description of features of the larger objects in that chart refer to Pink 2015. Data in this section related to the density and gravitational attraction of these moons is based on this article. For a tongue-in-cheek egalitarian analysis of the moons of the solar system, see Block 2014.

[30] This statement and most of the comments in this sub-section refer to the Mars-sized moons of the outer planets. For tiny celestial bodies around Mars, like Phobos and Deimos, much of the discussion about asteroids in Chap. 9 applies.

provide a valuable resource, plus a jumping off point, for exploration of the outer solar system and beyond. This would only require the use of the well-understood technology of desalinization. One could build colonies on either the darker and older surfaces or on the more recent icy crust[31] of the seas. One very interesting possibility would be that with a massive salt ocean, life compatible to Earth could already exist or could be introduced, though it would have to be halophile (high salt-friendly) which would limit the possible choices. Such life would have to be adapted to darkness as sunlight, already much dimmer than at Earth, could not penetrate miles of dirty ice (further limiting choices). The thin atmosphere consists mainly of elemental oxygen plus O_2 molecules with a trace of O_3. In short, such atmosphere as there is would be quite corrosive. Escape velocity from the planet would be fairly low, but Jupiter's gravity could be an issue. Nevertheless, the orb's resources plus the potential for it to host natural or introduced life as a food source will one day make it an attractive location for a base of operations. Europa, smaller than Earth's Moon, is also large and similar to Ganymede except that its surface is much younger, though it suffers from higher radiation (Schirber 2009).

Callisto is the second largest and located the farthest away from the home planet of the Galilean[32] moons (Zimmerman 2012a). As evidenced by its heavily cratered surface, it is the oldest in the solar system. It is also the least dense. Its distance from Jupiter means that the tidal forces and radiation emanating from that giant are much lower. Like Ganymede, it appears to have a vast sub-surface ocean, and it has many of the same attractions and challenges. Since Callisto has the least radiation[33] and is farthest from Jupiter, it would make an even better base of operations. With all the water and the ability to produce fuel and possibly host life, it is the most attractive location of all Jovian moon candidates for a base of operations. A viable habitat could be built within the crust to protect against the low temperatures.

---

[31] About 60% of Ganymede's surface is more brilliant than the darker portions which are marked by significant numbers of impact craters. The more extensive lighter surfaces are known to be more recent because of the relative lack of such impacts. It is marked with ridges that are theorized to stem from tectonic activity and tidal forces (Kramer 2015).

[32] Jovian moon discovered by Galileo Galilei.

[33] The least radiation, especially when in conjunction with reduced tidal heating, also means that there is less heat available. This fact could mean that this moon is less suitable to host life than Ganymede.

Being the most volcanic body in the solar system, the third largest Jovian moon is Io which is entirely different from the other Galilean orbs and not very hospitable (Zimmerman 2012b). Some eruptions can cover the entire surface. At −202° F, it has sulfur dioxide snow fields. This chemical is the main component of its atmosphere. Unlike the other satellites in the Jupiter neighborhood, Io has little if any water because of its internal heat and because as the closest to Jupiter, the extreme radiation has driven water away. The internal heat results from the gravitational effects of the largest planet in the solar system on a body with an elliptical path. In addition, by cutting across Jupiter's field lines of magnetic forces, it is in effect an electric generator. In terms of colonization, the conditions would be hellish and the gravitational issues for approach and take-off would be the most difficult in this celestial neighborhood.

Titan, a moon of Saturn and the second largest after Ganymede in the solar system, is the only other body in the Sun's neighborhood besides Earth known to have large bodies of liquid on the surface (Redd 2015). Its oceans consist of liquid methane (CH_4) and ethane (C_2H_6). Titan's atmosphere is deeper than Earth's and consists mostly of nitrogen with a sizeable portion of methane. It has methane and cyanide (CN perhaps in the form of HCN) clouds and rain. Other hydrocarbons form great sandy deserts with dunes. The presence of a liquid water and ammonia (NH_3) ocean below the surface is suspected but not confirmed. These facts make Titan a worthy contender for colonization. The abundance of fuel alone is a big draw. Incidentally, there is speculation that as our Sun approaches red giant phase, Titan would warm to the point of supporting liquid oceans of H_2O on the surface and thus become an alternative home for humanity, though the gravity would be much lower.

References

Abramson, Michael. 2004. *Expectorations*. Volume V. A Collection of Poetry and Prose. Bloomington, IN: Xlibris Corporation.

Amundsen, Roald, Thorvald Nilsen, Kristian Prestrud, and A.G. Chater, Trans. 1976 [1912]. *The South Pole: An Account of the Norwegian Expedition in the Fram, 1910–12*. Vols. I and II. London: C. Hurst & Company.

Bates, Clair. 2012. Up and Away! World's Largest Airship Lifts Off for the First Time. *Daily Mail*. June 25. http://www.dailymail.co.uk/sciencetech/article-1279831/Up-away-Worlds-largest-airship-lifts-time.html. Accessed 23 Oct 2015.

Block, Walter. 1986. *The U.S. Bishops and Their Critics: An Economic and Ethical Perspective*. Vancouver: The Fraser Institute.

———. 1991. "Old Letters and Old Buildings," *The Freeman Ideas on Liberty* 96. http://www.fee.org/vnews.php?nid=2363. Accessed 20 Apr 2016.

———. 2012. Rozeff on Privacy: A Defense of Rothbard. December 13. http://archive.lewrockwell.com/blog/lewrw/archives/128349.html. Accessed 20 Apr 2016.

———. 2013a. There Is No Right to Privacy. July 13. http://archive.lewrockwell.com/2013/07/walter-block/there-is-no-right-to-privacy/. Accessed 20 Apr 2016.

———. 2013b. *Defending the Undefendable II: Freedom in All Realms*. Terra Libertas Publishing House.

———. 2014. Book Review Essay of Steven Pinker's: *The Better Angels of Our Nature: Why Violence Has Declined*. New York, N.Y. Penguin; Part II. *Management Education Science Technology Journal MEST* 2 (1): 141–160.

Block, Walter, Stephan Kinsella, and Roy Whitehead. 2006. The Duty to Defend Advertising Injuries Caused by Junk Faxes: An Analysis of Privacy, Spam, Detection and Blackmail. *Whittier Law Review* 27 (4): 925–949. http://www.walterblock.com/wp-content/uploads/publications/block-etal_spam_whittier-2006.pdf; http://www.walterblock.com/wp-content/uploads/2009/06/faxesduty.pdf. Accessed 20 Apr 2016.

Chang, Kenneth. 2015. Mars Shows Signs of Having Flowing Water, Possible Niches for Life, NASA Says. September 28. http://www.nytimes.com/2015/09/29/science/space/mars-life-liquid-water.html?_r=0.

Chappell, Matt. 2014. 15 Famous Predictions that Were Spectacularly Wrong. April 14. http://www.news.com.au/technology/gadgets/famous-predictions-that-were-spectacularly-wrong/story-fn6vihic-1226889769437. Accessed 25 Aug 2015.

Choi, Charles Q. 2014a. Planet Jupiter: Facts About Its Size, Moons and Red Spot. *Space.com*. November 14. http://www.space.com/7-jupiter-largest-planet-solar-system.html. Accessed 7 Dec 2015.

———. 2014b. Planet Venus Facts: A Hot, Hellish & Volcanic Planet. *Space.com*. November 4. http://www.space.com/44-venus-second-planet-from-the-sun-brightest-planet-in-solar-system.html. Accessed 28 Oct 2015.

Czech, Kenneth P. 2006. Roald Amundsen and the 1925 North Pole Expedition. June 12. http://www.historynet.com/roald-amundsen-and-the-1925-north-pole-expedition.htm. Accessed 25 Aug 2015.

Dark Government. n.d. Moons of Our Solar System Scaled to Earth's Moon. http://www.darkgovernment.com/moons.html. Accessed 19 Nov 2015.

Ferdinand Magellan Timeline. 2015. Ferdinand Magellan Timeline. March. http://www.datesandevents.org/people-timelines/13-ferdinand-magellan-timeline.htm. Accessed 27 Aug 2015.

Glasscock, Carl Burgess. 2011. Car History—Get a Horse! http://www.americanautohistory.com/Articles/Article005.htm.

Gordon, David. 2004. Liberty and Obedience. *The Mises Review*. Fall. http://mises.org/misesreview_detail.aspx?control=262. Accessed 20 Apr 2016.

History.com. 2016. 1789; Mutiny on the HMS Bounty. April 28. http://www.history.com/this-day-in-history/mutiny-on-the-hms-bounty. Accessed 27 Aug 2015.

———. n.d. Ferdinand Magellan. http://www.history.com/topics/exploration/ferdinand-magellan. Accessed 25 Aug 2015.

Jessa, Tega. 2010. How Fast Is Mach 1. *Universe Today*. 10–31. http://www.universetoday.com/77077/how-fast-is-mach-1/. Accessed 17 Nov 2015.

Katz, Joshua. n.d. Why Libertarians Should Reject Positive Rights. http://mises.org/journals/scholar/katz.pdf. Accessed 20 Apr 2016.

Kramer, Miriam. 2015. Jupiter's Moon Ganymede Has a Salty Ocean with More Water than Earth. *Space.com*. March 12. http://www.space.com/28807-jupiter-moon-ganymede-salty-ocean.html. Accessed 19 Nov 2015.

Light Sail. n.d. Solar Sailing—Flight by Light. The Planetary Society. http://sail.planetary.org/. Accessed 2 Dec 2015.

Long, Roderick T. 1993. Abortion, Abandonment, and Positive Rights: The Limits of Compulsory Altruism. *Social Philosophy and Policy* 10 (1): 166–191. http://praxeology.net/RTL-Abortion.htm. Accessed 20 Apr 2016.

Mason, Betsy. 2010. The Tragic Race to Be First to the South Pole. *Science*. May 10. http://www.wired.com/2010/05/polar-race-gallery/.

Mercer, Ilana. 2001. Stealing Our Words. August 8. http://mises.org/story/750. Accessed 20 Apr 2016.

Pearson, Michael. 2015. Liquid Water Exists on Mars, Boosting Hopes for Life There, NASA Says. September 29. http://www.cnn.com/2015/09/28/us/mars-nasa-announcement/.

Pegg, David. 2014. 25 Famous Predictions that Were Proven to Be Horribly Wrong. March 13. http://list25.com/25-famous-predictions-that-were-proven-to-be-horribly-wrong/. Accessed 25 Aug 2015.

Pink, Roger. 2015. Understanding the Gravity of the Situation. *Roger's Equations.* March 10. http://cr4.globalspec.com/blogentry/25919/Understanding-the-Gravity-of-the-Situation. Accessed 19 Nov 2015.

Rader, Andrew. 2014. *Leaving Earth: Why One-Way to Mars Makes sense.* Amazon Digital Services LLC.

Rao, Joe. 2015. Planet Mercury: Some Surprising Facts for Skywatchers. *Space. com.* April 29. http://www.space.com/29265-mercury-planet-facts-for-sky-watchers.html. Accessed 18 Nov 2015.

Redd, Nola Taylor. 2015. Titan: Facts About Saturn's Largest Moon. *Space.com.* February 4. http://www.space.com/15257-titan-saturn-largest-moon-facts-discovery-sdcmp.html. Accessed 20 Nov 2015.

Regis, ed. 2015. Let's Not Move to Mars. *New York Times.* September 21. http://www.nytimes.com/2015/09/21/opinion/lets-not-move-to-mars.html?_r=0.

Rothbard, Murray N. 1982b. Law, Property Rights, and Air Pollution. *Cato Journal* 2 (1). Reprinted in *Economics and the Environment: A Reconciliation,* Walter E. Block, ed., Vancouver: The Fraser Institute, 1990, pp. 233–279. http://mises.org/story/2120; http://www.mises.org/rothbard/lawproperty.pdf. Accessed 20 Apr 2016.

Sample, Ian. 2015. Nasa Scientists Find Evidence of Flowing Water on Mars. September 28. http://www.theguardian.com/science/2015/sep/28/nasa-sci-entists-find-evidence-flowing-water-mars. Accessed 25 Aug 2016.

Schirber, Michael. 2009. Hiding from Jupiter's Radiation. *Astrobiology Magazine.* January 19. http://www.astrobio.net/news-exclusive/hiding-from-jupiters-radiation/. Accessed 2 Dec 2015.

Schlenoff, Daniel C. 2011. Amundsen Becomes First to Reach South Pole, December 14, 1911. December 4. http://www.scientificamerican.com/article/south-pole-discovered-december-14-1911/.

Selick, Karen. 2014. Housing Rights Case Illustrates Why Positive Rights Are Phony Rights. *National Post.* December 29. http://business.financialpost.com/2014/12/29/housing-rights-case-illustrates-why-positive-rights-are-phoney-rights/. Accessed 20 Apr 2016.

UOH. 2002. University of Hawaii. Ham Club. Balloon Lift with Lighter than Air Gases. May. http://www.chem.hawaii.edu/uham/lift.html. Accessed 20 Apr 2016.

Warhaft, Z. 1997. *The Engine and the Atmosphere: An Introduction to Engineering.* Cambridge and New York: Cambridge University Press.

Whiteway, J.A., et al. 2009. Mars Water-Ice Clouds and Precipitation. *Science* 325 (5936): 68–70. http://www.sciencemag.org/content/325/5936/68.short.

Williams, David R. 2016. NASA, Space Science Data Coordinated Archive. Planetary Fact Sheets. National Aeronautics and Space Administration. February 29. http://nssdc.gsfc.nasa.gov/planetary/factsheet/uranusfact.html; http://nssdc.gsfc.nasa.gov/planetary/factsheet/saturnfact.html. Accessed 18 Apr 2016.

WNET. 2008. Marco Polo's Journey. October 30. http://www.wliw.org/marcopolo/2008/10/30/timeline-marco-polos-journey/. Accessed 25 Aug 2015.

Zimmerman, Kim. 2012a. Callisto: Facts About Jupiter's Dead Moon. Space.com. February 13. http://www.space.com/16448-callisto-facts-about-jupiters-dead-moon.html. Accessed 19 Nov 2015.

———. 2012b. Io: Facts About Jupiter's Volcanic Moon. Space.com. July 3. http://www.space.com/16419-io-facts-about-jupiters-volcanic-moon.html. Accessed 20 Nov 2015.

———. 2014. Ganymede: Facts About Jupiter's Largest Moon. *Space.com*. February 13. http://www.space.com/16440-ganymede-facts-about-jupiters-largest-moon.html. Accessed 19 Nov 2015.

Zubrin, Robert. 2011. *The Case for Mars, The Plan to Settle the Red Planet and Why We Must*. New York: Free Press, Simon & Schuster.

8

The Gas Giants

After looking at most of the other objects in the solar system, surely colonizing a gas giant planet ought to be beyond the pale. As described below, high gravitational attraction and atmospheres with excessive pressure will challenge any voyagers.

With the distances involved in approaching these orbiting megaspheres, certain obscure practical problems with space travel make themselves felt more strongly than for nearby destinations. After a five-year voyage, the Juno space probe (NASA 2016a) has arrived at its destination. Probes (Chap. 5) are fine for their purposes, but in contemplating a manned spacecraft, explorers must solve some issues that are not immediately apparent. Shockingly for some, your authors maintain that private organizations are best able to develop the required solutions.

The first issue is a standard scientific challenge: the lack of gravitationally induced weight. To some extent the effects of weightlessness are well understood from previous studies including one just completed at the International Space Station (NASA 2016b) in which astronaut Scott Kelly spent nearly an entire year in space with zero gravity. An example of the effects on the human body includes fluid shift that can cause increasing pressure in the cranium and the eyes. The usual approach to solving this issue is to propose a rotating disk that induces centrifugal force. Any

© The Author(s) 2018
P. L. Nelson, W. E. Block, *Space Capitalism*, Palgrave Studies in Classical Liberalism,
https://doi.org/10.1007/978-3-319-74651-7_8

deleterious results to the human body after 10 or more years (round trip of five years each way plus the residence time at the destination) will become much more pronounced than felt in a mere one year. A similar structure or some other means of providing artificial gravity must be planned to keep the staff healthy. Assembling this mass in space at a reasonable cost requires free-thinking individuals of the sort that only entrepreneurs can provide.

For that year in space, Kelly was accompanied by Mikhail Kornienko, a Russian cosmonaut. Apparently, they could live together in confined quarters without one killing the other. That is an accomplishment. However, they were near Earth. Radio calls, normally paced conversations with numerous people were possible. Such discussions will not feel normal if it takes a few hours to receive a response to one's last statement. Isolation, severe as it may have been on the ISS, will be compounded by the drawn-out communications with earthlings. In addition, the travelers to the outer planets face a deprivation of many cultural activities. Granted they can stream a live sports event on TV, but they cannot attend a live concert. They will be unable to browse a book store or feel a sea breeze on their faces. For the sake of variety and mental health, there must be more than just two people. They must have some way to resolve conflicts. They must be able to get away from each other. And those 10 years? That is for a Jupiter run—to the closest large orb. The others are even further away. This potential boredom suggests a need for the type of varied services and a vibrant, engaging society at which commercial enterprises excel. It will be more of an ecology than a machine. This chapter dwells on a few of the challenges that might be experienced on or near the large planets themselves.

Jupiter

Jupiter, aside from its moons discussed in Chap. 7, may well be the least promising planet in the solar system for colonization. This is not to say that at some point in the far distant future some entrepreneur may not devise a technology to approach this orb. The problem falls into two broad categories—attractive resources and difficult challenges.

While the solar system's giant may contain a rocky core with resources similar to those of Earth, most of the planet consists of hydrogen and some helium.[1] These assets exist elsewhere in the solar system where they are much easier to access. Surrounding the hypothetical rocky core, the Jovian globe has a layer of metallic hydrogen (Seligman n.d.)[2] which is a state wherein the electrons become independent of the nucleus. It then becomes a conductor of electricity which explains the intense magnetic field at about 20,000 times as strong as that of Earth's (Choi 2014a).[3] However, one enticing possibility is that the deep atmosphere could support carbon rain in the form of diamonds.

The challenges are manifold. First the pull of gravity is 2.4 times that of Earth. This means that the energy required to approach and take off would be gargantuan. Furthermore, the weight of the atmosphere there is much greater than even at the center of Earth. The strong magnetic field traps radiation of high-energy particles into large belts capable of damaging even heavily shielded space probes. Due to this radiation, Jupiter broadcasts radio waves. The winds in the atmosphere exceed 400 miles per hour and are very turbulent.

Perhaps the biggest challenge of Jupiter is that it is so big. That is to say, it is not scarce. There is more than enough of it to go around, even if a Malthusian nightmare overtook humanity, and we were trillions or quadrillions of people, instead of a mere seven billion, and somehow could overcome the physical impossibilities mentioned above. In fact, just to show how silly we can be, Jupiter is so large that if we assigned one cubic mile of it to each person, that planet could accommodate over 340 trillion people.

Saturn

Saturn is much like Jupiter in terms of composition.[4] As such, the benefits from colonization are likewise limited. Challenges are similar but somewhat reduced. Gravity at the surface is not that much more than

---

[1] Facts about Jupiter can be verified by reference to Choi 2014a and Trefil 2012.

[2] An alternative view is that hydrogen does not form a liquid metal at high pressures but takes on one of two other forms: an unusual solid in which molecules associate weakly with neighbors and another in which they bond with adjacent particles to form planar sheets (Foley 2013).

[3] We greatly rely on this author for our discussion of these large planets.

[4] Facts about Saturn can be verified by reference to Choi 2014b and Trefil 2012.

that on Earth.[5] Winds have even greater velocity, reaching up to about 1200 miles per hour. The magnetic field of this ringed planet is only about 600 times as strong as ours.[6]

Uranus

Among the four gaseous outer planets, Uranus, along with Neptune, is sometimes referred to as an ice giant since its atmosphere is made up of ice instead of gas (Redd 2012).

The troposphere is a methane haze that imparts to it a blueish-green color (Harrison 2010).[7] Even though this planet is much larger and more massive than Earth, its gravity is about 10% less (Williams 2016). This is because it is composed of much lighter materials than is our home: ices comprised of water, methane, and ammonia. However, the atmosphere is mostly hydrogen with about 15% helium.[8] The weather is rather life-threatening with winds at the equator exceeding 500 miles per hour. The extreme axial tilt, 98 degrees,[9] results in extended 21-year-long seasons. The ensuing spring time storms are both massive and potent.

The methane haze limits our ability to know what is inside the planet.[10] One of the first challenges would be to further explore the interior to ascertain its contents. This orb emits slightly more heat than it gains from the Sun.[11] It most likely has a small rocky core, but that is uncertain at this time.[12] The bulk of its mass is made up of an icy mantle. The "ice" is

---

[5] Saturn's gravity is only about 7% higher than Earth's according to Williams 2016. This sounds counterintuitive. The reason is that most of the mass is farther away from the surface (i.e. deeper) than Earth and in net consists of much lighter materials such as hydrogen and helium instead of our planet's iron, silicon, lead, and such.

[6] Ibid.

[7] Facts about Uranus can be verified by reference to Harrison 2010 and Williams 2016.

[8] Williams, Ibid.

[9] Williams, Ibid. The tilt means that once every 84 Earth years (the length of one Uranian year) the North Pole is aimed almost directly at the Sun. Also of interest, the direction of spin is opposite to that of every other planet of the solar system except Venus.

[10] Harrison, op. cit.

[11] Ibid.

[12] Ibid.

not of the sort with which humans are familiar. Due to the extreme weight, the surface of the mantle is well above freezing (0° C).[13] The surface pressure at the ice mantle exceeds 1000 bars.[14] In other words, the mantle of water and ammonia results from high pressure more than cold temperatures. While the temperature is not prohibitive, colonization would require the ability to withstand those horrific pressures.

Other than its moons,[15] how could this planet be colonized? The first step would likely be a probe wherein the internal workings would not be deformed by the hostile environment. We cannot say this for sure, since it is our belief that the best way to approach any such effort is via the free-enterprise system. And it is impossible for mere theoreticians of capitalism, such as the present authors, to fully anticipate what actual entrepreneurs will do.[16] If, hypothetically, shoe stores, or restaurants, had always been the task of government, and then it came to pass that these industries were suddenly privatized, it would be beyond our ability to predict where such stores would be located, what, precisely, they would sell, etc. The statists would ask the usual questions:

- Who will provide them?
- How much will it cost?
- Where and how will manufacturers obtain the resources and labor?
- We have always done it this way, why change?
- Etc. *ad nauseam.*

---

[13] Ibid.

[14] Williams, op. cit. One bar equals 14.5 pounds per square inch (29.5 inches of mercury) or slightly less than the earthly average atmospheric pressure at sea level.

[15] The Uranian moons are quite small and consist mostly of water and rock. Refer to Chap. 9 regarding the colonization of small celestial bodies.

[16] The concern expressed in this paragraph relates to the very common desire of statists to demand specific, though ossified, answers. Free thinkers tend to accept uncertainty and enthusiastically "go with the flow." They know that people are always thinking of how to improve their lives and that this constant series of acts improves the lot of everyone. In sharp contrast, both left-leaning socialists and rightist neo-conservatives (fascists) incline towards the need for a plan laid out in detail in advance. They fail to appreciate that their "clever" proposals will invariably be undone by the mere fact that people act to promote a future better in their view than that which would otherwise have obtained (Mises 1998). Among the latter, a frozen rigidity of thought is all too common.

Since these questions can never be answered in advance of entrepreneurial activity, fearful and wimpy statists will inevitably resist privatization as unfeasible, or worse.[17]

Neptune

Neptune is much like Uranus but warmer (Harrison 2010).[18] It has a similar ice mantle and atmosphere. Under present technology its pressure will inhibit colonization. A probe like that described above might be possible to investigate the interior. As with Uranus, much needs to be learned.

Triton is a large moon of this planet (Harrison 2010) that bears many similarities to Pluto, mentioned in Chap. 9.

Why even discuss these four planets, given that, even under much more advanced technology, it will neither be years nor decades, and possibly not even centuries, before human beings can incorporate them into our economy? There are several reasons. For one thing, we wish to be thorough in our description of likely colonization targets. To ignore these gas giants would be to overlook the greater portion of the mass of planets in our solar system. For another, no one can determine in advance when (or if) members of our species will be able to survive in these far-away places. Sometimes, scientific and engineering advancement can occur rather quickly. Who would have thought, years ago, that men could fly or travel in space or walk on the Moon? Third, we wish to demonstrate in this way the power and potential of free enterprise; we dare to contemplate, perhaps long in advance, a time when capitalism will be able to do the seeming impossible and render this forbidding real estate amenable to consumerism. Just think of the boost to the tourism industry afforded by Saturn's rings!

---

[17] While many do not have the imagination to overcome challenges on their own and readily assume others cannot, the worst of the statists are perfectly willing to injure, cage, or even kill those who emerge from Plato's cave and see the light, especially if they then proclaim what they see.

[18] Yes, it is warmer even though farther away from the center of our little solar system. It emits more heat than it receives from the Sun. The source of the internal energy is a matter of speculation.

References

Choi, Charles Q. 2014a. Planet Jupiter: Facts About Its Size, Moons and Red Spot. *Space.com*. November 14. http://www.space.com/7-jupiter-largest-planet-solar-system.html. Accessed 7 Dec 2015.

———. 2014b. Planet Venus Facts: A Hot, Hellish & Volcanic Planet. *Space.com*. November 4. http://www.space.com/44-venus-second-planet-from-the-sun-brightest-planet-in-solar-system.html. Accessed 28 Oct 2015.

Foley, James A. 2013. New Solid Form of Hydrogen Discovered at Extreme Pressures. Nature World News. June 4. http://www.natureworldnews.com/articles/2260/20130604/new-solid-form-hydrogen-discovered-extremepressures.htm. Accessed 7 Dec 2015.

Harrison, Thomas Edward. 2010. The Jovian Planets: Uranus, and Neptune. University of New Mexico, Astronomy 105. http://astronomy.nmsu.edu/tharriso/ast105/UranusandNeptune.html. Accessed 11 Dec 2015.

NASA., 2016a. National Space and Aeronautics Administration. Juno. February 11. https://www.nasa.gov/mission_pages/juno/main/index.html. Accessed 25 Mar 2016.

———., 2016b. National Space and Aeronautics Administration. Astronaut Scott Kelly Returns Safely to Earth After One-Year Mission. March 1. http://www.nasa.gov/press-release/nasa-astronaut-scott-kelly-returns-safely-to-earth-after-one-year-mission. Accessed 25 Mar 2016.

Redd, Nola Taylor. 2012. What Is the Temperature of Uranus? *Space.com*. November 30. http://www.space.com/18707-uranus-temperature.html. Accessed 7 Dec 2015.

Seligman, Courtney. n.d. Planetary Magnetic Fields and Metallic Hydrogen. *Online Astronomy eText: The Planets*. http://cseligman.com/text/planets/metallichydrogen.htm. Accessed 7 Dec 2015.

Trefil, James. 2012. *Space Atlas*. Washington, DC: National Geographic Society.

von Mises, Ludwig. 1998 [1949]. *Human Action, Scholars' Edition*. Auburn: Mises Institute. http://www.mises.org/humanaction.asp.

Williams, David R. 2016. NASA, Space Science Data Coordinated Archive. Planetary Fact Sheets. National Aeronautics and Space Administration. February 29. http://nssdc.gsfc.nasa.gov/planetary/factsheet/uranusfact.html; http://nssdc.gsfc.nasa.gov/planetary/factsheet/saturnfact.html. Accessed 18 Apr 2016.

9

Asteroids, Comets, and Other Non-Planetary Objects

Asteroids, comets, dwarf planets, and other non-planetary objects (including centaurs)[1] exist in a wide variety of sizes from near planetary to small rocks and ice chunks.[2] The larger objects could be treated like the smaller planets such as Mars or Mercury. Smaller objects could be homesteaded[3] in their entirety. As we consider larger denizens of space, a continuum (Block and Barnett, 2008) exists where conceivably any number of owners could divide up ownership in them either by shares or spatial lots. The object of traveling to these small, and not so small, orbiting bodies is to set foot[4] on them and earn a living in a new and exhilarating

---

[1] The mythical centaurs were descendants of Centaurus, a son of the music god Apollo, half man, half beast (horse). We are not here discussing those creatures. We discuss, instead, small celetial bodies in an elibtical orbit about the sun with a semi-major axis inside the Kiuper Belt and near or outside Jupiter's orbit.

[2] Even grains of sand are included in this inventory, if it is to be complete.

[3] For the libertarian theory of homesteading, see Block 1990, 2002a, b; Block and Edelstein 2012; Nelson 2015; Block and Yeatts 1999–2000; Block vs. Epstein 2005; Bylund 2005, 2012; Grotius 1625; Hoppe 1993, 2011; Kinsella 2003, 2006, 2009; Locke 1948; Paul 1987; Pufendorf 1673; Rothbard 1973, p. 32; Rozeff 2005; Watner 1982.

[4] On Earth, the homesteading tradition is indeed to "set foot" on virgin territory, so that it can be brought into ownership status. This may or may not be possible for the heavenly bodies. We advocate an extension of homesteading theory to space by allowing for additional techniques, such as robots. If an entrepreneur never "sets foot," personally, on an asteroid, but develops it mechanically, we claim he would be the rightful owner of whatever territory with which his robots mix their

© The Author(s) 2018
P. L. Nelson, W. E. Block, *Space Capitalism*, Palgrave Studies in Classical Liberalism,
https://doi.org/10.1007/978-3-319-74651-7_9

environment, one that challenges the assumptions and experiences of the settlers. Granted, the robotic probes of governments and state-run universities send back interesting information; but it is not the same as being there. More to the point, it is not the same as employing the object for useful purposes.[5]

It is personal exploring, living, engineering mines, building factories, and constructing houses that inspire the emotions, not robots. This cannot be denied; however, we argue that mechanical means of justifying property titles would also be legitimate. The knowledge that men and/or their machines belong in space unbeholden to others drives exploration.

Dwarf Planets

"Dwarf planets are spherical, or nearly so, and orbit the Sun just like the eight major planets. But unlike planets, Planetoids are not able to clear their orbital path[6] so there are similar objects and smaller debris at roughly the same distance from the Sun. A dwarf planet is much smaller than a planet (smaller even than Earth's moon), but it is not a moon. Pluto is the best known of this type of space body" (Erickson 2015).

Eris (Williams 2015) is a good example.[7] It is the largest, known, Kuiper belt object. The orbit takes 558 earth years. This body holds definite interest for space explorations in that a theory of internal heating via

---

"labor." Should a developer construct an automated device capable of mining platinum, send the contraption to an asteroid, and put the metal to beneficial use, then he has indeed become the proprietor, in our view. Should said person devise a loading procedure and transport the mineral to Earth, the same would apply. For a similar extension of "classical" Lockean-Rothbardian-Hoppean libertarian homesteading theory to nature preservation, see Block and Edelstein 2012.

[5] A useful purpose is defined by the owner. So-called stakeholders have no stake and, therefore, should have no say.

[6] This definition is somewhat slippery in that it could be said that planets also do not entirely clear their path. Consider asteroid 2010 SO16. From Earth's point of view, it follows a horseshoe orbit crossing over our path alternating between slightly inside our orbit for about 175 years until it starts to catch up, then because of Earth's gravity is propelled to a higher energy level where it falls behind us for the next 175 years (Atkinson 2011). Our planet has not cleared this object from its orbit.

[7] Formerly known as Xena. Other known Kuiper belt objects of substantial, small-world size include in size order: Pluto, Makemake, Haumea, Sedna, and Quaoar (Erickson 2015). (The designation of Pluto as a dwarf planet remains controversial.)

radioactive decay suggests that it may sustain an internal ocean.[8] If there is such an underground sea, life compatible with mankind's earthly experience is possible. Williams goes on to describe the surface as containing frozen methane. With a potential energy source[9] and water, the plutoid[10] could be used as a base for further exploration. Some mini-planets might have hot or warm cores. The valleys and polar areas could be filled with ice or non-dense material. Some could even have a thin atmosphere and geysers spewing H_2O. Enterprising entrepreneurs will eventually explore in more detail the surficial and internal composition and find first hand, additional resources.

Another dwarf planet, in this case in the asteroid belt, is Ceres. According to Marder and Scuiletti (2015) it has roughly the surface area of Alaska, Texas, and California combined. It rotates with a 9-hour day and appears to have quite a bit of water. In fact, it may be expelling H_2O through geysers. That would suggest a heat source such as that caused by radioactive decay. All these properties, combined with the fact that it is much closer to Earth than plutoids in the Kuiper belt, makes it very attractive for development. As with Eris, Ceres is easily large enough to support exploration by multiple entrepreneurs with diverse businesses. No currently known reason would prohibit development of its own independent economy.[11]

Challenges that developers will have to overcome involve low gravity and lack of atmosphere. However, with sufficient water, a rocky core to explore for minerals, heat, and relatively abundant sunlight, Ceres could become quite productive and self-sustaining. To do so would certainly be easier than developing Eris. But for this to occur, freedom from power freaks, especially terra-bound bureaucrats, is necessary. The reason is that

---

[8] An internal ocean is a body of liquid water beneath the surface of an otherwise frozen planet which is warmed above the melting point by heat generated by an internal source such as radioactive decay.

[9] It may be that we should not count methane as an energy source. It cannot generate energy without an oxidizer. Here we assume that if such does not already exist on Eris, it can be obtained elsewhere and imported. Besides oxygen, fluorine, sulfur, or chlorine can serve as efficient elemental oxidizers along with a variety of chemical radicals.

[10] Plutoid, meaning "resembling Pluto," is an alternative name for a dwarf planet.

[11] That is other than governmental hegemony and statist attempts to assert control.

the funds required to build pressurized greenhouses for agriculture, a permanent space port, and mines beneath the sub-surface oceans, etc. could only be raised in an environment of secure property rights.[12]

With a celestial body of this size, one would expect Ceres over the eons to have intercepted many asteroids and to have multiple types of minerals for exploitation. The mining opportunities would be almost endless. It would avoid such challenges as zero gravity[13] that would be expected on mere asteroids. On the other hand, the structures required to support underground mines would be minor compared to similar ones on our planet. If efficiency and self-reliance can be achieved, mining and manufacturing, let alone low transportation costs, could render mineral extraction competitive or even cheaper than earth excavations. Ownership could resemble a Martian scheme (See Chap. 7). There is no reason an off-world society would not resemble that of our present planet because individuals would exhibit a broad variety of personalities and interests and at the same time share in communities with parties and fellowship.

Large Asteroids

The larger asteroids, such as 704 Interamnia (Sato et al. 2014) or 121 Hermione (Marchis et al. 2009), have sufficient gravity for men to work on the surface.[14] They are large enough to have variegated physical properties

[12] An argument against the concept that funding requires secure property rights is that it would require vast funding, and only government has sufficient wherewithal to accomplish anything like these Herculean tasks. We respond in two ways. One, from where did government obtain these revenues in the first place? Obviously from the private sector. If it would stop doing so—better yet, also return these mulcted funds—the free-enterprise system would face far less of a challenge. Secondly, has anyone ever heard of a stock market? This is the way, par excellence, for private people to amalgamate financial resources.

[13] Many might wonder why zero or near-zero gravity would be an intractable issue. One might have thought it would not be, since it would be easy to move otherwise heavy machines around. The reason is that it would take no effort to accidentally launch oneself or one's equipment into outer space. All operations would require tethers, personal rockets, and/or other clumsy equipment. Without a method to gain purchase, such simple tasks as tightening a screw become major challenges. Of course, all such challenges can be overcome; the only point here is that even the minimal gravity of a plutoid would make life easier.

[14] Some regard the minor planets of the asteroid belt as asteroids; herein we have discussed them separately because (1) they share certain characteristics such as being spherical unlike smaller

both in terms of depth and surface irregularities.[15] They likely would have hills and mountains. For these, the larger they are the less chance a single entity could homestead the entire asteroid.[16]

Miners would test for and follow veins of minerals. Even farming might be possible. For example, it could take place inside a greenhouse with an artificial carbon dioxide rich atmosphere at earth-like pressure and temperature. Possibly, surface lots could be surveyed and developed.

Similarly, bases for staging further exploration could be developed. This would be true especially if such a celestial body had usable resources with which to build and fuel vehicles. Imagine the energy savings for a launch when the gravity is a twentieth that of Earth. Manufacturing in cases where low gravity is beneficial would perform even better than on plutoids. Consider the simplification if the object were in a state of tidal lock (discussed previously in Chap. 6, note 14) with respect to the Sun. All the work could be completed on the sunny side. With such bodies, though a self-sustaining economy is difficult to visualize, permanent residence would be a clear possibility.

Small Asteroids

Small asteroids present a wealth of intriguing opportunities and challenges (Planetary Resources n.d.). The first test of human endurance and efficient work relates to the lack of adequate gravity and atmosphere. A human could accidentally launch himself from the object by simply jumping or running a jackhammer. Spacesuits and anchors are required. A small dyna-

---

objects, and (2) the smaller they are, the more difficult it is to imagine a multi-owner, self-sustaining, self-contained economy with many-faceted enterprises.

[15] One rather startling irregularity of interest is the variation of gravity on the surface. For a dumbbell-shaped object of sufficient size for gravity to be significant and able to hold gases, a person would weigh more near the waist than at the far extremities (depending on the exact shape there might even be spots on the surface with negative gravity, i.e. one would be pulled away from the surface). If it had an atmosphere, gases might accumulate at the midriff while leaving a near vacuum farther out: that suggests some interesting possibilities for manufacturing processes that could never be attained on a planet such as Earth.

[16] Rothbard (1982a, b) discusses the "technological unit." This refers to the minimal (and by implication maximum) size of property necessary to be viable. The point is that in this context, it might well be that it would be "one per customer" in terms of owning an entire heavenly body, if it is small enough.

mite explosion could, for a loosely cemented entity, separate it into multiple pieces.[17] At the same time, these limitations provide boundless prospects. Unlike for large space objects, both landing and launching are simple, low-energy affairs. There would be no chance to burn up in the atmosphere during entry. Low gravity would mean that lifting precious material to the surface and loading it onto a vessel would be cheap and easy. The small size that would enable industrialists to avoid the expenses of survey is but one more example of the benefits. Perhaps most important is being far away from aggressors who might wish to intrude.

An asteroid lodged at (or orbiting) a Lagrange point[18] would have additional advantages. Competition for their occupation would be expected. One use for these points in space, as discussed in Chap. 5 on space probes, would be to install satellites such as a telescope at Earth's L-2. Located there, it would remain constantly in the Earth's shadow. Similarly, two telescopes orbiting any L-2 point[19] but within the shadow of a large planet such as the Jupiter L-2 locus could offer a stereo view[20] for quite a long distance into space. Through the use of direct propulsion or a gravity tractor (Wall 2014), an asteroid could be moved to any of these locations with respect to each of the planets. A body small enough to be moved, but large enough to provide a stable and workable surface area, would provide a wealth of opportunities. It would offer a base at a

---

[17] The libertarian analysis of gun control, dynamite, and the legitimacy of nuclear weapons, depend intimately on the size of the planet on which human habitation exists. See on this Block and Block (2000).

[18] Refer to Chap. 5, for more on Lagrange points. For a reminder, L-2 is in direct solar orbit outside of Earth's orbit but keeps pace rather than falling behind.

[19] An orbit of L-2 (called a halo orbit) would be unstable, and the satellite would tend to drift out of position anytime it was perturbed. Therefore, the telescopes would require thrusters to aid in station keeping.

[20] A stereo view is one where two visual sensors at some distance from each other provide depth perception. Human eyes are a case in point. The greater the separation from each other, the greater the ability to judge distances. Here the idea is to take one photograph aimed at the same object when on one side of the Sun and another from the other side. The same thing is now done from Earth, but the stereoscopic effect would be more powerful when these two photos were from Jupiter's shadow. For just as our two eyes help us discern distances by looking at an object from two directions, so can taking a photo from two such locations. Another illustration is the old stereoscopic double photo viewers that were the rage in the late nineteenth century. Each of the two photos was taken from several feet apart to exaggerate the perception of three dimensions. Further, being in the shadow of the planet helps to reduce interfering light.

predicable position; it would remain where it was initially placed.[21] The essential requirement for such use is that the property rights to the asteroid and the location in space are secure so that it is worth the investment to move the asteroid and install the equipment.

Entrepreneurs can be expected to find mining asteroids a worthwhile endeavor. For example, small Type M[22] space objects might prove to be pure, uniform nickel or iron requiring little or no refining (Planetary Resources n.d.).[23] One huge benefit to mining an object in space is that no NIMBYs[24] would interfere with the operation. Could it be that the real reason governments wish to restrict private space development with provisions such as those outlined in the United Nations Treaties and Principles on Outer Space (2002), is that they cannot abide the idea of people being outside of their control.[25] Be that as it may, only private parties tend to have the wisdom and foresight to find resources in space and to overcome the obstacles necessary to convert them into valuable assets rather than mere objects of curiosity.

Comets

Comets are distinguished by their properties and erratic orbits. Choi (2014e) describes them as "dirty snow balls." They vary in composition, but usually contain water and typically consist of the ices of ammonia,

---

[21] That is an asteroid at a LaGrange Point would keep position with respect to the Sun and planets with the use of thrusters for station keeping.

[22] Type M refers to a metallic asteroid and usually consists of one uniform element such as molybdenum or osmium but generally not both.

[23] Little or no refining is needed because asteroids date from the very beginning of the formation of the solar system. They were part of the star-forming dust cloud for our Sun. The most dominant nickel and iron Type M asteroids originally emanated from dying stars. During the last stages of stellar fusion circumferential zones of uniform elements existed so that pure chunks, our proto asteroids, would be part of the nebula formed by the blast. The heavier elements such as platinum, lead, and thorium may have come from the collision of stellar remnants such as neutron stars (Grossman 2013). They too would likely be pure. Since that time, they have not undergone erosion or mixing as they would were they part of a larger planet.

[24] Not In My Back Yard.

[25] Perish the thought. On a serious note, this strikes us as similar to the concept of the Berlin Wall (or Donald Trump's wall which the Mexicans will supposedly pay to construct) or charging an exit tax to emigrate. How dare someone move away? For more on this see Chap. 2 on man's inhumanity to man.

carbon dioxide, methane and other less-common elements and compounds. The orbits of the ones with which men are familiar are typically
elliptical in shape and extend from the inner solar system to beyond
Jupiter to the Kuiper belt or the Oort[26] cloud. Containing both water
and energy-rich chemicals, they, too, offer prospects for enterprising
explorers.

Comets provide some very interesting opportunities for private space
explorers. Imagine a relatively large comet. On the outward journey from
the inner solar system, one could hitch a ride to the Kuiper belt or Oort
cloud orbiting outside of Pluto and Neptune. Find a likely inbound
comet, calculate its orbit, and determine a path to meet it somewhere
near one's base. Then ride it out along its usual path. Think of the potential energy savings. It would be, in effect, a quasi-free spaceship.[27]

The more volatile materials of the comet, when heated, become gases.
As space bodies containing gases such as water, methane, and even more
complex long-chain hydrocarbons and amino acids, they provide usable
resources. Hitching a ride could provide time to mine such chemicals and
use them together with an oxidizer for generating heat during the trip
outward and thereafter. For interstellar travel, one could travel to the
outer reaches of the solar system where one could launch towards a destination with minimal gravity from the Sun after having accumulated vast
resources for the trip.

Centaurs share may of the properties of comets and are often regarded
as comets but have some of the properties of large asteroids and even
minor planets (Clavin and Harrington 2013; Erickson 2015). They have
unstable orbits that cross that of one of the gas giants. These large planets
can perturb their path around the Sun and thereby cause permanent
changes that result in travel to the inner solar system or expulsion from
the solar system.

What of the danger of a comet impacting with the third planet from
the Sun? The movie *Armageddon* depicted just that scenario. In it, our

---

[26] The Oort cloud is the spherical collection of space objects that lies beyond the Kuiper belt. It
tends to extend about half way to the neighboring stars.

[27] A widely used phrase in economics is "free rider." That means something quite different in the
context of the dismal science, but it might readily be employed with regard to riding a comet to the
outer reaches of the solar system.

heroes saved the Earth, of course. But which occurrence is more likely? That this protection could be achieved by government, or the private sector of the economy? Most neo-classical economists would choose the former, due to the so-called public goods "market failure."[28] This is the "free-rider" challenge: each entrepreneur will presumably wait for someone else to undertake the costs of an action that will benefit all (saving the Earth from the comet in this case) and no one will actually do it.[29] This "let George do it" philosophy presumably creates a "market failure." But mainstream economists cannot hide behind this mischievous doctrine, since precisely the same phenomenon will afflict nations in the present scenario. In other words, the United States will wait for China, Russia, Europe, Japan, Israel, to deal with the comet,[30] while that expectation will afflict all the others with inaction. That is, China, Russia, etc., *each country* capable of dealing with such an eventuality, will attempt to "free ride" on the efforts of anyone foolish enough to undertake it. As in the case of Buridan's Ass (Rothbard 2010) that perished from a similar inaction, so will the human population.

Such a scenario is unlikely in the extreme. There are all sorts of reasons to expect that the "externality will become internalized." That is, that private firms, more likely than the state apparatus, will prove flexible enough to overcome this impasse. Private railroad companies, not governments, created standard gauge, so that cargo no longer had to be loaded and unloaded each time it passed onto the property of a different firm. This benefitted *all* of them, and yet, somehow,[31] they could overcome

---

[28] For an Austrian economic critique of the public goods market failure fallacy, see Barnett and Block 2007, 2009; Block 1983, 2000a, b, 2003; Cowen 1988; De Jasay 1989; Holcombe 1997; Hoppe 1989; Hummel 1990; Osterfeld 1989; Pasour 1981; Rothbard 1985, 1997b; Schmidtz 1991; Sechrest 2003, 2004a, b, 2007; Tinsley 1998–1999. Rothbard's (1997b, p. 178) *reductio ad absurdum* of public goods is as follows: "A and B often benefit, it is held, if they can force C into doing something… [A]ny argument proclaiming the right and goodness of, say, three neighbors, who yearn to form a string quartet, forcing a fourth neighbor at bayonet point to learn and play the viola, is hardly deserving of sober comment."

[29] In the more sophisticated versions of this economic fallacy, some will indeed undertake the needed activity, but will invest too few resources in so doing.

[30] Blow it up, divert it from a course that will impact the Earth, etc.

[31] The Transcontinental Railroad 2012; Neu and Taylor 1956; Puffert 2000.

the tendency toward inaction. In like manner, the railroad firms also got together[32] and created the now-familiar time zones. Not only did they themselves gain by being better able to coordinate with each other, but these vast benefits "spilled over" into society as a whole. We cannot rule out of consideration such cooperation on the part of governments on praxeological grounds,[33] but it seems more probable that space companies could sort out a comet aimed at the Earth than a bunch of statist politicians and bureaucrats.

Hazards

Space debris is a major challenge to space exploration (Goldsmith 2015). The higher the speed (see Chap. 1 on the need for hyper speeds), the worse will be the issue of impact avoidance or damage in the event of impact. It is through the unregulated free market that solutions to intractable problems are found. Explorers will be well motivated to develop methods for detection of both minuscule and massive invisible objects and quick reaction mechanisms for avoidance of things large and small.

If Bruce Willis[34] can do it, then so can (some of) the rest of us. Only, in the case of the movie, there were no positive benefits to be garnered. Rather, the goal was to prevent a negative from occurring, a disastrous collision of the asteroid and our home. But the economic analysis is similar. Attaining a gain or avoiding a loss comes down to the same thing; if it is worth doing, the "magic of the market" is most likely the best way to undertake it. There is an argument to be made to the contrary, however,

---

[32] Happily, this took place during an epoch before anti-trust stopped "collusion." See on this Anderson et al. 2001; Armentano 1999; Barnett et al. 2005, 2007; Block 1977, 1982, 1994; Block and Barnett 2009; Boudreaux and DiLorenzo 1992; Costea 2003; DiLorenzo 1996; DiLorenzo and High 1988; Henderson 2013; High 1984–1985; McChesney 1991; McGee 1958; Rothbard 2004; Shugart 1987; Smith 1983; Tucker 1998a, b.

[33] Block 1973, 1980, 1999; Batemarco 1985; Fox 1992; Hoppe 1989, 1991, 1992, 1995; Hülsmann 1999; Von Mises 1969, 1998; Polleit 2008, 2011; Rizzo 1979; Rothbard 1951, 1957, 1960, 1971, 1973, 1997a, b, c, d; Selgin 1988.

[34] In the movie *Armageddon* a Texas-sized asteroid is scheduled to crash into the Earth. The protagonist is sent to outer space to intercept and split out this intruder.

in the present case. Why should anyone, call him Bruce Willis Inc., undertake any such protection of the home planet? All the costs would fall upon him, whereas the benefits would be dispersed to practically everyone else in our world.[35] According to the most widely held view, known as the Alvarez hypothesis,[36] the dinosaurs became extinct due to a similar occurrence approximately 66 million years ago when an asteroid crashed into what is now the Gulf Coast of the Yucatan Peninsula. How, then, to address what economists would call the market failure of positive externalities, or free-riding effects? Why would the Willis Corporation undertake protecting the Earth all on his own? There are several motivations. He would be not merely a national hero, but an international one. He would be given all sorts of prizes from a thankful world's population. He might even do well from a purely financial perspective: private donations would shower on his head. Would other corporations and rich people want to contribute to his efforts? They would have every incentive to do so. On the positive side, this would constitute free advertising for all other contributors. On the negative side, people might boycott any large firm that did not help fund the rescue. Think of a Honda, or Coca-Cola, or a Microsoft that refused to donate money, vast amounts of it, to this enterprise. Whether or not the Earth survived the impact of the asteroid, their businesses might not.

But the asteroids have positive aspects as well. According to Reynolds (2014): "Asteroid 3554 is estimated to contain $20 trillion worth of valuable metals. And there are many other asteroids containing similar wealth." He continues: "But nothing is likely to be developed unless investors can expect to own what they mine. Just as the miners of the

---

[35] Of course, including Willis too. He wants to have a home to come back to, and, also, presumably, has loved ones stationed here.

[36] Luis Alvarez, with the help of Walter Alvarez, proposed a theory that a massive asteroid of approximately 10-kilometer diameter collided with the Earth. This kicked up a cloud of dust that remained airborne for several years. As a result of the reduced sunlight reaching the Earth's surface, photosynthesis was suppressed and much of the vegetation which constituted the base of the food chain for the dinosaurs died. The die-off is called the K-T extinction event (Cretaceous-Tertiary Boundary). For more information and for the reasons the hypothesis is convincing refer to Alvarez et al., 1980 and to University of California 2007. The latter article also includes brief discussions of alternative causes such as a supernova, volcanism, plate tectonics, and global climate change (the dinosaurs must have been using their gas-guzzling cars too intensively for their own good).

nineteenth century gold rushes would have stayed home if they expected their nuggets to be seized by authorities, people investing in space mining operations need similar property rights. The 1967 Outer Space Treaty forbids 'national appropriation' of 'the moon and other celestial bodies.'" Are asteroids "celestial bodies?" Who knows? But if there is any question about this, it will retard space exploration in this regard. There is also the issue of whether "space people" would be bound by the laws of earthlings. Presumably, they would be, since although it is unlikely cops from the home planet would "visit" them on their celestial bodies, when and if they revisited Earth, compulsion could be used against them. Even more reason, then, to modify our local planetary laws regarding off-world private property.

Summary

For astronomers, the distinction between a planet, a moon, a comet, an asteroid, a dwarf planet is crucial. These differences are as important to them as are those between the periodic elements to the chemist, the difference between species, or genus and order, to the biologist. But categories of celestial bodies are of lesser moment to the entrepreneur. It makes trivial difference to him if he mines platinum from one or the other of these extra-terrestrial orbs. A similar phenomenon takes place when the economist attempts to explain the endangerment of species due to the tragedy of the commons. It matters not whether the subject is the extinction of the buffalo, the rhinoceros, or the elephant. For him, insofar as the pure economics of the matter is concerned, the elephant is merely a big buffalo with a funny looking nose.

Something of the same order occurs in the present context. So, we must take the distinctions made in this chapter with at least a small grain of salt. They are all-important for some purposes, but perhaps less so for our own analysis: the prospects of putting space exploration, exploitation, and colonization on a private property, profit-making basis. In this and other chapters, we speculate on the mechanisms that such entrepreneurs might use to access resources.

References

Alvarez, Luis, et al. 1980. Extraterrestrial Cause for the Cretaceous-Tertiary Extinction. *Science* 208 (4448): 1095–1108.

Anderson, William, Walter E. Block, Thomas J. DiLorenzo, Ilana Mercer, Leon Snyman, and Christopher Westley. 2001. The Microsoft Corporation in Collision with Antitrust Law. *The Journal of Social, Political and Economic Studies* 26 (1): 287–302.

Armentano, Dominick T. 1999. *Antitrust: The Case for Repeal*. Revised 2nd ed. Auburn, AL: Mises Institute.

Atkinson, Nancy. 2011. Earth Has a Companion Asteroid with a Weird Orbit. *Universe Today*. April 6. http://www.universetoday.com/84652/earth-has-a-companion-asteroid-with-a-weird-orbit/. Accessed 17 Nov 2015.

Barnett, William, Walter E. Block, and Michael Saliba. 2005. Perfect Competition: A Case of 'Market-Failure'. *Corporate Ownership & Control* 2 (4): 70–75.

Barnett, William, II, Walter E. Block, and Michael Saliba. 2007. Predatory Pricing. *Corporate Ownership & Control* 4 (4), Continued—3, Summer: 401–406.

Batemarco, Robert. 1985. Positive Economics and Praxeology: The Clash of Prediction and Explanation. *Atlantic Economic Journal* 13 (2): 31–27.

Block, Walter E. 1973. A Comment on 'The Extraordinary Claim of Praxeology,' by Professor Gutierrez. *Theory and Decision* 3 (4): 377–387.

Block, Walter. 1977. Austrian Monopoly Theory—A Critique. *The Journal of Libertarian Studies* I (4): 271–279.

Block, Walter E. 1980. On Robert Nozick's 'On Austrian Methodology'. *Inquiry* 23 (4): 397–444.

Block, Walter. 1982. *Amending the Combines Investigation Act*. Vancouver: The Fraser Institute.

———. 1983. Public Goods and Externalities: The Case of Roads. *The Journal of Libertarian Studies: An Interdisciplinary Review* VII (1): 1–34. http://www.mises.org/journals/jls/7_1/7_1_1.pdf. Accessed 23 Apr 2016.

———. 1990. Earning Happiness Through Homesteading Unowned Land: A Comment on 'Buying Misery with Federal Land' by Richard Stroup. *Journal of Social Political and Economic Studies* 15 (2): 237–253.

———. 1994. Total Repeal of Anti-trust Legislation: A Critique of Bork, Brozen and Posner. *Review of Austrian Economics* 8 (1): 35–70.

Block, Walter E. 1999. Austrian Theorizing, Recalling the Foundations: Reply to Caplan. *Quarterly Journal of Austrian Economics* 2 (4): 21–39.

———. 2000a. Watch Your Language. February 21. http://www.mises.org/fullarticle.asp?control=385&month=17&title=Watch+Your+Language&id=19; http://mises.org/daily/385. Accessed 11 June 2016.

———. 2000b. Word Watch. April 20. http://www.mises.org/fullstory.asp?control=414&FS=Word+Watch. Accessed 23 Apr 2016.

Block, Walter. 2002a. Homesteading City Streets; An Exercise in Managerial Theory. *Planning and Markets* 5 (1): 18–23. http://www-pam.usc.edu/volume5/v5i1a2s1.html; http://www-pam.usc.edu/. Accessed 23 Apr 2016.

———. 2002b. On Reparations to Blacks for Slavery. *Human Rights Review* 3 (4): 53–73.

———. 2003. National Defense and the Theory of Externalities, Public Goods and Clubs. In *The Myth of National Defense: Essays on the Theory and History of Security Production*, ed. Hans-Hermann Hoppe, 301–334. Auburn: Mises Institute. http://www.mises.org/etexts/defensemyth.pdf. Accessed 23 Apr 2016.

———. 2007. Anarchism and Minarchism; No Rapprochement Possible: Reply to Tibor Machan. *The Journal of Libertarian Studies* 21 (1): 91–99. http://www.mises.org/journals/jls/21_1/21_1_5.pdf. Accessed 11 June 2016.

Block, Walter E. 2009. *The Privatization of Roads and Highways: Human and Economic Factors*. Auburn, AL: The Mises Institute. http://www.amazon.com/Privatization-Roads-And-Highways-Factors/dp/1279887303/; http://mises.org/books/roads_web.pdf; http://mises.org/daily/3416. Accessed 23 Aug 2016.

Block, Walter, and William Barnett. 2009. Monopsony Theory. *American Review of Political Economy* 7 (1/2): 67–109.

Block, Walter E., and Matthew Block. 2000. Toward a Universal Libertarian Theory of Gun (Weapon) Control. *Ethics, Place and Environment* 3 (3): 289–298.

Block, Walter E., and Michael R. Edelstein. 2012. Popsicle Sticks and Homesteading Land for Nature Preserves. *Romanian Economic and Business Review* 7 (1): 7–13. http://www.rebe.rau.ro/REBE%207%201.pdf. Accessed 29 Sep 2016.

Block, Walter, and Richard Epstein. 2005. Debate on Eminent Domain. *NYU Journal of Law & Liberty* 1 (3): 1144–1169.

Block, Walter, and William Barnett II. 2008. Continuums. *Journal Etica e Politica/Ethics & Politics* 1: 151–166. http://www2.units.it/~etica/; http://www2.units.it/~etica/2008_1/BLOCKBARNETT.pdf. Accessed 23 Apr 2016.

Block, Walter and Guillermo Yeatts. 1999–2000. The Economics and Ethics of Land Reform: A Critique of the Pontifical Council for Justice and Peace's 'Toward a Better Distribution of Land: The Challenge of Agrarian Reform'. *Journal of Natural Resources and Environmental Law* 15 (1): 37–69

Boudreaux, Donald J., and Thomas J. DiLorenzo. 1992. The Protectionist Roots of Antitrust. *Review of Austrian Economics* 6 (2): 81–96.

Bylund, Per. 2005. Man and Matter: A Philosophical Inquiry into the Justification of Ownership in Land from the Basis of Self-Ownership. Master thesis, Lund University, Spring Semester (June). http://www.uppsatser.se/uppsats/a7eb17de8f/; http://perbylund.com/academics_polsci_msc.pdf; http://www.essays.se/essay/a7eb17de8f/; http://www.lunduniversity.lu.se/o.o.i.s?id=24965&postid=1330482. Accessed 23 Apr 2016

———. 2012. Man and Matter: How the Former Gains Ownership of the Latter. *Libertarian Papers* 4 (1). http://libertarianpapers.org/articles/2012/lp-4-1-5.pdf. Accessed 23 Apr 2016.

Choi, Charles Q. 2014e. Comets: Facts About the 'Dirty Snowballs' of Space. *Space.com.* November 15. http://www.space.com/53-comets-formation-discovery-andexploration.html. Accessed 30 July 2015.

Clavin, Whitney, and Harrington, J. D. 2013. NASA's WISE Finds Mysterious Centaurs May Be Comets. California Institute of Technology—Jet Propulsion Laboratory. July 25. http://www.jpl.nasa.gov/news/news.php?release=2013-234. Accessed 4 Aug 2015.

Costea, Diana. 2003. A Critique of Mises's Theory of Monopoly Prices. *The Quarterly Journal of Austrian Economics* 6 (3): 47–62.

Cowen, Tyler, ed. 1988. *The Theory of Market Failure: A Critical Examination.* Fairfax, VA: George Mason University Press. http://www.amazon.com/Theory-Market-Failure-Critical-Examination/dp/0913969133/ref=sr_1_1?ie=UTF8&s=books&qid=1200191409&sr=1-1. Accessed 23 Apr 2016.

De Jasay, Anthony. 1989. *Social Contract, Free Ride: A Study of the Public Goods Problem.* Oxford: Oxford University Press. http://www.amazon.com/Social-Contract-Free-Ride-Paperbacks/dp/0198239122/ref=sr_1_1?ie=UTF8&s=books&qid=1200191531&sr=1-1. Accessed 23 Apr 2016.

DiLorenzo, Thomas J. 1996. The Myth of Natural Monopoly. *Review of Austrian Economics* 9 (2): 43–58.

DiLorenzo, Tom, and Jack High. 1988. Antitrust and Competition, Historically Considered. *Economic Inquiry* 26 (1): 423–435.

Erickson, Kristen. 2015. NASA. National Aeronautics and Space Administration. *Solar System Exploration.* Eris. http://solarsystem.nasa.gov/planets/profile.cfm?Object=Dwa_Eris; https://solarsystem.nasa.gov/planets/profile.cfm?

Object=Ast_10199Chariklo;   http://solarsystem.nasa.gov/planets/profile.
cfm?Object=Dwarf. Accessed 24 July 2015.

Fox, Glenn. 1992. The Pricing of Environmental Goods: A Praxeological Critique of Contingent Valuation. *Cultural Dynamics* V (3): 245–259.

Goldsmith, Donald. 2015. Does Humanity's Destiny Lie in Interstellar Space Travel? Space.com. January 27. https://solarsystem.nasa.gov/planets/profile.cfm?Object=Ast_10199Chariklo. Accessed 4 Aug 2015.

Grossman, Lisa. 2013. Cosmic Collisions Spin Stellar Corpses into Gold. *New Scientist-Daily News.* July 17. https://www.newscientist.com/article/dn23886-cosmic-collisions-spin-stellar-corpses-into-gold/. Accessed 29 Feb 2015.

Grotius, Hugo. 1625. *Law of War and Peace (De Jure Belli ac Pacis)*, 3 volumes. Trans. A.C. Campbell, London, 1814.

Henderson, David R. 2013. The Robber Barons: Neither Robbers nor Barons. *Library of Economics and Liberty.* March 4. http://www.econlib.org/cgi-bin/printarticle2.pl?file=Columns/y2013/Hendersonbarons.html. Accessed 9 Aug 2015.

High, Jack. 1984–1985. Bork's Paradox: Static vs Dynamic Efficiency in Antitrust Analysis. *Contemporary Policy Issues* 3: 21–34.

Holcombe, Randall. 1997. A Theory of the Theory of Public Goods. *Review of Austrian Economics* 10 (1): 1–10. http://www.mises.org/journals/rae/pdf/RAE10_1_1.pdf. Accessed 23 Apr 2016.

Hoppe, Hans-Hermann. 1989. Fallacies of the Public Goods Theory and the Production of Security. *The Journal of Libertarian Studies* IX (1): 27–46. http://www.mises.org/journals/jls/9_1/9_1_2.pdf. Accessed 23 Apr 2016.

———. 1991. Austrian Rationalism in the Age of the Decline of Positivism. *Journal des Economistes et des Etudes Humaines* 2 (2). Reprinted as Hoppe, Hans-Hermann. 1994. Austrian Rationalism in the Age of the Decline of Positivism. In *Austrian Economics: Perspectives on the Past and Prospects for the Future*, ed. Richard M. Ebeling, vol. 17, 59–96. Hillsdale, MI: Hillsdale College Press.

———. 1992. On Praxeology and the Praxeological Foundation of Epistemology and Ethics. In *The Meaning of Ludwig von Mises*, ed. J. Herbener. Boston: Dordrecht.

———. 1993. *The Economics and Thics of Private Property. Studies in Political Economy and Philosophy*. Boston: Kluwer Academic Publishers.

———. 1995. *Economic Science and the Austrian Method*. Auburn, AL: The Ludwig von Mises Institute.

————. 2011. Of Private, Common, and Public Property and the Rationale for Total Privatization. *Libertarian Papers* 3 (1). http://libertarianpapers.org/2011/1-hoppe-private-common-and-public-property/. Accessed 23 Aug 2016.

Hülsmann, Jörg Guido. 1999. "Economic Science and Neoclassicism." *Quarterly Journal of Austrian Economics*, Vol. 2 Num. 4, pp. 1–20.

Hummel, Jeffrey. 1990. National Goods vs. Public Goods: Defense, Disarmament and Free Riders. *The Review of Austrian Economics* IV: 88–122. http://www.mises.org/journals/rae/pdf/rae4_1_4.pdf. Accessed 23 Apr 2016.

Kinsella, Stephan N. 2003. A Libertarian Theory of Contract: Title Transfer, Binding Promises, and Inalienability. *Journal of Libertarian Studies* 17 (2): 11–37. http://www.mises.org/journals/jls/17_2/17_2_2.pdf. Accessed 23 Apr 2016.

————. 2006. How We Come to Own Ourselves. September 7. http://www.mises.org/story/2291. Accessed 23 Apr 2016.

————. 2009. Homesteading, Abandonment, and Unowned Land in the Civil Law. May 22. http://blog.mises.org/10004/homesteading-abandonment-and-unowned-land-in-the-civil-law/. Accessed 23 Apr 2016.

Locke, John. 1948. *An Essay Concerning the True Origin, Extent and End of Civil Government*. In *Social Contract*, ed. E. Barker, 17–19. New York: Oxford University Press.

Marchis, F., et al. 2009. The Cybele Binary Asteroid 121 Hermione Revisited. 40th Lunar and Planetary Science Conference. http://www.lpi.usra.edu/meetings/lpsc2009/pdf/1336.pdf. Accessed 29 July 2015.

Marder, Jenny, and Sciuletti, Justin. 2015. Dawn over Ceres, a Mission of Humankind. *PBS Newshour* 6–24. http://www.pbs.org/newshour/updates/mission-humankind/. Accessed 27 July 2015.

McChesney, Fred. 1991. Antitrust and Regulation: Chicago's Contradictory Views. *Cato Journal* 10 (3): 775–778.

McGee, John S. 1958. Predatory Price Cutting: The Standard Oil (New Jersey) Case. *The Journal of Law and Economics*, October, 137–169.

Nelson, Peter Lothian. 2015. To Homestead a Nature Preserve. Liberty.me. July 14. https://peterlothiannelson.liberty.me/to-homestead-a-nature-preserve/. Accessed 29 Aug 2015.

Neu, Irene D., and George Rogers Taylor. 1956. *The American Railroad Network, 1861–1890*. Cambridge: Harvard University Press.

Osterfeld, David. 1989. Anarchism and the Public Goods Issue: Law, Courts and the Police. *The Journal of Libertarian Studies* 9 (1): 47–68. http://www.mises.org/journals/jls/9_1/9_1_3.pdf. Accessed 23 Apr 2016.

Pasour, Jr., E.C., 1981, "The Free Rider as a Basis for Government Intervention," *The Journal of Libertarian Studies*, Vol. V, No. 4, pp. 453–464. http://www. mises.org/journals/jls/5_4/5_4_6.pdf. Accessed 23 Apr 2016.

Paul, Ellen Frankel. 1987. *Property Rights and Eminent Domain*. Livingston, NJ: Transaction Publishers.

Polleit, Thorsten. 2008. Mises's Apriorism Against Relativism in Economics. April 25. http://blog.mises.org/archives/008051.asp. Accessed 9 Aug 2015.

———. 2011. True Knowledge from a Priori Theory. June 8. http://mises.org/daily/5349/True-Knowledge-from-A-Priori-Theory. Accessed 9 Aug 2015.

Pufendorf, Samuel. 1673. Natural Law and the Law of Nations (De officio hominis et civis prout ipsi praescribuntur lege naturali).

Puffert, Douglas J. 2000. The Standardization of Track Gauge on North American Railways, 1830–1890. *The Journal of Economic History* 60 (4): 933–960.

Reynolds, Glenn Harlan. 2014. Mine Asteroids in Space to Help Us on Earth. *USA Today*. September 16. http://iucat-test.uits.iu.edu/iupui/articles/edsgsc/edsgcl.382537991/?resultId=4&highlight=%22Mines%20and%20mineral%20resources%20--%20Economic%20aspects%22. Accessed 15 Nov 2015.

Rizzo, Mario. 1979. Praxeology and Econometrics: A Critique of Positivist Economics. In *New Directions in Austrian Economics*, ed. Louis Spadaro, 40–56. Kansas City: Sheed Andrews and McMeel.

Rothbard, Murray N. 1951. Praxeology: Reply to Mr. Schuller. *American Economic Review* 41 (5): 943–946.

———. 1957. In Defense of Extreme Apriorism. *Southern Economic Journal* 23 (1): 314–320.

———. 1960. The Mantle of Science. Reprinted from *Scientism and Values*, ed. Helmut Schoeck and James W. Wiggins. Princeton, NJ: D. Van Nostrand; *The Logic of Action One: Method, Money, and the Austrian School*. Cheltenham: Edward Elgar, 1997, pp. 3–23.

———. 1971. Freedom, Inequality, Primitivism and the Division of Labor. Modern Age, Summer, 226–245. Reprinted in Kenneth S. Templeton, Jr. (ed.), *The Politicization of Society*. Indianapolis: Liberty Press, 1979, pp. 83–126. Reprinted in *The Logic of Action Two: Applications and Criticism from the Austrian School*. Glos, UK: Edward Elgar Publishing Ltd., 1997, pp. 3–35. http://mises.org/fipandol.asp.

———. 1973. *For a New Liberty*. New York: Macmillan. http://mises.org/rothbard/newlibertywhole.asp. Accessed 23 Aug 2016.

———. 1982a. *The Ethics of Liberty*. Atlantic Highlands, NJ: Humanities Press.

———. 1982b. Law, Property Rights, and Air Pollution. *Cato Journal* 2 (1). Reprinted in *Economics and the Environment: A Reconciliation*, Walter E.

Block, ed., Vancouver: The Fraser Institute, 1990, pp. 233–279. http://mises. org/story/2120; http://www.mises.org/rothbard/lawproperty.pdf. Accessed 20 Apr 2016.

———. 1985. Airport Congestion: A Case of Market Failure? The Free Market. Auburn, AL: The Ludwig von Mises Institute. http://www.mises.org/ econsense/ch52.asp.

———. 1997a. Toward a Reconstruction of Utility and Welfare Economics. Reprinted in *The Logic of Action One: Method, Money, and the Austrian School*, 211–254. Glos, UK: Edward Elgar Publishing Ltd.

———. 1997b. *The Logic of Action: Applications and Criticism from the Austrian School*. Vol. II. Cheltenham: Edward Elgar.

———. 1997c. Praxeology, Value Judgments, and Public Policy. In *The Logic of Action One*, ed. Murray N. Rothbard, 78–99. Cheltenham, UK: Edward Elgar Publishing Limited.

———. 1997d. In Defense of 'Extreme Apriorism'. *Southern Economic Journal*, January 1957, 314–320. Reprinted in *The Logic of Action One*, ed. Murray N. Rothbard, 100–108. UK: Edward Elgar Publishing Limited.

———. 2010. Jean Buridan and the Theory of Money. *Mises Daily Articles*. January 1. Auburn, AL.

———. 2004 [1962]. *Man, Economy and State*. Auburn, AL: Ludwig von Mises Institute, Scholar's Edition.

Rozeff, Michael S. 2005. Original Appropriation and Its Critics. September 1. http://www.lewrockwell.com/rozeff/rozeff18.html. Accessed 23 Apr 2016.

Sato, Isao, et al. 2014. A 3-D Shape Model of (704) Interamnia from Its Occultations and Lightcurves. Scientific Research—An Academic Publisher. March. http://www.scirp.org/journal/PaperInformation.aspx?paperID=43533. Accessed 29 July 2015.

Schmidtz, David. 1991. *The Limits of Government: An Essay on the Public Goods Argument*. Boulder, CO: Westview Press.

Sechrest, Larry. 2003. Privateering and National Defense: Naval Warfare for Private Profit. In *The Myth of National Defense: Essays on the Theory and History of Security Production*, ed. Hans-Hermann Hoppe, 239–274. Auburn, AL: The Ludwig von Mises Institute.

———. 2004a. Public Goods and Private Solutions in Maritime History. *The Quarterly Journal of Austrian Economics* 7 (2): 3–27. http://www.mises.org/ journals/qjae/pdf/qjae7_2_1.pdf; https://dev.mises.org/journals/qjae/pdf/ qjae7_2_1.pdf. Accessed 23 Apr 2016.

———. 2004b. Private Provision of Public Goods: Theoretical Issues and Some Examples from Maritime History. *ICFAI Journal of Public Finance* II (3): 45–73. http://www.mises.org/journals/scholar/Sechrest7.pdf. Accessed 23 Apr 2016.

————. 2007. Privately Funded and Built U.S. Warships in the Quasi-War of 1797–1801. *The Independent Review* 12 (1): 101–113.

Selgin, George A. 1988. Praxeology and Understanding: An Analysis of the Controversy in Austrian Economics. *Review of Austrian Economics* 2: 19–58; and Praxeology and Understanding, Auburn, AL: Ludwig von Mises Institute, 1990.

Shugart, William F., II. 1987. Don't Revise the Clayton Act, Scrap It! *Cato Journal* 6: 925.

Smith, Jr., Fred L. 1983. Why Not Abolish Antitrust? *Regulation*, Jan–Feb, 2.

The Transcontinental Railroad. 2012. *A History of Railroad Technology. Standardization of American Rail Gauge.* http://railroad.lindahall.org/essays/rails-guage.html. Accessed 18 May 2017.

Tinsley, Patrick. 1998–1999. With Liberty and Justice for All: A Case for Private Police. *Journal of Libertarian Studies* 14 (1): 95–100. http://www.mises.org/journals/jls/14_1/14_1_5.pdf. Accessed 23 Aug 2016.

Tucker, Jeffrey. 1998a. Controversy: Are Antitrust Laws Immoral? *Journal of Markets & Morality* 1 (1): 75–82.

————. 1998b. Controversy: Are Antitrust Laws Immoral? A Response to Kenneth G. Elzinga. *Journal of Markets & Morality* 1 (1): 90–94.

United Nations. 2002. Treaties and Principles on Outer Space. United Nations Publication Sales No. E.02.I.20 ISBN 92-1-100900-6. http://www.unoosa.org/pdf/publications/STSPACE11E.pdf. Accessed 3 Aug 2015.

University of California Museum of Paleontology. 2007. *Asteroids and Dinosaurs: Unexpected Twists and an Unfinished Story.* Berkeley: Regents of the University of California. http://undsci.berkeley.edu/lessons/pdfs/alvarez_woflow.pdf. Accessed 16 Nov 2015.

Von Mises, Ludwig. 1969. *Theory and History: An Interpretation of Social and Economic Evolution.* New Rochelle, NY: Arlington House.

————. 1998 [1949]. *Human Action: The Scholar's Edition.* Auburn, AL: The Mises Institute.

Wall, Mike. 2014. NASA's Asteroid-Capture Mission May Test New Method to Defend Earth. *Space.com.* May 16. http://www.space.com/25897-asteroid-deflection-enhanced-gravity-tractor.html. Accessed 30 July 2015.

Watner, Carl. 1982. The Proprietary Theory of Justice in the Libertarian Tradition. *Journal of Libertarian Studies* 6 (3–4): 289–316. http://mises.org/journals/jls/6_3/6_3_6.pdf. Accessed 23 Apr 2016.

Williams, Matt. 2015. Meet Eris, The Solar System's Largest Dwarf Planet. *Universe Today.* 5–30. http://io9.com/meet-eris-the-solar-systems-largestd-warf-planet-1707948972. Accessed 27 July 2015.

10

Space Boondoggles: NASA, STEM Subsidies

What is a boondoggle? A common definition is "work or activity that is wasteful or pointless but gives the appearance of having value."

How, in turn, is "value" determined? The answer emanating from the dismal science is that it is determined by a person who values, or an evaluator. For example, if Jones purchases a wristwatch for $20, we as economists, or as persons exhibiting common sense, may conclude that Jones valued the time piece at an amount greater than his out of pocket expense. He would have scarcely purchased it at this price if he did not.[1] Similarly, the vendor rated this part of his stock at less than that amount, for a similar reason. Each party to this transaction, then, earned a profit from it: the difference between what was paid (received) and the value placed on this implement.[2] That is how price is determined in the market: through voluntary exchange.

---

[1] Strictly speaking, all we are entitled to deduce is that there was *something* about the watch he valued more highly than the $20. It need not have been the piece of jewelry itself. For example, he didn't really care about the watch, but he wanted to get a date with the saleswoman, and made the purchase for this reason.

[2] In sharp contrast, both Marx (1867) and Smith (1776) suffered under an objective theory of value, namely, labor. In this view, goods and services are valued in proportion to workmen's hours embodied in them. But this is easily shown to be fallacious. Mud pies and cherry pies require the

© The Author(s) 2018
P. L. Nelson, W. E. Block, *Space Capitalism*, Palgrave Studies in Classical Liberalism,
https://doi.org/10.1007/978-3-319-74651-7_10

Furthermore, the evaluator, at the instant of the exchange with the knowledge he possessed, desired that particular watch more than anything else he could have purchased. For example, he could have exchanged his $20 for the shirt nearby in the same department store, one that was on sale. The economist would conclude that the chronometer was worth more to him than the shirt otherwise he would have exchanged his money for that instead. In short, that time piece exceeded not only the value of the money but of everything else available to him at that moment.

Matters are very different in the government sector of the economy. Here, there are no willing buyers and sellers. Rather, the state imposes compulsory levies on the citizenry, and then gives[3] them goods and services based on its tax collections. But the people never *agreed* to pay even one red cent for any of the "largesse" showered upon them.[4] Therefore, we are not entitled to deduce that they value the product at any given level, let alone at all, and certainly not at a level exceeding the taxes mulcted from them. For all we know, the long-suffering taxpayer despises the artifact or service he receives from his rulers.

NASA

Take the $1.8 billion 2015 budget of the National Aeronautics and Space Administration (NASA 2015) as an example. Does this mean that this organization provided benefits equal to that amount? It implies no such thing. All we are entitled to deduce from this fact is that those in power

---

same amount of effort to bake, but one is worth a lot, and the other nothing. Suppose 100 hours went into manufacturing an X. So, according to this theory, it is worth a certain amount of money. But later on, the prices of a complement or a substitute change, and X becomes valued at a different rate. But, it still has 100 hours of effort incorporated into it, contrary to this theory.

[3] This "giving" of services amounts to a form of propaganda. It is the typical ploy of predators and parasites to give something enticing to the victim. Like the attractive blue bulb of the angler fish, the state offers, say, roadways. When the dupe bites, he is eaten alive.

[4] This lack of agreement on the price applies even if the individual in question voted in favor of a tax to pay for the certain benefit. The voter has merely indicated that he would like to have the good or service as long as the lion's share is paid by others. If he had been willing to pay the full price himself, he would have done so without taking the time to petition the government.

transferred the hard-earned $1.8 billion of the populace to itself, and then engaged in various and sundry activities. It is conceivable that the value of these efforts was a multiple of its costs to the citizenry.[5] The other end of the spectrum is also plausible, probable in fact: there was no value created at all to anyone who paid for it.[6]

Consider the moon landing of 1969 as a case in point. This cost some $25.4 billion (Anthony 2014).[7] Did the population gain an amount more, equal to, less than, or zero, as a result? There is nothing in the science of economics that can definitively deny the last: no gain in value at all—the complete waste of this entire amount of money unless one counts "Tang®"[8] and national pride: WE were there FIRST!

The economic welfare of Neil Armstrong and Buzz Aldrin certainly improved. They were volunteers (paid "volunteers" that is) in this enterprise. But the rest of us were forced to subsidize their vacation against our will.[9] But even apart from such a radical analysis of the issue, mainstream commentators offer reasons for maintaining it was not an economical use of funds. Why not? In the view of Kaku (2009):

> Back in the mid-1950s, President Dwight Eisenhower actually laid down a sober and methodical timetable for space exploration. He envisioned a fleet of robotic probes that would scout out the moon and beyond. Astronauts would join them later, launched on small, fast space planes. Like fighter pilots, our astronauts would be able to blast into space at the drop of a hat.

---

[5] If the value were indeed greater than the cost, there would have been no need for the state to compel these payments. Under a regime of economic freedom, the consumers would have volunteered these monies to attain these benefits because they would have been perceived as truly beneficial. What of the free rider or public goods objection to this claim? This is refuted below under "neighborhood effects" and "public goods" in Chap. 11.

[6] We do not count NASA employees in this calculation. We know that they valued the monies they received in salary more than the opportunity costs of their time (otherwise they would quit their jobs or not take them up in the first place). As for the taxes, in effect they paid none. It was just a book-keeping arrangement. To refer to levies paid on governmental salaries as payments is meaningless newspeak. The employee actually received as his real salary the nominal amount minus the withheld sum. The same applies to "taxes" on social security.

[7] In 1973 dollars. In terms of present (2016) costs, the cost of the moon landing is about $150 billion.

[8] Tang® was, in fact, not developed for the space program (Kramer 2013).

[9] Taxes are compulsory, the views of critics of this claim to the contrary notwithstanding.

But when Sputnik's launch was splashed over every front page in October 1957, all of that changed.[10] Suddenly, the race to the moon was all about proving the superiority of capitalism over communism. Arthur C. Clarke, the British author of *2001: A Space Odyssey*, once commented that he would have never imagined there would be a push to put men on the moon if it hadn't became (sic) the focus of competition between two nations.

At the height of the Cold War, the superpowers spared no expense in funding the latest space spectacular. Dazzling stunts in space, not cost-cutting, were the order of the day. No one bothered to read their price tag.[11]

Precisely. You will not find, ever, capitalist entrepreneurs ignoring a price tag. Or, if you do, you will find them soon in the throes of bankruptcy, therein no longer able[12] to effectively serve their customers.[13]

It cannot be denied that millions of people, nay, hundreds of millions, were thrilled that members of their species walked on the Moon.[14] Such persons were particularly proud that "we," our nation, had performed this adventure. But, they had no way of plunking down any cash on the barrel-head to *demonstrate* (Rothbard 1997a) that this was so. In contrast, every time they go to a movie, or a Super Bowl, matters are entirely different. In these latter cases, we have direct, objective evidence as to the benefits of these expenditures. In the case of the moon landing, we did not.

---

[10] This is reminiscent of the hysteria of the time. During a visit by the senior author of this book to one Dr. Weddell in 1957, he lectured us 11-year-old children about how Sputnik proved that the U.S. education system had failed by falling behind those "Commies." It did nothing of the kind. It merely demonstrated that the Russians wanted to score a propaganda talking point in an area that the Americans were not at the time pursuing. This vignette is not to suggest that public schools are not seriously deficient.

[11] Once again, we are reminded of a highschool sporting competition.

[12] Unless, of course, they are deemed by the government "too big to fail," yet another difficulty with statism.

[13] And precisely *who* are their customers? Stockholders? No. Stakeholders? No. Government? No. The general public? Again no. Then who? Those who *purchase* their products! See on this Simons 2013.

[14] No one, perhaps more so than Rand (1969). But this is exceedingly curious. One would think that a small government advocate such as she would chastise the state for going beyond what she regards as its very limited proper role: armies, courts, and the police.

Of course, the Challenger and Columbia debacles[15] must be counted on the debit side of the ledger for NASA. Were a calamity of this sort to have taken place in the private sector, it might well have spelled the death knell for the company responsible. But this rarely occurs in the so-called public sector. There, catastrophes abound, and there is no automatic feedback mechanism of profit and loss that all but guarantees the exit of those responsible.[16]

The fact to keep in mind is that Challenger, and even Columbia, by itself does not represent half the problem. The Space Shuttle is designed to fail and do so spectacularly with excessive bells and whistles. The first obvious failure mechanism is lift-off. Once achieved,[17] it allows no escape method for about two minutes until booster separation. Even then the crew could not simply stop. They would have had to burn off excess fuel from the external tank prior to jettisoning it, which is then followed by nearly impossible maneuvers (Dunn 2014). Engineers call a system with no way out or no backup plan: "designed to fail." For two minutes, on the most dangerous part of the flight, there was no plan B.

As if that were not bad enough, there is really no reasonable way to retro-fit an escape mechanism. Since the crew cabin was an integral part of the spaceship, such a system would require the ability to lift the entire unit with payload. Presumably, the external fuel tank and boosters could be jettisoned at the same time, but then NASA would have had two uncontrolled rockets doing cartwheels in the sky with a massive explosive bomb (the external fuel tank) in the middle of it all. Any Mercury-style escape tower would have had to be sufficiently large compared to the size

---

[15] Axelrod 2008; Ceglowski 2005; Hudgins 2012; Futron 2002; Kinnucan 1983; Krauss 2011; Rapp 2015; Vaughan 1996; Winsor 1988; Zeeberg 2011. Even here, no one can be sure that it counted on the debit side for everyone. A onetime friend of one of the present authors loved mishaps because he could use them in arguments proving the need for humility. He avidly scoured the newspapers for disasters and all of the details he could get. He liked to point to the pericope (a short extract from a larger work) of the Tower of Babel (לְבָב), Genesis 11: 1–9. The point is that without a payment mechanism, there is no way to tell whether any good or service has any value positive or negative let alone its proper price.

[16] A case in point is the Katrina disaster. Actually, that storm missed New Orleans by some 40 miles. The approximately 1900 deaths were caused by failure of the levees to hold. And which organization was responsible for that malfeasance? The Army Corp of Engineers which is, at last look, still in existence? For more in this vein see Rockwell and Block 2010; Block and Rockwell 2007.

[17] Technically, the cut-off time for an abort was solid fuel booster ignition.

of the vehicle to lift it out of the maelstrom prior to the impending collision of one of the missiles with the tank. The only genuine answer would have been a complete redesign to include an escape pod for the astronauts. One wonders whether a good system would also include the ability to recover the payload when the launch was aborted.

In addition, the practicality of the entire spaceplane is questionable for simple tasks. It has a huge cargo bay plus a seven-person crew cabin. Thus, it is an exceedingly large and expensive transportation system that can only achieve low earth orbit. In addition to being impractical, with a 1.5% failure rate,[18] it can be regarded as unreliable.

A less spectacular NASA failure is represented by the Liberty Bell. This Mercury capsule splashed down in the Atlantic Ocean on July 21, 1961. The official, disputed, story is that the hatch malfunctioned and admitted sea water causing it to sink. Gus Grissom narrowly managed to escape (NASA 2000).

A hair-raising event on Apollo 13 garnered worldwide attention when a liquid oxygen tank exploded. The crew managed to survive by using the lunar lander as a "lifeboat." Prior to the flight, the problem container had suffered numerous glitches, but was deemed "safe" and used anyway (NASA 2009).

A truly bad day for NASA and the European Space Agency was when the Hubble Space Telescope started to broadcast images from space. They were blurry. The device was proclaimed to be able to produce exceptionally clear photographs free from atmospheric distortion. These pictures were anything but. The Hubble became the butt of jokes (Fox News 2009). Its mirror had the incorrect focal length making it nearsighted. Some people suggested it had been designed by Mr. Magoo.[19] This was an optical error, of the most basic, bone-headed variety, rendering the

---

[18] There were two fatal failures, Challenger and Columbia, out of a total of 135 missions (NASA n.d.). Consider this fact in terms of lives lost per mission. With seven aboard, that is 14 lives or slightly more than one death for every 10 missions. Who seriously wants to face those odds? Compare these with one's odds of dying in an automobile (0.72 deaths per 100 million passenger miles) (Maass 2013). Converting that to the number of outings, the average car trip is 14.6 miles (Green 2015). That means there is about 0.0001 (1 per 10,000) fatality per car trip as opposed to 0.1 per shuttle excursion.

[19] Jim Backus's Mr. Magoo was a puppet afflicted with near sightedness. It was serialized as an animated TV series (IMDb n.d.).

exceedingly expensive instrument useless. Fortunately, it could be fixed by the installation of some corrective lenses. Oops, that meant an additional high-cost, high-risk, space shuttle launch and spacewalk to install the fix (Pearce 2012).

The preceding incidents amount to nothing more than a brief sampling of NASA's boondoggles.[20]

STEM Subsidies and Neighborhood Effects

STEM stands for Science, Technology, Engineering, and Mathematics. Many commentators have pushed to promote this sort of education, in significant part so that it can promote space exploration.[21] Does a case exist for neighborhood effects resulting from government subsidization of *any* education, STEM or otherwise? Given that the answer to that question is yes,[22] what is the justification for a heavy focus on science, technology, engineering, and math, above all other disciplines? Before we move on to discuss more deeply those two questions, we point out that feminists have long been gnashing their teeth that, due to capitalism's[23] supposed discrimination against the fairer sex; females remain[24] underrepresented in these fields; and proposed subsidies should seek to address that effect. Women (we are talking about generalizations and trends here;

---

[20] For more on this as well as lapses of other space agencies see Space Safety (2016).

[21] A new field trip to Mars immerses school children in the red planet for the purpose of inspiring future astronauts. (Unreal 2016). For further information on the relation of STEM education and space exploration, see NASA n.d.; Heller 2012; Hohler 2009; Alexander and Buchsbaum 2007; Aldrin 2011.

[22] We argue that it is not.

[23] Typically, "capitalism" is the "usual suspect" of feminists. One must constantly remind himself that the conflation of *laissez-faire* with cronyism, diametric opposites, is nearly ubiquitous. In no way does the system of *laissez-faire* capitalism put down women for they are completely free to compete on an equal basis as is everyone else. Rather, it is the socialistic tendencies embedded within Otto von Bismarck's welfare laws, the Fabian Society, the British Labour Party, the Democratic Party, and the Republican Party that create the need to exploit entire groups of people, such as females. Even when the political winds change and previously disparaged demographics become favored, such favoritism takes a form proclaimed to be compensation for past injustice but which in fact leads to dependency.

[24] Proportionately, more of them than men will be working only part time as they have babies; or will quit entirely.

many individuals do not go along with the crowd) are fully capable of making their own way in the free market. To assume they must be coddled or led into "preferred" STEM choices constitutes an insult and an injustice to the very people such programs are intended to help.

The highest profile voice long calling for governmental subsidization of education in general has been that socialist, Milton Friedman[25] (1962, p. 86–88). He opines:

A stable and democratic society is impossible without a minimum degree of literacy and knowledge on the part of most citizens and without widespread acceptance of some common set of values. Education can contribute to both. In consequence, the gain from the education of a child accrues not only to the child or his parents but also to other members of the society. The education of my child contributes to your welfare by promoting a stable and democratic society. It is not feasible to identify the particular individuals (or families) benefitted and so to charge for services rendered. There is therefore a significant 'neighborhood effect.'

What kind of governmental action is justified by this particular neighborhood effect?…government has…assumed the financial costs of providing schooling. It has paid, not only for the minimum amount of schooling required of all, but also for additional schooling at higher levels available to youngsters but not required of them. One argument for both steps is the

---

[25] Friedman a socialist? Was he not one of the foremost and well known capitalists (Friedman/ Donahue 1979)? So he was reputed to be. Yet, we have the temerity to refer to him as a socialist. The reason is much deeper than the cited passage which indicates approval of state-run schools. More essential to the Chicago monetarist school, his philosophy, is the approval of a state-owned central bank. Banks and schools are first-order means of production. Government ownership of them is an important aspect of socialism. If a nation's money is socialized, how can that country be free? If a legal tender law mandates the use of a single currency, then, obviously, the system is not that of *laissez-faire*. For further critiques of this author along these lines see Berliner 19991995, p. 326; Block 1999, 2003, 2006, 2010, 2011, 2013; Block and Barnett 2012–2013; Block and Friedman 2006; Friedman 2000; Kinsella 2009; Lind 2012; Long 2006; Marcus 2007; McChesney 1991; North 2012; Machan 2010; McChesney 1991; Rand n.d.; Rothbard 2002; Sennholz 2006; Vance1996, 2005; Wapshott 2012; Wenzel 2012; Wilcke 1999. States Friedman (2000)himself: "In the middle of a debate on the subject of distribution of income, in which you had people who you would hardly call socialist or egalitarian—people like Lionel Robbins, like George Stigler, like Frank Knight, like myself—Mises got up and said, 'You're all a bunch of socialists,' and walked right out of the room." Here is Rand's (n.d.) view of Friedman and Stigler 1946: "'collectivist propaganda' and 'the most pernicious thing ever issued by an avowedly conservative organization'" (cited in Skousen 2001).

'neighborhood effects' discussed above. The costs are paid because this is the only feasible means of enforcing the required minimum. Additional schooling is financed because other people benefit from the schooling of those of greater ability and interest, since this is a way of providing better social and political leadership. The gain from these measures must be balanced against the costs, and there can be much honest difference of judgment about how extensive a subsidy is justified. Most of us, however, would probably conclude that the gains are sufficiently important to justify some government subsidy.

What are the difficulties with this position? Several come to mind. "A stable and democratic society is impossible without a minimum" of shoes, pencils, paper clips, underwear; apples, chicken, barbers, carpenters, indeed, a whole host of goods and services. Does this mean that government should provide them all, or subsidize them? Hardly. But by implication this would appear to be Friedman's view.

What is a "democratic society"? Is it one where two foxes and a chicken vote on what to have for dinner? Is it acceptable for a small group of people (say, *arguendo*, five) to take possession of the automobile of one of their members by force? If we add one more member making it six, is it then okay for the five to oppress the sixth? Are there any number of characters where such an action is unacceptable but if one more is added then it is? Libertarians answer with a firm "NO WAY!" Should even one dissenter remain, then in a democracy everyone else, the majority, is an oppressor. The only way for a democracy or any (state) organization to be just is that members of the minority, even individuals, initially agree to be bound by the vote. Also necessary is that signatories may subsequently withdraw support, such as payment of taxes, and sufferance of regulations without having violent sanctions imposed upon them. This is the libertarian principle of secession written into the American Declaration of Independence:

> That whenever any Form of Government becomes destructive of these ends [the rights to Life, Liberty and the pursuit of Happiness], it is the Right of the People to alter or to abolish it, and to institute new Government, laying its foundation on such principles and organizing its powers in such form, as to them shall seem most likely to effect their Safety and Happiness.

Prudence, indeed, will dictate that Governments long established should not be changed for light and transient causes; and accordingly, all experience hath shewn, that mankind are more disposed to suffer, while evils are sufferable, than to right themselves by abolishing the forms to which they are accustomed. But when a long train of abuses and usurpations, pursuing invariably the same Object evinces a design to reduce them under absolute Despotism, it is their right, it is their duty, to throw off such Government, and to provide new Guards for their future security.

Libertarians would go further than Thomas Jefferson and proclaim that even the individual may secede. That is very far from a national democracy as normally understood.[26]

"Neighborhood effects" are typically characterized as externalities in the neo-classical economic literature. Rothbard (1997b, p. 178) dismissed them as a justification for government intervention in the free market: His *reductio ad absurdum* is as follows: "A and B often benefit, it is held, if they can force C into doing something... [A]ny argument proclaiming the right and goodness of, say, three neighbors, who yearn to form a string quartet, forcing a fourth neighbor at bayonet point to learn and play the viola, is hardly deserving of sober comment." Friedman does not favor compelling anyone to take viola lessons; but he does support the notion that they can be forced to become educated. Friedman only resorts to subsidies, which compel taxpayers to pony up the necessary funds, instead of legally requiring all and sundry to become educated, since the latter would be unfeasible in his opinion.

Another difficulty is that economically mischievous laws such as rent control and minimum wages, which Friedman (1962), happily, opposes, are most popular precisely in areas where education of the sort he favors predominate. For example, in the People's Republics of Cambridge,

---

[26] Could one make the case, and many people do, that the repeated reciting of the Pledge of Allegiance commits one to remain a ward of the state? Not bloody likely. First of all, it is mainly children that do so. They can hardly be considered capable of making such thorough and far-reaching commitments. Secondly, for so momentous an agreement, any sensible court would likely rule that it would have to be in writing, signed, and notarized.

Massachusetts; Berkeley,[27] California; Boulder, Colorado; or Ann Arbor, Michigan; where there are tens if not hundreds of thousands of students in small geographical areas. Here, too, is where support for the economically illiterate Bernie Sanders was most popular. Perhaps "education" of this sort is really an external diseconomy, and would be more appropriately taxed, not subsidized? There is nothing in Friedman's analysis that could prevent reaching such a conclusion, the exact opposite of what he recommended. The point here is that there is a great amount of subjectivity[28] involved in making the claim that education benefits others who cannot be forced to pay for it; that people with no children gain from the education of other people's progeny, and therefore should be compelled to pay for it. Do not people gain when others smile at them? Take showers? Wear clothes?[29] Using the "logic" employed by Friedman, government should intervene in these cases too, lest not enough of these "neighborhood effects" occur. These benefits, too, "accrue... not only to" smilers, shower takers, clothes wearers "but also to other members of the society."

We must conclude that there is no warrant for statist support of education. However, assume, *arguendo*, that there is. Should STEM be promoted *vis-à-vis* the humanities? It is to that question that we now turn.

---

[27] Why do we characterize these widely-esteemed institutions of higher learning as "people's republics"? The lead author of this book attended the University of California, Berkeley, starting in 1967 and found it the most provincial community he ever experienced. There was, at the time of his residence, an orthodoxy which could not be publicly challenged. Even private disputation of the accepted convention with a professor was verboten. It appears to us that many other highly ranked colleges and universities have adopted the same or a similar ethos. That canon was leftist, even Marxist, in nature. The term "people's republics" is widely used by communist regimes which restrict free speech and, hence, constitutes an apt metaphor for these communities. More recently, non-leftist speakers such as Milo Yianopolous and Ann Coulter have been in effect banned from this institution of "higher learning" as has been Charles Murray from its sister school, Vermont's Middlebury College.

[28] States Hayek (1979, pp. 52–53): "And it is probably no exaggeration to say that every important advance in economic theory during the last hundred years was a further step in the consistent application of subjectivism."

[29] Of course, as unbelievable as it is, states do make demands in such topics as appropriate clothing, bathing, etc. sometimes sending out police to take measurements (The Young Turks 2016). Libertarians disapprove.

STEM vs. Humanities

Prominent among the alarmists in the STEM "crisis" are Holdren and Lander (2012). They whine that there is a shortfall looming of one million college graduates with degrees in these technical fields. In their view, the "sky really will be falling" if monies for education are not diverted from alternative studies to these more technical fields.

In the view of Zakaria (2015), however: "A broad general education helps foster critical thinking and creativity. Exposure to a variety of fields produces synergy and cross fertilization. Yes, science and technology are crucial components of this education, but so are English and philosophy."

There are problems here. For one thing, English and philosophy at most universities have, to a great degree, been taken over by cultural Marxists. Their motto is that dead white males must be ignored or avoided; that live ones should abandon their untoward "privilege"; professors of literature and philosophy are pre-eminent among those who have supported and even inculcated the demands for trigger warnings, safe spaces, and the right to shout down any opinion on campus not to the liking of their "snowflake" students. The liberal arts, all of them,[30] have been overtaken by cultural studies, feminist studies, queer studies, multicultural studies, black studies, and other whining studies.

Once we assume away the argument against government support for education, we really are at sea without a rudder. There are no prices to guide us. We are in, roughly, the position of the central planning board of the U.S.S.R.[31] Yes, there are both "benefits and costs" as Friedman

---

[30] With the possible exception of economics, which has one foot in the humanities, but another in more technical disciplines. Whether for good or not, the two co-authors of this book have between them degrees in engineering, economics, history, and divinity. Speaking authoritatively from personal experience, STEM generally amounts to technical training whereas the humanities tends towards education per-se so long as the student can see through the propaganda that all too often passes for education. The current modern usage of the term "education" encompasses no fewer than three at best marginally related concepts: education (learning how to function in the world in which we exist: philosophy, history, etc.), technical training (learning how to perform specific tasks: engineering, cooking, etc.), and propaganda (exposure to the preferred myths of the powers who wish to impose their will on others: civics, political studies, etc.).

[31] See on this Boettke 2001; Ebeling 1993; Hayek 1948; Hoff 1981; Hoppe 1989; Von Mises 1922, 1977.

would have it, to public instruction. But without market-generated prices, without profit and loss, without exit due to bankruptcy for entrepreneurs who cannot satisfy consumers, there is no non-arbitrary answer to the question of how to allocate resources between STEM and the humanities. States Ridley (2015, p. 138) in this regard: "To most people, the argument for public funding of science rests on a list of the discoveries made with public funds, from the internet…to the Higgs' boson[32]… But that's highly misleading. Given that government has funded science munificently, it would be odd if it had not found out something. We learn nothing about what would have been discovered by alternative funding arrangements. And we can never know what discoveries were not made because government funding of science inevitably crowded out much of the philanthropic and commercial funding, which might have had different priorities." But most importantly, government funding typically prostitutes science with political correctness. One's conclusions must conform to current political preferences if funding is desired. Thus, rigorous investigation of reality is annulled.

References

Alexander, Sonja, and Esther Buchsbaum. 2007. NASA and M.A.D. Science Partner to Promote Science Education. September 5. http://www.nasa.gov/home/hqnews/2007/sep/HQ_07185_Mad_Science.html. Accessed 7 July 2016.

Anthony, Sebastian. 2014. The Apollo 11 Moon Landing, 45 Years on: Looking Back at Mankind's Giant Leap. July 21. http://www.extremetech.com/extreme/186600-apollo-11-moon-landing-45-years-looking-back-at-mankinds-giant-leap. Accessed 23 May 2016.

Axelrod, Alan. 2008. *Profiles in Folly: History's Worst Decisions and Why They Went Wrong*. Sterling Publishing Company.

Berliner, Michael S., ed. 1995. *Letters of Ayn Rand*. New York: Dutton.

Block, Walter E. 1999. Austrian Theorizing, Recalling the Foundations: Reply to Caplan. *Quarterly Journal of Austrian Economics* 2 (4): 21–39.

———. 2003. National Defense and the Theory of Externalities, Public Goods and Clubs. In *The Myth of National Defense: Essays on the Theory and History*

---

[32] A sub-atomic particle predicted by Peter Higgs.

of Security Production, ed. Hans-Hermann Hoppe, 301–334. Auburn: Mises Institute. http://www.mises.org/etexts/defensemyth.pdf. Accessed 23 Apr 2016.

———. 2006. Kevin Carson as Dr. Jekyll and Mr. Hyde. *The Journal of Libertarian Studies* 20 (1). http://mises.org/journals/jls/20_1/20_1_4.pdf. Accessed 11 June 2016.

———. 2011. Review Essay of Ostrom, Elinor. 1990. *Governing the Commons: The Evolution of Institutions for Collective Action.* Cambridge and New York: Cambridge University Press. In *Libertarian Papers*, Vol. 3, Art. 21. http://libertarianpapers.org/2011/21-block-review-of-ostroms-governing-the-commons/.

———. 2010. Review of Huebert's Libertarianism Today. *Libertarian Papers*. http://libertarianpapers.org/2010/19-block-review-of-hueberts-libertarianism-today/. Accessed 29 June 2016.

———. 2013. *Defending the Undefendable II: Freedom in All Realms.* Terra Libertas Publishing House.

Block, Walter, and Llewellyn H. Rockwell Jr. 2007. Katrina and the Future of New Orleans. *Telos* 139: 170–185. http://tinyurl.com/2wv8lc; http://journal.telospress.com; http://journal.telospress.com/cgi/reprint/2007/139/170.

Block, Walter E., and Milton Friedman. 2006. Fanatical, Not Reasonable: A Short Correspondence Between Walter Block and Milton Friedman (on Friedrich Hayek). *Journal of Libertarian Studies* 20 (3): 61–80 http://www.mises.org/journals/jls/20_3/20_3_4.pdf; https://mises.org/system/tdf/20_3_4.pdf?file=1&type=document.

Block, Walter E., and William Barnett II. 2012–2013. Milton Friedman and the Financial Crisis. *American Review of Political Economy* 10 (1/2): 2–17. https://sites.bemidjistate.edu/arpejournal/wp-content/uploads/sites/2/2015/11/v10n1-block.pdf.

Boettke, Peter J. 2001. *Calculation and Coordination: Essays on Socialism and Transitional Political Economy.* London: Routledge. http://www.mises.org/etexts/cc.pdf. Accessed 23 May 2016.

Cegłowski, Maciej. 2005. A Rocket to Nowhere. August 3. http://www.idlewords.com/2005/08/a_rocket_to_nowhere.htm.

Dunn, Terry. 2014. The Space Shuttle's Controversial Launch Abort Plan. February 26. http://www.tested.com/science/space/460233-space-shuttles-controversial-launch-abort-plan/. Accessed 29 June 2016.

Ebeling, Richard M. 1993. Economic Calculation Under Socialism: Ludwig von Mises and His Predecessors. In *The Meaning of Ludwig von Mises*, ed. Jeffrey Herbener, 56–101. Norwell, MA: Kluwer Academic Press.

Fox News. 2009. Hubble Telescope Almost Was Billion-Dollar Joke. May 11. http://www.foxnews.com/story/2009/05/11/hubble-telescope-almost-was-billion-dollar-joke.html. Accessed 1 July 2016.

Friedman, David. 1979. Private Creation and Enforcement of Law: A Historical Case. *University of Chicago Law Review.* http://www.daviddfriedman.com/Academic/Iceland/Iceland.html. Accessed 23 Apr 2016.

Friedman, Milton. 1962. The Role of Government in Education. In *Capitalism and Freedom.* Chicago IL: University of Chicago Press.

———. 2000. Interview. Commanding Heights. October 1. http://www.pbs.org/wgbh/commandingheights/shared/minitextlo/int_miltonfriedman.

Futron Corporation. 2002. Space Transportation Costs: Trends in Price Per Pound to Orbit 1990–2000. September 6. https://web.archive.org/web/20110711061933/http://www.futron.com/upload/wysiwyg/Resources/Whitepapers/Space_Transportation_Costs_Trends_0902.pdf. Accessed 23 May 2016.

Green, Michael. 2015. New Study Reveals When, Where and How Much Motorists Drive. *AAA News Room.* April 16. http://newsroom.aaa.com/2015/04/new-study-reveals-much-motorists-drive/. Accessed 6 July 2016.

Hayek, F.A. 1948. Socialist Calculation I, II, & III. In *Individualism and Economic Order.* Chicago: University of Chicago Press.

Hayek, Friedrich A. 1979. *The Counter-Revolution of Science.* 2nd ed. Indianapolis: Liberty Press.

Heller, Chris. 2012. Neil deGrasse Tyson: How Space Exploration Can Make America Great Again. March 5. http://www.theatlantic.com/technology/archive/2012/03/neil-degrasse-tyson-how-space-exploration-can-make-america-great-again/253989/. Accessed 7 July 2016.

Hoff, Trygve J.B. 1981. *Economic Calculation in a Socialist Society.* Indianapolis: Liberty Press.

Hohler, Daniel. 2009. Top 5 Reasons Why Space Exploration Is Important for the World. July 26. http://planetsave.com/2009/07/26/top-5-reasons-why-space-exploration-is-important-for-the-world/. Accessed 7 July 2016.

Holdren, John P., and Eric Lander. 2012. Report to the President: Engage to Excel: Producing One Million Additional College Graduates with Degrees in Science, Technology, Engineering, and Mathematics. February. https://www.whitehouse.gov/sites/default/files/microsites/ostp/pcast-engage-to-excel-final_2-25-12.pdf. Accessed 23 May 2016.

Hoppe, Hans-Hermann. 1989. Fallacies of the Public Goods Theory and the Production of Security. *The Journal of Libertarian Studies* IX (1): 27–46. http://www.mises.org/journals/jls/9_1/9_1_2.pdf. Accessed 23 Apr 2016.

Hudgins, Edward L. 2012. Time to Privatize NASA. http://www.cato.org/publications/commentary/time-privatize-nasa. Accessed 23 May 2016.

IMDb. n.d. Jim Backus Biography. IMDb. http://www.imdb.com/name/nm0000822/bio?ref_=nm_ov_bio_sm. Accessed 7 July 2016.

Kaku, Michio. 2009. The Cost of Space Exploration. July 16. http://www.forbes.com/2009/07/16/apollo-moon-landing-anniversary-opinions-contributors-cost-money.html. Accessed 23 May 2016.

Kinnucan, P. 1983. Push to Commercialize Space Runs into Budget Cutbacks, Boondoggle Charges, and Fear of High Risks. *High Technology* 3: 43–45.

Kinsella, Stephan N. 2009. What Libertarianism Is. August 21. https://mises.org/library/what-libertarianism. Accessed 23 Apr 2016.

Kramer, Miriam. 2013. To Moonwalker Buzz Aldrin, 'Tang Sucks'. *Space.com*. June 12. http://www.space.com/21538-buzz-aldrin-tang-spaceflight.html. Accessed 30 June 2016.

Krauss, Lawrence. 2011. The Space Shuttle Programme Has Been a Multi-billion-dollar Failure. *The Guardian*. July 21. https://www.theguardian.com/science/2011/jul/21/space-shuttle-programme. Accessed 23 May 2016.

Lind, Michael. 2012. Thank You, Milton Friedman: How Conservatives' Economic Hero Helped Make the Case for Big Government. August 7. http://www.salon.com/2012/08/07/thank_you_milton_friedman/.

Long, Roderick T. 2006. Realism and Abstraction in Economics: Aristotle and Mises Versus Friedman. *The Quarterly Journal of Austrian Economics* 9 (3): 3–23 http://www.mises.org/journals/qjae/pdf/qjae9_3_1.pdf.

Maass, Harold. 2013. The Odds Are 11 Million to 1 that You'll Die in a Plane Crash [sic]. *The Week*. July 8. http://theweek.com/articles/462449/odds-are-11-million-1-that-youll-die-plane-crash. Accessed 6 July 2016.

Machan, Tibor R. 2010. Milton Friedman and the Human Good, June 7; http://mises.org/daily/4451/Milton-Friedman-and-the-Human-Good.

Marcus, B. K. 2007. "The Tepid Movement Before Mises" April 12; http://www.mises.org/story/2530.

Marx, Karl. 1906 [1867]. *Das Capital*. New York: Modern Library.

McChesney, Fred. 1991. Antitrust and Regulation: Chicago's Contradictory Views. *Cato Journal* 10 (3): 775–778.

NASA. 2000. National Aeronautics and Space Administration. Liberty Bell 7 MR-4 (19). September 29. http://www.nasa.gov/externalflash/the_shuttle/. Accessed 1 July 2016.

———. 2009. National Aeronautics and Space Administration. Apollo 13. July 8. http://www.nasa.gov/externalflash/the_shuttle/. Accessed 1 July 2016.

———. 2015. National Aeronautics and Space Administration. https://www.nasa.gov/sites/default/files/files/FY15_Summary_Brief.pdf. Accessed 24 Apr 2016.

———. n.d. National Aeronautics and Space Administration. The Shuttle. http://www.nasa.gov/externalflash/the_shuttle/. Accessed 1 July 2016.

North, Gary. 2012. "Detours on the Road to Freedom: Where Milton Friedman Went Wrong." http://archive.lewrockwell.com/north/north1178.html.

Pearce, Rohan. 2012. What Went Wrong with the Hubble Space Telescope (and What Managers Can Learn from It). *CIO*. March 29. http://www.cio.com. au/article/420036/what_went_wrong_hubble_space_telescope_what_managers_can_learn_from_it_/?pp=3. Accessed 1 July 2016.

Rand, Ayn. n.d. http://books.google.ca/books?id=QV2OJqbt45oC&pg=PA38 7&lpg=PA387&dq=%22the+most+pernicious+thing+ever+issued+by+an+a vowedly+conservative+organization%22&source=web&ots=DV4j_dhJA&si g=DZYoo1KjulTGviiR7kFGINFrbnY&hl=en&sa=X&oi=book_result&res num=1&ct=result.

Rand, Ayn. 1969. Apollo 11. *The Objectivist* (September). https://ari.aynrand. org/issues/science-and-industrialization/scientific-and-technological-progress/Apollo-11.

Rapp, Donald. 2015. Why the NASA Approach Will Likely Fail to Send Humans to Mars for Many Decades to Come. October 30. http://link.springer.com/ chapter/10.1007/978-3-319-22249-3_7. Accessed 23 May 2016.

Ridley, Matt. 2015. *The Evolution of Everything: How New Ideas Emerge.* New York: Harper.

Rothbard, Murray N. 1997a. Toward a Reconstruction of Utility and Welfare Economics. Reprinted in *The Logic of Action One: Method, Money, and the Austrian School,* 211–254. Glos, UK: Edward Elgar Publishing Ltd.

———. 1997b. *The Logic of Action: Applications and Criticism from the Austrian School.* Vol. II. Cheltenham: Edward Elgar.

Rothbard, Murray N. 2002. Milton Friedman Unraveled. *Journal of Libertarian Studies* 16 (4): 37–54 http://www.mises.org/journals/jls/16_4/16_4_3.pdf; https://www.lewrockwell.com/2016/02/murray-n-rothbard/totaldemolition-milton-friedman/.

Sennholz, Hans F. 2006. Milton Friedman, 1912–2006. December 16. http:// mises.org/story/2414.

Simons, Robert. 2013. The Business of Business Schools: Restoring a Focus on Competing to Win. *Capitalism and Society* 8 (1): Art. 2. http://www.hbs.edu/ faculty/publication%20files/cap%20and%20soc%20simons_054781c5-4cd0-4c99-bf9e-94cebf404a8d.pdf. Accessed 8 June 2016.

Skousen, Mark. 2001. *The Making of Modern Economics.* New York: M. E. Sharpe.

Smith, Adam. 1979 [1776]. *An Inquiry into the Nature and Causes of the Wealth of Nations.* Indianapolis, IN: Liberty Fund.

Space Safety. 2016. New Chart of Space Incidents and Close Calls. *Space Safety Magazine*. April 12. http://www.spacesafetymagazine.com/space-disasters/new-chart-space-incidents-close-calls/. Accessed 7 July 2016.

The Young Turks. 2016. Police Force Muslim Woman to Strip at Beach. August 24. https://www.youtube.com/watch?v=3kJcFYsxW4Y. Accessed 1 Sep 2016.

Unreal. 2016. Field Trip to Mars: Framestore's Shared VR Experience Delivered with Unreal Engine 4. August 15. https://www.youtube.com/watch?v=e0XNlsXnKp0. Accessed 1 Sep 2016.

Vaughan, Diane. 1996. *The Challenger Launch Decision: Risky Technology, Culture, and Deviance at NASA*. Chicago: University of Chicago Press.

Vance, Laurence M. 1996. Friedman's Mistake. *The Free Market* 14 (11). http://www.mises.org/freemarket_detail.asp?control=158&sortorder=articledate.

Vance, Laurence. 2005. The Curse of the Withholding Tax. April 21. http://www.mises.org/story/1797.

Von Mises, Ludwig. 1977. *A Critique of Interventionism*. New Rochelle, NY: Arlington House. http://www.mises.org/etexts/mises/interventionism/contents.asp.

Von Mises, Ludwig. 1981 [1922]. *Socialism: An Economic and Sociological Analysis*. Trans. J. Kahane. Indianapolis: Liberty Fund. http://mises.org/books/socialism/contents.aspx.

Wapshott, Nicholas. 2012. A Lovefest Between Milton Friedman and J.M. Keynes. July 30. http://www.thedailybeast.com/articles/2012/07/30/nicholas-wapshott-a-lovefest-between-milton-friedman-and-j-mkeynes.html.

Wenzel, Robert. 2012. How Milton Friedman Helped Make the Case for Big Government. August 9. http://www.economicpolicyjournal.com/2012/08/how-milton-friedman-helped-make-case.html.

Winsor, Dorothy A. 1988. Communication Failures Contributing to the Challenger Accident: An Example of for Technical Communicators. *Professional Communication, IEEE Transactions on* 31 (3): 101–107.

Wilcke, Richard R. 1999. An Appropriate Ethical Model for Business, and a Critique of Milton Friedman. http://mises.org/journals/scholar/Ethics.PDF.

Zakaria, Fareed. 2015. Why America's Obsession with STEM Education Is Dangerous. March 26. https://www.washingtonpost.com/opinions/why-stem-wont-make-us-successful/2015/03/26/5f4604f2-d2a5-11e4-ab77-9646eea6a4c7_story.html. Accessed 23 May 2016.

Zeeberg, Amos. 2011. How to Avoid Repeating the Debacle That Was the Space Shuttle; It Promised the Moon but Delivered Low Earth Orbit at Exorbitant Cost. And It's Partly Your Fault. July 22. http://discovermagazine.com/2011/jul-aug/22-how-to-avoid-repeating-debacle-of-space-shuttle. Accessed 23 May 2016.

11

Public Goods: Basic Research and Terraforming

The theses of this book are (1) that free enterprise, and it alone, is the last best hope for space travel, colonization, and getting some significant numbers of humans off our home planet, and (2) that relying on government to pursue this goal is a snare and a delusion. However, critics will point to the doctrine of "public goods" to denigrate this case of ours. We will now consider that perspective, and then apply it to two crucial aspects of the space program, basic research[1] as a public good and terraforming.

---

[1] Basic research includes such concepts as Einstein's general theory of relativity, Pythagoras' theorem, and Euclid's geometry. It is not specific research, for example, regarding the development of a medication to cure cancer. When Newton set down the principles of calculus, he was trying to find a way to address mathematical problems he was facing: to wit how to find solutions related to the limits of equations where the denominator of a fraction approached zero. (The result of a real number divided by zero is indeterminate. See the mathematical "proof" that 2 = 1 at the end of this chapter.) No one asked Sir Isaac to do that; so, other than the opportunity to sell a few books, he had no hope of financial gain. Certainly, the British Crown did not ask for it.

© The Author(s) 2018
P. L. Nelson, W. E. Block, *Space Capitalism*, Palgrave Studies in Classical Liberalism,
https://doi.org/10.1007/978-3-319-74651-7_11

Public Goods

The Theory

To see the fallacy of the "public goods" contentions, a clear understanding of the doctrine is required; then the fallacy will become evident. This chapter demonstrates that the basic research necessary for the conquest of space can be generated by private enterprise, as can terraforming. Indeed, only those with personal investments have the motivation to seek out what categorically works and does so efficiently.

What, then, is the claim that there is a market failure regarding public goods? First, we must distinguish between two types of goods. Private ones may be defined as those for which it is possible to exclude non-payers and which are rivalrous. For example, it is entirely possible, actually easy, to exclude non-payers of hot dogs from consuming them. The merchant has a very credible threat to offer against any person who wishes to enjoy his product, without paying: he will call the police (hopefully private ones).[2] Does this mean that no thief ever got away with stealing one of these foodstuffs? No, of course not. Excludability need not be 100%. But as long as the overwhelming proportion of consumers actually pay for their hotdogs, this criterion is satisfied. In contrast, it is very difficult, according to this argument, to omit from the enjoyment of the benefits of a crowded city street, a lighthouse, national defense, and, of present interest, basic research and terraforming. By their very nature, it is argued, these items partake of non-excludability. Non-payers will not be able to be prohibited from enjoying the benefits, direct, or indirect, of these goods and services.

What is rivalrousness; and what does excludable mean? A good is rivalrous if there are competitors for its enjoyment. It is non-rivalrous if all of us, together, can benefit from it. If A eats a hotdog, then B cannot also do so. If B wears a pair of pants, then A cannot do so. A and B are rivals for the use or consumption of these items. In contrast, radio and television waves

---

[2] See on this Gregory 2011; Guillory and Tinsley 2009; Hoppe 2011; Huebert 2010; Murphy 2005; Rothbard 1973a, b, 1975, 1998 [1982]; Stringham 2007; Tannehill and Tannehill 1984 [1970]; Tinsley 1998–1999; Wiśniewski 2014; Wollstein 1969; Woolridge 1970.

are non-rivalrous. If 1000 people are accessing one of these broadcasts, and a few or even many additional consumers tune in, the latter in no way reduce, let alone end, the enjoyment of the former. They are not rivalrous with one another.[3] However, if extra commuters enter the crowded sidewalk or roadway, they slow down everyone else. Here, then, there is competition, or rivalrousness.

When an item is non-rivalrous and non-excludability applies, it is a pure public good. If only one or the other criterion is applicable, it would be characterized as a semi-public good. If the market failure of public goods does not apply, these are pure private goods, where both excludability and rivalrousness hold true. Let it not be thought that each of these four cases describes roughly 25% all items. At least in the view of most economists, the overwhelming majority of products are private.[4]

According to this perspective, with busy streets or highways there is rivalrousness, and the marginal costs of adding one more person to them would be greater than zero. Thus, we should exclude at least some of these additional users. Whereas adding one utilizer of either the empty highway or street will not slow anyone down. The marginal or additional costs of them doing so would be zero, and therefore they should not be excluded. Similarly, we are indeed able to exclude motorists from limited access highways, whether busy or empty, while this supposedly does not apply to city streets, either busy or not.[5] Government intervention is supposedly justified in all non-private goods cases since the market will fail to provide these goods either at all or will do so inadequately. With this introduction to public goods theory, we are now ready to explore the fallacies involved.

---

[3] Notice that those who pay for radio waves have an interest in reaching the widest audience possible. Sponsorship *is* rivalrous in that only so many commercials can be broadcast without driving away too many potential listeners. The radio station thus excludes advertisers. But viewing is made to be non-competitive on purpose. This discussion isolates from paid TV where all or part of the income is directly from the viewer.

[4] The proportion of goods for which there is market failure depends upon the judgement of the economist. Presumably the Marxist economist (a contradiction in terms) would see very few purely private goods relative to others in this profession; whereas, this book you are now reading demonstrates that *all* things are privately created and that the concept of market failure is devoid of meaning.

[5] That local access streets may not be set up to exclude motorists, or even pedestrians, is a misconception. We see already in our day, access to streets limited in gated communities. Limitation of access can be accomplished not only by fences but by no-trespassing signs, guards, or technologies not yet devised. Availability of access should be determined by the owner(s) of the street.

The Critique

According to extreme interpretation of this doctrine, no public goods could ever have been produced in a free economy because the entrepreneur either cannot exclude non-payers or the good is non-rivalrous, or both. But this is highly problematic in the case of basic research. Yet it would be exceedingly difficult to credit government for these accomplishments. Therefore, perforce, they were created in the private sector, contrary to this viewpoint. The public goods argument is incorrect at least in these cases. There are numerous other such counter examples: the music of Mozart, the idea of the conservation of angular momentum,[6] etc.

In contrast, there is also the moderate claim that yes, the market is indeed capable of producing public goods, but it can only produce less or fewer of them than is optimal. The difficulty with this position is that there is no objective criterion for what would be the optimal amount, and it simply will not do to say that this is whatever does not occur under free enterprise.

So far, we have only superficially considered criticism of this public goods doctrine.[7] Now, let us dig deeper. Consider, first, the busy city street. According to mainstream economists, non-payers cannot be excluded from entry. While it may well be true that the *government* is so inept that it cannot do so, it by no means follows that a private owner could not succeed.[8] If he could not, he would lose money, ultimately go bankrupt, and be replaced by someone who could. We even have some quasi-analogous cases of private enterprises succeeding in doing exactly that. For instance, con-

---

[6] A bicycle in motion stays upright because of the conservation of angular momentum. If a rotating wheel tilts to the right, then it will veer to the right to compensate. For a video of a demonstration refer to Physilicious (2009). For the reader who is unfamiliar with it, we strongly recommend reviewing the YouTube demonstration listed in the bibliography—it is fun.

[7] For an extensive literature on this see Barnett and Block 2007, 2009; Block 1983, 2000a, b, 2003; Cowen 1988; De Jasay 1989; Holcombe 1997; Hoppe 1989; Hummel 1990; Osterfeld 1989; Pasour 1981; Rothbard 1997; Schmidtz 1991; Sechrest 2003, 2004a, b, 2007; Stringham 2015; Tinsley 1999.

[8] This assumes that the owner wishes to exclude users. Let us consider a street in a commercial district. The merchants want as many people as possible to use the street. Therefore, they would consider it part of the overhead of conducting business and charge their customers nothing. Should the street become so busy that people are driven away, they would improve the street at their own expense and thank their blessings for such success.

sider the Boston or New York City marathons. There are several tens of thousands of entries in each. Thus, the streets and sidewalks become very crowded. How do the *private* organizers of these events preclude free riders? Simple. They issue a bib, some six inches by eight inches in size, and a few safety pins, to all those who pay a fee to enter for them to affix to their shirts. If there is any runner without such adornment, he is easily seen as a thief of services, and dealt with accordingly.

Then, there are the problems with rivalrousness. Consider a hotel, apartment, ballfield, concert hall, movie theater, classroom with less than 100% occupancy. That pretty much describes actual practice, except for World Series, Super Bowl, Mardi Gras, or similar events. But this means there is no rivalrousness regarding the unoccupied seats, or rooms! According to the specious and pernicious doctrine of public goods, these institutions ought to be nationalized, since economic inefficiency abounds. The point is, it would cost nothing whatsoever to place an additional marginal person in one of these empty places.[9] But this is silly. Hotels and movie theaters, etc. are viable concerns. There is no need to engage in the sovietization of them. Nor is it clear that there are no costs to filling an empty seat in a movie theater; the owners might well see matters entirely differently. It will likely impose severe psychic costs on their proprietors. The thought that they must issue freebies might drive them to apoplexy.

Nor is the lighthouse protected from this sort of criticism. In the days of sailing ships, the owner of this facility had a credible threat to offer non-payers: "(With fist raised) One of *these* days"[10] he will *turn off the light*. This, possibly, may never come to pass. But the mere possibility will tend to raise the salaries of the sailors on such vessels, due to the added risk. And, too, when word gets out that there are some who are not pulling their weight, they will lose goodwill and standing in the community. It might well be cheaper to pay the lighthouse fee than undergo these costs.

---

[9] There would be only tiny costs for empty hotel rooms; sweeping the floor, laundering the sheets, etc. This is a small proportion of the total price of these amenities. More to the point, empty seats might be a signal to the capitalist that he is charging too much. To maximize profits by achieving 100% occupancy, he could lower the price. However, he will likely find it more efficient, or at least easier to manage, if he charges a single price that sometimes results in long lines while at other times, seats go unoccupied.

[10] With apologies to Ralph Kramden, a character created in the 1950s by Jackie Gleason.

Nor is the pure public good of national defense immune from this criticism. A private defense agency[11] may indeed exclude from its benefits those who refuse to pay for this service. All it needs to do is to announce[12] to the terrorist du jour, the Hitler, the Stalin, or the ISIL, that the Jones corporation refuses to subscribe. They are fair game, as far as this private police-army corporation is concerned. And this works on the macro-level too. Suppose that those in Massachusetts, *en masse*, refuse to pay for this service, while those in Texas, do so. The protection firm makes a similar proclamation to the "usual suspects." Of course, unanimity is usually not attained in the real world. Posit, then, that 99% of Texans subscribe, but only 1% of those in the Bay State do so. Public pressure in the Lone Star State will presumably deal with the outliers, and their counterparts in Massachusetts will have to migrate, if they wish to be protected. In any case, a private defense agency need not enroll 100% of all those they protect. Some lesser percentage will typically allow the enterprise to be a going concern.

We have seen that the public good doctrine is dead from the neck up. This is the theory, the basis on which the claim is made that the market cannot (sufficiently) supply basic research. It is to this subject that we next turn.[13]

Basic Research

Space exploration and colonization[14] will require two types of research: basic[15] and engineering. There are few who would doubt that private enterprise is capable of the latter. Indeed, to call this into question would

[11] Here is bibliographical support for this contention: Block 2003; Cowen 1988; De Jasay 1989; Hoppe 1989; Hummel 1990; Pasour 1981; Rothbard 1997; Schmidtz 1991; Sechrest 2003, 2004a, b, 2007.

[12] An actual announcement is not strictly necessary and might be risky from a liability point of view. A would-be aggressor will discover on his own who is unprotected.

[13] One process of the colonization of celestial bodies would be terraforming. If anything were a public good a "terraformed" planet would seem to be it. For the reasons cited above, this too would also be provided by the free market. For more on this, refer to the discussion below.

[14] "Colonization" has a bad press. It is associated with exploiting helpless people. Happily, no such implication can attach in the present case, unless there are Martians or Venusians who will be ground down by human beings. For the argument that this process was actually helpful to its supposed victims back here on Earth, see Ferguson (2011).

[15] For an important critique of government supported basic research, see Accad (2016).

seem unusual, in that there are vast numbers of engineers who work in the private sector.

Basic research, however, is another matter. Not only is it acceptable to question whether such activities could occur under the direction of private entrepreneurs, it is the overwhelming conclusion of virtually the entire economics profession either that this cannot take place at all or, at best, only in a severely curtailed manner. Why has this delusion taken hold of the minds of the purveyors of the dismal science? It is due to the claim that basic research is a public good; in the extreme, the market is incapable of providing any goods and services that partake in this "market failure." At the very least, too little of it will be forthcoming if society relies on the profit motive. The public sector, then, will have to make good the shortfall.

Mazzucato (2013) seemingly takes a position contrary to the one being articulated here. She argues that government has participated in many, many of the scientific and engineering breakthroughs we have witnessed. This cannot be denied. We acknowledge that she makes a good case for this hypothesis. However, it does not so much as lay a glove on the argument we are making. It would be strange indeed if, given the gigantic proportion of the world's GDP that funnels through this institution[16] that, despite it, *some* good did not result. President Obama made a similar claim what he said: "You didn't build that," referring to public sector amenities without which private enterprise supposedly could not function. He continued: "Somebody invested in roads and bridges. If you've got a business—you didn't build that. Somebody else made that happen. The Internet didn't get invented on its own. Government research created the Internet so that all the companies could make money off the Internet" (Kiely 2012).

As to the facts of the matter, the professor and the president are correct; both parties, government and the private sector, had a hand in the accomplishments of modern capitalism. But there is also a hidden-between-the-lines implication of what they were saying: that were it not for the state apparatus, these achievements could not have been attained. They are engaging in a contrary to fact conditional. They in effect claim that subtract government from history, and we would be far worse off

---

[16] This funneling of economic activity through the government occurs only at the state's own insistence, through compulsory levies.

economically than we are now; few or none of these benefits would have been forthcoming.[17] But this conclusion does not at all follow from the premise. For it is a virtual certainty that had not the government been involved in the creation of roads, bridges, tunnels,[18] the Internet and other such elements relied upon by markets, private enterprise would have accomplished these tasks. In fact, there is no government product, none, that has not, at some time in our history, also been produced by the private sector (Woolridge 1970) and invariably at a lower cost.[19] There is also another hidden assumption on the part of Mazzucato and Obama: on net balance, government's contribution to this process was a positive one. This is hard to sustain. Yes, of course the statists diverted part of the monies they mulcted from private individuals at gun-point to this social overhead capital. But they also engaged in numerous programs that lowered GDP. When *both* effects are considered, we see that government was a net drag on economic development. With no doubt, none of the truths uttered by Obama and Mazzucato obviate this. Rothbard (1963, pp. 339–348) explicitly made this case when he argued that to get a better measure of GDP we ought not to add government expenditures, but rather *subtract* them.[20] So much for the views of Obama and Mazzucato. Quite the contrary:

---

[17] "But here I want to address a companion argument that is often used to justify not only expansive government per se, but a large military sector specifically. It's the argument that war is an important, and even necessary, source of scientific progress, because technologies developed by the state to fight wars often have important civilian uses. Innovation is a side benefit of war, say war's defenders. By mobilizing all the resources of society, through coercion, repression, and exploitation, we get not only civic pride and the martial spirit, but also great new technologies" (Klein 2013). Yes, Tang® and radar (an acronym for RAdio Detection And Ranging) came to us "courtesy" of the ever-loving government. But what wonders would the free market have produced instead, or rather in addition, had the statists not spent vast amounts of treasure on these discoveries. Oh, and Tang® did not come from the government (see Chap. 10).

[18] For an examination of private roads, bridges, and tunnels in terms of privatization, see Block (2009).

[19] See on this Anderson and Hill 1996; Block 2002c, 2009; Butler 1988; Carnis 2003; Ebeling 2013; Hanke 1987a, b; Hannesson 2004, 2006; Hoppe 2011; Karpoff 2001; Megginson and Netter 2001; Moore 1987; Moore and Butler 1987; Motichek et al. 2008; Ohashi 1980; Ohashi et al. 1980; Pirie 1986; Savas 1987; Walker 1988; White 1978.

[20] Salerno (2015) avers: "Now it is certainly true that a reduction in real government spending causes a reduction in real GDP, as it is officially calculated. But…the reduction in government spending does not retard the growth of production of goods that satisfy consumer demands and, in fact, most likely accelerates it. In addition, real incomes and living standards of producers/consum-

Today, when we look at private companies like Google, Apple, and Facebook and marvel at their innovations, we should remember that these companies are constantly subject to market tests, and that the goods and services they innovate must be accepted by consumers to be profitable. When they succeed, we know that they are creating value for society because consumers have chosen their products and services over others.

The goods and services produced by the Rand Corporation, the Pentagon, and the National Science Foundation do not face any kind of market test. The goods and services they produce are valuable to the directors, and members of Congress, and to the researchers themselves who are on the payroll, but the value of this research is determined arbitrarily. (Klein 2015)

Terraforming

According to this public goods argument, only government could terraform an extraterrestrial body such as the Moon or Mars. Why? To do so would imply giving these orbs an atmosphere in which humans could survive, land upon which crops could be planted, rivers and lakes and perhaps oceans to support our habitation, and in every other way make them replicas of the Earth. But then free riders would appear to take over the terrain; they would have undertaken none of the costs, and be able to benefit from the great investment of the terraformer. The latter could not exclude the former, it is alleged. Therefore, he would not undertake this effort in the first place. Or, he would only do so if he could own the entire planet, and this would appear to be incompatible, at the very least, with libertarian homesteading theory.

At the outset, there is at least some superficial plausibility to this objection. After all, no libertarian would acquiesce in the notion that Columbus, for example, could own the entire North America[21] merely by planting a flag on its border. Nor, even, could he do so if he homesteaded

---

ers in the private sector rise as a direct result of the decline in government spending. The reason for this seeming paradox lies in the conventional method used to calculate real output in the economy." And what is this "conventional method?" It is to *add* to the GDP all government expenditure regardless of whether it promotes economic progress. For example, if all the state did was dig holes and fill them up again, and there were no other reverberations from such an act, this would *boost* officially measured well-being, while obviously *reducing* real goods and services available to the public. See also on this Casey 2015; Rothbard 1970, p. 201; Strow and Strow 2013.

[21] The pernicious notion that a claim of homesteading is plausible from the planting of a flag by a conquistador abstracts from the rights of the indigenous peoples.

a one-mile-deep perimeter around these lands. Here, he would own, only, that territory he had made his own, and not the entire interior of the continent. Let us briefly review libertarian homesteading theory to see if we cannot see our way clear to maintaining that the private terraformer would indeed have an incentive to improve the planet to the extent necessary for human habitation.

We start with human persons. Who should own them? There are only four possibilities: no ownership, joint or common possession, slavery, or individual self-ownership. First, if no one owned anyone, even himself, then he would have no interest in maintaining anyone. We would all die. Since no one owns us, we would have no right to use ourselves. We would not be able to attain food. We could not so much as breathe. Second, we could all own one-seven-billionth of everyone, since there are roughly that many inhabitants on our planet. Unfortunately, the same result would ensue. To get permission to engage in any acts, we would have to get unanimous consensus, but we could not even begin to obtain agreement from the local committee meetings. Third, some could own others as slaves. This is better than the previous two options since, at least, the human race would not perish holus-bolus. However, unless someone could put forth a justification other than "might makes right," which it certainly does not, this option, too, must be rejected for lack of support. That leaves only the fourth possibility, we each own ourselves, which is difficult to dismiss. This is buttressed by the fact that we each "homestead" ourselves. We mix our labor with our bodies. We control them through an act of will, which does not occur in any of the other cases.

That settled, we move on to the issue of who may own which swathes of land. Again, we confront similar possibilities. First, no one may own, and therefore have the right to interact with, any territory or even matter. This may be rejected out of hand since we would not be entitled to sit or stand anywhere, a manifest absurdity. A second alternative is that we each own one-seven-billionth of the entire Earth. Again, we would all perish since the vast committee meetings necessary to determine what should be done on each acre would never settle anything. A third option is that we divide the land into seven billion bits, each of equal value.[22] This is the most preferable so far, but what did each person do to justify land titles to "his" share.

---

[22] That is, an acre in fertile Kentucky would be worth two or more in less fertile Wyoming, and many acres in the desert of Nevada or the arctic tundra.

"Nothing" would be the answer. The best system for allocating land to people has been furnished by Locke (1690, chapter 5, sec. 27) who states:

> "...every man has a property in his own person: this nobody has any right to but himself. The labour of his body, and the work of his hands, we may say, are properly his. Whatsoever then he removes out of the state that nature hath provided, and left it in, he hath mixed his labour with, and joined to it something that is his own, and thereby makes it his property. It being by him removed from the common state nature hath placed it in, it hath by this labour something annexed to it, that excludes the common right of other men: for this labour being the unquestionable property of the labourer, no man but he can have a right to what that is once joined to...."

In the eyes of the critic, however, this statement leads to more questions than answers. For example, just how intensive must this "mixing" be. Is it one corn plant every square foot, every square yard, every acre, every square mile, every square hundred miles, one per continent, one per entire world? The answer emanating from the libertarian community on this matter[23] is that it all depends? On what? On the culture, on the previous practices, on the established mores, etc. For example, East of the Mississippi, where the land is relatively fertile, a government-determined homestead typically comprised 160 acres. West of this river, something of the order of 10 times that amount was necessary to keep body and soul together for the farmers who were the initial homesteaders. In the desert of Nevada, or the wilds of northern Alaska, perhaps another 10-fold increase would be in order. The point is, there are no hard and fast rules to the last decimal place as to exactly how much land[24] may be taken through this process; how intensive the "mixing" must be. The specifics are to be determined by adjudication.[25] All we can say without fear of contradiction is that the more isolated, uninhabited, infertile a given piece of land is, the less intensive must be the homesteading, to claim ownership of it.

---

[23] Block 1990, 2002a, b; Block and Edelstein 2012; Block and Yeatts 1999–2000; Block vs Epstein 2005; Bylund 2005, 2012; Grotius 1625; Hoppe 1993, 2011; Kinsella 2003, 2006, 2009; Locke 1948; Paul 1987; Pufendorf 1673; Rothbard 1973a, b, p. 32; Rozeff 2005; Watner 1982.

[24] For a libertarian analysis of grey areas and continua, see Block and Barnett (2008).

[25] For the argument that adjudication could be done privately, see Benson 1990a, b, 2002; Friedman 1979, 1989; Hoppe 2001; Osterfeld 1989; Peden 1977; Rothbard 1973a, b, 1982a, b, 1991; Stringham 1998–1999; Tannehill and Tannehill 1984; Woolridge 1970.

Now, there is nothing that fits this bill as it does on (a non-terraformed) Mars. Assume then that the first firm to occupy Mars terraforms the entire planet. Do they own it all? No! But they certainly do have a valid claim to a good part of it. That consideration and that alone ought to absolve this process from the public goods objection that private terraforming could not take place on the Red Planet. How much, exactly? In the early phases of settlement, we would expect that the transformation of Mars would be of limited scope. The idea that the first firm to occupy Mars would terraform the whole planet to the extent that it is a perfect copy of Earth is utterly unrealistic. Unless the process was so simple that the project hardly qualified as labor, a highly unlikely assumption, then there would be no profitable advantage to converting the ruddy orb to imitate the Earth in this manner. And if it were that simple, then no one could claim to have invested the labor necessary. No, the initial occupants would much more likely set up a colony of tent-like or underground structures in which the cost to develop a breathable environment would be as cheap as possible. Thus, they would legitimately take possession of the village itself plus some surrounding infrastructure incidental to their community's viability. At this early stage, the drawing of a boundary line would be the very last thing on their minds. It is only after many settlers competing to create ever better environments that Mars would gradually become "terraformed." During this extensive procedure boundary lines would become progressively more important.

The idea that others are not benefitted by the achievement of an actor is preposterous. All trades benefit both participants. An innovator might realize that he would like green vegetation outside his habitable dome for aesthetic purposes. How would he achieve this since there is no oxygen? He would need heat, obviously, plus nitrogen, oxygen, and carbon dioxide. With an almost pure CO_2 atmosphere, and much less solar heat than Earth, his goal might appear impossible. However, if he could use reflectors to concentrate sunlight and provide artificially generated or imported air and water to the root system, he could conceivably grow wetland plants outside his bubble. If he did so, these plants would add oxygen to the atmosphere. On its own, this act would have an insignificant impact. But if millions of residents did it, the atmosphere would eventually become breathable. As more and more residents came to the planet, an ever-increasing portion would become habitable until at last a vast expanse was a completely welcoming environment for humans. The areal extent of that first hamlet would then belong to the initial colonizers. Suppose now that these intrepid trail blazers started homesteading the fourth planet at roughly the same time.

It would appear churlish, not to say difficult to imagine, for one of them to attempt to "free ride" by standing idly by while the others engaged in the expensive process of terraforming that would of course benefit them all. Clearly, he would suffer the consequences of his own lethargy for he would have no right to trespass into communities of his fellow settlers; they would prohibit his entry. 'Tis true, it cannot be denied, that when we posit more and more economic actors to be involved in this process the challenges become more difficult. However, the perfect is the enemy of the good, and it would appear unlikely that so many colonizers would be involved to make this process untenable.

An Aside, Bonus Material: The Proof that 1 = 2 or an Example of How a Real Number Cannot Be Divided by Zero

This sub-section is an aside intended to demonstrate the principle referred to in footnote 1 above. The demonstration requires knowledge of simple algebra. An introductory knowledge of calculus will be helpful but not necessary. To begin, let us make two simple assumptions:

$a = 1$
$b = 1$
If that is the case, then:
$a = b$
Multiplying both sides by b:
$ab = b^2$
Subtracting a^2:
$ab - a^2 = b^2 - a^2$
Factoring:
$a(b - a) = (b + a)(b - a)$
Canceling identical terms:
$a\cancel{(b - a)} = (b + a)\cancel{(b - a)}$
$a = b + a$
$1 = 2$

Considering that each step looks valid, why does this "proof" yield an obviously incorrect result? The operation of "canceling identical terms" is merely a fancy way of referring to division. The result of (b − a) where a and b are equal is zero. Therefore, that step amounts to division by zero which is indeterminate. When we find a case in nature, such as finding the location where a projectile stops going up and begins descending, where division by zero appears necessary, we can approximate the answer by running a series of calculations where the denominator approaches zero and see at what distance it closes. Or we can use the calculus invented by Newton.

References

Accad, Michael. 2016. Peer-Review and Science's Funding Problem. April 17. https://mises.org/blog/peer-review-and-science%E2%80%99s-funding-problem. Accessed 23 Apr 2016.

Anderson, Terry L., and Peter J. Hill, eds. 1996. *The Privatization Process: A Worldwide Perspective*. Lanham, MD: Rowman & Littlefield Publishers.

Benson, Bruce L. 1990a. Customary Law with Private Means of Resolving Disputes and Dispensing Justice: A Description of a Modern System of Law and Order Without State Coercion. *The Journal of Libertarian Studies* IX (2): 25–42. http://mises.org/journals/jls/9_2/9_2_2.pdf. Accessed 11 June 2016.

———. 1990b. *The Enterprise of Law: Justice Without the State*. San Francisco: Pacific Research Institute for Public Policy.

———. 2002. Justice Without Government: The Merchant Courts of Medieval Europe and Their Modern Counterparts. In *The Voluntary City: Choice, Community and Civil Society*, ed. David T. Beito, Peter Gordon, and Alexander Tabarrok, 127–150. Oakland, CA: The Independent Institute.

Block, Walter. 1983. Public Goods and Externalities: The Case of Roads. *The Journal of Libertarian Studies: An Interdisciplinary Review* VII (1): 1–34. http://www.mises.org/journals/jls/7_1/7_1_1.pdf. Accessed 23 Apr 2016.

———. 1990. Earning Happiness Through Homesteading Unowned Land: A Comment on 'Buying Misery with Federal Land' by Richard Stroup. *Journal of Social Political and Economic Studies* 15 (2): 237–253.

———. 2000a. Watch Your Language. February 21. http://www.mises.org/fullarticle.asp?control=385&month=17&title=Watch+Your+Language&id=19; http://mises.org/daily/385. Accessed 11 June 2016.

———. 2000b. Word Watch. April 20. http://www.mises.org/fullstory.asp?control=414&FS=Word+Watch. Accessed 23 Apr 2016.

————. 2002a. Homesteading City Streets; An Exercise in Managerial Theory. *Planning and Markets* 5 (1): 18–23. http://www-pam.usc.edu/volume5/v5i1a2s1.html; http://www-pam.usc.edu/. Accessed 23 Apr 2016.

————. 2002b. On Reparations to Blacks for Slavery. *Human Rights Review* 3 (4): 53–73.

————. 2002c. Radical Privatization and Other Libertarian Conundrums. *The International Journal of Politics and Ethics* 2 (2): 165–175. http://www.walter-block.com/publications/radical_privatization.pdf. Accessed 23 Aug 2016.

————. 2003. National Defense and the Theory of Externalities, Public Goods and Clubs. In *The Myth of National Defense: Essays on the Theory and History of Security Production*, ed. Hans-Hermann Hoppe, 301–334. Auburn: Mises Institute. http://www.mises.org/etexts/defensemyth.pdf. Accessed 23 Apr 2016.

————. 2007. Anarchism and Minarchism; No Rapprochement Possible: Reply to Tibor Machan. *The Journal of Libertarian Studies* 21 (1): 91–99. http://www.mises.org/journals/jls/21_1/21_1_5.pdf. Accessed 11 June 2016.

————. 2009. *The Privatization of Roads and Highways: Human and Economic Factors*. Auburn, AL: The Mises Institute. http://www.amazon.com/Privatization-Roads-And-Highways-Factors/dp/1279887303/; http://mises.org/books/roads_web.pdf; http://mises.org/daily/3416. Accessed 23 Aug 2016.

Block, Walter E., and Michael R. Edelstein. 2012. Popsicle Sticks and Homesteading Land for Nature Preserves. *Romanian Economic and Business Review* 7 (1): 7–13. http://www.rebe.rau.ro/REBE%207%201.pdf. Accessed 29 Sep 2016.

Block, Walter, and Richard Epstein. 2005. Debate on Eminent Domain. *NYU Journal of Law & Liberty* 1 (3): 1144–1169.

Block, Walter, and William Barnett II. 2008. Continuums. *Journal Etica e Politica/Ethics & Politics* 1: 151–166. http://www2.units.it/~etica/; http://www2.units.it/~etica/2008_1/BLOCKBARNETT.pdf. Accessed 23 Apr 2016.

Block, Walter and Guillermo Yeatts. 1999–2000. The Economics and Ethics of Land Reform: A Critique of the Pontifical Council for Justice and Peace's 'Toward a Better Distribution of Land: The Challenge of Agrarian Reform'. *Journal of Natural Resources and Environmental Law* 15 (1): 37–69

Butler, Eamonn, ed. 1988. *The Mechanics of Privatization*. London: Adam Smith Institute.

Bylund, Per. 2005. Man and Matter: A Philosophical Inquiry into the Justification of Ownership in Land from the Basis of Self-Ownership. Master thesis, Lund University, Spring Semester (June). http://www.uppsatser.se/uppsats/a7eb17de8f/; http://perbylund.com/academics_polsci_msc.pdf;

http://www.essays.se/essay/a7eb17de8f/; http://www.lunduniversity.lu.se/o.o .i.s?id=24965&postid=1330482. Accessed 23 Apr 2016

———. 2012. Man and Matter: How the Former Gains Ownership of the Latter. *Libertarian Papers* 4 (1). http://libertarianpapers.org/articles/2012/ lp-4-1-5.pdf. Accessed 23 Apr 2016.

Carnis, Laurent. 2003. The Case for Road Privatization: A Defense by Restitution. *Journal des Economistes et des Etudes Humaines.* 13 (1): 95–116.

Casey, Christopher P. 2015. How GDP Metrics Distort Our View of the Economy. May 15. http://www.thedailybell.com/editorials/36294/Mises-Institute-How-GDP-Metrics-Distort-Our-View-of-the-Economy/. Accessed 23 Apr 2016.

Cowen, Tyler, ed. 1988. *The Theory of Market Failure: A Critical Examination.* Fairfax, VA: George Mason University Press. http://www.amazon.com/ Theory-Market-Failure-Critical-Examination/dp/0913969133/ref=sr_1_1?-ie=UTF8&s=books&qid=1200191409&sr=1-1. Accessed 23 Apr 2016.

De Jasay, Anthony. 1989. *Social Contract, Free Ride: A Study of the Public Goods Problem.* Oxford: Oxford University Press. http://www.amazon.com/Social-Contract-Free-Ride-Paperbacks/dp/0198239122/ref=sr_1_1?ie=UTF8&s=-books&qid=1200191531&sr=1-1. Accessed 23 Apr 2016.

Ebeling, Richard. 2013. Why Not Privatize Foreign Policy? http://epictimes. com/article/127064/why-not-privatize-foreign-policy. Accessed 23 Aug 2016.

Ferguson, Niall. 2011. *Civilization: The West and the Rest.* Penguin Books.

Friedman, David. 1979. Private Creation and Enforcement of Law: A Historical Case. *University of Chicago Law Review.* http://www.daviddfriedman.com/ Academic/Iceland/Iceland.html. Accessed 23 Apr 2016.

———. 1989. *The Machinery of Freedom: Guide to a Radical Capitalism.* 2nd ed. La Salle, IL: Open Court.

Gregory, Anthony. 2011. Abolish the Police. May 26. http://www.lewrockwell. com/gregory/gregory213.html. Accessed 23 Aug 2016.

Grotius, Hugo. 1625. *Law of War and Peace (De Jure Belli ac Pacis),* 3 volumes. Trans. A.C. Campbell, London, 1814.

Guillory, Gil, and Patrick Tinsley. 2009. The Role of Subscription-Based Patrol and Restitution in the Future of Liberty. *Libertarian Papers* 1 (12). http:// libertarianpapers.org/2009/12-the-role-of-subscription-based-patrol-and-restitution-in-the-future-of-liberty/. Accessed 23 Aug 2016.

Hanke, Steve H. 1987a. Privatization. In *The New Palgrave: A Dictionary of Economics,* ed. J. Eatwell, M. Milgate, and P. Newman, vol. 3, 976–977. London: The Macmillan Press, Ltd.

————., ed. 1987b. *Privatization and Development*. San Francisco: Institute for Contemporary Studies.

Hannesson, Rögnvaldur. 2004. The Privatization of the Oceans. In *Evolving Property Rights in Marine Fisheries*, ed. D.R. Leal, 25–48. Lanham, MD: Rowman and Littlefield.

————. 2006. *The Privatization of the Oceans*. Cambridge, MA: MIT Press.

Holcombe, Randall. 1997. A Theory of the Theory of Public Goods. *Review of Austrian Economics* 10 (1): 1–10. http://www.mises.org/journals/rae/pdf/RAE10_1_1.pdf. Accessed 23 Apr 2016.

Hoppe, Hans-Hermann. 1989. Fallacies of the Public Goods Theory and the Production of Security. *The Journal of Libertarian Studies* IX (1): 27–46. http://www.mises.org/journals/jls/9_1/9_1_2.pdf. Accessed 23 Apr 2016.

————. 1993. *The Economics and Thics of Private Property. Studies in Political Economy and Philosophy*. Boston: Kluwer Academic Publishers.

————. 2001. *Democracy—The God That Failed: The Economics and Politics of Monarchy, Democracy, and Natural Order*. Rutgers University, NJ: Transaction Publishers.

————. 2011. Of Private, Common, and Public Property and the Rationale for Total Privatization. *Libertarian Papers* 3 (1). http://libertarianpapers.org/2011/1-hoppe-private-common-and-public-property/. Accessed 23 Aug 2016.

Huebert, Jacob. 2010. *Libertarianism Today*. Santa Barbara, CA: Praeger.

Hummel, Jeffrey. 1990. National Goods vs. Public Goods: Defense, Disarmament and Free Riders. *The Review of Austrian Economics* IV: 88–122. http://www.mises.org/journals/rae/pdf/rae4_1_4.pdf. Accessed 23 Apr 2016.

Karpoff, Jonathan M. 2001. Public Versus Private Initiative in Arctic Exploration: The Effects of Incentives and Organizational Structure. *The Journal of Political Economy* 109 (1): 38–78.

Kiely, Eugene. 2012. 'You Didn't Build That,' Uncut and Unedited. July 23. http://www.factcheck.org/2012/07/you-didnt-build-that-uncut-and-unedited/. Accessed 17 Aug 2015.

Kinsella, Stephan N. 2003. A Libertarian Theory of Contract: Title Transfer, Binding Promises, and Inalienability. *Journal of Libertarian Studies* 17 (2): 11–37. http://www.mises.org/journals/jls/17_2/17_2_2.pdf. Accessed 23 Apr 2016.

————. 2006. How We Come to Own Ourselves. September 7. http://www.mises.org/story/2291. Accessed 23 Apr 2016.

————. 2009. Homesteading, Abandonment, and Unowned Land in the Civil Law. May 22. http://blog.mises.org/10004/homesteading-abandonment-and-unowned-land-in-the-civil-law/. Accessed 23 Apr 2016.

Klein, Peter G. 2013. Without the State, Who Would Invent Tang? *The Free Market* 31 (3): 1–3. https://mises.org/system/tdf/March2013_0.pdf?file=1; https://mises.org/library/without-state-who-would-invent-tang. Accessed 23 Apr 2016.

Locke, John. 1690 [1955]. *Second Treatise on Government*. Chicago: Henry Regnery.

———. 1948. *An Essay Concerning the True Origin, Extent and End of Civil Government*. In *Social Contract*, ed. E. Barker, 17–19. New York: Oxford University Press.

Mazzucato, Mariana. 2013. *The Entrepreneurial State: Debunking Public vs. Private Sector Myths*. Anthem.

Megginson, W., and J. Netter. 2001. From State to Market: A Survey of Empirical Studies on Privatization. *Journal of Economic Literature* 39 (2): 321–389.

Moore, Stephen. 1987. Privatizing the U.S. Postal Service. In *Privatization*, ed. Stephen Moore and Stuart Butler. Washington, DC: Heritage Foundation.

Moore, Stephen, and Stuart Butler, eds. 1987. *Privatization*. Washington, DC: Heritage Foundation.

Motichek, Amy, Walter E. Block, and Jay Johnson. 2008. Forget Ocean Front Property, We Want Ocean Real Estate! *Ethics, Place, and Environment* 11 (2): 147–155.

Murphy, Robert P. 2005. A Free Market in Space. *The Free Market* 53 (1), January.

Ohashi, T.M. 1980. *Privatization, Theory and Practice: Distributing Shares in Private and Public Enterprise*. Vancouver, BC: The Fraser Institute.

Ohashi, T.M., T.P. Roth, Z.A. Spindler, M.L. McMillan, and K.H. Norrie. 1980. *Privation Theory & Practice*. Vancouver, BC: The Fraser Institute.

Osterfeld, David. 1989. Anarchism and the Public Goods Issue: Law, Courts and the Police. *The Journal of Libertarian Studies* 9 (1): 47–68. http://www.mises.org/journals/jls/9_1/9_1_3.pdf. Accessed 23 Apr 2016.

Pasour, Jr., E.C., 1981, "The Free Rider as a Basis for Government Intervention," *The Journal of Libertarian Studies*, Vol. V, No. 4, pp. 453–464. http://www.mises.org/journals/jls/5_4/5_4_6.pdf. Accessed 23 Apr 2016.

Paul, Ellen Frankel. 1987. *Property Rights and Eminent Domain*. Livingston, NJ: Transaction Publishers.

Peden, Joseph R. 1977. Property Rights in Celtic Irish Law. *The Journal of Libertarian Studies* 1 (2): 81–96.

Physilicious. 2009. Conservation of Angular Momentum. *Geddes Physics*. February 22. https://www.youtube.com/watch?v=UZlW1a63KZs. Accessed 2 Sep 2016.

Pirie, Madson. 1986. *Privatization in Theory and Practice*. London: Adam Smith Institute.

Pufendorf, Samuel. 1673. Natural Law and the Law of Nations (De officio hominis et civis prout ipsi praescribuntur lege naturali).

Rothbard, Murray N. 1963. *America's Great Depression*. Kansas City: Sheed Andrews. http://www.mises.org/rothbard/agd.pdf. Accessed 23 May 2016.

———. 1970. *Power and Market: Government and the Economy*. Menlo Park, CA: Institute for Humane Studies.

———. 1973a. Free Market, Police, Courts, and Law. *Reason*: 5–19.

———. 1973b. *For a New Liberty*. New York: Macmillan. http://mises.org/rothbard/newlibertywhole.asp. Accessed 23 Aug 2016.

———. 1975. Society Without a State. *The Libertarian Forum* 7 (1), January. http://www.lewrockwell.com/rothbard/rothbard133.html. Accessed 23 Aug 2016.

———. 1982a. *The Ethics of Liberty*. Atlantic Highlands, NJ: Humanities Press.

———. 1982b. Law, Property Rights, and Air Pollution. *Cato Journal* 2 (1). Reprinted in *Economics and the Environment: A Reconciliation*, Walter E. Block, ed., Vancouver: The Fraser Institute, 1990, pp. 233–279. http://mises.org/story/2120; http://www.mises.org/rothbard/lawproperty.pdf. Accessed 20 Apr 2016.

———. 1997. *The Logic of Action: Applications and Criticism from the Austrian School*. Vol. II. Cheltenham: Edward Elgar.

———. 1991. On Denationalizing the Courts. *Rothbard-Rockwell Report*, vol. 2, no. 10. Burlingame, CA: Center for Libertarian Studies.

———. 1998 [1982]. Isaiah Berlin on Negative Freedom. In *The Ethics of Liberty*, chapter 27, 215–218. New York: New York University Press. http://www.mises.org/rothbard/ethics/ethics.asp. Accessed 20 Apr 2016.

Rozeff, Michael S. 2005. Original Appropriation and Its Critics. September 1. http://www.lewrockwell.com/rozeff/rozeff18.html. Accessed 23 Apr 2016.

Salerno, Joseph T. 2015. How Reducing GDP Increases Economic Growth. Mises Daily. January 2. https://mises.org/library/how-reducing-gdp-increases-economic-growth. Accessed 17 Aug 2015.

Savas, E.S. 1987. *Privatization*. Chatham, NJ: Chatham House Publishers.

Schmidtz, David. 1991. *The Limits of Government: An Essay on the Public Goods Argument*. Boulder, CO: Westview Press.

Sechrest, Larry. 2003. Privateering and National Defense: Naval Warfare for Private Profit. In *The Myth of National Defense: Essays on the Theory and History of Security Production*, ed. Hans-Hermann Hoppe, 239–274. Auburn, AL: The Ludwig von Mises Institute.

———. 2004a. Public Goods and Private Solutions in Maritime History. *The Quarterly Journal of Austrian Economics* 7 (2): 3–27. http://www.mises.org/journals/qjae/pdf/qjae7_2_1.pdf; https://dev.mises.org/journals/qjae/pdf/qjae7_2_1.pdf. Accessed 23 Apr 2016.

———. 2004b. Private Provision of Public Goods: Theoretical Issues and Some Examples from Maritime History. *ICFAI Journal of Public Finance* II (3): 45–73. http://www.mises.org/journals/scholar/Sechrest7.pdf. Accessed 23 Apr 2016.

———. 2007. Privately Funded and Built U.S. Warships in the Quasi-War of 1797–1801. *The Independent Review* 12 (1): 101–113.

Stringham, Edward. 1998–1999. Justice Without Government. *Journal of Libertarian Studies* 14 (1): 53–77.

Stringham, Edward., ed. 2007. *Anarchy and the Law: The Political Economy of Choice.* Somerset, NJ: Transaction Publishers.

———. 2015. *Private Governance: Creating Order in Economic and Social Life.* New York: Oxford University Press.

Strow, Brian Kent, and Claudia Wood Strow. 2013. Gross Actual Product: Why GDP Fosters Increased Government Spending and Should Be Replaced. *The Journal of Private Enterprise* 29 (1): 53–71.

Tannehill, Morris, and Linda Tannehill. 1984 [1970]. *The Market for Liberty.* New York: Laissez Faire Books. http://www.lewrockwell.com/orig11/tannehill1.html. Accessed 23 Aug 2016.

Tinsley, Patrick. 1998–1999. With Liberty and Justice for All: A Case for Private Police. *Journal of Libertarian Studies* 14 (1): 95–100. http://www.mises.org/journals/jls/14_1/14_1_5.pdf. Accessed 23 Aug 2016.

Walker, Michael A., ed. 1988. *Privatization: Tactics and Techniques.* Vancouver, Canada: The Fraser Institute.

Watner, Carl. 1982. The Proprietary Theory of Justice in the Libertarian Tradition. *Journal of Libertarian Studies* 6 (3–4): 289–316. http://mises.org/journals/jls/6_3/6_3_6.pdf. Accessed 23 Apr 2016.

White, Lawrence H. 1978. Privatization of Municipally-Provided Services. *The Journal of Libertarian Studies* 2 (2): 187–197.

Wiśniewski, Jakub Bożydar. 2014. Defense as a Private Good in a Competitive Order. *Review of Social and Economic Issues* 1 (1): 2–35. http://rsei.rau.ro/images/V1N1/Jakub%20Bozydar%20Wisniewski.pdf. Accessed 27 Apr 2016.

Wollstein, Jarret B. 1969. Society Without Coercion. In *Society Without Government.* New York: Arno Press.

Woolridge, William C. 1970. *Uncle Sam the Monopoly Man.* New Rochelle, NY: Arlington House.

12

Space Law

There should be no difference between law as it applies to space or any-thing else.[1] From the libertarian point of view, law should consist, solely, of promoting and defending the non-aggression principle (NAP). This means that anyone may do anything he wishes to all other people, pro-vided only that he refrains from threatening or initiating violence against fellow human beings, and does not interfere with their justly owned property.[2] In this perspective, the following acts would be unlawful: mur-der, rape, theft, kidnapping, trespass, assault, battery, fraud, enslavement, etc. Car-jacking on land, boat-jacking in the water, and spaceship-jacking amongst the heavenly bodies would be equally against the law, and for the same reason: they all violate the NAP.

---

[1] Seemingly, anyone who writes a book about space and interplanetary relations must think that there is something unique about that arena. And, yes, this is indeed the case in many regards as pretty much the entirety of the present book makes clear. But this does not apply in our view to the law. It should apply in the same manner to any area of our galaxy; on Earth, on Jupiter, and every-where else. We go further: it should also not be upheld any differently depending upon the histori-cal epoch under consideration. Libertarian law should apply, equally, to the caveman in the past, the modern man at present, and to the spaceman in the future.

[2] "Threatening or initiating violence" would include any purposeful and knowing act or threat thereof which is a violation of the rights of the person on the receiving end.

© The Author(s) 2018
P. L. Nelson, W. E. Block, *Space Capitalism*, Palgrave Studies in Classical Liberalism,
https://doi.org/10.1007/978-3-319-74651-7_12

This of course does not mean that people may not use violence against each other. Indeed, they may do so. But only if it is agreed upon by both parties, the initiator and the target. Thus, boxing and voluntary sadomasochism between consenting adults constitute legally acceptable behavior.[3] In gambling, one party "takes" the property of another. But if these interactions are consensual, libertarian theory says nay to legally prohibiting any of these interactions.[4] Nor would there be any victimless "crimes" in this philosophy. There are no justified laws concerning consensual adults against prostitution, pornography, gambling, drugs, etc., and this too would apply equally to land, water, and space.

Why, then, even have a chapter at all in this book entitled "space law?" As it turns out, there is such a thing as actual space law and, unfortunately, it deviates to a great degree from what would hold true under libertarianism. It is the burden of this chapter to document this divergence, and make the case for a shift from state dictation to radical liberty.

What, then, is extant space law? First, recent entries in this history start off with the resolution adopted by the U.N. General Assembly (1962a, p. XVIII) *Declaration of Legal Principles Governing the Activities of States in the Exploration and Use of Outer Space* (Treaty on Principles, 1966). It reads (in part) as follows:

The General Assembly,…

Recognizing the common interest of all mankind in the progress of the exploration and use of outer space for peaceful purposes,

---

[3] Some might even use the term "laudable behavior." Why would, say, boxing be considered by anyone to be praiseworthy conduct? Prizefighting is after all nothing more that hitting another person in the hopes of personal financial gain: despicable, ought we not say? Yet the prizes come from willing customers who are entertained by the event. Many of the attendees experience a vicarious release of emotion. Otherwise these people might act out their anger in real life were they unable observe this performance in a ring. Still others might enjoy watching the boxers' skill and strategy. Laudable indeed is the provision of these services. For more on the sometimes-commendable nature of activities widely viewed as depraved, see Block 1976, 2013a, b.

[4] On libertarian law, see Benson 1989a, b, 1990a, b, 1993, 2001; Hoppe 1993; Kinsella 1992, 1995, 1996, 1997, 1998–1999, 2001; Rothbard 1982b. As applied to space, see Huebert and Block 2007a, b, 2008.

Believing that the exploration and use of outer space should be carried on for the betterment of mankind and for the benefit of States irrespective of their degree of economic or scientific development,…

Solemnly declares that in the exploration and use of outer space States should be guided by the following principles:

1. The exploration and use of outer space shall be carried on for the benefit and in the interests of all mankind.
2. Outer space and celestial bodies are free for exploration and use by all States on a basis of equality and in accordance with international law.
3. Outer space and celestial bodies are not subject to national appropriation by claim of sovereignty, by means of use or occupation, or by any other means.
4. The activities of States in the exploration and use of outer space shall be carried on in accordance with international law, including the Charter of the United Nations, in the interest of maintaining international peace and security and promoting international co-operation and understanding.
5. States bear international responsibility for national activities in outer space, whether carried on by governmental agencies or by non-governmental entities, and for assuring that national activities are carried on in conformity with the principles set forth in the present Declaration. The activities of non-governmental entities in outer space shall require authorization and continuing supervision by the State concerned. When activities are carried on in outer space by an international organization, responsibility for compliance with the principles set forth in this Declaration shall be borne by the international organization and by the States participating in it.
6. In the exploration and use of outer space, States shall be guided by the principle of co-operation and mutual assistance and shall conduct all their activities in outer space with due regard for the corresponding interests of other States. If a State has reason to believe that an outer space activity or experiment planned by it or its nationals would cause potentially harmful interference with activities of other States in the peaceful exploration and use of outer space, it shall undertake appropriate international consultations before proceeding with any such

activity or experiment. A State which has reason to believe that an outer space activity or experiment planned by another State would cause potentially harmful interference with activities in the peaceful exploration and use of outer space may request consultation concerning the activity or experiment.

7. The State on whose registry an object launched into outer space is carried shall retain jurisdiction and control over such object, and any personnel thereon, while in outer space. Ownership of objects launched into outer space, and of their component parts, is not affected by their passage through outer space or by their return to the earth....

To briefly summarize this travesty[5] of a document, the international bureaucrats oppose private property rights, the system that has done so much good for the well-being and wealth of people on Earth. First, in their view, these principles shall not be applied to heavenly bodies. Instead, without using the word, they say we shall adopt for space the principles of communism, and opposition to private property and economic freedom, which always lead to disastrous economies, actual starvation, and mass murder. They seek to impose on space the system from which the U.S.S.R. could free itself only after the loss of life on a gargantuan scale.

Second, in this short legal history is the 1967 Outer Space Treaty, entitled: *Treaty on Principles Governing the Activities of States in the Exploration and Use of Outer Space, including the Moon and Other Celestial Bodies* (U.N. General Assembly (1962b). Written along much the same lines as its U.N. predecessor of 1962, it provided the following:

The Outer Space Treaty provides the basic framework on international space law, including the following principles:

---

[5]We use the word "travesty" because the document is essentially dishonest; it almost perfectly expresses a Marxian view of fair use without openly saying so. Furthermore, it fails to note that "States" (in the second paragraph: "*Believing...*") are necessarily based on the negation of the NAP. It proclaims as compatible goals, high-sounding principles which are in irreconcilable conflict, to wit "the betterment of mankind" and "the benefit of States." The list of dishonest usages within this one small passage could go on to fill many pages.

- the exploration and use of outer space shall be carried out for the benefit and in the interests of all countries and shall be the province of all mankind;
- outer space shall be free for exploration and use by all States;
- outer space is not subject to national appropriation by claim of sovereignty, by means of use or occupation, or by any other means;
- States shall not place nuclear weapons or other weapons of mass destruction in orbit or on celestial bodies or station them in outer space in any other manner;
- the Moon and other celestial bodies shall be used exclusively for peaceful purposes;[6]
- astronauts shall be regarded as the envoys of mankind;
- States shall be responsible for national space activities whether carried out by governmental or non-governmental entities;
- States shall be liable for damage caused by their space objects; and
- States shall avoid harmful contamination of space and celestial bodies.

Note that this, too, is much in keeping with the U.N.'s viewpoint on the oceans and waterways of our home planet. They, too, shall be the "common heritage of all mankind." Under the U.N. Convention on the Law of the Sea (UNCLOS n.d.),[7] the peoples of the land-locked nations, who rarely ventured out onto the world's waters, such as Bolivia, Paraguay, Mali, Niger, Chad, Congo, Austrian, Hungary, Serbia, Mongolia, and Kazakhstan would have as much claim to property rights and ocean wealth as those such as Spain, Holland, England, and the United States whose citizens had been sea-farers and nautical explorers for centuries. The difficulties in such a doctrine are manifest. First, they are clearly unfair. Why should those who have had no truck with the waters or with outer space have any share in them, let alone one based on equality? Second, they are uneconomical, in that incentives are blunted. This is easier to see in space than in the oceans, since most exploration of the former lies in the future, and of the latter in the past. So, which nations

---

[6] For a rather unusual but "peaceful" purpose of moons, see Block 2014a, c. These essays constitute a tongue-in-cheek attack on egalitarianism. Some planets, it turns out, have more than their fair share of moons; others are relatively deprived in this regard. These publications make the case for redistributing moons from the "rich" (when measured in moons) to the "poor."

[7] For support of the UNCLOS initiative, see Brisman 2011; Colombos 1967; Klein 2004.

have taken the lead in extra-planetary ventures? Obviously, Russia, the United States, and China. Suppose the benefits of these expenditures were going to be shared, and equally so with countries so under-developed that their contribution to this effort consists mainly of looking at the Moon. What would that do to the incentives of the former to continue their massive investments in this sector of the economy? To ask this is to answer it: they would come to a screeching halt.

Nevertheless, as cogent as the preceding argument is, it largely misses the crucial point. Those relatively wealthy governments did their exploration with stolen funds. Thus, they too have no rights. It is the still to be identified entrepreneurial explorers who will rightly one day take possession of and put to beneficial use celestial bodies and other valuable assets. Only they, and they alone, would have the right to exclude the governments of all three of those nations and the U.N. Should the General Assembly and respective governments continue to assert unjustifiable and oppressive control, the end result may well be the very war they profess a desire to avoid. It has always been so, the United States being a pre-eminent example.

Next in the batter's box is the Moon Agreement of 1979.[8] Its main provisions concern the peaceful non-military use of this heavenly body. As regards our own concerns, Article 4 maintains that: "The exploration and use of the moon shall be the province of all mankind and shall be carried out for the benefit and in the interests of all countries, irrespective of their degree of economic or scientific development." Thus, we observe more of the same. It is difficult to see the justification for yet another treaty, when the previous two in this series were so similarly defective.

Moreover, regardless of whether all of mankind has taken any role whatsoever in developing new property, defense of any and all legislative findings taking charge of such resources[9] is difficult at best. This mindset would appear to be based in equal measure on two emotions, neither of which is very salutary. The first is envy. This is one of the seven deadly

---

[8] Its formal name is: "Agreement Governing the Activities of States on the Moon and Other Celestial Bodies." See on this "Moon Agreement," 1979. For generally supportive commentary on applying UNCLOS to space see Asamoah 1966; Christol 1980, 1982, 1985; Dembling 1979; Goedhuis 1981; Jasentuliyana 1995; Joyner 1986; Kopal 1968, 1996; Rana 1994; Vlasic 1967.

[9] Whether in the seas of the Earth or on heavenly bodies to everyone on Earth, legislation usurping possession of assets remains indefensible.

sins, but we do not hear too much about this in these politically correct times where the top 1% of the wealth distribution is seen as the devil incarnate.[10] The second is egalitarianism. But this, too, is subject to fatal objections. If people really oppose inequality, why do they still sport two eyes? If they gave up one to a blind man, all they would lose is depth perception. Then they could no longer be racing car drivers, target shooters, or basketball players. But we believe most people would regard the gains of one eye to the blind man as gargantuan in comparison. Similarly, unequal intelligence is a strong determinant of wealth inequality. One wonders how many of those responsible for the U.N. declarations as to the oceans and heavenly bodies being the inheritance of all of mankind, equally, would be willing to give up, oh, 35 IQ points to the less well-endowed in this regard to promote greater equality if this were but possible. Our prediction: not too many at all. Thus, hypocrisy arises in our assessment of this philosophy.

A real breakthrough occurred more recently, and this was by no means "more of the same." This refers to the U.S. Commercial Space Launch Competitiveness Act (2015), signed by President Obama on November 25 of that year. It allows not only for private property in off-earth worlds, but contains no provision whatsoever for sharing wealth garnered in this manner with those too under-developed economically and technologically to even think of participating in space exploration. Of course, there are other nations that are economically developed which did not engage in space exploration. They, too, were uninvolved in the process of homesteading, which alone under libertarian theory generates property rights.

Stimers (2015) cannot say enough good things about this initiative. According to that author, this law constitutes no less than "one giant leap for law." He continues: "One provision of the law…has gotten most of the headlines. It says, quite simply, that if an American company retrieves minerals, metals or resources from an asteroid or other location in space, it owns them as far as the U.S. is concerned. That single sentence, which applies to all nonliving matter in the cosmos, appears to be the most sweeping legislative recognition of property rights in human history."

---

[10] For a critique of those who want to incorporate envy into public policy, see Fedako 2011; Gordon 2008; Hayek 1960; Hazlitt 2013; Klein 2014; Levin 1996; Mathews 2002; Reisman 2005; Sennholz 2001; Schoeck 1966.

No truer words were uttered than these by Olinga (2015): "…the Space Act breaks with the concept that space should be shared by everyone on Earth for scientific research and exploration, it establishes the rights of investors to profit from their efforts, at least under US law."

What say the present authors about this new law? Good riddance to previous space law predicated upon egalitarianism[11] and envy. If we want to put outer space resources on a paying and thus beneficial basis, we do well to jettison laws based on socialism (Mises 1922). These mandate that factors of production belong to "all of mankind," for example, should be controlled by the state apparatus. If we want extra-terrestrial land and assets to be productive, we should embrace the requirements of *laissez-faire*: private property and no government regulation or control.[12]

However, as positive as is this new development, there are flaws in it, from the perspective of the free-market philosophy which animates the present book. First, the private property rights apply only to materials taken from the heavenly bodies, and brought back to Earth. This is all well and good, but what about territory in-situ? That is, a bill more in keeping with the requirements of the free market would apply property rights not only to that sort of material, but also to the source of them: parts of or whole asteroids themselves, and as much of the Moon and Mars people are able to homestead.[13]

Second, there is the matter of regulations. While the government is not for the moment inaugurating them, these are on the cards. Part of the title of Stockton (2015) is a bit misleading ("No to Rocket Regulations"), but

[11] Egalitarianism as commonly used is, in itself, false and hypocritical. Additionally, it is materialistic in its focus because it speaks only to the sharing of material assets. Its falsehood stems in part from the common belief of its advocates that they are not materialistic. Meanwhile, it silently posits "an elite corps of impudent snobs" (Spiro Agnew) to control the distribution of wealth while hypocritically garnering power to themselves at the expense of the less fortunate. See on this Rothbard (1971).

[12] "Liberalism: b: a theory in economics emphasizing individual freedom from restraint and usually based on free competition, the self-regulating market, and the gold standard. c: a political philosophy based on belief in progress, the essential goodness of the human race, and the autonomy of the individual and standing for the protection of political and civil liberties"—Merriam Webster online 2013. Those who call themselves "liberal" but who in fact advocate massive government control are at best pseudo-liberal.

[13] For an explication and defense of homesteading see Block 1990, 2002a, b; Block and Edelstein 2012; Block and Yeatts 1999–2000; Block vs Epstein 2005; Bylund 2005, 2012; Grotius 1625; Hoppe 1993, 2011; Kinsella 2003, 2006, 2009; Locke 1948 (pp. 17–19), 1955 (chapter 5); Paul 1987; Pufendorf 1673; Rothbard 1973, p. 32; Rozeff 2005; Watner 1982.

this author contradicts himself in his text: "First and foremost, the bill protects private spaceflight from regulatory oversight, giving the industry up to 8 years to get its innovations in place before government overseers step in and start counting rivets." What happens in almost a decade from now? Presumably, the state will stick its big fat nose into the business of private entrepreneurs. This can hardly be counted on the positive side of the ledger. But matters are even worse. Griffin (2015) correctly states of this law: "It also requires that US authorities specify the way that asteroid mining will be regulated and organized." Economically speaking, socialism is government ownership of the means of production. But from the *laissez-faire* point of view, fascism consists of heavy regulation. Thus, while the U.S. Commercial Space Launch Competitiveness Act of 2015 at least partially eschews the former, it is part and parcel of the latter.[14]

Third, overall it cannot be denied that this law is a step forward from a libertarian perspective, at least compared to what went before it. However, let us offer one last criticism: this is over-reach. What business does the U.S. government have passing legislation concerning off-world entities? According to the U.S. Constitution, our government claims sovereignty over the territory of that country, and nothing else. Well, the Moon, Mars, asteroids, comets, etc. do not at all fall within this purview. It is audacious and insolent on the part of those responsible for the passage of this law to in effect maintain they have some sort of righteous control over any of the heavenly bodies. Let those who travel and work there set up their own rules, hopefully fully upon libertarian lines.

Finally, let us consider intellectual property (patents, copyrights). The Wright brothers spent the latter part of their careers trying to protect their patents instead of improving aircraft (Boldrin and Levine 2008); let's not allow that to happen with rocket ships.[15]

---

[14] In popular parlance, "fascism" depicts goose stepping, militarism, destruction of non-Aryans, gays, etc. But from an economics point of view, it indicates something quite different, government regulation and control, not ownership. For example, Krupp, BMW, Mercedes, Stuka, Volkswagen, were all "private" companies under Hitler's rule. That is, there was a thin veneer of private ownership with regard to them. But they were far from free agents, working in a *laissez-faire* economy. Rather, the German government highly regulated all of them. Despite protestations to the contrary, functional control implies practical ownership. In short, fascism is virtually identical to socialism, maybe even communism.

[15] For the case against intellectual property, see Boldrin and Levine 2008; De Wachter 2013; Kinsella 2001, 2012; Long 1995; Menell 2007a, b; Mukherjee and Block 2012; Navabi 2015; Palmer 1989.

There is a case in favor of patents leading to more research and development. After all, supply curves slope in an upward direction: the more compensation that is offered, the more likely that which is compensated will be forthcoming. If inventors are promised a monopoly privilege, other things being equal, more inventions are likely to be attempted, and then made. On the other hand, the longer the system continues, the less strong is this argument. In the long run, matters tend to be reversed. Why? There are several reasons. For one thing, with no intellectual property, scientists can ignore everything else in their creative search for new products. But when the patent system is in force, and more and more of these monopoly privileges are granted, then the would-be inventor can no longer focus solely on his research. Now he must run a gauntlet of other patents. For another, there are now lawsuits with people squabbling over whether or not a given advance infringed upon someone else's property rights. This means that more and more engineers and scientists are in court, instead of in their labs. Third, there are now released upon the scientific community patent trolls, who apply for these entitlements, not to bring forth new products, but rather to sue others for violations.

But this is merely the empirical case for and against this system. Far worse for the case in favor of patents is the deontological realm. The point here is that private property rights only properly apply when *scarcity* is applicable. But ideas, once known, are no longer scarce. If someone else learns that $E = MC^2$, Einstein still has that knowledge. Both he and we can "own" this. In contrast, if someone takes Einstein's shoes, he has them, and the physicist no longer does. Shoes—private property; ideas—not. Further, the view that ideas can be owned is subject to a *reductio ad absurdum*. Every word in every language is an idea; if they can be owned, then words can be. The word "every," presumably, was invented by Mr. Every. The word "word," presumably, was invented by Mr. Word. The word "in," presumably, was invented by Mr. In. Thus, a person who supports this doctrine would be prevented, from using the phrase "every word in…." But he would be obliged not to use any other extant word either. In a word, so to speak, he could not so much as speak or write. But a doctrine which cannot licitly be expressed by its proponent is subject to a fatal philosophical flaw. Then, too, patents are typically subject to a time limitation; sometimes 25 years. Copyrights run out after a while, sometimes a decade or two after the creator's death. In sharp contrast, shoes, books, pencils, bicycles, and other scarce objects are not time denominated. They can be passed from parent to child; property rights in them are unlimited. If patents were really property rights they, too, would stretch forever. That they are not is indication that even in the view of advocates of this pernicious doctrine, they are not valid property rights.

References

Benson, Bruce L. 1989a. Enforcement of Private Property Rights in Primitive Societies: Law Without Government. *The Journal of Libertarian Studies* IX (1): 1–26. http://mises.org/journals/jls/9_1/9_1_1.pdf. Accessed 11 June 2016.

———. 1989b. The Spontaneous Evolution of Commercial Law. *Southern Economic Journal* 55: 644–661.

———. 1990a. Customary Law with Private Means of Resolving Disputes and Dispensing Justice: A Description of a Modern System of Law and Order Without State Coercion. *The Journal of Libertarian Studies* IX (2): 25–42. http://mises.org/journals/jls/9_2/9_2_2.pdf. Accessed 11 June 2016.

———. 1990b. *The Enterprise of Law: Justice Without the State.* San Francisco: Pacific Research Institute for Public Policy.

———. 1993. The Impetus for Recognizing Private Property and Adopting Ethical Behavior in a Market Economy: Natural Law, Government Law, or Evolving Self-Interest. *Review of Austrian Economics* 6 (2): 43–80.

———. 2001. Restitution as an Objective of the Criminal Justice System. *The Journal of the James Madison Institute* Winter: 17–22.

Block, Walter E. 1976. *Defending the Undefendable.* Auburn, AL: The Mises Institute.

Block, Walter. 1990. Earning Happiness Through Homesteading Unowned Land: A Comment on 'Buying Misery with Federal Land' by Richard Stroup. *Journal of Social Political and Economic Studies* 15 (2): 237–253.

———. 2002a. Homesteading City Streets; An Exercise in Managerial Theory. *Planning and Markets* 5 (1): 18–23. http://www-pam.usc.edu/volume5/v5i1a2s1.html; http://www-pam.usc.edu/. Accessed 23 Apr 2016.

———. 2002b. On Reparations to Blacks for Slavery. *Human Rights Review* 3 (4): 53–73.

———. 2013a. There Is No Right to Privacy. July 13. http://archive.lewrockwell.com/2013/07/walter-block/there-is-no-right-to-privacy/. Accessed 20 Apr 2016.

———. 2013b. *Defending the Undefendable II: Freedom in All Realms.* Terra Libertas Publishing House.

Block, Walter E. 2014a. A Collection of Essays on Libertarian Jurisprudence: Sunshine and Property Rights. *Saint Louis University Law Journal* 58 (2):

541–547. http://slu.edu/Documents/law/Law%20Journal/Archives/LawJournal58-2/Block_Article.pdf. Accessed 20 Apr 2016.

———. 2014b. Block Discovers New Source of Inequality; Calls for Government Action. June 3. https://www.lewrockwell.com/2014/06/walter-e-block/walter-block-discovers-a-new-source-of-inequality/. Accessed 2 Dec 2015.

Block, Walter E., and Michael R. Edelstein. 2012. Popsicle Sticks and Homesteading Land for Nature Preserves. *Romanian Economic and Business Review* 7 (1): 7–13. http://www.rebe.rau.ro/REBE%207%201.pdf. Accessed 29 Sep 2016.

Block, Walter and Guillermo Yeatts. 1999–2000. The Economics and Ethics of Land Reform: A Critique of the Pontifical Council for Justice and Peace's 'Toward a Better Distribution of Land: The Challenge of Agrarian Reform'. *Journal of Natural Resources and Environmental Law* 15 (1): 37–69

Boldrin, Michele, and David K. Levine. 2008. *Against Intellectual Monopoly.* http://levine.sscnet.ucla.edu/general/intellectual/against.htm; http://mises.org/store/Against-Intellectual-Monopoly-P552.aspx.

Brisman, Avi. 2011. United Nations Convention on the Law of the Sea. *Encyclopedia of Global Justice* 1103–1104. http://link.springer.com/reference workentry/10.1007%2F978-1-4020-9160-5_661. Accessed 13 Dec 2015.

Bylund, Per. 2005. Man and Matter: A Philosophical Inquiry into the Justification of Ownership in Land from the Basis of Self-Ownership. Master thesis, Lund University, Spring Semester (June). http://www.uppsatser.se/uppsats/a7eb17de8f/; http://perbylund.com/academics_polsci_msc.pdf; http://www.essays.se/essay/a7eb17de8f/; http://www.lunduniversity.lu.se/o.o.i.s?id=24965&postid=1330482. Accessed 23 Apr 2016

———. 2012. Man and Matter: How the Former Gains Ownership of the Latter. *Libertarian Papers* 4 (1). http://libertarianpapers.org/articles/2012/lp-4-1-5.pdf. Accessed 23 Apr 2016.

Christol, Carl Q. 1980. The Common Heritage of Mankind Provision in the 1979 Agreement Governing the Activities of States on the Moon and Other Celestial Bodies. *The International Lawyer* 14 (3): 429–483. Published by: American Bar Association. http://www.jstor.org/stable/40706663?seq=1#page_scan_tab_contents. Accessed 13 Dec 2015.

———. 1982. *The Modern International Law of Outer Space.* New York: Pergamon Press.

———. 1985. The Moon Treaty Enters into Force. *The American Journal of International Law* 79 (1): 163–168. Published by: American Society of International Law. http://www.jstor.org/stable/2202679?seq=1#page_scan_tab_contents. Accessed 13 Dec 2015.

Colombos, Constantine John. 1967. *The International Law of the Sea*. Longmans.

De Wachter, Joren. 2013. IP Is a Thought Crime. At TEDxLeuven. June 6. http://www.youtube.com/watch?feature=player_detailpage&v=E5BOBs3Nmbw.

Dembling, P. G. 1979. Treaty on Principles Governing the Activities of States in the Exploration and Use of Outer Space, Including the Moon and Other Celestial Bodies. In *Manual on Space Law*, vol. I, compiled and ed. N. Jasentuliyana and R.S.K. Lee. Dobbs Ferry, NY: Oceana Publications.

Fedako, Jim. 2011. Envy, the State, and My Fellow Man. September 28. https://mises.org/library/envy-state-and-my-fellow-man. Accessed 13 Dec 2015.

Goedhuis, D. 1981. Some Recent Trends in the Interpretation and the Implementation of the Rules of International Space Law Essays in Honor of Oliver J. Lissitzyn. *Columbia Journal of Transnational Law* 19: 213–233.

Gordon, David. 2008. Should the State Regulate Envy? January 15. https://mises.org/library/should-state-regulate-envy. Accessed 13 Dec 2015.

Griffin, Andrew. 2015. Asteroid Mining Made Legal After Barack Obama Gives US Citizens the Right to Own Parts of Celestial Bodies. November 26. http://www.independent.co.uk/news/science/asteroid-mining-made-legal-after-barack-obama-gives-us-citizens-the-right-to-own-parts-of-celestial-a6750046.html. Accessed 13 Dec 2015.

Grotius, Hugo. 1625. *Law of War and Peace (De Jure Belli ac Pacis)*, 3 volumes. Trans. A.C. Campbell, London, 1814.

Hayek, Friedrich A. 1960. *The Constitution of Liberty*. Chicago: University of Chicago Press.

Hazlitt, Henry. 2013. On Appeasing Envy. July 30. https://mises.org/library/appeasing-envy. Accessed 13 Dec 2015.

Hoppe, Hans-Hermann. 1993. *The Economics and Thics of Private Property. Studies in Political Economy and Philosophy*. Boston: Kluwer Academic Publishers.

Huebert, J.H., and Walter E. Block. 2007a. Space Environmentalism, Property Rights, and the Law. *Memphis Law Review* 37 (2): 281–309. http://www.jhhuebert.com/articles/SpaceEnvironmentalism.pdf. Accessed 13 Dec 2015.

Huebert, J. H. and Walter E. Block. 2007b. In Defense of Advertising in Space. Proceedings of the 49th Colloquium on the Law of Outer Space: International Institute of Space Law, 479–489. http://adage.com/article?article_id=112401; http://www.jhhuebert.com/articles/In%20Defense%20of%-20Advertising%20in%20Space.pdf; http://www.commercialalert.org/issues/culture/outer-space/an-ad-space-odyssey;   http://thelede.blogs.nytimes.com/2006/11/22/space-marketing/. Accessed 13 Dec 2015.

Huebert, J. H. and Walter E. Block. 2008. "Environmentalists in Outer Space." *The Freeman: Ideas on Liberty*, March, Vol. 58, No. 2; http://fee.org/freeman/detail/environmentalists-in-outer-space. Accessed on 12-13-15.

Jasentuliyana, N. 1995. A Survey of Space Law as Developed by the United Nations. In *Perspectives on International Law*, ed. N. Jasentuliyana. London, The Hague, and Boston: Kluwer Law International.

Joyner, C.C. 1986. Legal Implications of the Concept of the Common Heritage of Mankind. *International and Comparative Law Quarterly* 35 (1): 190–199. http://journals.cambridge.org/action/displayAbstract?fromPage=online&aid=1507532&fileId=S0020589300044201. Accessed 13 Dec 2015.

Kinsella, Stephan. 1992. Estoppel: A New Justification for Individual Rights. *Reason Papers* 17 (Fall): 61.

———. 1995. Legislation and the Discovery of Law in a Free Society. *Journal of Libertarian Studies* 11 (Summer): 132.

Kinsella, Stephen. 1996. Punishment and Proportionality: The Estoppel Approach. *The Journal of Libertarian Studies* 12 (1): 51–74. http://www.mises.org/journals/jls/12_1/12_1_3.pdf. Accessed 8 June 2016.

Kinsella, Stephan. 1997. A Libertarian Theory of Punishment and Rights. 30 *Loy. L.A. L. Rev.* 607–645.

Kinsella, N. Stephan. 1998–1999. Inalienability and Punishment: A Reply to George Smith. *Journal of Libertarian Studies* 14 (1): 79–93. http://www.mises.org/journals/jls/14_1/14_1_4.pdf. Accessed 8 June 2016.

Kinsella, N. Stephan. 2001. Against Intellectual Property. *Journal of Libertarian Studies* 15 (2): 1–53. http://www.mises.org/journals/jls/15_2/15_2_1.pdf.

Kinsella, Stephan N. 2003. A Libertarian Theory of Contract: Title Transfer, Binding Promises, and Inalienability. *Journal of Libertarian Studies* 17 (2): 11–37. http://www.mises.org/journals/jls/17_2/17_2_2.pdf. Accessed 23 Apr 2016.

———. 2006. How We Come to Own Ourselves. September 7. http://www.mises.org/story/2291. Accessed 23 Apr 2016.

Kinsella, N. Stephan. 2012. Economic Freedom of the World Rankings and Intellectual Property: The United States' Bad Ranking Is Even Worse Than Reported. http://c4sif.org/2012/09/economic-freedom-of-the-world-indexes-and-intellectual-property-the-united-states-bad-ranking-is-even-worse-than-reported/.

Klein, Natalie. 2004. *Dispute Settlement in the U.N. Convention on the Law of the Sea*. Cambridge Studies in International and Comparative Law. Cambridge University Press.

Klein, Peter J. 2014. Inequality and Envy. May 30. https://mises.org/blog/inequality-and-envy. Accessed 13 Dec 2015.

Kopal, Vladimir. 1968. Treaty on Principles Governing the Activities of States in the Exploration and Use of Outer Space, Including the Moon and Other Celestial Bodies. In *Yearbook of Air and Space Law 1966* (Annuaire de droit aérien et spatial), ed. R.H. Mankiewicz. Montreal: McGill University Press.

———. 1996. United Nations and the Progressive Development of International Space Law. In *The Finnish Yearbook of International Law*, ed. M. Koskenniemi and K. Takamaa, vol. VII. The Hague, Boston, and London: Martinus Nijhoff Publishers and Kluwer Law International.

Levin, Michael. 1996. Capitalism, Envy, and the Inner City. February 1. https://mises.org/library/capitalism-envy-and-inner-city. Accessed 13 Dec 2015.

Locke, John. 1948. *An Essay Concerning the True Origin, Extent and End of Civil Government*. In *Social Contract*, ed. E. Barker, 17–19. New York: Oxford University Press.

Long, Roderick. 1995. The Libertarian Case Against Intellectual Property Rights. *Formulations* 3 (1). http://libertariannation.org/a/f31l1.html.

Mathews, Don. 2002. The Price of Envy. April 11. https://mises.org/library/price-envy. Accessed 13 Dec 2015.

Menell, Peter S. 2007a. Intellectual Property and the Property Rights Movement. *Regulation*, Fall. http://www.cato.org/pubs/regulation/regv30n3/v30n3-6.pdf.

———. 2007b. The Property Rights Movement's Embrace of Intellectual Property: True Love or Doomed Relationship? *Ecology Law Quarterly* 34.

Mukherjee, Jay, and Walter E. Block. 2012. Libertarians and the Catholic Church on Intellectual Property Laws. *Journal of Political Philosophy Las Torres de Lucca* (1): 59–75. http://www.lastorresdelucca.org/index.php?option=com_k2&view=item&id=93:libertarios-y-la-iglesia-católica-en-las-leyes-de-propie-dad-intelectual&Itemid=24&lang=en&Itemid=23.

Navabi, Ash. 2015. To Taylor, Love Freedom. June 23. https://mises.ca/posts/blog/to-taylor-love-freedom/. Accessed 4 Aug 2016.

Olinga, Luc. 2015. New US Space Mining Law to Spark Interplanetary Gold Rush. December 8. http://phys.org/news/2015-12-space-law-interplanetary-gold.html. Accessed 13 Dec 2015.

Palmer, Tom. 1989. Intellectual Property: A Non-Posnerian Law and Economics Approach. *Hamline Law Review* 12 (2): 261–304.

Paul, Ellen Frankel. 1987. *Property Rights and Eminent Domain*. Livingston, NJ: Transaction Publishers.

Pufendorf, Samuel. 1673. Natural Law and the Law of Nations (De officio hominis et civis prout ipsi praescribuntur lege naturali).

Rothbard, Murray N. 1982b. Law, Property Rights, and Air Pollution. *Cato Journal* 2 (1). Reprinted in *Economics and the Environment: A Reconciliation*, Walter E. Block, ed., Vancouver: The Fraser Institute, 1990, pp. 233–279.

http://mises.org/story/2120;   http://www.mises.org/rothbard/lawproperty.
    pdf. Accessed 20 Apr 2016.

Rana, Harminderpal Singh. 1994. Common Heritage of Mankind & the Final
    Frontier: A Revaluation of Values Constituting the International Legal
    Regime for Outer Space Activities, The Note. *Rutgers Law Journal.* 26 (1):
    225–250.

Reisman, George. 2005. Envy Unleashed at the New York Times. June 6. https://
    mises.org/library/envy-unleashed-new-york-times. Accessed 13 Dec 2015.

Rozeff, Michael S. 2005. Original Appropriation and Its Critics. September 1.
    http://www.lewrockwell.com/rozeff/rozeff18.html. Accessed 23 Apr 2016.

Schoeck, Helmut. 1966. *Envy: A Theory of Social Behavior.* New York: Harcourt
    Brace and World.

Sennholz, Hans F. 2001. The Envy Tax. August 1. https://mises.org/library/
    envy-tax. Accessed 13 Dec 2015.

Stimers, Paul. 2015. One Small Step for Man, One Giant Leap for Law. *Wall
    Street Journal*: A15. December 7. http://www.wsj.com/articles/one-small-
    step-for-man-one-giant-leap-for-law-1449444596. Accessed 13 Dec 2015.

Stockton, Nick. 2015. Congress Says Yes to Space Mining; No to Rocket
    Regulations. November 18. http://www.wired.com/2015/11/congress-says-
    yes-to-space-mining-no-to-rocket-regulations/. Accessed 13 Dec 2015.

U.N. General Assembly. 1962a. *Declaration of Legal Principles Governing the
    Activities of States in the Exploration and Use of Outer Space.* http://www.
    unoosa.org/oosa/en/ourwork/spacelaw/treaties/introouterspacetreaty.html.
    Accessed 8 June 2016.

———. 1962b. Treaty on Principles Governing the Activities of States in
    the Exploration and Use of Outer Space, Including the Moon and Other
    Celestial Bodies. http://www.unoosa.org/oosa/en/ourwork/spacelaw/treaties/
    introouterspacetreaty.html. Accessed 8 June 2016.

U.S. Commercial Space Launch Competitiveness Act (USCSLCA). 2015.
    https://www.congress.gov/bill/114th-congress/house-bill/2262/text.
    H.R.2262. Accessed 13 Dec 2015.

Vlasic, Ivan A. 1967. The Space Treaty: A Preliminary Evaluation. *California
    Law Review* 55 (2): 507–519.

Von Mises, Ludwig. 1981 [1922]. *Socialism: An Economic and Sociological
    Analysis.* Trans. J. Kahane. Indianapolis: Liberty Fund. http://mises.org/
    books/socialism/contents.aspx.

Watner, Carl. 1982. The Proprietary Theory of Justice in the Libertarian
    Tradition. *Journal of Libertarian Studies* 6 (3–4): 289–316. http://mises.org/
    journals/jls/6_3/6_3_6.pdf. Accessed 23 Apr 2016.

13

Timing

There are three dimensions in which allocative cooperation is needed in economics: geographic, allocation in terms of types of goods, and then through
time.[1] Consider the first allocation regarding geographic cooperation. This
pertains to the fact that goods and services must be allocated throughout the
areas in which the economy functions. For example, oranges, grown in
California and Florida, must not stay in those states if we are to have an
economy worthy of the name. Rather, they must percolate throughout the
entire country and the world, for the sake of economic efficiency. How is this
to be done? The central planning mode would feature a bureaucrat in
Washington D.C., London, or similar location ordering farmers to deliver
this citrus fruit to consumers located elsewhere. He would have to determine
how much of this product would be delivered to each of the states, to which
cities and small towns in the country, and, ultimately, to which grocery stores.

Happily, there is another way of allocating oranges: the free market's
price system. This "magic of the market" is undertaken by arbitrage
through space.[2] If citrus is plentiful at the South-western and South-eastern

---

[1] We are inspired in this chapter by the 1960 Jimmy Jones rock and roll song "Good timin'."

[2] Not interstellar space, the focus of most of this book. Rather, in this case our purview is limited to
more earthly arenas. We are now referring to geographical arbitrage: bringing goods from areas
where they are selling for a low price, to those "spaces" where they are dear, in order to earn a profit.

© The Author(s) 2018

P. L. Nelson, W. E. Block, *Space Capitalism*, Palgrave Studies in Classical Liberalism,
https://doi.org/10.1007/978-3-319-74651-7_13

corners of our country, and rarely seen elsewhere, then its price will be low in these two places, and high elsewhere. Assuming that transportation costs are less than the value of this good, entrepreneurs will purchase where it is cheap, and deliver to where it is expensive. The former will raise the low prices, and the latter will decrease the high prices. In equilibrium, prices will be the same throughout, abstracting from the costs of these rearrangements. It makes no economic sense for this fruit to remain where it was grown. Consumers in these two states can only eat so many oranges. Without this geographic rearrangement, growers could not take advantage of the economies of scale. Why allow a basket of this fruit to remain in Florida, for example, selling for $1, when it could garner, say, $20 in New Hampshire? Arbitrageurs will purchase it in the former place, sell it in the latter, and the price will tend to settle between these two points.

The second type of allocation takes place in terms of types of goods and services. Suppose we decide we are all too fat and need to go on a diet. This means we now want to eat more rabbit food such as lettuce, carrots, tomatoes, cucumbers, spinach (ugh!),[3] etc., and reduce our intake of all foods that make life worth living: chocolate, candies, cookies, cakes, ice cream for example. But if we all live up to our New Year's resolutions, the farmers will have to be induced, somehow, to accommodate our new wishes. The central planning method of ensuring this is that we all write letters to our esteemed leaders asking them to order members of the agricultural industry to shift from one type of crop to another. If they demur, force will have to be used on them to force compliance. However, if there is anything we have learned from the failure of Soviet agriculture, it is that the bayonet is not a good farm implement.[4]

How would such a changeover be accomplished under *laissez-faire* capitalism? It is simple.[5] We would just stop purchasing fattening foods

---

[3] The second author of this book insists upon "ugh!" The first author objects and hereby admits he channels *Popeye*, declares that he loves spinach, and assigns to the other writer the moniker: "J. Wellington Wimpy." Have we gone wholly puerile? Probably, but then what else is new? (We acknowledge and thank Elzie Crisler Segar for his wonderful creativeness and the entertainment he has bestowed on Americans.)

[4] It is this reliance on the bayonet and similar instruments of destruction to kill and oppress that we regard as both immoral and illicit.

[5] The beauty of *laissez-faire* is that not everyone needs to engage in uniform practices such as dieting. "We" refers to those who wish to make this change, not those who do not. Block can have all the

and beverages, and start buying those that steer towards belt-tightening. Prices of the former would fall, and of the latter, rise. Profits would follow a similar path. Thanks to Smith's (1776) "invisible hand" farmers will be led, by the lure of maximizing returns, to switch from what customers purchased in the past to what they now want to consume.

Of what does the third allocation, through time, consist? Not only must goods be allocated geographically, and in terms of types and kinds, but, if the economy is to be at all efficient, events must take place in a certain order of time. While most people appreciate the first two allocative necessities, the same cannot be said for this third type.

Consider. In an advanced culture before chairs can be manufactured, factories must be set up, we must have tools to cut wood, raw timber must be transported to the workplace, laborers must be assembled, land amassed, etc.[6] And this is to say nothing of the longer-term requirements. Trees must first be grown, workers educated, and the material that comprise the tools must be mined. Rubber and other raw materials that go into the creation of trucks, and transportation systems, must be brought to bear, etc. But in what proportions, and at which times? Again, we can contrast a central planning mode to resolve these quandaries with one emanating from the free-market system. In the former case, the bureaucrat simply arbitrarily determines these decisions. The "decider" allocates so much of the national treasure to this or that alternative, and hopes for

---

cake he wishes and Nelson can have his spinach too. More generally, some could join hippie communes, based on the notion "from each according to his ability, to each in accordance with his need." Others would be free to go it alone, or on behalf of their families. In contrast, in a socialist society, the means of production are nationalized, and no one is free to set up shop for himself under pure communism. In attenuated versions of this system, some small enterprises might be allowed, but not large ones. The "need" to control others as exhibited in the socialist polity in turn stems from the idea of fellowship gone wrong. In prehistoric times where one of the leading causes of death was being eaten alive, close association with others within a tribe provided an evolutionary advantage and enhanced the ability to survive. Cooperation is therefore deeply ingrained in the human psyche. This working together is strongest where free association reigns. The desire for community becomes warped and destructive when it focuses on ensuring that everyone dresses the same, expresses only one opinion, and eats only approved foods. Where failure to toe the party line can result in death, people become dishonest, resentful, rebellious, and silent loners. The intimidated sit in dark rooms watching television. Prognoses for survival is then threatened rather than enhanced.

[6] In the most basic state of development, a log may be rolled to the desired location. No need for factories and no special training would be required. In a slightly more advanced community a single person could collect sticks and vines. He would then lash them together, weave a seat, and create a far more comfortable chair. It would take more time than the log and require at least minimum training.

the best. The type of chaos that results has been well-documented in the economic literature (Von Mises 1947; Murphy 2002; Salerno 2010).[7]

Consider these three triangles:

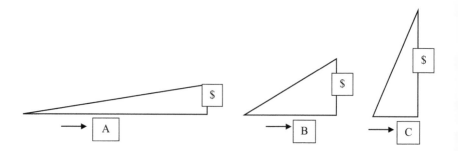

How does the free enterprise system solve this problem of time ordering? Simple. It is via interest rates, freely determined in the marketplace. They are based on an economic phenomenon called "time preference." When people are relatively impatient, interest rates tend to be higher. This places a premium on goods and services deliverable in the short run. Triangle C illustrates this. The period of production from the time of the first investment, the lower left part of this geometrical figure, to the lower right, the date when the good is available for consumption, is relatively short. In the extreme, this is typically a hand-to-mouth poverty-stricken economy, in which people are desperate for consumable items, and think along the lines of now, now, now! B illustrates an intermediate position in this regard, while A depicts an economy marked by the relatively wealthy, who can afford to wait for final goods, and as a result receive more, and a growing amount of them.[8] The height of each triangle represents the value of the total consumption of the economy. The area of

---

[7] In addition to documentation, chaos has been experienced every time a shortage occurs such as following a hurricane when insufficient building contractors are available because bureaucrats forbid gouging by "outsiders."

[8] These triangles are the mainstay of the Austrian business cycle theory. To delve deeply into the intricacies of this intellectual apparatus would take us too far afield from our present concerns. Our purpose in this chapter is to apply some of these insights to the matter at hand, space exploration. The reader interested in ABCT may consult this article (Barnett and Block 2009), which, although critical of the triangle for technical reasons that do not concern us here, lists a large bibliography of how this geometrical figure is used in ABCT.

the triangle depicts the total value of consumption plus intermediate goods and basic factors of production. It is equal in all three cases. Right now, all three societies are equally wealthy. But A saves and invests more than B, and B more than C. Eventually, other things being equal, A will be the richest, and B the poorest. The angle of the hypotenuse signifies the interest rate (it is highest in C, lowest in A). Other things being equal, A will have the greatest growth rate, and C the lowest. This is because the former has more capital goods relative to consumers' goods, and the latter, the least.

Think in terms of goods moving from left to right. At the beginning of the production process, on the left side of the triangle are basic industries; these are ones whose products will not be available for a great amount of time: mining, education, cement, etc. The next stage in this process are industries closer and closer to the end of production, when the consumer purchases the final product. For example, moving from left to right we might find the farmer who produces the wheat, the miller who refines it into flour, the commercial bakery that turns this product[9] into bread and cake, the jobber who is next in the process, the wholesaler who brings it one step further to the consumer, and finally the retailer who makes final delivery. Interspersed with these producers would be those who transport it from stage to stage, those who insure it, etc. The point is, the interest rate differs from society to society. There is a very high rate of interest in C, a low one in A. The interest rate is akin to a price, the price of time.[10]

A practical day-to-day experience of this principle is copying. Version C would be a person with a quill pen copying the text from one sheet to another. Process B would be a printing press where the operator mounts a sheet of paper, inks the type, and presses the paper. He can do that repeatedly and turn out dozens of sheets in the same time span. But he must first set up the press so it takes much longer to get the first copy. System A would be a copy machine. Put lots of original pages in the feed and turn out hundreds of sheets per minute. But the mechanism must first be manufactured and the factory built to produce those copiers.

---

[9] Along with numerous others.

[10] Actually, the relative price of otherwise identical goods at different stages of production.

Finally, we attempt to relate these considerations to the topic of the present volume. Was this system of interest rates as an indicator allowed to operate in the development of space travel? To ask this question is to answer it: of course not. And, this, for two reasons. First, the Federal Reserve System determines interest rates. The Fed is an equivalent to the central planning board of the U.S.S.R. This central bank imparts more than just a little bit of calculational chaos to the economic system. It brings a strong measure of Sovietization to the Western economy. If it makes a mistake, can it be automatically weeded out of the economic system through bankruptcy? Of course not. No more than the central planning bureau can be made to disappear in any country that remains true to its communistic ideals. This centrally determined interest rate pattern is as incompatible with free enterprise as would be price controls for oranges or candy and cake versus salads. Perhaps it is even more serious, since the interest rate permeates the entire economy in a way that no single good, or even several of them, can.[11]

The second reason is that even if we had a market-determined interest rate, the government could blithely ignore it, if its plans were incompatible with it. For example, if it wanted to invest in interest-sensitive goods, basic factors of production located at the left side of the triangle, it could do so with impunity. Let us consider an analogy: the development of the automobile. In the actual pattern, engineers in the early stages of car manufacture at the beginning of the twentieth century worked on the clutch and starting mechanisms. But suppose instead, they had devoted the lion's share of their efforts on features that came much later in history: air conditioning and automatic transmission, or self-driving cars which are only now being seriously contemplated. If so, they would have misallocated resources regarding the time dimension. They would have been putting the cart before the horse, so to speak. They would have been doing something akin to asking your wife to marry you on the first date. Who would have wanted an automobile with modern radios, even if such were possible, in the vehicle of 1912, for example, when so many more basic elements were still to be introduced?

---

[11] Even money is not as pervasive in the economy as is the interest rate. For barter takes place without the intermediation of money, while each and every price, without exception, depends upon the interest rate.

What are the specifics regarding the purpose of the present chapter? It is our claim that by sending men to the Moon in 1969, the government engaged in space exploration prematurely, and this undermined the entire effort. It is always difficult to engage in contrary-to-fact history, but let's take a crack at it. What could have been done instead of following the actual time horizon of space flight? Some possibilities would have been to work on better fuels, more modern rocketry, the space elevator. If this pattern ensued, perhaps men would have landed on the Moon in 1999 instead of 1969,[12] and then there would have been enough momentum to continue to Mars in 2009 with this improved technology. Or, perhaps, instead of the massive amount of resources spent on the 1969 event, more money should have been allocated to an even more basic approach: more Ph.D.s in physics and engineering. The point is, President Kennedy's decision to land a man on the Moon in the 1960s was a political one; it did not emanate from purely economic considerations. As such, it may well have set back, or maybe rendered forever impossible, our goal of extra-terrestrial colonization, not promoted it. And, this can only be seen and appreciated if we keep in mind that not only must resources be allocated sensibly from a geographical and type-of-good perspective, but also from one that places *time* front and center.

Consider the electric light. It was invented over a century ago. It effectively converted nighttime within houses and factories to daytime; darkness into brightness. The increase in safety, productivity, and level of knowledge brought in its wake was phenomenal. At first it was done with the incandescent lightbulb,[13] a wire that got hot enough to glow and which was enclosed in a vacuum-filled glass orb so that oxygen deprivation would forestall it from burning. The bureaucracy in Washington decided that because of that heat, the bulb constituted a horrific waste of energy. It happened that there was at the time a recent technology, the compact fluorescent light (GFL), that could produce lots of illumination

---

[12] But then of course we may not have been able to beat the Russians, which was the real Kennedian goal. But it was thus a dead-end objective because once the United States was victorious, there was no follow-up—nowhere to go.

[13] Thank you, Thomas Edison. Previously, dim and dangerous open flames in the form of candles, whale oil, or kerosene lamps, made popular by Rockefeller (Chernow 2004), were used for that purpose.

with relatively little heat. A law was passed mandating these "marvels." However, they were notoriously expensive, ecologically unfriendly (they contain mercury and thus cannot be disposed of both easily and safely), deteriorated by emitting less light as time went on, and too often failed completely in a matter of minutes[14] (Berendsohn[15] 2008). Many people refused to use them. Aside from basic libertarian concerns that the prohibition of incandescent lights constituted a violation of the non-aggression principle, the mandate was, from a practical viewpoint, premature. Why? Because there was already a much more promising technology in existence: the light emitting diode (LED). At the time, that technique was exceedingly expensive. However, with further research, LEDs have become much better and cheaper, though they too have problems such as fickering that makes the incandecent bulb remain attractive. As usual, our statist friends jumped the gun and foisted on the population a terrible product that should have never seen the light of day.[16]

Here is another example of premature bureaucratic interference: California's Senate Bill 1298 directing its Department of Motor Vehicles to draft regulations mandating safety features for self-driving automobiles (California 2015). The first phase, testing, mandates requirements for manufacturers to meet with each other prior to allowing these vehicles to operate on state roads. These regulations require a licensed driver on board who will be able to take over control immediately, if needed. In the first place, such an operation is exceedingly dangerous. Why, one might ask? The "driver" would be sitting in the car with nothing to do for an extended period. All at once, after say two hours of idleness (reading or texting to occupy the time would obviously not be allowed), the car makes an unexpected maneuver, such as slowing down because of a traffic jam. The monitoring human feels the sudden slow down, looks up and sees a mass of brake lights and panics. Upon taking over he conducts unsafe maneuvers to deal with a situation that the car had well under control. Furthermore,

---

[14] The first author of this book has personal experience that indicates a vast degree of variable performance of GFLs. Most of them burn out within two to six months, one has lasted four years so far, and one (the last one he ever bought) had a life span of only 10 minutes.

[15] Many of Berendsohn's expert fixes are difficult to manage in that each lamp is designed as it is. Some point up, others down. Customers cannot change that without throwing out the existing lamp; this is especially difficult if it is built-in. Many of his "expert fixes" do require *experts* to implement. It is easier to avoid the use of such products in the first place.

[16] Pardon the pun.

the requirement for a driver and a full set of controls is foolish. It is like prohibiting a truck from carrying merchandise. The whole purpose of the former is to do the driving and do it safely just as the latter is intended to move freight. The effect is to forbid the very device that the law is supposed to enable.[17]

References

Barnett, William, and Walter E. Block. 2009. Coase and Bertrand on Lighthouses. *Public Choice* 140 (1–2): 1–13. https://doi.org/10.1007/s11127-008-9375-x. Accessed 23 Apr 2016.

Berendsohn, Roy. 2008. 3 Compact Fluoresent Light Bulb Problems—And Expert Fixes. *Popular Mechanics*. August 31. http://www.popularmechanics.com/home/how-to/a3474/4276104/. Accessed 22 Aug 2016.

California, DMV. 2015. Summary of Draft Autonomous Vehicles Deployment Regulations. Department of Motor Vehicles. December 16.

Chernow, Ron. 2004. *Titan: The Life of John D. Rockefeller, Sr.* New York: Vintage.

Juma, Calestous. 2016. *Innovation and Its Enemies, Why People Resist New Technologies*. New York: Oxford University Press.

Murphy, Robert P. 2002. *Chaos Theory: Two Essays on Market Anarchy*. New York: RJ Communications LLC. http://mises.org/books/chaostheory.pdf. Accessed 21 Mar 2016.

Salerno, Joseph T. 2010 [1998]. Beyond Calculational Chaos: Sound Money and the Quest for Economic Order in Ex-Communist Europe. In *Money: Sound and Unsound*, 467–496. Auburn, AL: Ludwig von Mises Institute.

Von Mises, Ludwig. 1947. *Planned Chaos*. Auburn: The Mises Institute. https://mises.org/library/planned-chaos. Accessed 21 Mar 2016.

---

[17] For more on this refer to Juma 2016.

14

Who Are the Libertarians in the Space Initiative?

Introduction

This chapter attempts to establish who the libertarians are who are actively working on the space initiative. Or, perhaps better stated, which people are acting compatibly with the free-market philosophy, and which are not.

By the time the reader gets to this chapter, late in the book, he will be familiar with the basic premises of libertarianism.[1] To summarize, it is predicated upon the non-aggression principle (NAP) which states that it is a crime to threaten or initiate violence against innocent people or their property,[2] and the latter is based on homesteading or a chain of purchasing agreements from an original settler. Thus, we can immediately rule out NASA, and all the folk directly employed by this governmental orga-

---

[1] See on this Bergland 1986; Block 2008; Hoppe 1993; Huebert 2010; Narveson 1988; Nozick 1974; Rockwell 2014; Rothbard 1973, 1978; Woods 2013; Woolridge 1970.

[2] In David Nolan's words: "I hereby certify that I do not believe in or advocate the initiation of force as a means of achieving political or social goals." Source: http://int.search.myway.com.

© The Author(s) 2018
P. L. Nelson, W. E. Block, *Space Capitalism*, Palgrave Studies in Classical Liberalism,
https://doi.org/10.1007/978-3-319-74651-7_14

nization. The funds utilized by these people have been mulcted from the general taxpayer under duress.[3]

The reader will also have been acquainted with the likes of Elon Musk and other businessmen who are at present involved in the attempt to lift human beings off their home planet, and settle them onto some of the closer heavenly bodies. But which of them are part and parcel of the marketplace? And, to what degree? Before we can answer these questions, a few preliminary remarks are in order.

There is such a thing as libertarian ruling class theory. This may come as a surprise to many, since the concept is popularly thought to be a wholly owned subsidiary of Marxism. We have the temerity to make this claim because even though such historical figures as Caligula, Hisham ibn Abd al-Malik, and their ilk predate Marx by millennia, yet the methods used to implement the communist program strongly resemble those of the afore-named criminals. This cannot be denied. Our man Karl Marx did indeed have a communistic ruling class theory: the proletariat were the victims, and the bourgeoisie the exploiters.[4] However, notwithstanding the utter imbecility and vacuous nature of that perspective, we libertarians do indeed have our own theory of the ruling class. As for Marx's assertions, he did not understand that only those who violate the NAP are criminals, and only those who suffer from their depredations are the exploited. This, in a nutshell, is the libertarian class theory.[5]

---

[3] Happily, the budget for this state-run agency has been on the decline; all men of good will must look upon this decrease in compulsion favorably.

[4] This was based on the labor theory of value. Workers produced the entire product in this view, and any subtraction from GDP other than wages (rent, profits, etc.) was in effect a theft from them. For a critique of this malicious and fallacious viewpoint, see Block 2006; Bohm-Bawerk 1884, 2011; Cantillon 2011; Gordon 1991; Hoppe 1989; Maltsev 1993; Von Mises 1981; Murphy 2006, 2011; Reisman 2006; Steele 1981, 1992; Stigler 1958; Vaughn 1978. The theory is also based on the perverse belief that all members of a class necessarily have identical beliefs. All laborers *must* believe the same thing regarding wages. All women *must* hold identical interests. All members of a particular race *must* think alike. Libertarians and, indeed, all those with any modicum of common sense, reject this deterministic babel.

[5] For further reading on this see Block 2006; Burris 2012; Domhoff 1967, 1971, 1998; Donaldson and Poynting 2007; Hoppe 1990; Hughes 1977; Kolko 1963; Von Mises 1978; Oppenheimer 1975; Raico 1977; Rockwell 2001; Rothbard 2004. In the view of Rothbard 2004: "All States are governed by a ruling class that is a minority of the population, and which subsists as a parasitic and exploitative burden upon the rest of society. Since its rule is exploitative and parasitic, the State must purchase the alliance of a group of 'Court Intellectuals,' whose task is to bamboozle the public into accepting and celebrating the rule of its particular State. The Court Intellectuals have their

Private criminals, murderers, rapists, thieves, are all members of the predatory class. But government employees are far more powerful participants in the felonious brutality of forcing people to pay money against their will.[6] That is why NASA[7] cannot be considered on the side of the angels in the development of travel and settlement of space.

A good first approximation of libertarian class analysis was proposed by Calhoun (1853).[8] In his view, those who were net tax beneficiaries were the rulers, and those who paid more in assessments than they received in benefits were the ruled. His is a good start, since, given that government is the most powerful congregation of ruling-class members, and that taxation is its means of bilking the public, those who live off the avails of these payments must be scrutinized for membership of this category. Those whose net incomes are reduced by the state make good candidates for non-affiliation with the "biggest/baddest" criminal gang. But this cannot be all there is to the concept, since there are poor, helpless people, many welfare recipients, whose contribution to the state apparatus is miniscule, and whose intake from that source, for them, is relatively major. These individuals cannot be members of the libertarian ruling

---

work cut out for them. In exchange for their continuing work of apologetics and bamboozlement, the Court Intellectuals win their place as junior partners in the power, prestige, and loot extracted by the State apparatus from the deluded public. The noble task of Revisionism is to de-bamboozle: to penetrate the fog of lies and deception of the State and its apologists Court Intellectuals, and to present to the public the true history of the motivation, the nature, and the consequences of State activity. By working past the fog of State deception to penetrate to the truth, to the reality behind the false appearances, the Revisionist works to delegitimize, to desanctify, the State in the eyes of the previously deceived public."

[6] This is neither the time nor place to make the case for anarcho-capitalism. The interested reader may consult Rothbard 1973 and Spooner 1966 [1870]. Additional discussion on this subject may be found in Anderson and Hill 1979; Benson 1989, 1990a, b; Block 2007, 2010, 2011a, b; Casey 2010; DiLorenzo 2010; Gregory 2011; Guillory and Tinsley 2009; Hasnas 1995; Heinrich 2010; Higgs 2009, 2012; Hoppe 2008, 2011; Huebert 2010; King 2010; Kinsella 2009; Long 2004; McConkey 2013; Molyneux 2008; Murphy 2005; Rockwell 2013; Rothbard 1975, 1977, 1998; Stringham 2007; Tannehills 1984; Tinsley 1998–1999; Wenzel 2013; Woods 2014.

[7] Neither can the likes of the European Space Agency or the Russian Federal Space Agency be regarded as positive contributors.

[8] In this section, we write approvingly of Calhoun's views regarding taxpayers vs. recipients. Lest any confusion arise, let us make it clear that we decry his support of the First Bank of the United States, his initial praise of the Tariff of Abominations, and his supposed support of slavery (he really supported States Rights which historically is divided between staunch support of abolition and opposition to the same (Woods 2010)), and similar statist programs as well as the over-generalization of who constitutes the ruling class.

class, since that appellation implies at least a modicum of power in our society, and those on the dole can hardly qualify.[9]

In reality, poor people, who are receivers of state "largesse," must suffer major deprivation in order to receive these "benefits," i.e. they are made permanently dependent (Murray 1984). Sometimes they cannot marry their spouse or own too much or eat certain foods, etc. In short, unless one looks only at money flow and nothing else, wards of the government are not net payees. That narrow view is implicit in the essential materialism of socialists. Hold on! Are we to understand that socialists are materialists? Are not capitalists usually saddled with this appellation? Consider that the process of movement towards communism[10] is "Dialectic *Materialism*." It is a philosophy based on the belief that material is the sole reality. Fairness thus becomes not playing by the rules, but equal distribution of (financial) assets. Unequal dispersal of power and impartial umpires are of no concern; to statists only physical assets count.[11] Anarcho-capitalists, in contrast, focus their attention on the NAP. In this view, it is difficult in the extreme to see how voluntary commercial interaction, assuming no fraud, can be exploitative.[12] Austrian economists declare that value is subjective, that no deterministic or intrinsic properties such as the amount of labor or the input of resources create value. Rather it stems solely from the appreciation of the beholder. These are respectively a principled commitment to a peaceful approach to human relations and a spiritual relation to both

---

[9] Here it is important to note that self-appointed representatives of under-privileged citizens often *are* members of the ruling class and that their supposed dedication to poor people really enhances their own illicit political power.

[10] Communism is but one type of socialism (Von Mises 1922).

[11] The ubiquitous perversion of language by statists (Orwell 1949) contributes mightily to the destruction of civilization. Said Thatcher (1976): "They [socialists] always run out of other people's money."

[12] States Ridley (2015, pp. 31–32): "I once interviewed (Steven) Pinker in front of an audience in London, and was very struck by the passion of his reply when an audience member insisted that profit was a form of violence and was on the increase. Pinker simply replied with a biographical story. His grandfather, born in Warsaw in 1900, emigrated to Montreal in 1926, worked for a shirt company (the family had made gloves in Poland), was laid off during the Great Depression, and then, with his grandmother, sewed neckties in his apartment, eventually earning enough to set up a small factory, which they ran until their deaths. And yes, it made a small profit (just enough to pay the rent and bring up Pinker's mother and her brothers), and no, his grandfather never hurt a fly. Commerce, he said, cannot be equated with violence."

persons and things outside of one's self, not an enumeration of monetary units. We turn now to consider such men.

At the other end of the spectrum lie Hans-Hermann Hoppe and Ron Paul. They are the very paradigm instances of libertarians. Indeed, they are two of the foremost leaders of this entire movement. We choose them as examples to illustrate the weakness of Calhoun's theory. The former was a professor at the University of Nevada, Las Vegas, a public institution, and the latter for many years a U.S. Congressman from Texas. Under a strict Calhounian calculation, both would have had to have been relegated to the ruling class. After all, their entire salaries came to them courtesy of tax revenues, and the amount of money they paid back to the state was, we posit, far less than that amount. But to make any such categorization would amount to a thorough abnegation of the entire direction and personal commitment of their professional careers and, indeed, their very lives. If any two men spent their entire lives attempting to undermine statist plunder it was these two. To include them in the ruling class from a libertarian point of view would be an abject violation of this concept. It would be akin, from the opposite perspective, of claiming that Mao, Guevara, Stalin, and Hitler were good men. So, we must dig a bit deeper; we cannot accept Calhoun's definition as anything other than a first, good, but rough approximation.

And here we run into a bit of a problem. The ruling class may be defined as comprising those who have some significant power and (mainly) use the government as a means toward exploiting others, regardless of their net tax status. The difficulty is akin to that facing those who wished to define, so as to ban, pornography. They would say something along the lines of "I know it when I see it, but I can't objectively define it." Libertarian ruling-class theory is in something of a similar bind.[13] Both can point to clear cases. As to lascivious material, *The Devil in Miss*

---

[13] But not quite as bad. When the victorious army indicts the losing soldiers, the generals and colonels are typically found guilty, but not the privates and corporals. As for the intermediate officers, they lie in a gray area. There are no hard and fast objective rules that apply, but matters are not totally subjective either. A good illustration of the principle can be found in *Lilac Girls* (Kelly 2016). This is a novel based on the true stories of three women during WWII and refers to the Ravensbrück Concentration Camp. In it the senior medical overseer of Ravensbrück, Dr. Gebhardt, is sentenced to hang for crimes against humanity while Dr. Herta Oberheuser, a newly minted

Jones is pornographic, and the Bolshoi ballet is not.[14] Similarly, Hillary Clinton, Donald Trump, and Arthur Sulzberger, Jr.[15] are members of the ruling class; Rothbard, Paul, and Ayn Rand are clearly not. According to that old aphorism, "the devil is in the details." We must bear this in mind in what follows, when we attempt to separate the sheep from the goats.

Space-Oriented Entrepreneurs

With this introduction in mind, we now attempt to apply libertarian class analysis to the businessmen involved in the non-explicitly governmental space program. Who are the candidates for this category?

Elon Musk

No listing of businessmen involved in off-world enterprises would be complete without mentioning Mr. Musk. His company, Space X (http://www.spacex.com/) was launched in 2002. His reusable rocket, Falcon 9, was a great break-through, since, previously, such missiles could only be used once, at great cost. There is no doubt that when the definitive history of humanity's early attempts to get off the ground into the stars is written, this man will play a key role.

But, to what extent is he a member of the free-enterprise system in good standing, and to what degree is he guilty of "crony capitalism,"[16] the system whereby supposedly private businessmen are merely shills for the state? On the debit side of this particular ledger is the fact that Tesla Motors Inc., SolarCity Corp., and Space Exploration Technologies Corp., known as SpaceX, have all *together* been given some *$4.9 billion in subsi-*

---

doctor, one of the three women protagonists of the book, and the one who carried out the actual physical crimes, is sentenced to 20-years and only served five.

[14] Yes, we are aware that some in the world disagree with this assessment but believe that most do not equate ballerinas with gentlemen's club strippers.

[15] See Block (2014) on this.

[16] We could have said "guilty of 'rent seeking,'" but refrained. For justifications of this failure to use that nomenclature, see Bhagwati 1982; Block 2000, 2002; Henderson 2008; Pasour 1986; Wenzel 2016.

dies from government (Hirsch 2015) and are thus heavily dependent upon government largesse.[17]

States DeBord (2015): "If there's a consistent charge against Elon Musk and his high-flying companies—Tesla, SpaceX, SolarCity—it's that they're not really examples of independent, innovative market capitalism. Rather, they're government contractors, dependent on taxpayer money to stay afloat."

This, in and of itself, is not conclusive, since there are legitimate libertarian grounds for accepting money from the state. However, it is presumptively illicit, and to gain the free enterprise nod there must be massive evidence on the other side. Unfortunately, not much is forthcoming from this direction. Has Musk been outspoken and well-known in support of anarcho-capitalist principles? The Libertarian Party? The Mises Institute? The Free State Project? Sea-steading? Any of the libertarian think-tanks? There is no evidence we could uncover to demonstrate that, as a counterbalance to his acceptance of government money, he has shown any support whatsoever for the free-enterprise system.[18] In contrast, consider the contrary-to-fact conditional to the effect that the Koch brothers accepted massive amounts of government money. Can the claim be made on their behalf that despite this they are not crony capitalists, but, rather, have a bit of Ragnar Danneskjold[19] in them; that is, they have

---

[17] On subsidies to Tesla, see: Peters 2016; Jenkins 2016; Wynn and Lafleur 2009; Chandra et al. 2009; Kim 2014. Documentation in this regard for SolarCity and government grants to space X are evidenced by these authors: Richards 2015; Melchoir 2015; Chambers 2015. For a defense of government subsidies to Musk, and a critique of Hirsch (2015) on the grounds that pretty much every firm in the space and other high-tech firms are on the government dole, and therefore Musk is justified in doing so, see Autry (2015).

[18] We suspect that Mr. Musk is interested in proceeding with advanced scientific innovations including space exploration and that he would do so with or without state aid. He is impatient with bureaucratic foot-dragging. It may be simple expedience that results in his involvement with government. To illustrate this point, we refer to a quotation attributed to Musk: "To make an embarrassing admission, I like video games. That's what got me into software engineering when I was a kid. I wanted to make money so I could buy a better computer to play better video games—nothing like saving the world" (Hankoff 2014). This suggests a mindset compatible with libertarianism wherein Musk wishes to earn his own way to accomplish his goals. It reveals an impatience with waiting for others to provide for him (in this case a better computer).

[19] Danneskjold is a fictional seafaring pirate who attacks government ships (Rand 1957). He is a bit like Robin Hood (a pun, compare to: Robbin' Hood' or Robbing Hoodlum). Note that the latter did not simply take from the rich to give to the poor. He retrieved the ill-gotten goods taken with force by the nobility to return them to the victimized peasants. Ditto for the former: Ragnar, too,

used these funds to promote liberty? Of course they have. In Koch (2015), for example, and with a myriad of donations to free-enterprise oriented groups, they have confirmed, repeatedly, that the charge of crony capitalist would be difficult to attach to them. Musk has engaged in no such activities. This is not to say that the private recipient of tax revenues must use them to promote good libertarian ends if he is not to be considered a crony capitalist. It is sufficient that any innocent person relieves the government of its ill-gotten gains to establish himself as on the side of liberty. But, as a practical matter, we need to have some way to distinguish those who act compatibly with free enterprise from those who do not. The presumption is that recipients of massive amounts of government revenues are not on the side of the angels; rather, they are working hand in glove with the establishment. The acts of the Kochs, but not of Musk, go a long way in the direction of revealing the status of these two different entrepreneurs.[20]

Thus, Musk's enterprises to reach for the "stars," and colonize them too, cannot be counted as part of the free-market system. Indeed, they constitute the very opposite: economic fascism, government interventionism, crony capitalism. It is crucially important that institutional arrangements of this sort be sharply distinguished from capitalism. And, yet, all too often, this distinction is not made.[21] Yet, it is crucially important that this be done. For crony capitalism mulcts money from some people, taxpayers, and gives it to others, businessmen of the Musk ilk. How can this be justified? Certainly not on the basis of the progressive's

---

relieves the bad guys (statists) of their illicit gains and turns them over to the oppressed, only this time they are honest businessmen.

[20] For an alternative point of view, consider the words of Hamilton (2016) writing for Breitbart: "Yet make no mistake—the Planetary Resourcers [sic] are fully revolutionary. None of them are interested in waiting around to see what the federal government is willing to do in space—although, in their pragmatism, they are willing to work with NASA. Still, it has surely has crossed the mind of these investors that there's no EPA in space; indeed, space can be seen as one universe-sized enterprise zone."

[21] This is something that Vermont Senator Bernie Sanders and Pope Francis have in common. Neither makes this distinction. Indeed, they are oblivious to it. Joke: Do you know the difference between a living room and a bathroom? No? Then don't come to my house. Serious: Do you know the difference between crony and *laissez-faire* capitalism? No? Then don't get into political economy, for this constitutes one of the most vital distinctions in that entire field.

favorite principle: egalitarianism. For the recipient in this case is far wealthier than the average taxpayer. Nor can it be defended as promoting economic well-being. Indeed, the very opposite is the case. Rather, this constitutes a vast misallocation of resources from how these monies would otherwise be spent[22] and in the direction of a businessman who "cannot (be allowed) to fail." That is just the point. Musk enterprises are in this way propped up by government. It would be a great embarrassment to the state were they to go bankrupt.[23] In effect, they are no longer, if ever they were, passing any sort of market profit and loss test that all other firms must do every day. Instead, whether or not they are efficient, they will survive for another day as long as the taxman continues to subsidizes them.

The crony capitalism discussed herein is a good example of one reason why advocacy of state largesse for a favored project is self-defeating. When one promotes government support of a cause such as, say, feeding the hungry, one effectively gives moral permission for others to push their own favorite programs. The term for this is "moral hazard." An excellent maxim in this regard follows: "Deprivations from violence of the sort used by the state to attain 'noble' goals will always and everywhere fall most heavily on those least able to defend themselves." We can surmise that Musk is adept at this sort of manipulation. Without knowing it, the advocate for food stamps is ethically approving military expenditures, journeys to the Moon, and nuclear research, etc.; and he is enabling Musk and company.

That a sizable proportion of the subsidies given to Musk enterprises do not consist of cash handouts is one complication. Rather, some of the support comes to him in the form of lowered taxes, tax breaks, or "loopholes." That is, these corporations either pay less tax than other companies, or none at all. And this is a challenge to libertarian theory. For the latter favors lowering tax rates and revenues; indeed, eliminating them entirely.

---

[22] Presumably money not collected by the tax man would be spent on consumer goods such as bicycles, violins, computers, clothes, etc.; or invested in industries favored by the *owners* of these resources.

[23] Regarding embarrassing bankruptcies, think Solyndra. On this see Carden 2011; Holcombe 2014.

Jeff Bezos

Another strong contributor from the private sector to space flight is Jeff Bezos. He started his company, Blue Origin, in 2000, to develop a vertical take-off and landing apparatus, the New Shepard. His goal, among others, was space tourism; taking high-paying customers off the planet.

However, he too is hip-deep in subsidies from the government, taking in a cool $269.3 million. Perhaps, though, he is less guilty of violations of strict *laissez-faire* capitalism in that virtually all the money invested in his space-going firm is his own.[24] Only some 5% of it emanates from government tax coffers (Faust 2014).[25] Compared to $4.9 billion for Musk, this is chicken feed.

How does Bezos see this matter? Does he offer any defense, explanation, for his deviation from the straight and narrow? We found no speeches of his that touch upon this topic. The same holds true for his interviews. In the absence of any justification from him on this matter, we must conclude, tentatively, that his free-enterprise credentials are at least somewhat tarnished. On the positive side, he says: "It's not that rare to hear a junior leader defend a bad outcome with something like, 'Well, we followed the process.'…Good inventors and designers deeply understand their customer. They spend tremendous energy developing that intuition. They study and understand many anecdotes rather than only the averages you'll find on surveys" (Bezos 2017). This demonstrates a type of thinking that is not seen among bureaucrats.

Richard Branson

A nod to Richard Branson[26] is necessary for a complete listing of businessmen active in the space industry. Branson is the creator and CEO of Virgin Galactic, set up in 2004, utilizing "spaceship one" technology to promote off-world tourism. Seats were sold for some $200,000, a hefty

---

[24] Which Bezos earned from setting up and running Amazon, a private company that receives no known subsidies from the state.
[25] Is receiving only 5% financing from taxpayers akin to being a "little bit" pregnant?
[26] Sir Richard Charles Nicholas Branson.

price indeed, to some very famous people such as "Brad Pitt, Tom Hanks, Katy Perry, Paris Hilton, and Stephen Hawking" (Impey, p. 88).

However, Branson and government handouts are no strangers. According to Chakrabortty (2013): "[The] Virgin boss liked to move into industries sheltered from too much competition, pull subsidies out of taxpayers and then cash out… Branson has built his business empire with millions from you, me and other taxpayers."[27]

Is there anything exculpatory in his life that might resurrect his claim to libertarianism? There is not much, but there is something. Branson is on record as arguing that Britain should legalize drugs and follow the path of Portugal (Wintour 2015). Then, too, Sir Richard "had to cope with a long and brutal fight with government-subsidized British Airways" (Impey, p. 87). On the other hand, he pals around with Al Gore, and swallows whole, to the tune of $3 billion,[28] the philosophy of government restrictions as the necessary course for addressing climate change (Chibber 2009). Let us call that at least a complete offset of his free-enterprise credentials, if ever there were any.

Peter Diamandis

Medical doctor Diamandis is co-founder of the Zero Gravity Corporation, Space Adventures Ltd., International Space University, and Planetary Resources, and founder of Students for the Exploration and Development of Space and the Rocket Racing League. That ought to qualify him for membership as a space entrepreneur.

How does he stack up on the corporate welfare question? Not that well. Here is a statement from him (Diamandis 2015): "It's sad that the U.S. government doesn't fund risky research anymore." Why sad? Presumably, because, in his view, this is something that the U.S. government should do, once did, but no longer engages in. This is hardly a libertarian sentiment.

---

[27] See also on this Haymond 2014; Wheeler 2014; Runciman 2014; Bower 2014.
[28] At least in terms of promises, if not fulfillment (Runciman 2014).

On the other hand, there is some evidence of Diamandis' libertarianism. One is that he "… thought governments would never have the nimbleness or stomach for risk to take on the challenge of space. Worse, they prefer to smother innovation in red tape" (Impey, p. 93). Continues this author: "When Diamandis presented his idea[29] to the FAA, they said regulations wouldn't permit passengers to be in a diving airplane with their seat belts unstrapped." Then there is this gem: his "Lunar X Prize… offers $30-million to anyone who, *without government subsidy*, lands a robot on the moon" (emphasis added; see Reynolds 2012).

Of the four leaders of the space industry so far considered, it is fair to say that this candidate wins the free-market prize.

United Launch Alliance (ULA)

ULA is a joint venture between Lockheed Martin Space Systems and Boeing Defense, Space & Security. Formed in December 2006, this company is hand in glove with the U.S. military and its defense[30] establishment.

There is no one business person who stands out as the leader of this initiative, as in the cases mentioned above. As to an assessment from a libertarian perspective, it is difficult to avoid the conclusion that ULA, as in the case of its parent corporations, Boeing[31] and Lockheed Martin,[32] cannot be counted as stalwarts of the free-enterprise system.

---

[29] His Zero G Corporation would give paying customers "a nauseating but exhilarating experience" (Impey, p. 93) of weightlessness.

[30] This is the word usually associated with these companies, and it does indeed work with the U.S. Department of Defense. However, given the number of U.S. military bases abroad, a more accurate description might be Department of Offense. Previously, this institution was known as the Department of War. Perhaps "Department of Imperialism" would be yet more truthful, in that there are some 800 U.S. military bases in 140 countries. See on this Department of Defense 2007; Vance 2010.

[31] For critiques of the Boeing corporation from a free-market point of view see Dillow 2015a, b; Holler 2015; Steinhart 2014; Palmer and Herb 2015.

[32] For critiques of the Lockheed Martin corporation from a free-market point of view see Jopson 2014; Hartung 2016.

Burt Rutan

According to his review of Impey (2015), Foust (2015) states: "In the chapter celebrating entrepreneurial space, Impey places on a pedestal four individuals: Burt Rutan, Richard Branson, Peter Diamandis, and Elon Musk." Rutan, then, can take his rightful place amongst the space entrepreneurs we are vetting. How well does he do through the prism we are using as a focus? For the most part, his career is apolitical; in that regard, he is neutral on our scoresheet. However, as a somewhat peripheral matter, we must award him very, very high marks for this statement of his:

> I put myself in the (Those who fear expansion of Government control) group, and do not hide the fact that I have a clear bias on Anthropogenic global warming (AGW). My bias is based on fear of Government expansion and the observation of AGW data presentation fraud—not based on financial or any other personal benefit. I merely have found that the closer you look at the data and alarmists' presentations, the more fraud you find and the less you think there is an AGW problem....[33] (Rutan n.d.)

No one can be all bad from a free-enterprise point of view who says anything like that. True, this is a bit removed from privatized space exploration, but we have not been able to ascertain Rutan's views on that matter.

Paul Allen

This businessman is of course most noted for being a co-founder of Microsoft, along with Bill Gates. And, to be sure, computers are not unrelated to space exploration. However, we include him in this listing not for that company, but for SpaceShipOne (Howell 2013; Sharp 2014; Poeter 2015). This effort of his won the Ansari X-Prize in 2004. This is described as follows: "the Ansari XPRIZE challenged teams from around

---

[33] Why fraud? What do the deceivers hope to gain? The answer is power. The remedies to "climate change" recommended by statists inevitably involve increased restrictions and new, more draconian "laws." Thus, they have more ability to threaten people with jail and other sanctions in the hopes of controlling the actions of innocents. In addition, these purveyors of deception hope to, and do, collect fees and fines with which to line their pockets and further their agendas.

the world to build a reliable, reusable, privately financed, manned space-ship capable of carrying three people to 100 kilometers above the Earth's surface twice within two weeks" (Ansari Prize 2004). Thus, his credentials as a space entrepreneur are solid.

How does he do from a libertarian perspective? According to Martin (2010), Mr. Allen donates to candidates from both major parties, which does not exactly earn him any credit with libertarianism. However, he did oppose a tax increase for the very rich. But it is unclear if he did this out of self-preservation or because he philosophically favors low taxes. Either way, this most assuredly does earn him some credit with advocates of free enterprise and limited government.

On the other hand, and there is another hand, Mr. Allen also sup-ported Washington State's ballot initiative 1401 in the year 2015 (Detrick 2015; Brunner 2015; Doughton 2015; Banse 2015). This has the effect of banning the sale and "trafficking" of endangered species such as "any covered animal species or product, to include elephant, rhinoceros, tiger, lion, leopard, cheetah, pangolin, marine turtle, shark, and ray." Thus, we can view him as a sort of "watermelon";[34] he does not rely on the power of the free-enterprise system to save species, but instead depends upon governmental central planning. The reason for the endangerment of these animals is of course they are not allowed by law to be privately owned. Thus, the "tragedy of the commons" lays waste to them. Incentives to protect them are all but extinguished. The sheep and the vicuña[35] are similar species in many ways. The former, almost always privately owned, never approached extinction, while the latter, for many years prohibited from ownership, certainly did. Paul Allen is no friend of free enterprise (or of endangered species for that matter), at least in this regard,[36] To be sure, this field is rather removed from our main concern of outer space, but his behavior here gives an indication of his underlying philosophy.

---

[34] Green on the outside, but red on the inside.

[35] An Andes Mountains camelid. Their coats provide the ultimate in fine sartorial luxury (Coggins 2013).

[36] For the case that private ownership is the last best hope we have of preserving endangered species, see Anderson and Hill 1995; French 2012; Lora 2007; Kreuter and Platts 1996; Simmons and Kreuter 1989.

Orbital ATK

Here is a message from the CEO of this company, David W. Thompson (2016):

> Welcome to Orbital ATK! We are a new global aerospace and defense enterprise that combines two great companies—Orbital Sciences Corporation and ATK Aerospace and Defense—who have shared over 25 years of successful collaboration in developing and producing innovative and affordable technologies. Building on the storied history of both companies, Orbital ATK strives to be a global leader in space, defense, and aviation markets. The company's fundamental purpose is to create outstanding value for our customers by providing safe, reliable, and affordable products and systems that enable or enhance commercial, civil government, and defense operations. Guided by this goal, we aim to generate attractive financial returns for our investors, provide challenging and rewarding careers for our employees, create positive business opportunities for our suppliers and partners, *and support the men and women of our armed forces who protect our freedom every day.* By providing dependable and affordable aerospace and defense technologies, Orbital ATK is dedicated to being 'The Partner You Can Count On.'
>
> I hope you find the information about Orbital ATK on our web site to be useful. Please do not hesitate to contact our operating group leaders, business development managers, investor or public relations specialists, and human resource professionals if you would like to learn more about our company.[37]

If the U.S. military did indeed "protect our freedom every day" then Thompson's support for this institution would be unexceptionable; indeed, it would be fully compatible with libertarianism. But the facts of the matter simply do not support any such contention. Our armed forces occupy some 160 countries, with about 1000 military bases. The U.S. budget for soldiers, sailors, and marines is greater than the amount spent by the next 15 countries in terms of this type of expenditure (Department of Defense 2007; Vance 2010). This is hardly compatible with "protection" or defense. Rather, it reeks of *offense*, and imperialism. Thus, it is difficult to consider this entrepreneur as supportive of liberty and libertarianism.[38]

---

[37] Emphasis added by present authors.

[38] All too often libertarianism is conflated with conservatism, or neo-conservatism, or with the "right wing." Exhibit "A" on this is the Federalist Society which is predicated on an amalgamation

What Distinguishes a Libertarian from a Crony?

Some people might argue that our position is contradictory. On the contrary, we reject the favoritism meted out to these "capitalists." Why them?[39] Are there not otherwise deserving individuals who could benefit from government giving them a pass[40] on taxes? Of course there are. But on the other hand, we necessarily take the position that government revenues are morally and economically[41] suspect, and should be reduced as much as possible; and giving cash to, or lowering taxes paid by capitalists, or anyone else, accomplishes this goal. A similar challenge faces libertarians regarding the tax-exempt status of churches. There is no vindication for singling out that industry, *vis-à-vis* any other; but, we applaud the fact that some people are not paying taxes. This supposed problem is only one more reason for total and complete rejection of the tax system. The conflict would not arise in a libertarian society. So, without embarrassment we support "both/and." That is, first, the reduction or preferably the elimination of every single tax we can accomplish even if that implies the use of loopholes for that purpose. Second, we wish to reduce taxation as

---

of libertarians and conservatives. See on this Meyer (1962), Rothbard (1981). To be sure, these groups would indeed support a bloated military budget, and an armed force that throws its weight around the world. But, this is very different from the libertarian foreign policies of the founding fathers of our nation. For example, George Washington (1796): "The great rule of conduct for us in regard to foreign nations is in extending our commercial relations, *to have with them as little political connection as possible*" (emphasis added). Thomas Jefferson (1801): "Peace, commerce, and honest friendship with all nations, *entangling alliances with none*" (emphasis added). John Quincy Adams (2005): "America…goes not abroad seeking monsters to destroy."

[39] The explanation of this favoritism by the state is that Musk and the others are loot-seekers par excellence. In the Public Choice literature, this is called "rent-seeking" but our description is far more accurate. See on this Bhagwati 1982; Block 2000a, b, 2002; Henderson 2008; Pasour 1986; Wenzel 2016.

[40] This is sometimes called a "tax subsidy" or "tax expenditure." The idea here is that the government, in not collecting taxes that might otherwise accrue to it, is really subsidizing those folks privileged in this manner. Bosh and tosh. This only holds true if the state is the legitimate owner of the entire GDP. Then, yes, anything it gives back to the long-suffering taxpayers is indeed a subsidy to them. But where is the warrant to suppose that the state is the proper owner of everything, or anything, its residents have produced in any given year? Rather, the *people* are the proper owners of what they create, and taxes forcibly taken from them amount to no less than theft. See on this: Spooner 1966 [1870]; Napolitano 2013; Rothbard 1970, 1998.

[41] For the argument that government expenditures should be *subtracted* from the private sector see Rothbard 1963; Batemarco 1987.

much as possible, even if taxes cannot be entirely eliminated. We want to eradicate all taxes, *and* we do want to cut these revenues wherever we can, even if incompletely. Only where others, who do not share our view, have made it politically impossible to accomplish our preferred goal must we on a case-by-case basis choose the most pressing objective. That does not diminish our commitment to this aim.

Take another case. We are now back in the year 1861 and, for some reason, have the power to end slavery; but not for *all* innocent people victimized by this hideous crime, only for some of them. Posit, then, that we can free all slaves who are left-handed, but no others. Should we do so? Of course, we should! Freeing only, say, 5% of slaves is better than not allowing any of them to escape from this "curious institution." Our only choice, by stipulation, is to free this small group of people, or none at all. On the other hand, this scenario is exquisitely perturbing. Left-handed slaves are no more deserving of being freed than are right-handed ones. Choosing to free only members of the former category is unfair to all others.[42] Yet, we aver, the correct thing to do is to free only that small proportion of slaves over whom we have this ability. Given the limitations of this hypothetical scenario, we *must* stand idly by, and acquiesce in the continued, highly unjustified kidnapping of all the others. However, we would not *remain* idle or acquiescent. Oh, NO! We achieve what we can for the time being and continue to fight for the total elimination of this injustice without abatement.

We thus oppose direct government handouts,[43] *and* paradoxically applaud the fact that these innovators are protected from some taxes that will be levied on their competitors, even though this will undoubtedly misallocate resources. Better that some are not required to pay taxes, than none.

---

[42] This is sometimes called lack of horizontal justice.

[43] Again, a complication rears its head. Ragnar Danneskjold, a hero of Rand (1957), relieved the government of its ill-gotten (tax) gains and returned them to victims of state violence such as Midas Mulligan, Ken Danagger, Francisco d'Anconia, John Galt, and other fictional characters. (Rand does not explain how he killed no one, even state employees, but assures her readers that this was so.) The problem with Musk as a beneficiary of tax revenues is that he is a *crony* capitalist. Were matters otherwise, we would applaud this. For example, we see John Hospers (late chairman of the philosophy department at the University of Southern California, a state institution) as a non-crony capitalist. Block (2012) justifies him receiving tax monies.

Conclusion

We may have been a tad harsh on several of the businessmen we have discussed in this chapter. Yes, some of the transfers of funds from the state to their firms were outright subsidies. In the absence of any Ragnar Danneskjold type of defense, these are clearly outside the realm of private property and *laissez-faire* capitalism. However, a significant part of these payments concerns contracts between them and the government to provide specific services. Are these categorically incompatible with free markets? In the early days of flight, a significant part of commercial airline revenue emanated from contracts with the U.S. post office to transport mail. Were these firms banished from the honor roll of free enterprise for interacting with the state in this manner? No, to do so would amount to an extreme form of puritanism. Then, there is the case of Ron Paul and Ludwig von Mises[44] who also "contracted" with the government. To exclude these economic actors from the honorific of "libertarian" would be too narrow minded. Our solution to these conundrums is as follows. Having anything to do with government, anything at all, is to be, presumptively, a statist. However, this is only a presumption. It can be overturned. How so? By actively working to oppose, undermine, and denigrate socialism,[45] fascism,[46] and crony capitalism. Do Paul and von Mises meet these standards? Their lives were dedicated to fighting these criminal philosophies from within. What about Branson, Bezos, and Musk et al.? Alas, we doubt they can pass this more reasonable test.

---

[44] Many dozens of other libertarians in good standing were and are employed by public enterprises such as universities. This includes the second author of the present book, an employee of Loyola University New Orleans which accepts government largesse, and does nothing, officially, to mitigate this.

[45] From an economic point of view, socialism implies support for government ownership of all means of production; for example, Kim's North Korea, Stalin's U.S.S.R., Mao's China.

[46] From an economic point of view, this implies support for governmental heavy regulation of industry. The Nazi party, paradigm case of fascism, did not own Stuka, BMW, Volkswagen, or other German companies; it only exercised effective proprietary-like control of them. Thus, Barack Obama (apart from taking ownership in Detroit auto companies), Bernie Sanders, Hillary Clinton, are not really socialists. Rather, fascists. Of course, this is all from a technical economic point of view. In common parlance, "socialist" now means, in effect, egalitarians, and all three, at least verbally, qualify as socialists under that rubric.

A critic might object to the position we have taken on the following grounds. Consider the view of Murray Rothbard, who can be fairly characterized as "Mr. Libertarian" if anyone can be so labelled. In his view, teaching and writing and many other professions were functions that would occur even without the state, as opposed to fighting offensive wars, or creating a central bank, and therefore it would be compatible for libertarians to undertake such positions, even when organized by the state. That is a justification that sounds like the actions of the folks we have been lambasting for insufficiently supporting the free-enterprise system. The undeniable facts are, we must live in the society in which we exist, and the state has an immense presence. So even though we oppose state ownership, we yet drive along state-owned roads and eat food grown by government-subsidized farmers (which applies to the senior author of this book). Are we therefore statists because we take advantage of these amenities? Clearly that is what our critics would say. They would accuse us of hypocrisy. Should we not therefore lighten up, and simply live with the fact that space exploration has been overwhelmingly usurped by government? Yes, we must of course advocate against it, but maybe we should not blame those who do not.

While we have sympathy for this argument and understand the difficulties involved, we reject the criticism. It is not an entirely unreasonable one, but we are attempting to separate the sheep from the goats, and we must have some means of doing so. Calhounism and libertarian ruling-class theory are good first attempts. But if we are to truly distinguish between corporate monopoly, state crony capitalists, on the one hand, and those who are not guilty of these positions, we must employ *some* criteria, however imprecise. The criterion we have chosen is presumption of guilt. If you take vast sums of government money, mulcted from the long-suffering taxpayer at the point of a gun, you must do *something* to distinguish yourself from those who would be found guilty under libertarian law. If you do nothing and, to add insult to injury, use some of these vast riches to support measures incompatible with the free society, all we can say is that if the shoe fits, wear it.

References

Adams, John Quincy. 2005. *Congressional Record*. 109th Congress. First Session. Vol. 151, Part 4, March 11. https://books.google.com/books?id=eaCIX6d3Y 5YC&pg=PA4864&lpg=PA4864&dq=%22goes+not+abroad+seeking+mon sters%22&source=bl&ots=7y-SeZRFm0&sig=IoiE22eag3F5i3MFMGmVP qVaX5A&hl=en&sa=X&ved=0ahUKEwio-9D3yZfOAhUHbiYKHc-J0AyMQ6AEIKTAD#v=onepage&q=%22goes%20not%20abroad%20 seeking%20monsters%22&f=false. Accessed 28 July 2016.

Anderson, Terry, and P.J. Hill. 1979. An American Experiment in Anarcho-Capitalism: The Not So Wild, Wild West. *The Journal of Libertarian Studies* 3: 9–29. http://mises.org/journals/jls/3_1/3_1_2.pdf. Accessed 11 June 2016.

Anderson, Terry L., and Peter J. Hill, eds. 1995. *Wildlife in the Marketplace*. Lanham, MD: Rowman & Littlefield.

Ansari Prize. 2004. Funded by the Ansari Family, the Ansari XPRIZE Challenged Teams from Around the World to Build a Reliable, Privately Financed, Manned Spaceship Capable of Carrying Three People to 100 Kilometers Above the Earth's Surface Twice Within Two Weeks. The Prize Was Awarded in 2004 and Along with It, a Brand New Private Space Industry Was Launched. November 6. http://ansari.xprize.org/. Accessed 3 Aug 2016.

Autry, Greg. 2015. Everybody Hates a Winner: Elon Musk, the Government and the Damn Yankees Syndrome. June 4. http://www.huffingtonpost.com/greg-autry/everybody-hates-a-winner-_b_7508114.html. Accessed 29 June 2016.

Banse, Tom. 2015. Washington State Votes Overwhelmingly to Shut Down Ivory Trade. November 3. http://nwnewsnetwork.org/post/washington-state-votes-overwhelmingly-shut-down-ivory-trade. Accessed 28 July 2016.

Batemarco, Robert. 1987. GNP, PPR, and the Standard of Living. *The Review of Austrian Economics* 181–186. https://mises.org/library/gnp-ppr-and-standard-living.

Bensen, Bruse L. 1989. The Spontaneous Evolution of Commercial Law. *Southern Economic Journal* 55: 644–661.

———. 1990a. Customary Law with Private Means of Resolving Disputes and Dispensing Justice: A Description of a Modern System of Law and Order Without State Coercion. *The Journal of Libertarian Studies* IX (2): 25–42. http://mises.org/journals/jls/9_2/9_2_2.pdf. Accessed 11 June 2016.

———. 1990b. *The Enterprise of Law: Justice Without the State*. San Francisco: Pacific Research Institute for Public Policy.

Bergland, David. 1986. *Libertarianism in One Lesson*. Costa Mesa, CA: Orpheus Publications.

Bezos, Jeff. 2017. 2016 Letter to Shareholders. April 12. https://www.amazon.com/p/feature/z6o9g6sysxur57t. Accessed 18 May 2017.

Bhagwati, Jagdish N. 1982. Directly Unproductive, Profit-Seeking (DUP) Activities. *Journal of Political Economy* 90 (5): 988–1002. http://www.jstor.org/discover/10.2307/1837129?uid=3739400&uid=2&uid=3737720&uid=4&sid=21105317504383. Accessed 11 June 2016.

Block, Walter. 2007. Anarchism and Minarchism; No Rapprochement Possible: Reply to Tibor Machan. *The Journal of Libertarian Studies* 21 (1): 91–99. http://www.mises.org/journals/jls/21_1/21_1_5.pdf. Accessed 11 June 2016.

———. 2002. All Government Is Excessive: A Rejoinder to 'In Defense of Excessive Government' by Dwight Lee. *Journal of Libertarian Studies* 16 (3): 35–82. http://www.mises.org/journals/jls/16_3/16_3_3.pdf. Accessed 11 June 2016.

Block, Walter E. 2006. Radical Libertarianism: Applying Libertarian Principles to Dealing with the Unjust Government, Part II. Reason Papers 28 (Spring): 85–109. http://www.walterblock.com/publications/block_radical-libertarianism-rp.pdf; http://www.walterblock.com/wp-content/uploads/publications/block_radicallibertarianism-rp.pdf. (death penalty justified, net taxpayer, ruling class analysis, p. 87).

———. 2008. Homesteading, Ad Coelum, Owning Views and Forestalling. *The Social Sciences* 3 (2): 96–103. http://www.medwelljournals.com/fulltext/TSS/2008/96-103.pdf; http://medwelljournals.com/new/5/archivedetails.php?id=5&jid=TSS&theme=5&issueno=12. Accessed 20 Apr 2016.

———. 2000a. Watch Your Language. February 21. http://www.mises.org/fullarticle.asp?control=385&month=17&title=Watch+Your+Language&id=19; http://mises.org/daily/385. Accessed 11 June 2016.

———. 2000b. Word Watch. April 20. http://www.mises.org/fullstory.asp?control=414&FS=Word+Watch. Accessed 23 Apr 2016.

———. 2010. Review of Huebert's Libertarianism Today. *Libertarian Papers*. http://libertarianpapers.org/2010/19-block-review-of-hueberts-libertarianism-today/. Accessed 29 June 2016.

———. 2011a. Governmental Inevitability: Reply to Holcombe. *Journal of Libertarian Studies* 22: 667–688. http://mises.org/journals/jls/22_1/22_1_34.pdf. Accessed 11 June 2016.

———. 2011b. Review Essay of Ostrom, Elinor. 1990. *Governing the Commons: The Evolution of Institutions for Collective Action*. Cambridge and New York: Cambridge University Press. In *Libertarian Papers*, Vol. 3, Art. 21. http://libertarianpapers.org/2011/21-block-review-of-ostroms-governing-the-commons/.

———. 2012. *Yes to Ron Paul and Liberty*. New York: Ishi Press. http://www.amazon.com/dp/4871873234; http://libertycrier.com/education/walterblocksnew-book-on-ron-paul/; http://libertyunbound.com/node/862. Accessed 23 May 2016.

———. 2014. Book Review Essay of Steven Pinker's: *The Better Angels of Our Nature: Why Violence Has Declined.* New York, N.Y. Penguin; Part II. *Management Education Science Technology Journal MEST* 2 (1): 141–160.

Bohm-Bawerk, Eugen. 1959 [1884]. *Capital and Interest.* South Holland, IL: Libertarian Press. Trans. George D. Hunke and Hans F. Sennholz. See Particularly Part I, Chapter XII, Exploitation Theory of Socialism-Communism.

———. 2011. *Karl Marx and the Close of His System.* CreateSpace Independent Publishing Platform.

Bower, Tom. 2014. *Branson: Behind the Mask.* Faber.

Brunner, Jim. 2015. Paul Allen Bankrolls Initiative to Ban Rare-Species Trafficking. April 26. http://www.seattletimes.com/seattle-news/politics/paul-allen-backs-state-ban-on-rare-species-trafficking/. Accessed 28 July 2016.

Burris, Charles A. 2012. Who Rules America: Power Elite Analysis and American History. January 18. http://archive.lewrockwell.com/burris/burris21.1.html.

Calhoun, John C. 1953 [1853]. *A Disquisition on Government.* Ed.: Post, C. Gordon. *A Disquisition on Government and Selections from the Discourse.* Edited, with an Introduction. New York: Liberal Arts Press.

Cantillon, Richard. 2011. The Value of Labor. October 21. https://mises.org/library/value-labor.

Carden, Art. 2011. Who Could Have Predicted that the Solyndra Deal Wouldn't Work Out? October 10. https://mises.org/blog/who-could-have-predicted-solyndra-deal-wouldn%E2%80%99t-work-out.

Casey, Doug. 2010. Doug Casey on Anarchy. March 31. http://www.caseyresearch.com/cwc/doug-casey-anarchy. Accessed 23 Aug 2016.

Chakrabortty, Aditya. 2013. The Truth About Richard Branson's Virgin Rail Profits. June 10. http://www.theguardian.com/commentisfree/2013/jun/10/truth-richard-branson-virgin-rail-profits. Accessed 29 June 2016.

Chambers, Dean. 2015. Heavily Subsidized and Failing: Elon Musk and SolarCity. December 14. http://www.redstate.com/diary/qstarweb/2015/12/14/heavily-subsidized-failing-elon-musk-solarcity/. Accessed 17 June 2016.

Chandra, Ambarish, Sumeet Gulati, and Milind Kandlikar. 2009. Green Drivers or Free Riders? An Analysis of Tax Rebates for Hybrid Vehicles. February 24. SSRN: http://ssrn.com/abstract=1348808. Accessed 23 May 2016.

Chibber, Kabir. 2009. How Green Is Richard Branson? August 5. http://www.wired.co.uk/magazine/archive/2009/09/start/how-green-is-richard-branson. Accessed 29 June 2016.

Coggins, David. 2013. Why Does a Vicuña Jacket Cost $21,000? *Wall Street Journal*. September 20. http://www.wsj.com/articles/SB10001424127887323392204579073090614851288. Accessed 21 June 2016.

Dillow, Clay. 2015a. Boeing, GE Beat Tea Party as Congress Revives Export-Import Bank. December 4. http://fortune.com/2015/12/04/congressexport-import-bank. Accessed 29 June 2016.

———. 2015b. Obama Is About to Give Private Space Companies a Big Break. November 24. http://fortune.com/2015/11/24/obama-commercial-space-break/. Accessed 6 Dec 2015.

DeBord, Matthew. 2015. Elon Musk's Companies Have Always Depended on Government Money—And He's Has Always Been Up Front About It. June 8. http://www.businessinsider.com/elon-musk-always-depended-government-money-up-front-about-it-2015-6. Accessed 29 June 2016.

Department of Defense. 2007. Base Structure Report. http://www.defenselink.mil/pubs/BSR_2007_Baseline.pdf. Accessed 28 July 2016.

Detrick, Chloe. 2015. Washington Voters Approve Anti-Wildlife-Trafficking Initiative, I-1401, In a Landslide. November 4. http://www.humanesociety.org/news/press_releases/2015/11/washington-approves-wildlife-initative.html?referrer=https://www.google.com/. Accessed 28 July 2016.

Diamandis, Peter. 2015. Entrepreneurs, Not Government, Drive Innovation—Here's Why. July 14. https://www.linkedin.com/pulse/entrepreneurs-government-drive-innovation-heres-why-peter-diamandis?forceNoSplash=true. Accessed 29 June 2016.

DiLorenzo, Thomas J. 2010. The Culture of Violence in the American West: Myth Versus Reality. *The Independent Review* 15 (2): 227–239. http://www.independent.org/pdf/tir/tir_15_02_4_dilorenzo.pdf. Accessed 23 Aug 2016.

Domhoff, G. William. 1967. *Who Rules America?* Englewood Cliffs, NJ: Prentice-Hall.

———. 1971. *The Higher Circles: The Governing Class in America*. New York: Vintage Books.

———. 1998. *Who Rules America? Power and Politics in the Year 2000*. 3rd ed. Santa Cruz: University of California.

Donaldson, Mike, and Scott Poynting. 2007. *Ruling Class Men: Money, Sex, Power*. Peter Lang. http://books.google.com/books/about/Ruling_Class_Men.html?id=V-KjZ8p3N2oC.

Doughton, Sandi. 2015. Anti-poaching Campaign Is State's Richest this Year; Bankrolled by Billionaire Paul Allen, pro-Initiative-1401 Committee Has Raised more than Twice as much Money as Any Other Political Effort this

Year. October 29. http://www.seattletimes.com/seattle-news/politics/anti-poaching-campaign-is-states-richest-this-year/. Accessed 28 July 2016.

Faust, Jeff. 2014. Bezos Investment in Blue Origin Exceeds $500 Million. July 18. http://spacenews.com/41299bezos-investment-in-blue-origin-exceeds-500-million/. Accessed 29 June 2016.

Foust, Jeff. 2015. Book Review of *Beyond: Our Future in Space* by Chris Impey. May 11. http://www.thespacereview.com/article/2746/1. Accessed 29 June 2016.

French, Doug. 2012. Property Means Preservation. May 31. http://mises.org/daily/5960/. Accessed 11 June 2016.

Gordon, David. 1991. *Resurrecting Marx: The Analytical Marxist on Exploitation, Freedom and Justice.* Transaction Publishers.

Gregory, Anthony. 2011. Abolish the Police. May 26. http://www.lewrockwell.com/gregory/gregory213.html. Accessed 23 Aug 2016.

Guillory, Gil, and Patrick Tinsley. 2009. The Role of Subscription-Based Patrol and Restitution in the Future of Liberty. *Libertarian Papers* 1 (12). http://libertarianpapers.org/2009/12-the-role-of-subscription-based-patrol-and-restitution-in-the-future-of-liberty/. Accessed 23 Aug 2016.

Hamilton. 2016. The Two Kinds of Libertarianism: Calhounian and Heinleinian. *Breitbart.* November 16. http://www.breitbart.com/big-government/2013/11/16/the-two-kinds-of-libertarianism-calhounian-and-heinleinian/. Accessed 15 June 2016.

Hankoff, Nick. 2014. Top 5 Libertarian Quotes from Billionaire Elon Musk. *Voices of Liberty.* November 10. https://voicesofliberty.com/2014/11/10/top-5-libertarian-quotes-from-billionaire-elon-musk/6/. Accessed 20 June 2016.

Hartung, William. 2016. Lockheed Martin, Making Money the Old-Fashioned Way. March 17. http://www.huffingtonpost.com/william-hartung/lockheed-martin-making-mo_b_9486334.html. Accessed 29 June 2016.

Hasnas, John. 1995. The Myth of the Rule of Law. *Wisconsin Law Review* 199. http://faculty.msb.edu/hasnasj/GTWebSite/MythWeb.htm. Accessed 23 Aug 2016.

Haymond, Jeff. 2014. Top 1%'er Richard Branson Advocates for more Subsidies to the Rich! January 22. http://bereansatthegate.com/top-1er-richard-branson-advocates-for-more-subsidies-to-the-rich/. Accessed 29 June 2016.

Heinrich, David J. 2010. Justice for All Without the State. *The Libertarian Standard.* May 6. http://www.libertarianstandard.com/articles/david-j-heinrich/justice-for-all-without-the-state/. Accessed 23 Aug 2016.

Henderson, David R. 2008. Rent Seeking. In *The Concise Encyclopedia of Economics*, ed. David R. Henderson. Indianapolis, IN: The Liberty Fund. http://www.econlib.org/library/Enc/RentSeeking.html. Accessed 11 June 2016.

Higgs, Robert. 2009. Why We Couldn't Abolish Slavery Then and Can't Abolish Government Now. August 20. http://www.lewrockwell.com/higgs/higgs128. html. Accessed 23 Aug 2016.

———. 2012. What Is the Point of My Libertarian Anarchism? January 16. http://archive.lewrockwell.com/higgs/higgs180.html. Accessed 23 Aug 2016.

Hirsch, Jerry. 2015. Elon Musk's Growing Empire Is Fueled by $4.9 Billion in Government Subsidies. May 30. http://www.latimes.com/business/la-fi-hy-musk-subsidies-20150531-story.html#page=1. Accessed 29 June 2016.

Holcombe, Randall G. 2014. President Obama's Investment Skills. March 12. https://mises.org/blog/president-obama%E2%80%99s-investment-skills.

Holler, Dan. 2015. Don't Believe the Hype: Boeing Will Be Just Fine Without the Export-Import Bank; The Sky Isn't Falling, and Companies Like Boeing Certainly Don't Need You to Guarantee Their Business Model. August 27. https://sanantonioteaparty.us/dont-believe-the-hype-boeing-will-be-just-fine-without-the-export-import-bank/. Accessed 29 June 2016.

Hoppe, Hans-Hermann. 1989. Fallacies of the Public Goods Theory and the Production of Security. *The Journal of Libertarian Studies* IX (1): 27–46. http://www.mises.org/journals/jls/9_1/9_1_2.pdf. Accessed 23 Apr 2016.

———. 1990. Marxist and Austrian Class Analysis. *The Journal of Libertarian Studies* 9 (2): 79–94. http://mises.org/journals/jls/9_2/9_2_5.pdf.

———. 1993. *The Economics and Thics of Private Property. Studies in Political Economy and Philosophy*. Boston: Kluwer Academic Publishers.

———. 2008. Reflections on the Origin and the Stability of the State. June 23. http://www.lewrockwell.com/hoppe/hoppe18.html. Accessed 23 Aug 2016.

———. 2011. State or Private Law Society. April 10. http://www.lewrockwell. com/hoppe/hoppe26.1.html. Accessed 23 Aug 2016.

Howell, Elizabeth. 2013. Paul Allen: Billionaire Backer of Private Space Ventures. January 18. http://www.space.com/19333-paul-allen.html. Accessed 28 July 2016.

Huebert, Jacob. 2010. *Libertarianism Today*. Santa Barbara, CA: Praeger.

Hughes, Jonathan R.T. 1977. *The Governmental Habit: Economic Controls from Colonial Times to the Present*. New York: Basic Books.

Impey, Chris. 2015. *Beyond: Our Future in Space*. W. W. Norton & Company.

Jefferson, Thomas. 1801. Inaugural Address. March 4. http://avalon.law.yale. edu/19th_century/jefinau1.asp. Accessed 28 July 2016.

Jenkins, Holman W, Jr. 2016. Voters Should Be Mad at Electric Cars; If Trump and Sanders Fans Hate Absurd Handouts to Elites, the Tesla Economy Is the Place to Look. March 11. http://www.wsj.com/articles/voters-should-be-mad-at-electric-cars-1457737805. Accessed 23 May 2016.

Jopson, Barney. 2014. Roosevelt-era Bank Faces Tea Party Assault. June 25. http://www.ft.com/cms/s/0/5f0dbe14-fc89-11e3-86dc-00144feab7de. html#axzz4D0nfgjVt. Accessed 29 June 2016.

Kelly, Martha Hall. 2016. *Lilac Girls*. New York: Ballantine Books.

Kim, Kihoon. 2014. The Analysis of Government Financial Subsidies for the Electric Car Market. *The Korean Operations and Management Science Society* 39 (3): 41–49. http://www.koreascience.or.kr/article/ArticleFullRecord. jsp?cn=GOGGBB_2014_v39n3_41. Accessed 23 May 2016.

King, Seth. 2010. *Daily Anarchist* Interviews Walter E. Block. September 9. http://www.lewrockwell.com/block/block165.html. Accessed 23 Aug 2016.

Kinsella, Stephan N. 2009. What Libertarianism Is. August 21. https://mises. org/library/what-libertarianism. Accessed 23 Apr 2016.

Koch, Charles. 2015. The Good Profit: How Creating Value for Others Built One of the World's Most Successful Companies. Crown Business. https:// www.amazon.com/Good-Profit-Creating-Successful-Companies-ebook/dp/ B00TWEMGE8.

Kolko, Gabriel. 1963. *Triumph of Conservatism*. Chicago: Quadrangle Books.

Kreuter, Urs P., and Linda E. Platts. 1996. Why the Ivory Ban Is Failing. *Christian Science Monitor*. March 20. http://perc.org/articles/why-ivory-ban-failing. Accessed 11 June 2016.

Long, Roderick. 2004. Libertarian Anarchism: Responses to Ten Objections. http://www.lewrockwell.com/long/long11.html. Accessed 23 Aug 2016.

Lora, Manuel. 2007. If You Love Nature, Desocialize It. May 10. http://mises. org/daily/2539. Accessed 11 June 2016.

Maltsev, Yuri N. 1993. *Requiem for Marx*. CreateSpace Independent Publishing Platform.

Martin, Jonathan. 2010. Paul Allen gives $100,000 to Defeat Income-Tax Initiative. October 12. http://old.seattletimes.com/html/politicsnorthwest/2013139340_paul_allens_moment.html?syndication=rss. Accessed 11 June 2016.

McConkey, Michael. 2013. Anarchy, Sovereignty, and the State of Exception: Schmitt's Challenge. *The Independent Review*, v. 17, n. 3, pp. 415–428. http://www.independent.org/pdf/tir/tir_17_03_05_mcconkey.pdf. Accessed 23 Aug 2016.

Melchoir, Jillian Kay. 2015. SolarCity Can't Shine Without Subsidies. January 14. http://www.iwf.org/news/2799084/SolarCity-Can't-Shine-Without-Subsidies. Accessed 17 June 2016.

Meyer, Frank S. 1962. *In Defense of Freedom*. Chicago: Henry Regnery.

Molyneux, Stefan. 2008. The Stateless Society: An Examination of Alternatives. http://www.mail-archive.com/libertarianenterprise@yahoogroups.com/msg02056.html. Accessed 23 Aug 2016.

Murphy, Robert P. 2005. But Wouldn't Warlords Take Over? July 7. http://mises.org/story/1855; http://mises.org/library/wouldnt-warlords-take-over. Accessed 23 Aug 2016.

———. 2006. The Labor Theory of Value: A Critique of Carson's Studies in Mutualist Political Economy. *The Journal of Libertarian Studies* 20 (1). http://mises.org/journals/jls/20_1/20_1_3.pdf. Accessed 29 June 2016.

———. 2011. Problems with the Cost Theory of Value. May 23. https://mises.org/library/problems-cost-theory-value. Accessed 29 June 2016.

Murray, Charles. 1984. *Losing Ground: American Social Policy from 1950 to 1980*. New York: Basic Books.

Napolitano, Andrew. 2013. Taxation Is Theft; The Constitution Doesn't Permit the Feds to Steal Your Money. But Steal, the Feds Do. April 18. http://reason.com/archives/2013/04/18/taxation-is-theft. Accessed 28 July 2016.

Narveson, Jan. 1988. *The Libertarian Idea*. Philadelphia: Temple University Press.

Nozick, Robert. 1974. *Anarchy, State and Utopia*. New York: Basic Books.

Oppenheimer, Franz. 1975 [1914]. *The State*. New York: Free Life Editions.

Orwell, George. 1949. *Nineteen Eighty-Four*. London: Harvill Secker.

Palmer, Anna, and Jeremy Herb. 2015. Boeing, GE Cut Off Donations to Ex-Im Foes. August 5. http://www.politico.com/story/2015/08/boeing-ge-cut-off-donations-to-ex-im-opponents-121056. Accessed 29 June 2016.

Pasour, E.C., Jr. 1986. Rent Seeking: Some Conceptual Problems and Implications. *Review of Austrian Economics* 1: 123–143. http://mises.org/journals/rae/pdf/RAE1_1_8.pdf; http://mises.org/sites/default/files/rae1_1_8_5.pdf; http://mises.org/library/rent-seeking-some-conceptual-problems-and-implications. Accessed 11 June 2016.

Peters, Eric. 2016. Now Uncle Is 'Investing' in Tesla. Autos, Automobiles, Motorcycles, and Libertarian Politics. August 14. http://ericpetersautos.com/2016/08/14/now-uncle-investing-tesla/; https://www.lewrockwell.com/2016/08/eric-peters/champion-crony-capitalist/. Accessed 17 Aug 2016.

Poeter, Damon. 2015. Check Out Paul Allen's Giant Rocket-Toting Monster Plane. February 26. http://www.pcmag.com/article2/0,2817,2477458,00.asp. Accessed 28 July 2016.

Raico, Ralph. 1977. Classical Liberal Exploitation Theory: A Comment on Professor Liggio's Paper. *The Journal of Libertarian Studies* 1 (3): 179–184. http://mises.org/daily/4567/.

Rand, Ayn. 1957. *Atlas Shrugged*. New York: Random House.

Reisman, George. 2006. Freedom Is Slavery: Laissez-Faire Capitalism Is Government Intervention: A Critique of Kevin Carson's Studies in Mutualist Political Economy. *The Journal of Libertarian Studies* 20 (1). http://mises.org/journals/jls/20_1/20_1_5.pdf. Accessed 29 June 2016.

Reynolds, Neil. 2012. Waiting for the Age of Abundance. April 16. http://www.theglobeandmail.com/report-on-business/rob-commentary/waiting-for-the-age-of-abundance/article4100664/. Accessed 29 June 2016.

Richards, Tori. 2015. Sunset of Solar Subsidies Shadows SolarCity. June 23. http://watchdog.org/225430/solarcity/. Accessed 17 June 2016.

Ridley, Matt. 2015. *The Evolution of Everything: How New Ideas Emerge*. New York: Harper.

Rockwell, Lew. 2013. What Would We Do Without the State? March 31. http://www.lewrockwell.com/blog/lewrw/archives/134782.html. Accessed 23 Aug 2016.

Rockwell, Jr., Llewellyn H. 2001. Liberty and the Common Good. December 31. http://www.mises.org/article.aspx?Id=860.

———. 2014. What Libertarianism Is, and Isn't. March 31. http://www.lewrockwell.com/2014/03/lew-rockwell/what-libertarianism-is-and-isnt/. Accessed 29 June 2016.

Rothbard, Murray N. 1963. *America's Great Depression*. Kansas City: Sheed Andrews. http://www.mises.org/rothbard/agd.pdf. Accessed 23 May 2016.

———. 1970. *Power and Market: Government and the Economy*. Menlo Park, CA: Institute for Humane Studies.

———. 1973. *For a New Liberty*. New York: Macmillan. http://mises.org/rothbard/newlibertywhole.asp. Accessed 23 Aug 2016.

———. 1975a. *Conceived in Liberty, Volumes I & II—A New Land, A New People, The American Colonies in the Seventeenth Century*. New Rochelle, NY: Arlington House Publishers. With the Assistance of Leonard P. Liggio.

———. 1975b. Society Without a State. *The Libertarian Forum* 7 (1), January. http://www.lewrockwell.com/rothbard/rothbard133.html. Accessed 23 Aug 2016.

———. 1977. Do You Hate the State? *The Libertarian Forum* 10 (7), July. http://www.lewrockwell.com/rothbard/rothbard75.html. Accessed 23 Aug 2016.

———. 1981. Frank S. Meyer: The Fusionist as Libertarian Manque. *Modern Age* 352–363. https://mises.org/library/frank-s-meyer-fusionist-libertarian-manqu%C3%A9. Accessed 28 July 2016.

————. 1998 [1982]. Isaiah Berlin on Negative Freedom. In *The Ethics of Liberty*, chapter 27, 215–218. New York: New York University Press. http://www.mises.org/rothbard/ethics/ethics.asp. Accessed 20 Apr 2016.

————. 2004. The Case for Revisionism (and Against A Priori History). http://mises.org/library/case-revisionism-and-against-priori-history.

Runciman, David. 2014. The Stuntman. *London Review of Books* 36 (6): 21–25. http://www.lrb.co.uk/v36/n06/david-runciman/the-stuntman. Accessed 29 June 2016.

Sharp, Tim. 2014. SpaceShipOne: The First Private Spacecraft | The Most Amazing Flying Machines Ever. October 2. http://www.space.com/16769-spaceshipone-first-private-spacecraft.html. Accessed 28 July 2016.

Simmons, Randy, and Kreuter, Urs P. 1989. Herd Mentality: Banning Ivory Sales Is No Way to Save the Elephant. *Policy Review* (50): 46–49. http://agrilifecdn.tamu.edu/kreuter/files/2013/01/Simmons-Kreuter-1989_3.pdf. Accessed 11 June 2016.

Spooner, Lysander. 1966 [1870]. *No Treason: The Constitution of No Authority and A Letter to Thomas F. Bayard*. Larkspur, CO: Rampart College. http://jim.com/treason.htm. Accessed 23 Aug 2016.

Steele, David Ramsay. 1981. Posing the Problem: The Impossibility of Economic Calculation Under Socialism. *The Journal of Libertarian Studies* V (1): 7–22. http://www.mises.org/journals/jls/5_1/5_1_2.pdf. Accessed 29 June 2016.

————. 1992. *From Marx to Mises: Post Capitalist Society and the Challenge of Economic Calculation*. La Salle, IL: Open Court.

Steinhart, Dan. 2014. How the Tea Party Caused a Plane Crash. June 13. https://www.caseyresearch.com/articles/how-the-tea-party-caused-a-plane-crash. Accessed 29 June 2016.

Stigler, George J. 1958. Ricardo and the 93 Per Cent Labor Theory of Value. *American Economic Review* 48 (June): 357–367.

Stringham, Edward., ed. 2007. *Anarchy and the Law: The Political Economy of Choice*. Somerset, NJ: Transaction Publishers.

Tannehill, Morris, and Linda Tannehill. 1984 [1970]. The Market for Liberty, New York: Laissez Faire Books. http://www.lewrockwell.com/orig11/tannehill1.html. Accessed 23 Aug 2016.

Thatcher, Margaret. 1976. Interview for *Thames TV*, February 5.

Thompson, David W. 2016. CEO's Welcome. https://www.orbitalatk.com/about/ceos-welcome. Accessed 11 June 2016.

Tinsley, Patrick. 1998–1999. With Liberty and Justice for All: A Case for Private Police. *Journal of Libertarian Studies* 14 (1): 95–100. http://www.mises.org/journals/jls/14_1/14_1_5.pdf. Accessed 23 Aug 2016.

Vance, Laurence M. 2010. Same Empire, Different Emperor. February 11. http://www.lewrockwell.com/vance/vance195.html. Accessed 28 July 2016.

Vaughn, Karen I. 1978. John Locke and the Labor Theory of Value. *The Journal of Libertarian Studies* 2 (4): 311–325.

Von Mises, Ludwig. 1978. *The Clash of Group Interests and Other Essays.* New York: Center for Libertarian Studies. http://www.mises.org/etexts/mises/clash/clash.asp.

———. 1981 [1922]. *Socialism: An Economic and Sociological Analysis.* Trans. J. Kahane. Indianapolis: Liberty Fund. http://mises.org/books/socialism/contents.aspx.

Washington, George. 1796. Farewell Address. http://oll.libertyfund.org/quote/246. Accessed 28 July 2016.

Wenzel, Robert. 2013. Robert Ringer's Strawman Anarchist. February 2. http://archive.lewrockwell.com/wenzel/wenzel211.html. Accessed 23 Aug 2016.

———. 2016. Walter Block on the Intellectual War Path. April 25. http://www.economicpolicyjournal.com/2016/04/walter-block-on-intellectual-war-path.html?utm_source=feedburner&utm_medium=email&utm_campaign=Feed%3A+economicpolicyjournal%2FKpwH+%28EconomicPolicyJournal.com%29. Accessed 11 June 2016.

Wheeler, Joshua. 2014. Failure to Launch: How New Mexico Is Paying for Richard Branson's Space Tourism Fantasy. March 20. http://www.buzzfeed.com/jgwheel/failure-to-launch-how-new-mexico-is-paying-for-richard-brans#.sel3ryvP8. Accessed 29 June 2016.

Wintour, Patrick. 2015. UK Should Begin Decriminalising Drugs, Say Richard Branson and Nick Clegg. March 3. http://www.theguardian.com/politics/2015/mar/03/uk-should-begin-decriminalising-drugs-richard-branson-nick-clegg. Accessed 29 June 2016.

Woods, Tom. 2010. *Nullification: How to Resist Federal Tyranny in the 21st Century.* Washington, DC: Regnery Publishing.

———. 2013. The Question Libertarians Just Can't Answer. June 5. http://lewrockwell.com/woods/woods237.html. Accessed 29 June 2016.

———. 2014. Four Things the State Is Not. July 29. http://www.lewrockwell.com/2014/07/no_author/4-things-the-state-is-not/. Accessed 23 Aug 2016.

Woolridge, William C. 1970. *Uncle Sam the Monopoly Man.* New Rochelle, NY: Arlington House.

Wynn, Todd and Steve Lafleur. 2009. A Free Market Perspective on Electric Vehicles. October. http://cascadepolicy.org/pdf/env/FMPonElecVehicles_100109a.pdf. Accessed 23 May 2016.

15

Space-Oriented Writers

This chapter is devoted to a literature review of other books such as ours, whose subject matter is space travel and colonization of other heavenly bodies. But there are two caveats. First, there are not dozens or even scores of such volumes that have been published; rather, they number, literally, in the hundreds, if not thousands. We can thus only comment on a small sample of this gigantic literature. Our selection is biased in the direction of more recent publications. We do so for purposes of practicability. That is, we deal, solely, with books that focus on challenges faced by early space-farers and how to deal with them.

The second caveat is that we shall not merely be describing these other missives, as might be the practice of a professional book reviewer. Instead, we shall be looking at them from the vantage point of the same prism that motivates the present volume. What is the motivation for extra-planetary travel? Ours is primarily on the side of profitable human endeavor and to preserve our species from possible annihilation due, mainly, to governments and politicians. We also write from the free-enterprise perspective: to promote liberty in yet another manner. We maintain that the types of extra-terrestrial efforts which rely least of all on the apparatus of the state are better, and far preferable, to that which

© The Author(s) 2018
P. L. Nelson, W. E. Block, *Space Capitalism*, Palgrave Studies in Classical Liberalism,
https://doi.org/10.1007/978-3-319-74651-7_15

depends upon this apparatus to a greater degree. We favor completely private efforts as the best possible scenario of them all.

Third, many if not all the entries on this list have authors who may be characterized as space fans, not to say fanatics.[1] In their view, the race to other planets is now on, and the sooner humans set permanent foot off world, the better. In our view, in contrast, the timing of this mission should ideally depend only on the profit motive.[2] Whatever period entrepreneurs want to go boldly to hitherto unexplored regions is the best time for us as a species to go. But what about the urgency we feel for ensuring that at least some human beings reside elsewhere, so as to promote our preservation? We are supporters of Adam Smith's (1776) "invisible hand."[3] Thus, we maintain that the optimal date of departure for "greener" planets will tend to be precisely the one for which profits can expect to be maximized. And this applies, too, to other technological innovations such as warding off a mischievous asteroid intent upon crashing into our home planet. Too soon, and we are doomed to failure. Too late, and our beloved Earth takes on undue risk.

Why should that precise timing be necessary? No one could possibly have earned a profit from such endeavors 500 years ago. Anyone who tried would go broke, and their failure would discourage others from pursuing this goal. Successful entrepreneurs are precisely those who are *not* bankrupt. They are those who have, in the recent past, efficaciously evaluated the future better than others. Who can we place above them in terms of expecting success in the next time period? Bureaucrats who have never met a payroll? Politicians whose expertise lies in generating support from low-information voters? We speculate that undertaking these tasks 500 years from now will be way too late, in terms of optimal timing. Businessmen who wait that long have missed the bus; ok, the rocket ship. No, the best, least-biased estimator of the optimal time to pursue this goal lies with businessmen who have skin in the game and emerged from past commercial interaction with it intact, or enhanced. They have previously risked their own capital, or that voluntarily entrusted to them by other economic actors, and are now once again willing

---

[1] We the word "fan" in the non-critical sense of sports fans, opera fans, or chess fans.

[2] Of course, we by no means confine profit to monetary gains. Psychic income in economic parlance, or satisfaction in ordinary language, is an integral part of profits in our view.

[3] According to Rothbard (1987) the concept of the invisible hand was not original with Smith. Also, see Ahiakpor (1992, 1999, 2008) who defends Smith on this and many other grounds.

to roll the dice on this new project. With this introduction, we are now ready to begin commenting upon various contributions to this field. We start with

Petranek, Stephen L. 2015. *How we'll live on Mars*. New York: Simon and Schuster

This author starts out on the wrong foot with his dedication page showing the following quote:

> I want Americans to win the race for the kinds of discoveries that unleash new jobs…pushing out into the solar system not just to visit, but to stay. Last month, we launched a new spacecraft as part of a reenergized space program that will send American astronauts to Mars. —President Barack Obama, State of the Union Address, January 20, 2015

Nowhere in the U.S. Constitution, Obama's presumed contract[4] with the American people, does it mention space travel. The National Aeronautics and Space Administration (NASA) has been a disaster. Visiting or remaining on another planet is thus no proper part of any president's job description. However, Petranek quickly redeems himself with this passage on the very next page:

> Nearly a decade of anticipation has come down to this moment: the space-craft inches to the surface as the blast effect of braking rockets kicks up red dust. An Earth-bound audience waits eagerly as an announcer reminds them of a press conference that took place years earlier—a meeting that shocked the world and embarrassed NASA, which was still at least two years from testing its Mars spacecraft with humans aboard. On that day, the company behind this private effort to reach Mars revealed that it was about to build a series of huge rockets to transport people to Mars, and that within a decade it would launch one or two of them to effect the first manned landing on the Red Planet.

---

[4] For a critique of this way of looking at the matter see Spooner (1870) which claims there is no such valid contract in existence.

No author who extols "private effort" that "embarrassed NASA" can be all bad, no matter what else he says.

We also learn (pp. 2–3) that while Martian temperatures can reach a balmy 70 degrees Fahrenheit on a summer day (i.e. at the perihelion) at the equator, during the evening in the same season and place, the thermometer can fall to a not so idyllic negative 100 degrees Fahrenheit, and thus Earthlings on the fourth planet will need heavy and sophisticated protection from the weather. Whereupon this author shows his views about one aspect of settlement as perfectly congruent with our own. He states (pp. 5–6):

> When these rockets land on Mars in the near future, it will be far more than a great moment for exploration. It will not be nothing less than an insurance policy for humanity. There are real threats to the continuation of the human race on Earth, including our failure to save the home planet from ecological destruction[5] and the possibility of nuclear war. Collision with a single asteroid could eliminate most life, and eventually our own sun will enlarge and destroy Earth. Long before that happens, we must become a spacefaring species, capable of living not only on another planet but ultimately in other solar systems. The first humans who emigrate to Mars are our best hope for the survival of our species. Their tiny base will grow into a settlement, and perhaps even a new species that will expand rapidly. The company which built the rocket that brought them there is building hundreds more rockets. The intention is to create a viable population of 50,000 within a few decades. They can preserve the collective wisdom and achievement of humanity even if those of us back on Earth are annihilated.

---

[5] The current authors regard ecological destruction to be hyperbolic, which is not the same thing as non-existent. It is a ploy by statists to raise fear in order to justify a renewal of some form or other of eugenics. Symptomatic of their hubris is the assumption that humans are likely to destroy the Earth, not with nuclear weapons but with air-conditioners and underarm deodorants. From the time of Malthus (and perhaps earlier) one supposed disaster after another has been proposed as the end of humankind and the only solution to which was the imposition of harsh controls by the elite. Should disaster strike, the third rock will be destroyed, as Petranek suggests, by the cataclysmic impact of another massive space object such as a planetoid, a supermassive asteroid, or the evolution of the Sun to red giant status. As for the end of humanity, should the environment evolve towards one uninhabitable by men, they will adapt to the new conditions. A more likely cause would be the natural evolution of a superhuman species which will be able to cope. Regarding the claim that what real environmental problems do exist (e.g. pollution) this is the fault of government, not capitalism, see Rothbard (1982a, b).

We could have written those words ourselves, so in step with our own views are they. We especially appreciate Petranek speaking about "the company," yet another overlap between him and your present authors. However, we must demur from one small aspect of this otherwise splendid statement. We part company from him regarding the risk of "ecological destruction." We do so for three reasons. One, we doubt the evidence so far put forth for so pessimistic a conclusion. Second, weathermen have great difficulty predicting the temperature a few hours, let alone days or weeks, hence. How can we have any confidence about their assessments for a decade or two or even more? Third, we take note of the fact that there is not really a fair debate going on amongst those scholars contending over this issue. One side characterizes the other as "deniers,"[6] tries to get their opponents fired from their jobs, and even in extreme circumstances attempts to imprison those with whom they disagree.[7] Why is all this hysteria and nastiness employed if their gloomy predictions are correct? How can non-specialists in meteorology even begin to trust the supposed consensus of professionals that emanates from such a flawed process?

But, once again, our author (p. 6) soon redeems himself. He castigates "one U.S. president (who) stunted space travel for decades" and calls for progress "in a nonregulated way." Petranek's chapter 1 offers a history of the Mars Project, Sputnik, Carl Sagan's novel *Contact*, the Saturn V rocket, Werner von Braun, and once again (p. 14) quite properly attacks "NASA's years of slip-sliding away and the fact that it allowed contractors to work on a cost-plus basis." No, we applaud any author with so negative a view of government bureaucrats.

We are particularly grateful for chapter 2 of his book, entitled "The Great *Private*[8] Space Race," which starts out on a high note, not only criticizing government involvement, but also several crony capitalists along the way. He states (p. 15): "Getting into space has always seemed the province of governments that can afford the high cost of entry. The Boeing and Lockheed Martin space businesses, for example, largely happened because NASA and the US military were willing to write cost-plus contracts."

---

[6] Krugman 2015 piles it on a bit deeply, as can be seen, merely, from the title of his essay. We know full well from whence the word "denier" springs: from the history of the Holocaust.

[7] See on this Bastasch 2015a, b, Cook 2015; Delingpole 2015; Lewis 2015; Olson 2015.

[8] Emphasis added by present authors.

Other high points of this chapter include emphasis (p. 16) on essentially private actions in the space race including Orbital Sciences Corporation, Orbital ATK, Robert Zubrin,[9] and "Dutchmen Bas Lansdorp and Arno Wielders (who) formed the nonprofit Mars One[10] to launch one-way trips to the Red Planet." Compliments are also properly paid to (pp. 16–17), "Dennis Tito, the first private citizen to buy his way into space by paying the Russians a reported $20 million. His nonprofit organization, Inspiration Mars, optimistically plans to send a small spacecraft—perhaps the *Crew Dragon* spacecraft under development by SpaceX for manned flights to the International Space Station—to Mars with a married couple aboard in 2021." According to our author, other members of the honor roll include Jeff Bezos, Larry Page, Paul Allen, Sir Richard Branson, and Elon Musk,[11] businessmen all, something rarely mentioned in the literature.

However, we must once again take note of a jarring point made by our author. He states (p. 17): "Most of the efforts so far are as chaotic as the Wild West, but this time the frontier is space." Which efforts is Petranek speaking about? Why, those of the men mentioned in the previous paragraph regarding giving the human a *private* boost toward space exploration and colonization. But his assessment of the "wild west" is mistaken as a perusal of Anderson and Hill (1979, 2004) will demonstrate.[12] As per usual, our author once again recovers from this slip, ending this chapter on the following splendid note (p. 20):

---

[9] Zubrin is a bit of a space fan, see *supra*, but no one is perfect.

[10] The non-profits, along with profit-seeking corporations, together comprise the private sector of the economy. Both act compatibly with the non-aggression principle (NAP) of libertarianism.

[11] See above for a discussion as to whether or not Musk belongs on this list. Petranek (p. 19) says this of Musk. He "is in love with the idea that humans should become a spacefaring society. He is keenly aware that Earth will not be habitable forever. Musk seems frustrated by our denial about what we are doing to our habitat, and is ever cognizant of a simple fact: humans will become extinct if we do not reach beyond Earth."

[12] Why is it important, in a book about the future of space exploration, to be clear on what did or did not occur in the supposedly "wild west." For one thing, *all* publications should strive for accuracy. For another, when human beings set up off-world colonies, they will be as far removed, no, further, from the seats of power on earth as denizens of the "wild west" were from the centers of power in Washington D.C., or, generally, in the "East." Future interactions may well be analogous to those in the past, and if we cannot learn from them, what, oh what, is the benefit of history? According to that old aphorism, those who do not know or understand what has happened before are less likely to apply its lessons to their challenges. But if we are to do so successfully, we must have an accurate depiction of what actually occurred in that epoch.

No one can point a finger at the exact moment when NASA finally woke up and smelled the red dust, but when SpaceX's first *Dragon* capsule successfully reached the International Space Station in May of 2012, it immediately became obvious that a private company could probably do anything NASA could—and perhaps do it better.

We only quarrel with the "perhaps." Our reasoning is that private companies must pass a daily if not hourly market test of profit and loss (Hazlitt 1946) which is unknown in statist circles. If only for this one reason, the presumption must always and ever be that the former will be more efficient than the latter.[13]

Chapter 5 is devoted to the economics of setting up shop on Mars. We learn that rocket reusability will create (p. 30) "incredible cost savings" and that the sale of broadcasting rights (p. 36) can help finance this initiative. But now consider this (p. 31):

If reusability isn't achieved, Musk said, 'I just don't think we'll be able to afford it, because it's a difference between something costing a half a percentage each year of GDP and all the GDP.' Then he added: 'I think most people would agree, even if they don't intend to go themselves, that if we're spending something between a quarter to a half a percent of GDP on establishing a self-sustaining civilization on another planet [it] is probably worth doing. It's sort of a life insurance policy for life, collectively, and that seems like a reasonable insurance premium, and plus it would be a fun adventure to watch even if you don't participate.' Just as, when people went to the moon, only a few people actually went to the moon, but in a sense, we all went there vicariously. I think most people would say that was a good thing. When people look back and say, what were the good things that occurred in the twentieth century, that would have to be right near the top of the list. So I think there's value, even if someone doesn't go themselves.

---

[13] Then, too, there is a large empirical literature attesting to this conclusion. See Anderson and Hill 1996; Block 2002, 2009; Butler 1988; Carnis 2003; Ebeling 2013; Hanke 1987a, b; Hannesson 2004, 2006; Hoppe 2011; Karpoff 2001; Megginson 2001; Moore 1987; Moore and Butler 1987; Motichek et al. 2008; Ohashi 1980; Ohashi et al. 1980; Pirie 1986; Savas 1987; Walker 1988; White 1978.

Petranek quotes (p. 31) Musk's estimated one-way ticket price to Mars as $500,000. At first this sounds like a privately financed adventure (which libertarians would gladly support), especially because over the next few pages he goes on to discuss optimistically how many people there will be who will want to purchase fares. He even gives examples of likely types of adventurers. It sounds very good and positive: just what this book advocates. However, he extols (p. 38) "NASA's commitment to eventually using its *Orion* system to land humans on Mars."[14] He continues to praise similar efforts of European, Russian, and other state-run agencies. On page 29, he again looks to NASA as the group of officials who "are evaluating an increase in the limits of radiation astronauts are *allowed*[15] to experience as a way to get them to Mars *under operating guidelines*" (emphasis added). Imagine the uproar and penalties to be imposed should Space X change the rules. And he repeatedly looks to governmental initiatives for solutions to intractable problems with no mention of how private enterprises would do it.

The issue ignored by Petranek (and Musk as well) is that it is all well and good for individuals to decide for themselves whether to purchase insurance. But this is not at all what is under discussion in the present context. Rather, what is being talked about is whether people, all of us, should be *forced* to pony up the premiums. Whether it is 0.5% or 100% of GDP makes no difference. It is the principle that is important, at least from the libertarian perspective. And in that viewpoint, no one should be compelled to do anything at all, no matter how important such an action would be to others.[16]

But are we being unfair to both Petranek and Musk here? It might be argued by these two gentlemen and their defenders that opinions regarding inadequate GDP or reusable rockets do not themselves imply the use

---

[14] The full quote is as follows: "Prodded by Musk's bold plans and NASA's commitment to eventually using its *Orion* system to land humans on Mars, every spacefaring nation has joined the race to establish a presence on the Red Planet. In 2016, the European Space Agency will partner with Roscosmos, the Russian Federal Space Agency, to launch a Mars orbiter."

[15] The only person to determine whether a Mars traveler should be "allowed" to increase the allowable radiation dosage is the astronaut in person or his medical advisers, not some bureaucrat working in some neo-classical building in D.C., or a modern one in Cape Canaveral or Houston.

[16] We should all be constrained, prohibited, only from engaging in initiatory violence. Thus, laws against murder, theft, rape, arson, kidnapping, are the only ones that would be justified.

of force; neither does a statement that establishing a civilization on another planet is worth doing. Unless they themselves actually say that these concerns mandate a need for taxes or other form of coercion, then our criticism seems unjustified. We reject this possible defense of theirs. Musk says, and Petranek in quoting him does not demur, that the *government* moon landing was a "good thing." They double down: it was "right near the top of the list" of welcome initiatives. But they cannot plead ignorance of the fact that this so-called "good thing" was financed from taxes, which are compulsory. Suppose the present authors wrote that government expenditure on a park or museum would be a "good thing." They would then be guilty of supporting the use of force against innocent people, since this park or museum could only come into existence on the basis of taxation. If these two commentators feel so strongly about it, whatever it is, space exploration, health care, pensions, etc. let *them* pay for it, and/or ask for voluntary contributions toward these ends.[17] Taxation is not the only issue, Petranek decries certain private institutions and avers (page 74) that:

Any discussion of settling Mars needs to recognize the slippery slope between need and greed.[18] Although there are no native populations on Mars to overwhelm, there could easily be an unrestrained rush for material resources,[19] devastation of the environment,[20] destruction of sites valuable to scientific inquiry,[21] and even a temptation to re-create indentured servi-

---

[17] For the public good market failure objection see Chap. 11.

[18] Greed, the second of the Seven Deadly Sins, is often misunderstood especially since materialism has taken hold of Western and even worldwide philosophy. It is not, as commonly interpreted, a desire for material goods. That is an ingrained desire essential to human survival and well-being. It is a compulsive demand for the possessions (material or non-material) of other people even to the point of inspiring a willingness to rob or kill to obtain what is coveted. As such, greed for material goods can be of no concern during the early stages of Martian exploration when no material goods are yet owned.

[19] Horrors! "An unrestrained rush for material resources," what EVER would WE do then? Actually, there would be "restraints" if libertarian law is the order of the day. "First come, first served" would determine which homesteader came to own which property. And, no one would be allowed to interfere with anyone else's peaceful colonization of this unowned territory.

[20] What environment might be "destroyed?" Petranek urges in his chapter 7 how we can remake the planet into earth's image. That would amount to the wholesale substitution of one environment by another. We are reminded of the so-called "Genesis torpedo": *Star Trek IV, The Voyage Home*.

[21] The reference to "valuable" scientific sites suggests that he buys into some kind of intrinsic value theory. In this book, we maintain that land, or any good, has value only according to a human who appreciates it.

tude.[22] The Outer Space Treaty of 1967 and others that followed have attempted to make territory outside the of Earth common ground.[23] But humans have proven that they need laws to govern their behavior and enforcers as well.[24]

We mentioned in Chap. 6 that to live on Mars without support from Earth, we shall have to supply ourselves with air, water, food, shelter, special clothing, etc. But, not to worry: a dab of initiative and some technology now within reach will address these problems. The only jarring note, according to Petranek, is that unless we are willing to eat insects, yuck,[25] humans there will have to become vegans, double yuck. This pessimism is again based on the view of environmentalists that meat eating is intensely consumptive of resources combined with poor understanding of how problems are overcome. If interplanetary settlers want meat badly enough, they will figure it out. Humans are adaptable to many living conditions including those they will find on Mars.

Petranek's chapter 7 is devoted to terraforming, which we deal with in our own Chap. 11. His chapter 8 focuses on the new gold rush: asteroids. They contain valuable resources; so much so that private companies (Planetary Resources, Inc. and Deep Space Industries) have already been set up to exploit them.

Lewis, John S. 1997. *Mining the sky: Untold riches from the asteroids, comets and planets.* New York: Basic Books

---

[22] Indentured servitude is a private contractual agreement and is thus justified. If a man has such a strong desire to settle on Mars that he willingly subjects himself to years of service, who has the right to interfere? This sort of master/servant relationship should not be confused with chattel slavery based on kidnapping.

[23] While Petranek decries environmental destruction, here he hypocritically praises an ownership scheme known to aggravate the worst sort of ecological devastation: the tragedy of the commons.

[24] That humans need laws to govern their behavior is true enough: so long as we are discussing evolved law based on agreements between free people living and working together under the libertarian code. If, instead, as we expect, Petranek is referring to man-made laws not compatible with the non-aggression principle, our Chap. 2 offers the rebuttal.

[25] The more adventurous of the two current authors is open to the possibility that bugs may make good eating. Consider those ugly bug-like creatures called crabs, lobsters, or crayfish. One would think that a resident of New Orleans would better see the virtues of the latter. The less adventurous of the two current authors thinks that the more adventurous of the two current authors is…crazy.

There are three basic premises, or theses, of our present book. One, that it would be a good idea for man to colonize space (starting at the outset with the lowest-hanging fruit: the Moon and Mars). Two, the main reason for so doing is to enhance personal pleasure, increase profit, and preserve humans, of which the present authors, too, are inordinately fond. And three, this task should be undertaken by private enterprise, not government, and not by any unholy (fascistic) combination of the two. Lewis (1997) agrees with the last of these goals of ours. He does so enthusiastically, and provides a wealth of information as to its benefits. But these are, mainly, to attain more physical resources for the betterment and enrichment of those who remain on Earth. That is not part of our motivation at all. Indeed, we regard this as unnecessary, as "running out of resources" here, back on the home planet, is a fallacious notion. We are at present (2016) up to our armpits in resources, and hardly need to venture out into the heavenly bodies to obtain any more.[26] Another divergence we have with Lewis is his view that space exploration should primarily benefit Earthlings.[27] The case against this has been put forth, very dramatically, by Heinlein (1966). In his *The Moon is a Harsh Mistress*, fictional members of the Moon's community seek to separate from the dominion of the Earth, since they wish to keep raw materials from their terrain to themselves, and/or exchange them, but only on mutually agreeable terms of trade, not those determined by the home planet. Unless there are contractual arrangements that stipulate the very opposite, it smacks of colonialism for Earthlings to dictate commercial terms with the Mooniacs. This author has yet another concern which we do not share (p. 10): over-population on earth. Lewis, a latter-day Malthusian, thus sees the heavenly bodies as terrain to house excessive human population.[28]

---

[26] There was a famous bet between Paul Ehrlich and Julian Simon on this very matter. The former lost the wager, and his claim that there is any great likelihood of resource depletion in the near future thus took a dramatic hit. See on this Desrochers 2015; Kellard 1998; McClintick and Emmett 2005; Worstall 2013.

[27] On p. 128, one of his fictional (see explanation chapter introductions below) letter-writing characters views positively "the great worldwide effort to find clean, abundant new energy sources for Earth" in space. He mentions Earth as a mercantilist colonial power on several other occasions, such as (p. 130) where he extols the virtue of "transport(ing) back to Earth from space… commodities."

[28] For a critique of the Malthusian concern with over-population, see Desrochers 2015; Rothbard 2011; Say 1821.

What of our third plank, that off-earth ventures be predicated on free enterprise? Here, Lewis (1997, pp. 5–6), happily, is in accord with this view of ours: "Sadly, the domination of space activities by governments has caused the price of space travel to remain very high… Governments do not need to show a profit, and they have strong institutional incentives to keep costs (and therefore budgets) as high as possible… The cost of launching payloads from Earth into space can be brought down dramatically by using the most elementary principles of free enterprise, starting with free and open competition."

However, we find it difficult to agree with Lewis when he offers this as a reason for off-world exploration (pp. 10–11): "We must keep in mind planet Earth's ebbing supplies of fossil fuels… The exploitation of space technology offers the most attractive solution to the energy problem now visible."[29] We, the present authors, writing in late 2016 when the price of oil keeps dropping, and gasoline is as cheap as it has been in a long time[30] find this author's "the sky is falling" philosophy unconvincing. Also, Lewis seems blissfully unaware of the bet between Paul Ehrlich and Julian Simon on this running-out-of-resources business. The latter won this wager, successfully maintaining that "man's mind" (Simon 1981) is the "ultimate resource" and as long as we do not run out of that, diminutions of physical resources such as fuel present no real challenge.

We must also take issue with this sentiment expressed by the author (p. 11) where he calls for off-world "resources to keep our home planet alive and well." But, surely, at least from a libertarian point of view, the resources discovered on asteroids, comets, moons, etc. should belong to their owners. When and if they want to bring them back to the Earth, well and good. But this should be solely their decision. If, instead, they wish to use them to enrich their colonies elsewhere, that should be acceptable too. This idea that the people on Earth should necessarily be the beneficiaries of extra-planetary exploitation makes as much moral sense, namely none, as the medieval mercantilist system in which colonies existed only to enhance the wealth of the home country.

---

[29] Lewis states further (p. 217): "Millions of informed people are concerned about future energy supplies for Earth" and bewails "the dwindling supplies of crude oil and natural gas."
[30] Refer to commodity prices for "Crude Oil WTI (NYMEX) Price" on the Nasdaq.

Each of the chapters of Lewis' book starts with a fictional "letter" from one spaceman to another, typically dated several centuries in the future. We find these charming, as they give a glimpse to the reader of what life might be like many years from now, in far-away places. For example, the letter from chapter 2 is dated 2091, and tells of how a man born in 1941 (the birth year of the junior co-author of the present volume) came to take up an unearthly career. This chapter tells the story of early pioneers in our interest in space, such as Galileo, Huygens, Isaac Newton, Blaise Pascal, Copernicus, Bessel, Konstantin Tsiolkovsky, Robert Goddard, Hermann Oberth, Jules Verne, and Arthur C. Clarke. It provides an informative history.

In chapter 3 we learn of the Moon and the history of mankind's attempts to incorporate it into our economy. Chapter 4 is devoted to an eight-step plan leading to the provision of air, water, and food for people living on the Moon. An emphasis is placed on the importance of recycling to become self-sufficient.[31] We appreciate this bit of government-bashing on the part of the author (p. 58): "governmental programmatic decisions depend on political factors that often have nothing to do with the logic of mathematics, chemistry, physics, engineering, and economics. The Apollo missions were done not because they were the next logical step in space (they were not), but because of a political decision to beat the Soviet Union to a major space landmark." And again (p. 62): "That humankind should have reached mid-1990s without knowing how to grow food in space, how to deal with weightlessness, and how to counter the effects of cosmic radiation serves as a more powerful condemnation of the Soviet and American manned space programs from 1960 to 1995 than anything else a critic could say." However, unhappily from our point of view, Lewis supports a government bureaucracy (p. 64): "Unfortunately, for over

---

[31] In economic parlance, self-sufficiency is almost a curse word, as it apparently indicates an opposition to free trade. But in the present context, this does not at all apply. Ditto for "economic independence" (p. 73). Why do these two sets of concepts not relate? Both Lewis and the present authors are advocating a type of colonization which would enable survival even should the Earth become obliterated. Therefore, "self-sufficiency" is a long-term mandate. That being understood, the benefits of free trade apply after all. Rather than living in isolation, Martians would profit mightily from economic intercourse not only with each other but also with Earthlings, and so too the stay-behinds would experience gain.

twenty years it was impossible for NASA to get approval for this mission.[32] The proposed NASA mission would have cost no more than 1 percent of what was spent on Apollo." Why NASA should be exalted above practically every other government boondoggle can only be put down to space enthusiasm.[33]

Chapters 5 and 6 are devoted to asteroids and comets. Lewis waxes eloquent about just how valuable are the resources to be obtained from such sources in terms of platinum, iron, nickel, cobalt, osmium, iridium, palladium, etc. He calculates this (p. 112) as "…roughly equivalent to the gross global produce of Earth for the next thirty thousand years." Well, maybe. But, we shall have to deduct to costs of capturing these metals and, more importantly, factor into the equation the fact that when massive amounts of them come on stream, their present prices must inevitably fall.[34] It is more than passingly curious that this author would appear so ignorant of the basics of supply and demand analysis given that elsewhere in his book (p. 229) he seems fully aware of these niceties when he states: "There is so little…production that prices soar…."

We also delight in the title of his chapter 10: "Homesteading Mars." This means that not only will U.S. citizens be able to own materials they take away from other planets, they will also be able to claim as private property acreage on them. This goes quite a bit further down the path toward libertarianism in space than even the law passed in 2015[35] that overturns the idea that space is the equal and common heritage of all Earthlings, whether or not they have done anything to earn this wealth.

---

[32] Lewis (p. 64) describes this as "a small unmanned lunar satellite that would complete the mapping of the Moon's surface and its gravitational and magnetic fields and search for ice at the poles."

[33] In the debates for the Republican nomination for president leading up to the election of 2012, Texas Governor Rick Perry forgot the cabinet departments, agencies, and other government positions he would eliminate (see on this Hechtkopf 2011). NASA certainly was not one of them. The ones he remembered were Education and Commerce; he forgot Energy. The present authors would add NASA to his list.

[34] Lewis dramatically repeats this error with great verve on his pages 193–196. To give the reader the flavor of this over-the-top glee about the great wealth in store for us he states (p. 195) that the value of the iron alone in the asteroid belt is "10,000,000 times as large as the national debt!" Sorry Mr. Lewis, but that is almost certainly not so once expenses are deducted and price adjustments to this new abundance occur.

[35] See our discussion of the U.S. Commercial Space Launch Competitiveness Act in Chap. 12 on space law.

Let us conclude with a minor editing complaint. Lewis generously provides a glossary (pp. 262–264). This is needed, since he makes intensive use of abbreviations. The only difficulty is that not every one of them is listed there. For example LLO appears on page 121, but not in the glossary. Ditto for CELSS (p. 171) and HOOH (p. 170).

Rader, Andrew. 2014. *Leaving Earth: Why one-way to Mars makes sense.* Self-published

This book, as its title makes clear, has a narrow focus regarding settlement on the fourth planet: let us start off with a one-way, non-return trip there. Thus, it is rather orthogonal to our main interests. About its thesis, all we can say is that this decision should be made by the (hopefully) private firms that first venture forth to Mars, their employees, and their financial supporters. However, along the way Rader does have some things to say that overlap with our concerns. For example (p. 8):

> Since Earth is the most habitable planet we know of, why shouldn't we just stay here? There are many answers to this question, but perhaps the simplest is basic survival. We already know of many threats to our civilization, ranging from nuclear war, disease, and resource depletion, to environmental collapse, and impacts from space. Considering how the list has been growing over the past 50 years, it seems likely that there are other threats we aren't even aware of. As Carl Sagan famously said: in the long run, every civilization must become spacefaring to ensure its very survival. A sustainable off-Earth presence would provide an insurance policy which could ensure our continued existence, and prevent us from going the way of the dinosaurs. Considering how little it would cost (as a species, we spend less than 0.1% of our global economic output on spaceflight. We spend more on pet food) us, isn't it simply negligent not to take simple steps to avert potential extinction?

We heartily concur. An off-earth human presence increases the chances that at least some of us will survive.[36] However, we find difficulty in going

---

[36] Of course, if the "differently abled" and other such protected groups are forcibly included in the initial forays, this will reduce the chances of success for the entire enterprise. Were Christopher Columbus, Marco Polo, and those who first walked to the South Pole or climbed Mt. Everest compelled to embrace diversity, and take on people who "looked like" the average members of the

along with Rader completely on these matters. We have already commented, *supra*, on why we see no need to fear "environmental collapse." But what about "resource depletion?" This, in our view, is a fallacious concern on the part of this author. We have never, and never will, run out of resources, at least not if the free-enterprise system is allowed to operate. For as soon as there is any incipient tendency in the direction of unwanted resource reduction, the "magic of the market" comes into operation to obviate the danger. How? Its price rises, and this has several salutary effects. For example, suppose we start to run out of oil.[37] What, pray tell, will happen to its price? Why, it will increase of course, as its supply curve shifts to the left. This beneficial alteration will have several positive effects, all in the direction of preserving this commodity. For one thing, on the demand side people will use less of it. Automobiles will become smaller and more efficient, if the "invisible hand" has anything to say about the matter.[38] A premium will be placed on cars which garner more miles per gallon. On the supply side, it will pay for entrepreneurs to look for more oil deposits, and to dig deeper for them. As well, there will be a move toward substitutes, such as coal, gas, nuclear power, wind, water, solar, etc.[39] After these shifts take place and we are still witnessing a depletion of oil, its price will rise even further, thus empowering the strength of these salutary effects.

Rader offers other benefits of space-faring which, while not lying in the very bull's eye of our own concerns, are still of interest. There is the (p. 10) pursuit of scientific knowledge; the fact that (p. 11) it gives us a unique perspective about our home planet; and it would help improve our technology. Of course, these explanations are sufficient, but not necessary. There is plenty for humans to do on the third rock from the Sun to attain these goals. We need not venture elsewhere to accomplish them.

---

population from whence they sprang? The thought never would have occurred to anyone during those saner times. Furthermore, we regard it as an insult to foist upon someone a task which he is unwilling to undertake regardless of which side of the equation he occupies.

[37] The reader is invited to substitute for this factor of production anything else he wishes: trees, copper, zinc, watermelons, ham, human body parts, whatever.

[38] Increased automobile efficiency will occur automatically without any EPA mandates whatsoever.

[39] More to the point, some resource that is now totally unknown will very likely become available. Petroleum was completely unknown as a fuel to the hunters of whales even as the latter were approaching extinction. Further, consider the use of "sand" (silicon caulking) to take the place of coal tar.

Our author errs in his support for the thesis that "growing populations" (p. 15) place tremendous pressures on our planet. No. This Malthusian concern that subsistence living is just around the corner is unsustainable. If we were ever in all our recorded history, and even before that, faced with this danger on any systematic or massive scale, slavery would have been impossible. For who would go through the trouble of capturing, transporting, guarding, feeding people whose productivity was barely enough to support himself, as the subsistence theory requires. No one, that is who. And, yet, this curious institution has been with us all through written history and likely far before that, too. Therefore, widespread, barely sustainable living was impossible. It is contradicted by the fact of slavery. If this could not have occurred tens of thousands of years ago, it is fair to say that this danger is extremely unlikely to overcome us in the modern era, with technology vastly improved.[40] Nor is Rader's central planning perspective compatible with our own values. He states (pp. 17–18):

> In hindsight, even though people at the time questioned the value of sending people to the Moon, the Apollo program delivered a long-term economic stimulus that can still be traced today.

> Interest in the Apollo program dramatically increased the number of science and engineering graduates at all levels. Every technological field experienced as (sic) surge as a result of the Apollo program—not just those with a direct connection. Children, whose first taste of science was Neil Armstrong's small step, grew up to initiate a tech revolution twenty years later.

> Why not spend the money on Earth to do something like cure cancer instead? There is no doubt that there are other causes, some more important than space exploration. Clearly, sustaining human civilization on Earth is far more important than founding it on other worlds. However, this is a false dichotomy. Far from being in competition with the goal of preserving Earth civilization, establishing a human presence in space would significantly advance this goal.

---

[40] Why are considerations of the non-viability of slavery in the face of subsistence living important? Why are they even relevant to a book concerned with space exploration? We think it so because it is an invalid reason, justification for off-world colonization. We of course favor the latter, assuming profit considerations are in line with them. But, we insist, it is crucial to make the case for this initiative without errors in the premises, such as are now dealt with in the text.

Moreover, space exploration is not actually in competition with other critical tasks we face on Earth. We spend a negligible fraction of our resources exploring space. Going to Mars wouldn't require much—if any—additional investment, if we approach it in the right way.[41] In comparison to the several billions of dollars we spend on space per year (tens per person), critical problems like repairing infrastructure, replacing fossil fuels, or fixing health care, social security, and education require trillions of dollars. Space exploration is one of the highest leverage fields we can pursue in terms of return on investment. The global cost of maintaining a small human settlement on Mars would be insignificant, but the rewards could be immense.

Our problem with this passage is that it evinces a top-down management format that one would hope would be banished from the world after the fall of the Berlin Wall and the undoing of the U.S.S.R. There is simply no room, in this passage, for the decisions of individual entrepreneurs, customers, suppliers, etc.: the emphasis, instead, is on how GDP is "best" spent. Nor can we acquiesce with the notion that these alternative programs are not really "in competition" with each other. No. More money for cancer research necessarily means less for something else, perhaps space exploration, and vice versa of course. Every human action, no exceptions, has alternative or opportunity costs.

Nor can we see our way clear to agreeing with this author's (p. 31) claim that "We need to be bolder and less risk averse when we think about going to space." First, just who is the "we" here? Note that Rader is not saying *he* needs to make this change, perhaps by investing more of his own hard-earned money in companies now contemplating off-world exploration, settlement, mining. Perhaps the "we" is the entire human race. If so, then, this seems too audacious, not to say unmitigated effrontery or animated impudence. Who does he think he is to tell all the rest of us what attitude to adopt? Most likely though, reading between the lines, he is asking that government engages in a more aggressive policy, perhaps through NASA. In which case, this is incompatible with the

---

[41] The RIGHT way? Repeatedly, one statist or another tries to tell us that we only need competent administrators. No, the very nature of government administration and bureaucratic management precludes doing it the "right" way (Von Mises 1944). Another similar classic is "To ensure that it never happens again." When a law such as TARP is enacted to ensure that the financial crisis will never again occur, it inevitably fails to address the root cause, in this case the machinations of the Federal Reserve (Rothbard 1995).

libertarian message animating the present volume, in that virtually every penny spent by this organization is mulcted, at the point of a gun, from a hapless citizenry.

Second, this sort of support for the space program renders Rader an enthusiast. In contrast, the position we take is that the timing of ventures onto the heavenly bodies should emanate "from below" and be based not on dictatorial powers, but on individuals making these decisions for themselves.

An excerpt from his book (pp. 39–43) misleadingly labelled "private space," states (p. 39): "In the long run, space needs to pay for itself. However, large initial government investments in new transportation technologies are the norm rather than exception. Columbus' expeditions were government-funded as were the voyages of Hudson, Magellan, and the most other early explorers. Most historical colonization efforts, like the settlement of Jamestown, were government ventures. The European outposts established throughout the world have had a dramatic impact on the history of the world, and were all paid for by government entities."

Yes, none of this can be denied. However, just because it is indeed the norm for an illicit institution to funnel monies in directions not desired by their owners does not mean it is justified. To borrow a leaf from President Obama's runs for elected office in 2008 and 2012, we can "hope" for a genuine "change" from statists to private funding for reasons articulated all throughout the present book. But Rader is having none of this. He asserts (p. 39): "There are many ventures which have the potential to yield significant returns in the long run, but whose high initial costs make them unattractive to private investors. One of the primary roles of government is to promote long-term prosperity, even when returns are beyond the investment horizon of the private sector."

Sowell (2000) offers the perfect retort to this claim: "It is hard to imagine a more stupid or more dangerous way of making decisions than by putting those decisions in the hands of people who pay no price for being wrong." Indeed, when government errs[42] it cannot go bankrupt. It need not pass any stern market test of profit and loss. To expect the promotion of long-term prosperity from such an institution is indeed "stupid and dangerous." Economic progress stems from private enterprise, not because of the state,

---

[42] See our Chap. 10 for our list of the boondoggles of NASA and other government agencies in the air and in space.

but despite it. Nor is there anything untoward about "high initial costs." Yes, they sometimes are "unattractive to private investors," but certainly not always. Numerous successful industries—oil, steel, automobiles, real estate, hotels, transportation—are earmarked by "high initial costs." Imagine Edison's difficulties in trying to establish Edison Illuminating Company. He had to build both a power plant and a network of wires. He had to obtain control of the land in the middle of Manhattan for both. He had at first almost no customers. That was a difficult and unattractive proposition requiring an extensive sales job to bring financiers on board. Rader admits that (p. 39) "…the relative immunity from financial accountability is precisely why the government also tends to be horribly inefficient as compared with private industry." Does this deter him from his socialist public policy recommendations? No, it does not.[43]

However, this author is right on the money when he writes (p. 64): "The space treaties signed by many nations, including the United States, prohibit private ownership in space. This means that there might be legal troubles with claiming land…" on other heavenly bodies. Unhappily, the latest moves toward allowing off-world free enterprise, while allowing minerals from asteroids to be brought back to Earth, do not address this issue.[44]

We are also grateful to him for including a chapter on how to attract private investors for space exploration (pp. 71–75) and how this could sustain a settlement on Mars. Further, we welcome Rader's libertarian retort to those who object to endangering the first human inhabitants of Mars (p. 87): "What about the ethics of a one-way mission? Is it unethical to send people to somewhere where we can't bring them back? If people understand what they are getting into and agree to it, how could it possibly be unethical? As with medial matters, informed consent and personal liberty should supersede some conventional notion about what risks and sacrifices other people should be willing to tolerate." And again (p. 98): "In terms of a return to Earth, is it ethical to accept these potentially debilitating long term health

---

[43] Rader avers (p. 46): "I would love to see NASA funding doubled." Nor is it even clear that he can make the most elementary distinction between "private" and "public." He maintains (p. 40) "It is not always clear what people mean when they say 'private' or 'commercial' space. In one sense, we've had private space for decades—most military and NASA contractors have, after all, been private companies." But this is crony capitalism, not the *laissez-faire* variety thereof.

[44] On this see Chap. 12 in this book, where we discuss the present situation obtaining regarding space law.

effects? As long as it is voluntary, this seems to me to be a personal choice, a matter of informed consent. People who understand the risks must make the tradeoffs for themselves. Moreover, I fail to see why it is more ethical to subject people to cumulative doses of these effects far in the excess of a Mars mission by flying them in Earth orbit." And here is a further libertarian lagniappe from Rader (p. 99): "Assuming it's all voluntary, I'm not sure there's an ethical problem with any of this."

To conclude commentary on this author, what we have here in his book, from our point of view, is a "mixed bag." Rader is very congruent with our own views on some points, less so on others, and diametrically in opposition in several cases.

The Heinlein Crater

A Martian crater has been named After Robert A. Heinlein to honor the late author. Its diameter is approximately 83 kilometers or 52 miles.

The resolution was passed at the XXIInd triennial General Assembly of the International Astronomical Union (IAU), which was held in August 1994 in The Hague. The crater, to be officially known as the Heinlein Crater, is located at Martian latitude −64.6 degrees and longitude 243.8 degrees in Quad MC28SE on Mapt I-1453. ['Quad' defines the name of the map on which it appears and 'Map' is the U.S. Geological Survey number for that map.]—Heinlein (1997, p. 7)

What are we to make of this? Nomenclature may not seem too important, but, in this case, it represents something far more important. Namely, private property rights. Farmer Jones has a cow. He can name it anything he wants: Bossy, Marigold, whatever. The point is, it is *his* cow, so he gets to choose its appellation. But suppose someone else were to choose the designation for this cow and make it stick, against Jones' will; the cow is now called Susie. We would then have to say that a part of Jones' ownership rights over the bovine has now been abrogated. For a (small) part of the rights of private property consists of this privilege. The point is, owners, not anyone else, have the right to name their property.

Let us return to the "Heinlein Crater." Who named it thus? Well, 'twas the General Assembly of the International Astronomical Union. This means, if it means anything, that this group has seized at least partial ownership of the terrain in question. Did they homestead this territory? Of course not. Yet, they have in this way laid (again partial) claim to this property. The problem here is that this constitutes a chipping away at the libertarian homesteading justification for ownership.[45]

That is one side of a possible controversy regarding this phenomenon. However, there is also another side, a very powerful one. It goes like this.

The Mid-Atlantic Ridge, Jupiter, Neptune, Alpha-Centauri, Beetlejuice, Rigel, the Milky Way galaxy, the Andromeda galaxy, quasar ULAS J1120 + 0641, etc.—what do these places have in common? No human being owns them. Lots of names are given by someone who discovers something by observation, often from great distances, not by homesteading. The International Astronomical Union (IAU) is a private organization of astronomers (but includes nations as members), and in this respect is not unlike the Mont Pelerin Society.[46] It provides a uniform naming system to enable scientists to talk intelligently about specific objects. How is a crater on Mars any different? There are lots of places on Mars that have been named.[47] Indeed, Mars itself is a name given by someone who did not own it and who did not even set foot on it. Therefore, the preceding argument is fallacious. There is thus no problem with using common names such as the Heinlein Crater.

Is it possible to reconcile these two very different perspectives? Perhaps. At least from a libertarian point of view, we may say that, at the very least, governments should not be in the naming business, if only because they are illegitimate institutions in the first place.[48] As for all legitimate institutions and non-criminal individuals, let everyone name anything they want, and let's see what sticks.

---

[45] Let us say that if the present authors were to come to own a portion of a planet, or moon, or asteroid, or other heavenly body, and wanted to name it after someone who has done more than almost anyone else not only to popularize space travel, but to infuse it with a free-enterprise ethic, it would be none other than Robert A. Heinlein. His *The Moon is a Harsh Mistress* is a must read for all those who wish to be inspired by the libertarian vision, applied to an extra-terrestrial arena. We thus have no difficulty with naming a Martian crater after this very well-deserving novelist. Our objections, as can be seen, are otherwise.

[46] Although no government entities are members of the society.

[47] Peruse the image by Stinson (2016); numerous parts of Mars have already been named.

[48] For more on place names on Mars see this Chap. 14, note 5, *supra*.

References

Ahiakpor, James C.W. 1992. Rashid on Adam Smith: In Need of Proof. *The Journal of Libertarian Studies* 10 (2): 171–180.

———. 1999. Did Adam Smith Retard the Development of Economic Analysis? A Critique of Murray Rothbard's Interpretation. *The Independent Review* 3 (3): 355–383.

———. 2008. On Aspromourgos's Mistaken Reading of Adam Smith's Price Theory. *History of Economic Ideas* 16 (3): 119–124.

Anderson, Terry, and P.J. Hill. 1979. An American Experiment in Anarcho-Capitalism: The Not So Wild, Wild West. *The Journal of Libertarian Studies* 3: 9–29. http://mises.org/journals/jls/3_1/3_1_2.pdf. Accessed 11 June 2016.

Anderson, Terry L., and Peter J. Hill, eds. 1996. *The Privatization Process: A Worldwide Perspective*. Lanham, MD: Rowman & Littlefield Publishers.

Anderson, T.L., and P.J. Hill. 2004. *The Not So Wild, Wild West: Property Rights on the Frontier*. Stanford, CA: Stanford University Press.

Bastasch, Michael. 2015a. Dem. Senator Hopes the DOJ Sues Global Warming 'Deniers'. June 25. http://dailycaller.com/2015/06/25/dem-senator-hopes-the-doj-sues-global-warming-deniers/. Accessed 5 Dec 2015.

———. 2015b. Scientists Ask Obama to Prosecute Global Warming Skeptics. September 17. http://dailycaller.com/2015/09/17/scientists-ask-obama-to-prosecute-global-warming-skeptics/#ixzz3tVcjAMR1; http://dailycaller.com/2015/09/17/scientists-ask-obama-to-prosecute-global-warming-skeptics/. Accessed 5 Dec 2015.

Block, Walter. 2002. Radical Privatization and Other Libertarian Conundrums. The International Journal of Politics and Ethics 2 (2): 165–175. http://www.walterblock.com/publications/radical_privatiztion.pdf. Accessed 23 Aug 2016.

Block, Walter E. 2009. *The Privatization of Roads and Highways: Human and Economic Factors*. Auburn, AL: The Mises Institute. http://www.amazon.com/Privatization-Roads-And-Highways-Factors/dp/1279887303/; http://mises.org/books/roads_web.pdf; http://mises.org/daily/3416. Accessed 23 Aug 2016.

Butler, Eamonn, ed. 1988. *The Mechanics of Privatization*. London: Adam Smith Institute.

Carnis, Laurent. 2003. The Case for Road Privatization: A Defense by Restitution. *Journal des Economistes et des Etudes Humaines*. 13 (1): 95–116.

Cook, Russell. 2015. Those Scientists Who Want to Use RICO to Prosecute AGW 'Deniers' Have a Big Problem. October 1. http://www.americanthinker.com/articles/2015/10/those_scientists_who_want_to_use_rico_to_prosecute_agw_deniers_have_a_big_problem.html#ixzz3tVeVyG3S; http://www.americanthinker.com/articles/2015/10/those_scientists_who_want_to_use_rico_to_prosecute_agw_deniers_have_a_big_problem.html. Accessed 6 Dec 2015.

Delingpole, James. 2015. Twenty Alarmist Climate Scientists—Including UN IPCC Lead Author Kevin 'Travesty' Trenberth—Have Written a Letter to President Obama Urging Him to Use RICO Laws to Crush Dissent by Climate Skeptics. Their Hypocrisy and Dishonesty, Especially that of the Main Signatory, Almost Defies Belief. September 19. http://www.breitbart.com/big-government/2015/09/19/climate-alarmists-obama-use-rico-laws-jail-skeptics/. Accessed 6 Dec 2015.

Desrochers, Pierre. 2015. The Simon-Ehrlich Wager 25 Years on; as the Famous Environmentalist Bet Showed, Malthusians Are Always Wrong. http://www.spiked-online.com/newsite/article/the-simonehrlich-wager-25-years-on/17482#.Vm4zL09Ig5s.

Ebeling, Richard. 2013. Why Not Privatize Foreign Policy? http://epictimes.com/article/127064/why-not-privatize-foreign-policy. Accessed 23 Aug 2016.

Hanke, Steve H. 1987a. Privatization. In *The New Palgrave: A Dictionary of Economics*, ed. J. Eatwell, M. Milgate, and P. Newman, vol. 3, 976–977. London: The Macmillan Press, Ltd.

———., ed. 1987b. *Privatization and Development*. San Francisco: Institute for Contemporary Studies.

Hannesson, Rögnvaldur. 2004. The Privatization of the Oceans. In *Evolving Property Rights in Marine Fisheries*, ed. D.R. Leal, 25–48. Lanham, MD: Rowman and Littlefield.

———. 2006. *The Privatization of the Oceans*. Cambridge, MA: MIT Press.

Hazlitt, Henry. 2008 [1946]. *Economics in One Lesson*. Auburn, AL: Mises Institute. http://mises.org/books/economics_in_one_lesson_hazlitt.pdf. Accessed 29 June 2016.

Hechtkopf, Kevin. 2011. Rick Perry Fails to Remember What Agency He'd Get Rid of in GOP Debate. November 10. http://www.cbsnews.com/news/rick-perry-fails-to-remember-what-agency-hed-get-rid-of-in-gop-debate/.

Heinlein, Robert. 1997 [1966]. *The Moon Is a Harsh Mistress*. New York City: Tor Books.

Hoppe, Hans-Hermann. 2011. Of Private, Common, and Public Property and the Rationale for Total Privatization. *Libertarian Papers* 3 (1). http://libertarianpapers.org/2011/1-hoppe-private-common-and-public-property/. Accessed 23 Aug 2016.

Karpoff, Jonathan M. 2001. Public Versus Private Initiative in Arctic Exploration: The Effects of Incentives and Organizational Structure. *The Journal of Political Economy* 109 (1): 38–78.

Kellard, Joseph. 1998. Reason vs Faith: Julian Simon vs Paul Ehrlich. April 26. http://capitalismmagazine.com/1998/04/reason-vs-faith-julian-simon-vs-paul-ehrlich/.

Krugman, Paul. 2015. Republicans' Climate Change Denial Denial. December 4. http://www.nytimes.com/2015/12/04/opinion/republicans-climate-change-denial-denial.html?_r=0. Accessed 5 Dec 2015.

Lewis, John S. 1997. *Mining the Sky: Untold Riches from the Asteroids, Comets and Planets.* New York: Basic Books.

Lewis, Rob. 2015. Should Climate Change Deniers Be Prosecuted? September 20. http://www.dailykos.com/story/2015/9/20/1423309/-Scientists-ask-for-prosecution-of-climate-deniers-under-RICO-law. Accessed 6 Dec 2015.

McClintick, David, and Ross B. Emmett. 2005. Betting on the Wealth of Nature; The Simon-Ehrlich Wager. PERC Report 23 (3), September 29. http://www.perc.org/articles/betting-wealth-nature#sthash.M3R4F7jH.dpuf; http://www.perc.org/articles/betting-wealth-nature.

Megginson, W., and J. Netter. 2001. From State to Market: A Survey of Empirical Studies on Privatization. *Journal of Economic Literature* 39 (2): 321–389.

Moore, Stephen. 1987. Privatizing the U.S. Postal Service. In *Privatization*, ed. Stephen Moore and Stuart Butler. Washington, DC: Heritage Foundation.

Moore, Stephen, and Stuart Butler, eds. 1987. *Privatization.* Washington, DC: Heritage Foundation.

Motichek, Amy, Walter E. Block, and Jay Johnson. 2008. Forget Ocean Front Property, We Want Ocean Real Estate! *Ethics, Place, and Environment* 11 (2): 147–155.

Ohashi, T.M. 1980. *Privatization, Theory and Practice: Distributing Shares in Private and Public Enterprise.* Vancouver, BC: The Fraser Institute.

Ohashi, T.M., T.P. Roth, Z.A. Spindler, M.L. McMillan, and K.H. Norrie. 1980. *Privation Theory & Practice.* Vancouver, BC: The Fraser Institute.

Olson, Walter. 2015. Should Climate Change Deniers Be Prosecuted? October 1. http://www.newsweek.com/should-climate-change-deniers-be-prosecuted-378652. Accessed 6 Dec 2015.

Petranek, Stephen L. 2015. *How we'll live on Mars.* New York: Simon and Schuster.

Pirie, Madson. 1986. *Privatization in Theory and Practice.* London: Adam Smith Institute.

Rothbard, Murray N. 1987. Adam Smith Reconsidered. In *Austrian Economics Newsletter*, 5–7. Auburn, AL: The Ludwig von Mises Institute. Reprinted in *Austrian Economics* (Vol. 1) by S. Littlechild. Brookfield, VT: Edward Elgar Publishing Company (1990), pp. 41–44. http://mises.org/daily/2012. Accessed 23 Aug 2016.

———. 1982a. *The Ethics of Liberty*. Atlantic Highlands, NJ: Humanities Press.

———. 1982b. Law, Property Rights, and Air Pollution. Cato Journal 2 (1). Reprinted in *Economics and the Environment: A Reconciliation*, Walter E. Block, ed., Vancouver: The Fraser Institute, 1990, pp. 233–279. http://mises. org/story/2120; http://www.mises.org/rothbard/lawproperty.pdf. Accessed 20 Apr 2016.

———. 1995. *The Case Against the Fed*. Auburn, AL: Ludwig von Mises Institute.

———. 2011. Malthus and the Assault on Population. August 2. http://mises. org/daily/5501/. Accessed 10 Aug 2016.

Savas, E.S. 1987. *Privatization*. Chatham, NJ: Chatham House Publishers.

Say, Jean-Baptiste. 1821. *Letters to Mr. Malthus*. https://mises.org/library/letters-mr-malthus.

Simon, Julian. 1981. *The Ultimate Resource*. Princeton: Princeton University Press.

Smith, Adam. 1979 [1776]. *An Inquiry into the Nature and Causes of the Wealth of Nations*. Indianapolis, IN: Liberty Fund.

Sowell, Thomas. 2000. Wake Up, Parents! *Jewish World Review*. August 18. http://www.jewishworldreview.com/cols/sowell081800.asp. Accessed 14 Dec 2015.

Spooner, Lysander. 1966 [1870]. *No Treason: The Constitution of No Authority and A Letter to Thomas F. Bayard*. Larkspur, CO: Rampart College. http://jim.com/treason.htm. Accessed 23 Aug 2016.

Stinson, Liz. 2016. A Map of Mars That's Perfect for Everyday Earthlings. *Wired*. February 26. https://www.wired.com/2016/02/map-mars-thats-perfect-every-day-earthlings/. Accessed 2 Oct 2016.

Von Mises, Ludwig. 1944. *Bureaucracy*. New Haven: Yale University Press.

Walker, Michael A., ed. 1988. *Privatization: Tactics and Techniques*. Vancouver, Canada: The Fraser Institute.

White, Lawrence H. 1978. Privatization of Municipally-Provided Services. *The Journal of Libertarian Studies* 2 (2): 187–197.

Worstall, Tim. 2013. But Why Did Julian Simon Win the Paul Ehrlich Bet? January 13. http://www.forbes.com/sites/timworstall/2013/01/13/but-why-did-julian-simon-win-the-paul-ehrlich-bet/.

16

Conclusion

Sometimes, the writing of a book changes the minds of the authors. This is all to the good, since putting words down on a blank sheet of paper[1] is, hopefully, a creative process, and when this is working well, all bets are off. Writers may well start off with one thought in mind, but it becomes amended during the task of unburdening themselves.

Though we discovered many unexpected insights,[2] this did not occur in the present case. We like to think we were open to changing our minds on the benefits of private property rights and free enterprise regarding the colonization of the heavenly bodies, but, in the event, we did not. At the end of this process, we remain of the same opinion.

We see humanity poised at a fork in the road. Both highways lead in the direction of space travel. There is no doubt in our minds that in the next decade or two, man will be living, albeit in small numbers, on both

---

[1] In the modern era, filling up a blank monitor screen with verbiage.

[2] Perhaps how close we are to being fully capable of not only going to Mars but settling there in short order was the greatest surprise. But we came to the realization that other more exotic places lend themselves to colonization as well. We did not start with the idea that settlement of other star systems could happen within our lifetime or even within centuries. And it still might not ever take place. We found no fatal reason to assume it will not occur within a hundred years.

© The Author(s) 2018
P. L. Nelson, W. E. Block, *Space Capitalism*, Palgrave Studies in Classical Liberalism,
https://doi.org/10.1007/978-3-319-74651-7_16

the Moon and Mars. But there are two ways to get there. One is via the intermediation and leadership of the state. The other is through the organization of *laissez faire* capitalism.[3]

This entire book has been dedicated to making the case for the latter. For the first is the way of violence and death. It is putting the very organization most responsible for man's inhumanity to man in charge of what is perhaps the most promising adventure leading to a new birth of freedom. Throughout known history the state has led the way to genocide, war, oppression, and bereavement. Despite these deprivations, free men have always responded with services aimed at making life better for their fellow men.

What is our prognostication? Unhappily, it is not too good. At the time of this writing, neither major U.S. party candidate vying for the presidential suite can be fairly characterized as being an adherent of a limited government philosophy.[4] The same applies to the political trends throughout the world. Is Ali Khamenei of Iran a libertarian? Is Vladimir Putin dedicated to the freedom philosophy? How about Emmanuel Macron of France? Surely Angela Merkel must be committed to freedom?[5] To ask these questions is to answer them. The U.S. candidates who represented the Libertarian Party (Gary Johnson and William Weld) somewhat more closely track the philosophy of our book, but this group only garnered some 3% of the popular vote. Similar things might be said of Édouard Fillias a libertarian-leaning politician in France, Moshe Feiglin of Israel, or Tim Moen and Maxime Bernier in Canada. But way too much of the human populace looks to their government for salvation; so, we get Macron in France and Trump in the United States and their ilk. When most people say, as Ronald Reagan (1981) did "[G]overnment is the problem," they tend to be referring to *this government*. The worst of them will happily go out shooting government officers. Those who will

---

[3] A third option, of course, is a ménage à duo wherein both systems morph with one another to form that mongrel: economic fascism. Extrapolating from the present, this might well be the most likely path the United States and the world will take in future, but, as we have argued throughout this book, it is the worst path.

[4] The same, unhappily, can be said for almost all who are seeking other official offices including state and local.

[5] Clearly, we could name every country on Earth and make the same point.

vote for office seekers dedicated[6] to freedom are rare. People who argue for peaceful revolution are even more difficult to find. Private profit-searching explorers of the outer limits, as extraordinary as they are, are precisely those to whom the authors of this book turn.

Aside from losing the opportunity for showing how the freedom philosophy works, if free enterprise does not play a key role in space exploration and subsequent colonization, this process will be less efficient than otherwise it would have been. Indeed, the race to space may remain thoroughly misguided and end up mal-investing untold resources in an enterprise that resembles nothing more than an amateur sports car race and yielding only counter-productive results.[7]

As explained in the forgoing chapters, there is absolutely no reason why liberty-minded and self-financed people cannot lead the way. It was the state-financed explorers like Columbus and Pissarro who went astray, killed and enslaved the natives, and established nations of desperate poverty with violent cultures. One the other hand, while freedom seekers experienced many missteps,[8] they established a principled nation dedicated to the proposition that all men are endowed with rights not reliant on the state. This was a nation of great prosperity.[9] For these reasons, this book demonstrates ways in which entrepreneurship might work on various planets, moons, and even unoccupied locations and trails in the solar system and beyond. Scientifically, mankind has arrived. The technology exists or is easily foreseeable that allows habitation of Mars and other celestial bodies. Travel to other star systems and colonization of such untold worlds must occur before this century is out.

This promising future is put at risk by made-up, artificial "law" intended to stymie men. Likewise, the appropriation of basic research by bureaucrats who do not have anyone's interest at heart but their own,

---

[6] And here even Johnson/Weld fall very short of true libertarianism. Detailing their shortcomings would take us too far afield and would be counter-productive.

[7] If private entrepreneurs had reached the Moon in 1969, we strongly expect there would have been much faster and more intensive follow-up than in the event.

[8] The Salem witch trials for example, or the communistic agriculture of the first colony, or the warring with natives, or the beginnings of race-based chattel slavery, etc., etc. In the long term, these were mostly overcome because they could not survive in the face of people committed to liberty.

[9] Unfortunately, the worldwide reversion to the archaic tyranny of OBushama and their crews seems to be taking a new foothold. We look to libertarian space pioneers to reverse this trend.

does no good. We see both great promise as well as reasons for concern in the exploits of the foremost, start-up, space-oriented businesses. There is a continuum. At one end those who tend to lead the way on their own hold much more promise than those who look for state handouts.

Hopefully, this book will have played at least a small role in moving us in a positive economic and philosophical direction: toward freedom and liberty. We hope and pray that this will indeed occur. The fate of humanity hangs in the balance.

This, of course, is not to say that this book, all on its lonesome, can change the likely trajectory. However, our efforts are a small part of the libertarian movement, all of which is in the direction of less reliance on government. Evidence? Brexit shows almost a 180-degree change from the status quo. The people in the UK voting to leave the European Union can best be interpreted as an attempt to "take back our country."[10] A similar phenomenon may be responsible for the unpopularity of both Donald Trump and Hillary Clinton.[11] Remarkable was Sanders' long-running approval by many. Albeit the very opposite of libertarianism in many ways,[12] his was not exactly an example of politics as usual. Perhaps these portents, if writ large, can wean us from an entirely statist space exploration and colonization program. We look forward to humans living on other planets and distant solar systems. We look to a time when our entire species laps up this liberty and this libertarian perspective.

Reference

Reagan, Ronald. 1981. [first] Inaugural Address. January 20. http://www.presidency.ucsb.edu/ws/?pid=43130. Accessed 16 Sep 2017.

---

[10] While your authors decry the very concept of "our country," we are heartened by such full-scale rejection of the misguided leaders in Europe. But what is so bad about claiming possession of the territory in which we were born? It assumes that everyone homesteaded it and that there can be non-contractual shared proprietorship; it implies that the NIMBYs among us have a veto power over private citizens and their property.

[11] Although, of course, there is nothing about their candidacies that can be construed as a rejection of statism. The very opposite is the case. However, at least Trump's efforts, but not Hillary's, can be regarded as a rebuff of the establishment in the voters' minds if not in reality.

[12] Except for foreign policy.

Appendix: The Physics of Orbits

In this appendix, a brief and simplified explanation is given as to why orbits tend to be circular or elliptical and why they do not require a constant energy input. As the reader will have noticed in the main text of the book, paths through space are essential to travel and colonization: so important that efficient ones can be homesteaded. To aid understanding, the book includes this elementary discussion of orbits.[1]

We humans experience our environment as Euclidean[2] space. What does this have to do with interplanetary travel? Hold on, this will become clear in the next few paragraphs as your authors explain why what appears to be a curved path is in fact the shortest route, at least in terms of energy expenditure. In plane geometry, i.e. where all objects lie on a flat surface, two lines perpendicular to the same line are parallel and will never

---

[1] We authors worry that this material may seem too far removed from our main focus: colonizing space. Yet, we think it not entirely irrelevant. Our compromise: place this in an appendix. We readily acknowledge this is premature. Private property can only apply to scarce resources, and paths in space (outside of near-earth orbits) hardly qualify. But, they will, one of these days, hopefully sooner rather than later. And, in the meantime, what we say here has implications for airplane travel back on the home planet, right away, and for ocean paths, soon enough.

[2] Euclid (Εὐκλείδης) was a mathematician in the Hellenistic period, about 300 BC. He is widely considered the father of geometry. His analysis starts with a few assumptions called axioms, one of which is the principle that through a point off a given line, one and only one parallel line can be drawn.

© The Author(s) 2018
P. L. Nelson, W. E. Block, *Space Capitalism*, Palgrave Studies in Classical Liberalism,
https://doi.org/10.1007/978-3-319-74651-7

intersect. However, we humans live on a surface on which that is not true. If the Earth's shape is idealized to a perfect sphere with no hills or other undulations, two lines will connect with each other if extended far enough, namely 6225.25 miles.[3] One kind of non-Euclidean space is a spherical surface. In the special case where distances are small with respect to the diameter, Euclid's principles hold true to the extent that we can measure. If a person is living on such a surface, he would never know that the earth was not flat. There would still be straight lines as evidenced by the fact that he could look along the line and see that it did not veer to the right or left. In this spherical (Riemannian—after Bernhard Riemann) non-Euclidean space he would find that parallel lines always intersect eventually, when extended far enough.

In another kind of space, through a point off a given line, an infinite number of lines can be drawn that never intersect. Once again, if a person were living on such a plain, he would never know it except that it would be a fact that he would find that principle to be true. The name for this surface is a hyperbola (Lobachevskian).[4]

In both cases, one can determine the shape only by moving out of the two dimensions of the surface and looking at it in three dimensions. Then he can see the curvature of the surface.

Euclidean geometry and its principles can be applied to three-dimensional space. Within common human experience, it is still true that through a point off a given line, as indicated on three axes, one and only one parallel line may be formed. Likewise, both non-Euclidean principles can be envisioned, i.e. through that point (a) no such parallels exist or (b) an infinite number do.

Now consider certain features in the three-dimensional space as we know it. One feature is that planets orbit around stars. This would appear to violate Newton's first law.[5] Another is that if an apple is held above the Earth's surface and then dropped, it falls to the ground. We call this

---

[3] In other words, one-quarter of the Earth's circumference.

[4] Examples of hyperbolas include saddles and certain kinds of tents or tarps. They are characterized by curvature in one direction (let us say downward or negative, stirrup to stirrup so to speak) and upward (or positive, horn to cantle) when looking 90 degrees from the previous observation.

[5] Newton's first law: "An object at rest stays at rest and an object in motion stays in motion with the same speed and in the same direction unless acted upon by an unbalanced force."

apparent attraction gravity. We treat it like a force. It is unbalanced and appears to cause the orbiting body to constantly change direction and the apple to accelerate from rest to movement. However, we can detect forces. The attraction of magnets, for example, involves the movement of small particles.[6] No such particles appear to be related to gravity (Hawking, 1988, chapter 11). Rather, a better explanation is to forgo the idea that gravity is a force and posit that we live in a hyperbolic space. This could only be observed if we were able to move out of three-dimensional space and observe it from four or five dimensions.[7] From that perspective, the theory is that what looks to us like a circular or elliptical line is in fact straight.[8] Therefore, the most efficient path only appears curved in three dimensions in such a way as to require little or no energy.

The most oomph is used to divert from one natural, straight-line path to another, such as transferring from riding around the Earth while standing on its surface to, say, a stable orbit 100 miles above the Earth's surface. But once at the new elevation, no further energy is necessary to maintain that new trajectory.[9] Furthermore, the easiest way to change to a higher orbit is to accelerate for a short time along the direction of travel. This causes an elliptical trail (that does not need energy inputs once established) with the perihelion at the old height, and then add thrust as required when the aphelion is reached to make it circular again, but at an increased distance from the central object.

---

[6] For more on this refer to Hawking, 1988.

[7] The discussion in the text is intended to offer an analogy to help the reader better understand that more dimensions are needed to account for why a circular orbit might function like a straight line just like a third dimension is required in order to understand that the Earth is spherical rather than planar.

[8] Your authors apologize for the possible confusion. We attempt to simplify a theory that is not fully understood even by the most advanced physicists and astronomers to help the reader visualize the principles being discussed.

[9] That maintenance of a constant elevation requires no energy input is idealistic. In practice, orbits tend to decay because of losses caused by such forces as friction with interfering particles. For example, if a circling object is close enough to Earth, the rarified atmosphere causes drag. Similarly, while moving about the Sun, a body will suffer resistance from the solar wind. Because these effects are so weak (imagine the deleterious influence of a planet hitting a few protons), the deterioration tends to go unnoticed for generations on end and is ignored herein. Thus, though minimal, overcoming drag requires at least a bit of power.

References

Abramson, Michael. 2004. *Expectorations*. Volume V. A Collection of Poetry and Prose. Bloomington, IN: Xlibris Corporation.

Accad, Michael. 2016. Peer-Review and Science's Funding Problem. April 17. https://mises.org/blog/peer-review-and-science%E2%80%99s-funding-problem. Accessed 23 Apr 2016.

ACLU. 1999. 'No-Knock' Warrant Resulting in Denver Man's Death Should Not Have Been Issued. The American Civil Liberties Union. https://www.aclu.org/news/no-knock-warrant-resulting-denver-mans-death-should-not-have-been-issued-aclu-says. Accessed 25 June 2015.

———. 2015. The Prison Crisis. The American Civil Liberties Union. https://www.aclu.org/prison-crisis. Accessed 24 June 2015.

Adams, John Quincy. 2005. *Congressional Record*. 109th Congress. First Session. Vol. 151, Part 4, March 11. https://books.google.com/books?id=eaCIX6d3Y5YC&pg=PA4864&lpg=PA4864&dq=%22goes+not+abroad+seeking+monsters%22&source=bl&ots=7y-SeZRFm0&sig=IoiE22eag3F5i3MFMGmVPqVaX5A&hl=en&sa=X&ved=0ahUKEwio-9D3yZfOAhUHbiYKHcJ0AyMQ6AEIKTAD#v=onepage&q=%22goes%20not%20abroad%20seeking%20monsters%22&f=false. Accessed 28 July 2016.

© The Author(s) 2018

247

P. L. Nelson, W. E. Block, *Space Capitalism*, Palgrave Studies in Classical Liberalism,
https://doi.org/10.1007/978-3-319-74651-7

Adie, Douglas K. 1988. *Monopoly Mail: Privatizing the United States Postal Service*. New Brunswick, NJ: Transaction.

Ahiakpor, James C.W. 1992. Rashid on Adam Smith: In Need of Proof. *The Journal of Libertarian Studies* 10 (2): 171–180.

———. 1999. Did Adam Smith Retard the Development of Economic Analysis? A Critique of Murray Rothbard's Interpretation. *The Independent Review* 3 (3): 355–383.

———. 2008. On Aspromourgos's Mistaken Reading of Adam Smith's Price Theory. *History of Economic Ideas* 16 (3): 119–124.

Ahlbrandt, Roger. 1973. Efficiency in the Provision of Fire Services. *Public Choice* 16 (Fall): 1–15.

Aldrin, (Buzz) Edwin Eugene, Jr. 2011. The Buzz on Science Education and Space Exploration. January–February. http://www.iphonelife.com/issues/2011January-February/TheBuzzOnScience. Accessed 7 July 2016.

Alexander, Sonja, and Esther Buchsbaum. 2007. NASA and M.A.D. Science Partner to Promote Science Education. September 5. http://www.nasa.gov/home/hqnews/2007/sep/HQ_07185_Mad_Science.html. Accessed 7 July 2016.

Alperovitz, Gar. 1994. *Atomic Diplomacy: Hiroshima and Potsdam*. Pluto Press.

———. 1996. *The Decision to Use the Atomic Bomb*. Vintage.

Alvarez, Luis, et al. 1980. Extraterrestrial Cause for the Cretaceous-Tertiary Extinction. *Science* 208 (4448): 1095–1108.

Amundsen, Roald, Nilsen, Thorvald, Prestrud, Kristian, Chater, A.G. (tr.). 1976 [1912]. *The South Pole: An Account of the Norwegian Expedition in the Fram, 1910–12*, vol. I and II. London: C. Hurst & Company. ISBN 0-903983-47-8. Accessed 27 Aug 2015.

Anderson, William. 2005. Katrina and the Never-Ending Scandal of State Management. September 13. http://www.mises.org/story/1909.

Anderson, Chris. 2012. Elon Musk's Mission to Mars. Wired.com. October 21. http://www.wired.com/2012/10/ff-elon-musk-qa/. Accessed 27 April 2018.

Anderson, Chad. 2013. Rethinking Public–Private Space Travel. *Space Policy* 29 (4): 266–271. http://www.sciencedirect.com/science/article/pii/S0265964613000799. Accessed 11 July 2015.

Anderson, Terry, and P.J. Hill. 1979. An American Experiment in Anarcho-Capitalism: The Not So Wild, Wild West. *The Journal of Libertarian Studies* 3: 9–29. http://mises.org/journals/jls/3_1/3_1_2.pdf. Accessed 11 June 2016.

Anderson, Terry L., and Peter J. Hill, eds. 1995. *Wildlife in the Marketplace*. Lanham, MD: Rowman & Littlefield.

————, eds. 1996. *The Privatization Process: A Worldwide Perspective*. Lanham, MD: Rowman & Littlefield Publishers.

Anderson, T.L., and P.J. Hill. 2004. *The Not So Wild, Wild West: Property Rights on the Frontier*. Stanford, CA: Stanford University Press.

Anderson, William, Walter E. Block, Thomas J. DiLorenzo, Ilana Mercer, Leon Snyman, and Christopher Westley. 2001. The Microsoft Corporation in Collision with Antitrust Law. *The Journal of Social, Political and Economic Studies* 26 (1): 287–302.

Ansari Prize. 2004. Funded by the Ansari Family, the Ansari XPRIZE Challenged Teams from Around the World to Build a Reliable, Privately Financed, Manned Spaceship Capable of Carrying Three People to 100 Kilometers Above the Earth's Surface Twice Within Two Weeks. The Prize Was Awarded in 2004 and Along with It, a Brand New Private Space Industry Was Launched. November 6. http://ansari.xprize.org/. Accessed 3 Aug 2016.

Anthony, Sebastian. 2014. The Apollo 11 Moon Landing, 45 Years on: Looking Back at Mankind's Giant Leap. July 21. http://www.extremetech.com/extreme/186600-apollo-11-moon-landing-45-years-looking-back-at-mankinds-giant-leap. Accessed 23 May 2016.

Armentano, Dominick T. 1999. *Antitrust: The Case for Repeal*. Revised 2nd ed. Auburn, AL: Mises Institute.

Asamoah, Obed Y. n.d. Declaration of Legal Principles Governing the Activities of States in the Exploration and Use of Outer Space. *The Legal Significance of the Declarations of the General Assembly of the United Nations*: 129–160. Martinus Nijhoff http://link.springer.com/chapter/10.1007/978-94-011-9495-2_12. Accessed 13 Dec 2015.

Atkinson, Nancy. 2011. Earth Has a Companion Asteroid with a Weird Orbit. *Universe Today*. April 6. http://www.universetoday.com/84652/earth-has-a-companion-asteroid-with-a-weird-orbit/. Accessed 17 Nov 2015.

Autry, Greg. 2015. Everybody Hates a Winner: Elon Musk, the Government and the Damn Yankees Syndrome. June 4. http://www.huffingtonpost.com/greg-autry/everybody-hates-a-winner-_b_7508114.html. Accessed 29 June 2016.

Axelrod, Alan. 2008. *Profiles in Folly: History's Worst Decisions and Why They Went Wrong*. Sterling Publishing Company.

Bailout Tracker. 2015. Bailout Recipients. July 13. https://projects.propublica.org/bailout/list.

Banse, Tom. 2015. Washington State Votes Overwhelmingly to Shut Down Ivory Trade. November 3. http://nwnewsnetwork.org/post/washington-state-votes-overwhelmingly-shut-down-ivory-trade. Accessed 28 July 2016.

Barnes, Harry Elmer, ed. 1982. *Perpetual War for Perpetual Peace*. Institute for Historical Review.

———. 2004. *The Genesis of the World War an Introduction to the Problem of War Guilt*. Kessinger Publishing.

Barnett, William, II, and Walter E. Block. 2006. On Hayekian Triangles. *Procesos De Mercado: Revista Europea De Economia Politica* III (2): 39–141. http://mises.org/journals/scholar/block18.pdf; http://www.academia.edu/1359916/On_Hayekian_Triangles; http://papers.ssrn.com/sol3/papers.cfm?abstract_id=1880543. Accessed 21 Mar 2016.

Barnett, William, II, and Walter E. Block. 2007. Coase and Van Zandt on Lighthouses. *Public Finance Review* 35 (6): 710–733. http://pfr.sagepub.com/content/35/6/710.abstract; http://www.economist.com/blogs/freeexchange/2012/07/economic-fables. Accessed 23 Apr 2016.

Barnett, William, and Walter E. Block. 2009. Coase and Bertrand on Lighthouses. *Public Choice* 140 (1–2): 1–13. https://doi.org/10.1007/s11127-008-9375-x. Accessed 23 Apr 2016.

Barnett, William, Walter E. Block, and Michael Saliba. 2005. Perfect Competition: A Case of 'Market-Failure'. *Corporate Ownership & Control* 2 (4): 70–75.

Barnett, William, II, Walter E. Block, and Michael Saliba. 2007. Predatory Pricing. *Corporate Ownership & Control* 4 (4), Continued—3, Summer: 401–406.

Barry, Patrick L. 2005. Radioactive Moon. *NASA Science—Science News*. September 8. National Aeronautics and Space Administration. http://science.nasa.gov/science-news/science-at-nasa/2005/08sep_radioactivemoon/. Accessed 23 Nov 2015.

Bastasch, Michael. 2015a. Dem. Senator Hopes the DOJ Sues Global Warming 'Deniers'. June 25. http://dailycaller.com/2015/06/25/dem-senator-hopes-the-doj-sues-global-warming-deniers/. Accessed 5 Dec 2015.

———. 2015b. Scientists Ask Obama to Prosecute Global Warming Skeptics. September 17. http://dailycaller.com/2015/09/17/scientists-ask-obama-to-prosecute-global-warming-skeptics/#ixzz3tVcjAMR1; http://dailycaller.com/2015/09/17/scientists-ask-obama-to-prosecute-global-warming-skeptics/. Accessed 5 Dec 2015.

Batemarco, Robert. 1985. Positive Economics and Praxeology: The Clash of Prediction and Explanation. *Atlantic Economic Journal* 13 (2): 31–27.

———. 1987. GNP, PPR, and the Standard of Living. *The Review of Austrian Economics* 181–186. https://mises.org/library/gnp-ppr-and-standard-living. Accessed 23 May 2016.

Bates, Clair. 2012. Up and Away! World's Largest Airship Lifts Off for the First Time. *Daily Mail.* June 25. http://www.dailymail.co.uk/sciencetech/article-1279831/Up-away-Worlds-largest-airship-lifts-time.html. Accessed 23 Oct 2015.

Bauer, Peter. 1981. The Population Explosion: Myths and Realities. In *Equality, the Third World, and Economic Delusion.* Cambridge, MA: Harvard University Press.

Benson, Bruce L. 1989a. Enforcement of Private Property Rights in Primitive Societies: Law Without Government. *The Journal of Libertarian Studies* IX (1): 1–26. http://mises.org/journals/jls/9_1/9_1_1.pdf. Accessed 11 June 2016.

———. 1989b. The Spontaneous Evolution of Commercial Law. *Southern Economic Journal* 55: 644–661.

———. 1990a. Customary Law with Private Means of Resolving Disputes and Dispensing Justice: A Description of a Modern System of Law and Order Without State Coercion. *The Journal of Libertarian Studies* IX (2): 25–42. http://mises.org/journals/jls/9_2/9_2_2.pdf. Accessed 11 June 2016.

———. 1990b. *The Enterprise of Law: Justice Without the State.* San Francisco: Pacific Research Institute for Public Policy.

———. 1993. The Impetus for Recognizing Private Property and Adopting Ethical Behavior in a Market Economy: Natural Law, Government Law, or Evolving Self-Interest. *Review of Austrian Economics* 6 (2): 43–80.

———. 2001. Restitution as an Objective of the Criminal Justice System. *The Journal of the James Madison Institute* Winter: 17–22.

———. 2002. Justice Without Government: The Merchant Courts of Medieval Europe and Their Modern Counterparts. In *The Voluntary City: Choice, Community and Civil Society,* ed. David T. Beito, Peter Gordon, and Alexander Tabarrok, 127–150. Oakland, CA: The Independent Institute.

Berendsohn, Roy. 2008. 3 Compact Fluoresent Light Bulb Problems—And Expert Fixes. *Popular Mechanics.* August 31. http://www.popularmechanics.com/home/how-to/a3474/4276104/. Accessed 22 Aug 2016.

Bergland, David. 1986. *Libertarianism in One Lesson.* Costa Mesa, CA: Orpheus Publications.

Berliner, Michael S., ed. 1995. *Letters of Ayn Rand.* New York: Dutton.

Bezos, Jeff. 2017. 2016 Letter to Shareholders. April 12. https://www.amazon.com/p/feature/z6o9g6sysxur57t. Accessed 18 May 2017.

Bhagwati, Jagdish N. 1982. Directly Unproductive, Profit-Seeking (DUP) Activities. *Journal of Political Economy* 90 (5): 988–1002. http://www.jstor.

org/discover/10.2307/1837129?uid=3739400&uid=2&uid=3737720&uid =4&sid=21105317504383. Accessed 11 June 2016.

Billings, Linda. 2011. Commercial Space: Subsidies for Billionaires? April 19. https://doctorlinda.wordpress.com/2011/04/19/commercial-space-subsi-dies-for-billionaires/. Accessed 29 June 2016.

Block, Walter E. 1973. A Comment on 'The Extraordinary Claim of Praxeology,' by Professor Gutierrez. *Theory and Decision* 3 (4): 377–387.

———. 1976. *Defending the Undefendable*. Auburn, AL: The Mises Institute.

Block, Walter. 1977. Austrian Monopoly Theory—A Critique. *The Journal of Libertarian Studies* I (4): 271–279.

Block, Walter E. 1980. On Robert Nozick's 'On Austrian Methodology'. *Inquiry* 23 (4): 397–444.

Block, Walter. 1982. *Amending the Combines Investigation Act*. Vancouver: The Fraser Institute.

———. 1983. Public Goods and Externalities: The Case of Roads. *The Journal of Libertarian Studies: An Interdisciplinary Review* VII (1): 1–34. http://www. mises.org/journals/jls/7_1/7_1_1.pdf. Accessed 23 Apr 2016.

———. 1986. *The U.S. Bishops and Their Critics: An Economic and Ethical Perspective*. Vancouver: The Fraser Institute.

———. 1990. Earning Happiness Through Homesteading Unowned Land: A Comment on 'Buying Misery with Federal Land' by Richard Stroup. *Journal of Social Political and Economic Studies* 15 (2): 237–253.

Block, Walter E. 1991. "Old Letters and Old Buildings," *The Freeman Ideas on Liberty* 96. http://www.fee.org/vnews.php?nid=2363. Accessed 20 Apr 2016.

Block, Walter. 1994. Total Repeal of Anti-trust Legislation: A Critique of Bork, Brozen and Posner. *Review of Austrian Economics* 8 (1): 35–70.

Block, Walter E. 1998a. A Libertarian Case for Free Immigration. *Journal of Libertarian Studies: An Interdisciplinary Review* 13 (2): 167–186.

———. 1998b. Roads, Bridges, Sunlight and Private Property: Reply to Gordon Tullock. *Journal des Economistes et des Etudes Humaines* 8 (2/3): 315–326. http://141.164.133.3/faculty/Block/Blockarticles/roads2_vol8.htm; http:// www.walterblock.com/wp-content/uploads/publications/block_roads-bridges-sunlight-reply-tullock-1998.pdf. Accessed 20 Apr 2016.

———. 1999. Austrian Theorizing, Recalling the Foundations: Reply to Caplan. *Quarterly Journal of Austrian Economics* 2 (4): 21–39.

———. 2000a. Watch Your Language. February 21. http://www.mises.org/ful-larticle.asp?control=385&month=17&title=Watch+Your+Language&id=19; http://mises.org/daily/385. Accessed 11 June 2016.

Block, Walter. 2000b. Word Watch. April 20. http://www.mises.org/fullstory. asp?control=414&FS=Word+Watch. Accessed 23 Apr 2016.

———. 2002a. Homesteading City Streets; An Exercise in Managerial Theory. *Planning and Markets* 5 (1): 18–23. http://www-pam.usc.edu/volume5/ v5i1a2s1.html; http://www-pam.usc.edu/. Accessed 23 Apr 2016.

———. 2002b. On Reparations to Blacks for Slavery. *Human Rights Review* 3 (4): 53–73.

Block, Walter E. 2002c. All Government Is Excessive: A Rejoinder to 'In Defense of Excessive Government' by Dwight Lee. *Journal of Libertarian Studies* 16 (3): 35–82. http://www.mises.org/journals/jls/16_3/16_3_3.pdf. Accessed 11 June 2016.

Block, Walter. 2002d. Radical Privatization and Other Libertarian Conundrums. *The International Journal of Politics and Ethics* 2 (2): 165–175. http://www. walterblock.com/publications/radical_privatization.pdf. Accessed 23 Aug 2016.

———. 2003. National Defense and the Theory of Externalities, Public Goods and Clubs. In *The Myth of National Defense: Essays on the Theory and History of Security Production*, ed. Hans-Hermann Hoppe, 301–334. Auburn: Mises Institute. http://www.mises.org/etexts/defensemyth.pdf. Accessed 23 Apr 2016.

Block, Walter E. 2004. The State Was a Mistake. Book Review of Hoppe, Hans-Hermann, *Democracy, The God that Failed: The Economics and Politics of Monarchy, Democracy and Natural Order*, May 25, 2001. http://www.mises. org/fullstory.asp?control=1522. Accessed 11 July 2015.

Block, Walter. 2006a. Kevin Carson as Dr. Jekyll and Mr. Hyde. *The Journal of Libertarian Studies* 20 (1). http://mises.org/journals/jls/20_1/20_1_4.pdf. Accessed 11 June 2016.

———. 2006b. Deaths by Government: Another Missing Chapter. November 27. https://www.lewrockwell.com/2006/11/walter-e-block/deaths-by-government-anothermissingchapter/. Accessed 29 June 2015.

———. 2006c. Katrina: Private Enterprise, the Dead Hand of the Past, and Weather Socialism; An Analysis in Economic Geography. *Ethics, Place and Environment: A Journal of Philosophy & Geography* 9 (2): 231–241. Reprinted in 'Post-Katrina: Risk Assessment, Economic Analysis and Social Implications'—edited by Harry Richardson, Peter Gordon and James Moore. Edward Elgar Publishing.

Block, Walter E. 2006d. Radical Libertarianism: Applying Libertarian Principles to Dealing with the Unjust Government, Part II. *Reason Papers* 28 (Spring): 85–109.

http://www.walterblock.com/publications/block_radical-libertarianism-rp.pdf;
http://www.walterblock.com/wp-content/uploads/publications/block_radical-libertarianism-rp.pdf. (death penalty justified, net taxpayer, ruling class analysis, p. 87).

Block, Walter. 2007. Anarchism and Minarchism; No Rapprochement Possible: Reply to Tibor Machan. *The Journal of Libertarian Studies* 21 (1): 91–99. http://www.mises.org/journals/jls/21_1/21_1_5.pdf. Accessed 11 June 2016.

Block, Walter E. 2008. Homesteading, Ad Coelum, Owning Views and Forestalling. *The Social Sciences* 3 (2): 96–103. http://www.medwelljournals.com/fulltext/TSS/2008/96-103.pdf; http://medwelljournals.com/new/5/archivedetails.php?id=5&jid=TSS&theme=5&issueno=12. Accessed 20 Apr 2016.

———. 2009. *The Privatization of Roads and Highways: Human and Economic Factors.* Auburn, AL: The Mises Institute. http://www.amazon.com/Privatization-Roads-And-Highways-Factors/dp/1279887303/; http://mises.org/books/roads_web.pdf; http://mises.org/daily/3416. Accessed 23 Aug 2016.

———. 2010. Review of Huebert's Libertarianism Today. *Libertarian Papers.* http://libertarianpapers.org/2010/19-block-review-of-hueberts-libertarian-ism-today/. Accessed 29 June 2016.

———. 2011a. Hoppe, Kinsella and Rothbard II on Immigration: A Critique. *Journal of Libertarian Studies* 22: 593–623.

———. 2011b. Rejoinder to Hoppe on Immigration. *Journal of Libertarian Studies* 22: 771–792.

———. 2011c. Governmental Inevitability: Reply to Holcombe. *Journal of Libertarian Studies* 22: 667–688. http://mises.org/journals/jls/22_1/22_1_34.pdf. Accessed 11 June 2016.

———. 2011d. Rejoinder to Bertrand on Lighthouses. *Romanian Economic and Business Review* 6 (3): 49–67. http://www.rebe.rau.ro/REBE%206%203.pdf;http://www.economist.com/blogs/freeexchange/2012/07/economic-fables. Accessed 23 Apr 2016.

———. 2011e. Review Essay of Ostrom, Elinor. 1990. *Governing the Commons: The Evolution of Institutions for Collective Action.* Cambridge and New York: Cambridge University Press. In *Libertarian Papers*, Vol. 3, Art. 21. http://libertarianpapers.org/2011/21-block-review-of-ostroms-governing-the-commons/.

———. 2012a. Rozeff on Privacy: A Defense of Rothbard. December 13. http://archive.lewrockwell.com/blog/lewrw/archives/128349.html. Accessed 20 Apr 2016.

———. 2012b. *Yes to Ron Paul and Liberty*. New York: Ishi Press. http://www.amazon.com/dp/4871873234; http://libertycrier.com/education/walter-blocks-new-book-on-ron-paul/; http://libertyunbound.com/node/862. Accessed 23 May 2016.

———. 2013a. There Is No Right to Privacy. July 13. http://archive.lewrockwell.com/2013/07/walter-block/there-is-no-right-to-privacy/. Accessed 20 Apr 2016.

———. 2013b. *Defending the Undefendable II: Freedom in All Realms*. Terra Libertas Publishing House.

———. 2013c. Rejoinder to Todea on the 'Open' Contract of Immigration. *The Scientific Journal of Humanistic Studies* 8 (5): 52–55.

———. 2014a. Book Review Essay of Steven Pinker's: *The Better Angels of Our Nature: Why Violence Has Declined*. New York, N.Y. Penguin; Part II. *Management Education Science Technology Journal MEST* 2 (1): 141–160.

———. 2014b. A Collection of Essays on Libertarian Jurisprudence: Sunshine and Property Rights. *Saint Louis University Law Journal* 58 (2): 541–547. http://slu.edu/Documents/law/Law%20Journal/Archives/LawJournal58-2/Block_Article.pdf. Accessed 20 Apr 2016.

———. 2014c. Block Discovers New Source of Inequality; Calls for Government Action. June 3. https://www.lewrockwell.com/2014/06/walter-e-block/walter-block-discovers-a-new-source-of-inequality/. Accessed 2 Dec 2015.

———. 2014d. Responses to Critics of My Call for Interplanetary Welfare: Sharing Moons: Must We Resort to Interplanetary Warfare? June 5. http://www.lewrockwell.com/2014/06/walter-e-block/must-we-resort-to-interplanetary-warfare/; http://libertycrier.com/must-resort-interplanetary-welfare/; http://snewsi.com/id/1425596951. Accessed 11 July 2015.

———. 2014e. May I Sue the *New York Times*? A Libertarian Analysis of Suing for Libel. September 5. http://www.lewrockwell.com/2014/09/walter-e-block/may-i-sue-the-ny-times/. Accessed 29 June 2016.

———. 2014f. Evictionism and Libertarianism. *Journal of Medicine and Philosophy* 35 (2): 290–294. http://jmp.oxfordjournals.org/content/early/2014/04/27/jmp.jhu012.full?keytype=ref&ijkey=3n1zc8zcBRnT586; http://jmp.oxfordjournals.org/cgi/reprint/jhu012?ijkey=3n1zc8zcBRnT586&keytype=ref. Accessed 10 Aug 2016.

———. 2015. When Is It OK to Shoot Down a Drone? August 8. http://www.targetliberty.com/2015/08/when-is-it-ok-to-shoot-down-drone.html?utm_source=feedburner&utm_medium=email&utm_campaign=Feed%3A+TargetLiberty+%28Target+Liberty%29. Accessed 23 Aug 2016.

Block, Walter, and William Barnett. 2009. Monopsony Theory. *American Review of Political Economy* 7 (1/2): 67–109.

Block, Walter E., and Matthew Block. 1996. Roads, Bridges, Sunlight and Private Property Rights. *Journal Des Economistes Et Des Etudes Humaines* VII (2/3): 351–362.

———. 2000. Toward a Universal Libertarian Theory of Gun (Weapon) Control. *Ethics, Place and Environment* 3 (3): 289–298.

Block, Walter E., and Gene Callahan. 2003. Is There a Right to Immigration? A Libertarian Perspective. *Human Rights Review* 5 (1): 46–71.

Block, Walter E., and Milton Friedman. 2006. Fanatical, Not Reasonable: A Short Correspondence Between Walter Block and Milton Friedman (on Friedrich Hayek). *Journal of Libertarian Studies* 20 (3): 61–80 http://www.mises.org/journals/jls/20_3/20_3_4.pdf; https://mises.org/system/tdf/20_3_4.pdf?file=1&type=document.

Block, Walter E., and Michael R. Edelstein. 2012. Popsicle Sticks and Homesteading Land for Nature Preserves. *Romanian Economic and Business Review* 7 (1): 7–13. http://www.rebe.rau.ro/REBE%207%201.pdf. Accessed 29 Sep 2016.

Block, Walter, and Richard Epstein. 2005. Debate on Eminent Domain. *NYU Journal of Law & Liberty* 1 (3): 1144–1169.

Block, Walter E., and Michael Fleischer. 2010. How Would an Anarchist Society Handle Child Abuse? October 13. http://www.lewrockwell.com/block/block167.html. Accessed 23 Aug 2016.

Block, Walter E., and Peter Lothian Nelson. 2015. *Water Capitalism: The Case for Privatizing Oceans, Rivers, Lakes, and Aquifers.* New York: Lexington Books;RowmanandLittlefield.https://rowman.com/ISBN/9781498518802/Water-Capitalism-The-Case-for-Privatizing-Oceans-Rivers-Lakes-and-Aquifers. Accessed 14 Dec 2015.

Block, Walter, and Llewellyn H. Rockwell Jr. 2007. Katrina and the Future of New Orleans. *Telos* 139: 170–185. http://tinyurl.com/2wv8lc; http://journal.telospress.com; http://journal.telospress.com/cgi/reprint/2007/139/170.

Block, Walter, and William Barnett II. 2008. Continuums. *Journal Etica e Politica/Ethics & Politics* 1: 151–166. http://www2.units.it/~etica/; http://www2.units.it/~etica/2008_1/BLOCKBARNETT.pdf. Accessed 23 Apr 2016.

———. 2012–2013. Milton Friedman and the Financial Crisis. *American Review of Political Economy* 10 (1/2): 2–17. https://sites.bemidjistate.edu/arpejournal/wp-content/uploads/sites/2/2015/11/v10n1-block.pdf.

Block, Walter and Guillermo Yeatts. 1999–2000. The Economics and Ethics of Land Reform: A Critique of the Pontifical Council for Justice and Peace's 'Toward a Better Distribution of Land: The Challenge of Agrarian Reform'. *Journal of Natural Resources and Environmental Law* 15 (1): 37–69

Block, Walter, Stephan Kinsella, and Roy Whitehead. 2006. The Duty to Defend Advertising Injuries Caused by Junk Faxes: An Analysis of Privacy, Spam, Detection and Blackmail. *Whittier Law Review* 27 (4): 925–949. http://www.walterblock.com/wp-content/uploads/publications/block-etal_ spam_whittier-2006.pdf; http://www.walterblock.com/wp-content/ uploads/2009/06/faxesduty.pdf. Accessed 20 Apr 2016.

Boettke, Peter J. 2001. *Calculation and Coordination: Essays on Socialism and Transitional Political Economy.* London: Routledge. http://www.mises.org/ etexts/cc.pdf. Accessed 23 May 2016.

Bohm-Bawerk, Eugen. 1959 [1884]. *Capital and Interest.* South Holland, IL: Libertarian Press. Trans. George D. Hunke and Hans F. Sennholz. See Particularly Part I, Chapter XII, Exploitation Theory of Socialism-Communism.

———. 2011. *Karl Marx and the Close of His System.* CreateSpace Independent Publishing Platform.

Boldrin, Michele, and David K. Levine. 2008. *Against Intellectual Monopoly.* http://levine.sscnet.ucla.edu/general/intellectual/against.htm; http://mises. org/store/Against-Intellectual-Monopoly-P552.aspx.

Boudreaux, Donald. 2008. Optimal Population? April 8. http://cafehayek. com/2008/04/optimal-populat.html. Accessed 10 Aug 2016.

Boudreaux, Donald J., and Thomas J. DiLorenzo. 1992. The Protectionist Roots of Antitrust. *Review of Austrian Economics* 6 (2): 81–96.

Bower, Tom. 2014. *Branson: Behind the Mask.* Faber.

Boyle, Alan. 2015. Asteroid Mining Riches Await: President Obama Signs Space Resource Bill into Law. November 25. http://www.geekwire.com/2015/ asteroid-riches-president-obama-signs-space-resource-bill-into-law/. Accessed 6 Dec 2015.

Brandon, Russell. 2014. Cops Are Seizing Hundreds of Millions of Dollars from Drivers and Bragging About It in Chat Rooms. *The Verge.* September 8. http://www.theverge.com/2014/9/8/6120971/cops-are-seizing-hundreds-of-millions-of-dollars-from-drivers-and. Accessed 25 June 2015.

Branfman, Fred. 2013. World's Most Evil and Lawless Institution? The Executive Branch of the U.S. Government. *Alternet.* June 26. http://www.alternet.org/ investigations/executive-branch-evil-and-lawless?paging=off.

Brisman, Avi. 2011. United Nations Convention on the Law of the Sea. *Encyclopedia of Global Justice* 1103–1104. http://link.springer.com/reference workentry/10.1007%2F978-1-4020-9160-5_661. Accessed 13 Dec 2015.

Brunner, Jim. 2015. Paul Allen Bankrolls Initiative to Ban Rare-Species Trafficking. April 26. http://www.seattletimes.com/seattle-news/politics/paul-allen-backs-state-ban-on-rare-species-trafficking/. Accessed 28 July 2016.

Buchanan, Patrick J. 2014. Behind the Sinking of the Lusitania. September 3. http://www.lewrockwell.com/2014/09/patrick-j-buchanan/wilson-lied-us-into-wwi/.

Burris, Charles A. 2012. Who Rules America: Power Elite Analysis and American History. January 18. http://archive.lewrockwell.com/burris/burris21.1.html.

Butler, Eamonn, ed. 1988. *The Mechanics of Privatization.* London: Adam Smith Institute.

Bylund, Per. 2005. Man and Matter: A Philosophical Inquiry into the Justification of Ownership in Land from the Basis of Self-Ownership. Master thesis, Lund University, Spring Semester (June). http://www.uppsatser.se/uppsats/a7eb17de8f/; http://perbylund.com/academics_polsci_msc.pdf; http://www.essays.se/essay/a7eb17de8f/; http://www.lunduniversity.lu.se/o.o.i.s?id=24965&postid=1330482. Accessed 23 Apr 2016

———. 2012. Man and Matter: How the Former Gains Ownership of the Latter. *Libertarian Papers* 4 (1). http://libertarianpapers.org/articles/2012/lp-4-1-5.pdf. Accessed 23 Apr 2016.

Bystydzienski, Jill M., and Sharon R. Bird, eds. 2006. *Removing Barriers: Women in Academic Science, Technology, Engineering and Mathematics.* Bloomington and Indianapolis: Indiana University Press.

Calhoun, John C. 1853. *A Disquisition on Government.* Ed. C. Gordon Post. 1953. *A Disquisition on Government and Selections from the Discourse.* Edited, with an Introduction. New York: Liberal Arts Press.

California, DMV. 2015. Summary of Draft Autonomous Vehicles Deployment Regulations. Department of Motor Vehicles. December 16.

Campbell-Dollaghan, Kelsey. 2015. South China Sea Work Dredges Up Questions, Delays Planned IPO. August 21. http://gizmodo.com/chinas-dredging-in-the-south-china-sea-created-2-900-ac-1725604544. Accessed 11 Dec 2015.

Cantillon, Richard. 2011. The Value of Labor. October 21. https://mises.org/library/value-labor.

Caplan, Bryan. 2007. *The Myth of the Rational Voter: Why Democracies Choose Bad Policies*. Princeton, NJ: Princeton University Press.

Carden, Art. 2011. Who Could Have Predicted that the Solyndra Deal Wouldn't Work Out? October 10. https://mises.org/blog/who-could-have-predicted-solyndra-deal-wouldn%E2%80%99t-work-out.

Carnis, Laurent. 2003. The Case for Road Privatization: A Defense by Restitution. *Journal des Economistes et des Etudes Humaines*. 13 (1): 95–116.

Carr, Austin. 2013. SpaceX Founder Elon Musk Considered Buying Russian Ballistic Nukes?! FastCompany.com. March 9. http://www.fastcompany.com/3006829/spacex-founder-elon-musk-considered-buying-russian-ballistic-missiles-nukes. Accessed 11 July 2015.

Casey, Doug. 2010. Doug Casey on Anarchy. March 31. http://www.caseyresearch.com/cwc/doug-casey-anarchy. Accessed 23 Aug 2016.

Casey, Christopher P. 2015. How GDP Metrics Distort Our View of the Economy. May 15. http://www.thedailybell.com/editorials/36294/Mises-Institute-How-GDP-Metrics-Distort-Our-View-of-the-Economy/. Accessed 23 Apr 2016.

Castro III, Pablo. 2014. We Didn't Cross the Border, the Border Crossed Us. https://www.youtube.com/watch?v=DYsJzzPcVT0. Accessed 21 Oct 2015.

Cegłowski, Maciej. 2005. A Rocket to Nowhere. August 3. http://www.idlewords.com/2005/08/a_rocket_to_nowhere.htm.

Chakrabortty, Aditya. 2013. The Truth About Richard Branson's Virgin Rail Profits. June 10. http://www.theguardian.com/commentisfree/2013/jun/10/truth-richard-branson-virgin-rail-profits. Accessed 29 June 2016.

Chambers, Dean. 2015. Heavily Subsidized and Failing: Elon Musk and SolarCity. December 14. http://www.redstate.com/diary/qstarweb/2015/12/14/heavily-subsidized-failing-elon-musk-solarcity/. Accessed 17 June 2016.

Chamlee-Wright, Emily, and Daniel Rothschild. 2007. Disastrous Uncertainty: How Government Disaster Policy Undermines Community Rebound. Mercatus Center. http://www.mercatus.org/Publications/pubID.3579/pub_detail.asp; http://www.mercatus.org/repository/docLib/20070111_Disastrous_Uncertainty_complete.pdf.

Chandra, Ambarish, Sumeet Gulati, and Milind Kandlikar. 2009. Green Drivers or Free Riders? An Analysis of Tax Rebates for Hybrid Vehicles. February 24. SSRN: http://ssrn.com/abstract=1348808. Accessed 23 May 2016.

Chang, Kenneth. 2015. Mars Shows Signs of Having Flowing Water, Possible Niches for Life, NASA Says. September 28. http://www.nytimes.com/2015/09/29/science/space/mars-life-liquid-water.html?_r=0.

Chappell, Matt. 2014. 15 Famous Predictions that Were Spectacularly Wrong. April 14. http://www.news.com.au/technology/gadgets/famous-predictions-that-were-spectacularly-wrong/story-fn6vihic-1226889769437. Accessed 25 Aug 2015.

Charette, Robert M. 2013. The STEM Crisis Is a Myth; Forget the Dire Predictions of a Looming Shortfall of Scientists, Technologists, Engineers, and Mathematicians. August 30. http://spectrum.ieee.org/at-work/education/the-stem-crisis-is-a-myth. Accessed 23 May 2016.

Chernow, Ron. 2004. *Titan: The Life of John D. Rockefeller, Sr.* New York: Vintage.

Chibber, Kabir. 2009. How Green Is Richard Branson? August 5. http://www.wired.co.uk/magazine/archive/2009/09/start/how-green-is-richard-branson. Accessed 29 June 2016.

Choi, Charles Q. 2014a. Planet Jupiter: Facts About Its Size, Moons and Red Spot. *Space.com.* November 14. http://www.space.com/7-jupiter-largest-planet-solar-system.html. Accessed 7 Dec 2015.

———. 2014b. Planet Venus Facts: A Hot, Hellish & Volcanic Planet. *Space.com.* November 4. http://www.space.com/44-venus-second-planet-from-the-sun-brightest-planet-in-solar-system.html. Accessed 28 Oct 2015.

———. 2014c. Planet Mercury: Facts About the Planet Closest to the Sun. *Space.com.* November 4. http://www.space.com/36-mercury-the-suns-closest-planetary-neighbor.html. Accessed 28 Oct 2015.

———. 2014d. Planet Saturn: Facts About Saturn's Rings, Moons and Size. *Space.com.* November 17. http://www.space.com/48-saturn-the-solar-systems-major-ring-bearer.html. Accessed 7 Dec 2015.

———. 2014e. Comets: Facts About the 'Dirty Snowballs' of Space. *Space.com.* November 15. http://www.space.com/53-comets-formation-discovery-and-exploration.html. Accessed 30 July 2015.

Christol, Carl Q. 1980. The Common Heritage of Mankind Provision in the 1979 Agreement Governing the Activities of States on the Moon and Other Celestial Bodies. *The International Lawyer* 14 (3): 429–483. Published by: American Bar Association. http://www.jstor.org/stable/40706663?seq=1#page_scan_tab_contents. Accessed 13 Dec 2015.

———. 1982. *The Modern International Law of Outer Space.* New York: Pergamon Press.

———. 1985. The Moon Treaty Enters into Force. *The American Journal of International Law* 79 (1): 163–168. Published by: American Society of International Law. http://www.jstor.org/stable/2202679?seq=1#page_scan_tab_contents. Accessed 13 Dec 2015.

Clavin, Whitney, and Harrington, J. D. 2013. NASA's WISE Finds Mysterious Centaurs May Be Comets. California Institute of Technology—Jet Propulsion Laboratory.   July   25.   http://www.jpl.nasa.gov/news/news. php?release=2013-234. Accessed 4 Aug 2015.

Coffey, S. 2009. Establishing a Legal Framework for Property Rights to Natural Resources in Outer Space. *Case Western Reserve Journal of International Law* 41 (1): 119–147.

Coggins, David. 2013. Why Does a Vicuña Jacket Cost $21,000? *Wall Street Journal.* September 20. http://www.wsj.com/articles/SB10001424127 8873233922045790730906148512288. Accessed 21 June 2016.

Colgrass, Neal. 2014. Report: Hitler Was on Crystal Meth. *USA Today.* October 14. http://www.usatoday.com/story/news/world/2014/10/14/hitler-drugs-crystal-meth/17242185/. Accessed 8 Nov 2015.

Colombos, Constantine John. 1967. *The International Law of the Sea.* Longmans.

Conquest, Robert. 1986. *The Harvest of Sorrow.* New York: Oxford University Press.

———. 1990. *The Great Terror.* Edmonton, Alberta: Edmonton University Press.

Convention on International Liability for Damage Caused by Space Objects. 1971. United Nations General Assembly Resolution 2777 (XXVI), November 22.

Cook, Russell. 2015. Those Scientists Who Want to Use RICO to Prosecute AGW 'Deniers' Have a Big Problem. October 1. http://www.american-thinker.com/articles/2015/10/those_scientists_who_want_to_use_rico_to_prosecute_agw_deniers_have_a_big_problem.html#ixzz3tVeVyG3S; http://www.americanthinker.com/articles/2015/10/those_scientists_who_want_to_use_rico_to_prosecute_agw_deniers_have_a_big_problem.html. Accessed 6 Dec 2015.

Cooper, L.A. 2003. Encouraging Space Exploration Through a New Application of Space Property Rights. *Space Policy* 19 (2): 111–118.

Costea, Diana. 2003. A Critique of Mises's Theory of Monopoly Prices. *The Quarterly Journal of Austrian Economics* 6 (3): 47–62.

Courtois, Stephane, Nicolas Werth, Jean-Louis Panne, Andrzej Paczkowski, Karel Bartosek, and Jean Louis Margolin. 1999. *The Black Book of Communism: Crimes, Terror, Repression.* Trans. from French by Jonathan Murphy, and Mark Kramer. Cambridge, MA: Harvard University Press.

Cowen, Tyler, ed. 1988. *The Theory of Market Failure: A Critical Examination.* Fairfax, VA: George Mason University Press. http://www.amazon.com/

Theory-Market-Failure-Critical-Examination/dp/0913969133/ref=sr_1_1?i
e=UTF8&s=books&qid=1200191409&sr=1-1. Accessed 23 Apr 2016.
———. 2006. An Economist Visits New Orleans: Bienvenido, Nuevo Orleans.
April 19. http://www.mercatus.org/publications/pubID.2272/pub_detail.
asp.
Culpepper, Dreda, and Walter E. Block. 2008. Price Gouging in the Katrina
Aftermath. *International Journal of Social Economics* 35 (7): 512–520. http://
www.emeraldinsight.com/Insight/viewContentItem.do;jsessionid=D99C6D
908AEA5910439BB07AF99D0F48?contentType=Article&conten
tId=1729159.
Czech, Kenneth P. 2006. Roald Amundsen and the 1925 North Pole Expedition.
June 12. http://www.historynet.com/roald-amundsen-and-the-1925-north-
pole-expedition.htm. Accessed 25 Aug 2015.
Dark Government. n.d. Moons of Our Solar System Scaled to Earth's Moon.
http://www.darkgovernment.com/moons.html. Accessed 19 Nov 2015.
De Jasay, Anthony. 1989. *Social Contract, Free Ride: A Study of the Public Goods
Problem.* Oxford: Oxford University Press. http://www.amazon.com/Social-
Contract-Free-Ride-Paperbacks/dp/0198239122/ref=sr_1_1?ie=UTF8&s=b
ooks&qid=1200191531&sr=1-1. Accessed 23 Apr 2016.
De Wachter, Joren. 2013. IP Is a Thought Crime. At TEDxLeuven. June 6.
http://www.youtube.com/watch?feature=player_
detailpage&v=E5BOBs3Nmbw.
DeBord, Matthew. 2015. Elon Musk's Companies Have Always Depended on
Government Money—And He's Has Always Been Up Front About It. June 8.
http://www.businessinsider.com/elon-musk-always-depended-government-
money-up-front-about-it-2015-6. Accessed 29 June 2016.
Delingpole, James. 2015. Twenty Alarmist Climate Scientists—Including UN
IPCC Lead Author Kevin 'Travesty' Trenberth—Have Written a Letter to
President Obama Urging Him to Use RICO Laws to Crush Dissent by
Climate Skeptics. Their Hypocrisy and Dishonesty, Especially that of the
Main Signatory, Almost Defies Belief. September 19. http://www.breitbart.
com/big-government/2015/09/19/climate-alarmists-obama-use-rico-laws-
jail-skeptics/. Accessed 6 Dec 2015.
Dembling, P. G. 1979. Treaty on Principles Governing the Activities of States in
the Exploration and Use of Outer Space, Including the Moon and Other
Celestial Bodies. In *Manual on Space Law*, vol. I, compiled and ed.
N. Jasentuliyana and R.S.K. Lee. Dobbs Ferry, NY: Oceana Publications.

Department of Defense. 2007. Base Structure Report. http://www.defenselink. mil/pubs/BSR_2007_Baseline.pdf. Accessed 28 July 2016.

Derks, Belle, Naomi Ellemers, Colette van Laar, and Kim de Groot. 2011. Do Sexist Organizational Cultures Create the Queen Bee? *British Journal of Social Psychology* 50 (3): 519–535. http://onlinelibrary.wiley.com/doi/10.1348/014466610X525280/abstract. Accessed 23 May 2016.

Desrochers, Pierre. 2015. The Simon-Ehrlich Wager 25 Years on; as the Famous Environmentalist Bet Showed, Malthusians Are Always Wrong. http://www.spiked-online.com/newsite/article/the-simonehrlich-wager-25-years-on/17482#.Vm4zL09Ig5s.

Detrick, Chloe. 2015. Washington Voters Approve Anti-Wildlife-Trafficking Initiative, I-1401, In a Landslide. November 4. http://www.humanesociety. org/news/press_releases/2015/11/washington-approves-wildlife-initative. html?referrer=https://www.google.com/. Accessed 28 July 2016.

Diamandis, Peter. 2015. Entrepreneurs, Not Government, Drive Innovation— Here's Why. July 14. https://www.linkedin.com/pulse/entrepreneurs-government-drive-innovation-heres-why-peter-diamandis?forceNoSplash=true. Accessed 29 June 2016.

Dillow, Clay. 2015a. Boeing, GE Beat Tea Party as Congress Revives Export-Import Bank. December 4. http://fortune.com/2015/12/04/congress-export-import-bank. Accessed 29 June 2016.

———. 2015b. Obama Is About to Give Private Space Companies a Big Break. November 24. http://fortune.com/2015/11/24/obama-commercial-space-break/. Accessed 6 Dec 2015.

DiLorenzo, Thomas J. 1996. The Myth of Natural Monopoly. *Review of Austrian Economics* 9 (2): 43–58.

DiLorenzo, Thomas. 2006. Death by Government: The Missing Chapter. November 22. http://www.lewrockwell.com/dilorenzo/dilorenzo114.html. Accessed 11 July 2015.

DiLorenzo, Thomas J. 2010. The Culture of Violence in the American West: Myth Versus Reality. *The Independent Review* 15 (2): 227–239. http://www.independent.org/pdf/tir/tir_15_02_4_dilorenzo.pdf. Accessed 23 Aug 2016.

DiLorenzo, Tom, and Jack High. 1988. Antitrust and Competition, Historically Considered. *Economic Inquiry* 26 (1): 423–435.

Dolan, Chris. 1989. The Closest Star to the Earth, The Nearest Stars, as Seen from the Earth. http://www.astro.wisc.edu/~dolan/constellations/extra/nearest.html. Accessed 8 July 2015.

Domhoff, G. William. 1967. *Who Rules America?* Englewood Cliffs, NJ: Prentice-Hall.

———. 1971. *The Higher Circles: The Governing Class in America.* New York: Vintage Books.

———. 1998. *Who Rules America? Power and Politics in the Year 2000.* 3rd ed. Santa Cruz: University of California.

Donaldson, Mike, and Scott Poynting. 2007. *Ruling Class Men: Money, Sex, Power.* Peter Lang. http://books.google.com/books/about/Ruling_Class_Men.html?id=V-KjZ8p3N2oC.

Doughton, Sandi. 2015. Anti-poaching Campaign Is State's Richest this Year; Bankrolled by Billionaire Paul Allen, pro-Initiative-1401 Committee Has Raised more than Twice as much Money as Any Other Political Effort this Year. October 29. http://www.seattletimes.com/seattle-news/politics/anti-poaching-campaign-is-states-richest-this-year/. Accessed 28 July 2016.

Dunn, Terry. 2014. The Space Shuttle's Controversial Launch Abort Plan. February 26. http://www.tested.com/science/space/460233-space-shuttles-controversial-launch-abort-plan/. Accessed 29 June 2016.

Dunstan, J.E. 2002. Towards a Unified Theory of Space Property Rights: Sometimes the Best Way to Predict the Weather Is to Look Outside. In *Space: The Free-Market Frontier*, ed. E.L. Hudgins, 223–241. Washington: Cato Institute.

Ebeling, Richard M. 1993. Economic Calculation Under Socialism: Ludwig von Mises and His Predecessors. In *The Meaning of Ludwig von Mises*, ed. Jeffrey Herbener, 56–101. Norwell, MA: Kluwer Academic Press.

Ebeling, Richard. 2013. Why Not Privatize Foreign Policy? http://epictimes.com/article/127064/why-not-privatize-foreign-policy. Accessed 23 Aug 2016.

Encyclopædia Britannica. 2015. Nazi Party. June 8. https://www.britannica.com/topic/Nazi-Party. Accessed 4 Aug 2016.

Erickson, Kristen. 2015. NASA. National Aeronautics and Space Administration. *Solar System Exploration.* Eris. http://solarsystem.nasa.gov/planets/profile.cfm?Object=Dwa_Eris; https://solarsystem.nasa.gov/planets/profile.cfm?Object=Ast_10199Chariklo; http://solarsystem.nasa.gov/planets/profile.cfm?Object=Dwarf. Accessed 24 July 2015.

European Space Agency. 2013. What Are Lagrange Points? June 21. http://www.esa.int/Our_Activities/Operations/What_are_Lagrange_points. Accessed 23 Oct 2015.

FAR/AIM. 2016. *Federal Aviation Rules/Aeronautical Information Manual.* Aviation Supplies and Academics, Inc.; 2016 Edition (July 1, 2015). http://www.amazon.com/FAR-AIM-2016-Regulations-Aeronautical/dp/1619542501. Accessed 30 Nov 2015.

Faust, Jeff. 2014. Bezos Investment in Blue Origin Exceeds $500 Million. July 18. http://spacenews.com/41299bezos-investment-in-blue-origin-exceeds-500-million/. Accessed 29 June 2016.

Fay, Sidney Bradshaw. 1967. *The Origins of the World War.* The Free Press.

Fedako, Jim. 2011. Envy, the State, and My Fellow Man. September 28. https://mises.org/library/envy-state-and-my-fellow-man. Accessed 13 Dec 2015.

Federal Bureau of Prisons. 2015. Statistics, Offences. May 30. http://www.bop.gov/about/statistics/statistics_inmate_offenses.jsp. Accessed 24 June 2015.

Federalist Society. n.d.. http://www.fed-soc.org/ Accessed 28 July 2016.

Ferdinand Magellan Timeline. 2015. Ferdinand Magellan Timeline. March. http://www.datesandevents.org/people-timelines/13-ferdinand-magellan-timeline.htm. Accessed 27 Aug 2015.

Ferguson, Niall. 2000. *The Pity of War: Explaining World War I.* New York: Basic Books.

———. 2011. *Civilization: The West and the Rest.* Penguin Books.

Fleming, Thomas. 2004. *The Illusion of Victory: Americans In World War I.* New York: Basic Books.

Fleming, Nic. 2015. Should We Give Up on the Dream of Space Elevators? BBC. February 19. http://www.bbc.com/future/story/20150211-space-elevators-a-lift-too-far. Accessed 10 Nov 2015.

Foley, James A. 2013. New Solid Form of Hydrogen Discovered at Extreme Pressures. *Nature World News.* June 4. http://www.natureworldnews.com/articles/2260/20130604/new-solid-form-hydrogen-discovered-extreme-pressures.htm. Accessed 7 Dec 2015.

Foust, Jeff. 2015. Book Review of *Beyond: Our Future in Space* by Chris Impey. May 11. http://www.thespacereview.com/article/2746/1. Accessed 29 June 2016.

Fox, Glenn. 1992. The Pricing of Environmental Goods: A Praxeological Critique of Contingent Valuation. *Cultural Dynamics* V (3): 245–259.

Fox News. 2009. Hubble Telescope Almost Was Billion-Dollar Joke. May 11. http://www.foxnews.com/story/2009/05/11/hubble-telescope-almost-was-billion-dollar-joke.html. Accessed 1 July 2016.

Frank Fox, Mary, Deborah G. Johnson, and Sue V. Rosser, eds. 2006. *Women, Gender, and Technology.* Urbana and Chicago: University of Illinois Press.

French, Doug. 2012. Property Means Preservation. May 31. http://mises.org/daily/5960/. Accessed 11 June 2016.

Friedman, Milton. 1962. The Role of Government in Education. In *Capitalism and Freedom*. Chicago IL: University of Chicago Press.

Friedman, Milton. 2000. Interview. Commanding Heights. October 1. http://www.pbs.org/wgbh/commandingheights/shared/minitextlo/int_miltonfriedman.

Friedman, David. 1972. *Laissez Faire in Population: The Least Bad Solution*. New York: Population Council.

———. 1977. A Theory of the Size and Shape of Nations. *Journal of Political Economy* 85: 59–77.

———. 1979. Private Creation and Enforcement of Law: A Historical Case. *University of Chicago Law Review*. http://www.daviddfriedman.com/Academic/Iceland/Iceland.html. Accessed 23 Apr 2016.

———. 1989. *The Machinery of Freedom: Guide to a Radical Capitalism*. 2nd ed. La Salle, IL: Open Court.

Frontline World. 2003. Philippines, Islands Under Siege, 1898–1933 America's Colony. PBS. June. http://www.pbs.org/frontlineworld/stories/philippines/tl01.html. Accessed 23 June 2015.

Futron Corporation. 2002. Space Transportation Costs: Trends in Price Per Pound to Orbit 1990–2000. September 6. https://web.archive.org/web/20110711061933/http://www.futron.com/upload/wysiwyg/Resources/Whitepapers/Space_Transportation_Costs_Trends_0902.pdf. Accessed 23 May 2016.

Gajanan, Mahita. 2015. Going Up? Space Elevator Could Zoom Astronauts into Earth's Stratosphere. *The Guardian*. August 17. http://www.theguardian.com/science/2015/aug/17/space-elevator-thothx-tower. Accessed 10 Nov 2015.

Geron, Tomio. 2013. Elon Musk–SpaceX Testing New Reusable Rockets. March 9. Forbes.com. Accessed 25 May 2017.

Gibbs, Yvonne. 2015a. NASA Armstrong Fact Sheet: First Generation X-1. NASA. August 12. http://www.nasa.gov/centers/armstrong/news/FactSheets/FS-085-DFRC.html. Accessed 9 Nov 2015.

———. 2015b. NASA Armstrong Fact Sheet: X-15 Hypersonic Research Program. NASA. August 13. http://www.nasa.gov/centers/armstrong/news/FactSheets/FS-052-DFRC.html. Accessed 9 Nov 2015.

Glasscock, Carl Burgess. 2011. Car History—Get a Horse! http://www.americanautohistory.com/Articles/Article005.htm.

Goedhuis, D. 1981. Some Recent Trends in the Interpretation and the Implementation of the Rules of International Space Law Essays in Honor of Oliver J. Lissitzyn. *Columbia Journal of Transnational Law* 19: 213–233.

Goldsmith, Donald. 2015. Does Humanity's Destiny Lie in Interstellar Space Travel? Space.com. January 27. https://solarsystem.nasa.gov/planets/profile.cfm?Object=Ast_10199Chariklo. Accessed 4 Aug 2015.

Gordon, David. 1991. *Resurrecting Marx: The Analytical Marxist on Exploitation, Freedom and Justice*. Transaction Publishers.

———. 2004. Liberty and Obedience. *The Mises Review*. Fall. http://mises.org/misesreview_detail.aspx?control=262. Accessed 20 Apr 2016.

———. 2008. Should the State Regulate Envy? January 15. https://mises.org/library/should-state-regulate-envy. Accessed 13 Dec 2015.

Green, Michael. 2015. New Study Reveals When, Where and How Much Motorists Drive. *AAA News Room*. April 16. http://newsroom.aaa.com/2015/04/new-study-reveals-much-motorists-drive/. Accessed 6 July 2016.

Gregory, Anthony. 2011. Abolish the Police. May 26. http://www.lewrockwell.com/gregory/gregory213.html. Accessed 23 Aug 2016.

Gregory, Anthony, and Walter E. Block. 2007. On Immigration: Reply to Hoppe. *Journal of Libertarian Studies* 21 (3): 25–42.

Griffin, Andrew. 2015. Asteroid Mining Made Legal After Barack Obama Gives US Citizens the Right to Own Parts of Celestial Bodies. November 26. http://www.independent.co.uk/news/science/asteroid-mining-made-legal-after-barack-obama-gives-us-citizens-the-right-to-own-parts-of-celestial-a6750046.html. Accessed 13 Dec 2015.

Groove, S. 1969. Interpreting Article II of the Outer Space Treaty. *Fordham Law Review* 37 (3): 349–354.

Grossman, Lisa. 2013. Cosmic Collisions Spin Stellar Corpses into Gold. *New Scientist-Daily News*. July 17. https://www.newscientist.com/article/dn23886-cosmic-collisions-spin-stellar-corpses-into-gold/. Accessed 29 Feb 2015.

Grotius, Hugo. 1625. *Law of War and Peace (De Jure Belli ac Pacis)*, 3 volumes. Trans. A.C. Campbell, London, 1814.

Guillory, Gil, and Patrick Tinsley. 2009. The Role of Subscription-Based Patrol and Restitution in the Future of Liberty. *Libertarian Papers* 1 (12). http://libertarianpapers.org/2009/12-the-role-of-subscription-based-patrol-and-restitution-in-the-future-of-liberty/. Accessed 23 Aug 2016.

Hall, Joseph Lorenzo. 2003. Columbia and Challenger: Organizational Failure at NASA. *Space Policy* 19 (4): 239–247.

Hamilton. 2016. The Two Kinds of Libertarianism: Calhounian and Heinleinian. *Breitbart*. November 16. http://www.breitbart.com/big-government/2013/11/16/the-two-kinds-of-libertarianism-calhounian-and-heinleinian/. Accessed 15 June 2016.

Hanke, Steve H. 1987a. Privatization. In *The New Palgrave: A Dictionary of Economics*, ed. J. Eatwell, M. Milgate, and P. Newman, vol. 3, 976–977. London: The Macmillan Press, Ltd.

———., ed. 1987b. *Privatization and Development*. San Francisco: Institute for Contemporary Studies.

Hankoff, Nick. 2014. Top 5 Libertarian Quotes from Billionaire Elon Musk. *Voices of Liberty*. November 10. https://voicesofliberty.com/2014/11/10/top-5-libertarian-quotes-from-billionaire-elon-musk/6/. Accessed 20 June 2016.

Hannesson, Rögnvaldur. 2004. The Privatization of the Oceans. In *Evolving Property Rights in Marine Fisheries*, ed. D.R. Leal, 25–48. Lanham, MD: Rowman and Littlefield.

———. 2006. *The Privatization of the Oceans*. Cambridge, MA: MIT Press.

Harding, Sandra. 2006. *Science and Social Inequality: Feminist and Postcolonial Issues*. Urbana and Chicago: University of Illinois Press.

Harrison, Thomas Edward. 2010. The Jovian Planets: Uranus, and Neptune. University of New Mexico, Astronomy 105. http://astronomy.nmsu.edu/tharriso/ast105/UranusandNeptune.html. Accessed 28 April 2018.

Hartung, William. 2016. Lockheed Martin, Making Money the Old-Fashioned Way. March 17. http://www.huffingtonpost.com/william-hartung/lockheed-martin-making-mo_b_9486334.html. Accessed 29 June 2016.

Hasnas, John. 1995. The Myth of the Rule of Law. *Wisconsin Law Review* 199. http://faculty.msb.edu/hasnasj/GTWebSite/MythWeb.htm. Accessed 23 Aug 2016.

Hawking, Stephen. 1996. *A Brief History of Time*. New York: Bantam Books Trade Paperbacks.

Hayek, Friedrich A. 1935a. Socialist Calculation Debate: The Present State of the Debate. In *Collectivist Economic Planning: Critical Studies on the Possibility of Socialism*, ed. Friedrich A. Hayek, 201–243. London: Routledge and Kegan Paul.

———. 1935b. The Nature and History of the Debate. In *Collectivist Economic Planning: Critical Studies on the Possibility of Socialism*, ed. Friedrich A. Hayek, 1–40. London: Routledge and Kegan Paul.

———. 1940. Socialist Calculation: The Competitive 'Solution'. *Economica* 7 (May): 125–149.

Hayek, F.A. 1948. Socialist Calculation I, II, & III. In *Individualism and Economic Order*. Chicago: University of Chicago Press.

Hayek, Friedrich A. 1960. *The Constitution of Liberty*. Chicago: University of Chicago Press.

———. 1979. *The Counter-Revolution of Science*. 2nd ed. Indianapolis: Liberty Press.

Haymond, Jeff. 2014. Top 1%'er Richard Branson Advocates for more Subsidies to the Rich! January 22. http://bereansatthegate.com/top-1er-richard-branson-advocates-for-more-subsidies-to-the-rich/. Accessed 29 June 2016.

Hazlitt, Henry. 2008 [1946]. *Economics in One Lesson*. Auburn, AL: Mises Institute. http://mises.org/books/economics_in_one_lesson_hazlitt.pdf. Accessed 29 June 2016.

———. 2013. On Appeasing Envy. July 30. https://mises.org/library/appeasing-envy. Accessed 13 Dec 2015.

Hechtkopf, Kevin. 2011. Rick Perry Fails to Remember What Agency He'd Get Rid of in GOP Debate. November 10. http://www.cbsnews.com/news/rick-perry-fails-to-remember-what-agency-hed-get-rid-of-in-gop-debate/.

Heinlein, Robert. 1997 [1966]. *The Moon Is a Harsh Mistress*. New York: Tor Books.

Heinrich, David J. 2010. Justice for All Without the State. *The Libertarian Standard*. May 6. http://www.libertarianstandard.com/articles/david-j-heinrich/justice-for-all-without-the-state/. Accessed 23 Aug 2016.

Heller, Chris. 2012. Neil deGrasse Tyson: How Space Exploration Can Make America Great Again. March 5. http://www.theatlantic.com/technology/archive/2012/03/neil-degrasse-tyson-how-space-exploration-can-make-america-great-again/253989/. Accessed 7 July 2016.

Henderson, David R. 2008. Rent Seeking. In *The Concise Encyclopedia of Economics*, ed. David R. Henderson. Indianapolis, IN: The Liberty Fund. http://www.econlib.org/library/Enc/RentSeeking.html. Accessed 11 June 2016.

———. 2013. The Robber Barons: Neither Robbers nor Barons. *Library of Economics and Liberty*. March 4. http://www.econlib.org/cgi-bin/printarticle2.pl?file=Columns/y2013/Hendersonbarons.html. Accessed 9 Aug 2015.

Hertzfeld, H. 2011. Testimony for Hearing on the Office of Commercial Space Transportation's Fiscal Year 2012 Budget Request. May 5. http://science.

house.gov/sites/republicans.science.house.gov/files/documents/hearings/050511_Hertzfeld.pdf.

Higgs, Robert. 2009. Why We Couldn't Abolish Slavery Then and Can't Abolish Government Now. August 20. http://www.lewrockwell.com/higgs/higgs128.html. Accessed 23 Aug 2016.

———. 2012. What Is the Point of My Libertarian Anarchism? January 16. http://archive.lewrockwell.com/higgs/higgs180.html. Accessed 23 Aug 2016.

High, Jack. 1984–1985. Bork's Paradox: Static vs Dynamic Efficiency in Antitrust Analysis. *Contemporary Policy Issues* 3: 21–34.

Hirsch, Jerry. 2015. Elon Musk's Growing Empire Is Fueled by $4.9 Billion in Government Subsidies. May 30. http://www.latimes.com/business/la-fi-hy-musk-subsidies-20150531-story.html#page=1. Accessed 29 June 2016.

Hirschfeld, Bob. 2002. Space Elevator Gets Lift. *G4 Media—TechTV Vault.* January 31. http://web.archive.org/web/20050608080057/http://www.g4tv.com/techtvvault/features/35657/Space_Elevator_Gets_Lift.html. Accessed 10 Nov 2015.

History.com. 2015. Cultural Revolution. http://www.history.com/topics/cultural-revolution. Accessed 23 June 2015.

———. 2016. 1789; Mutiny on the HMS Bounty. April 28. http://www.history.com/this-day-in-history/mutiny-on-the-hms-bounty. Accessed 27 Aug 2015.

———. n.d. Ferdinand Magellan. http://www.history.com/topics/exploration/ferdinand-magellan. Accessed 25 Aug 2015.

Hoff, Trygve J.B. 1981. *Economic Calculation in a Socialist Society.* Indianapolis: Liberty Press.

Hohler, Daniel. 2009. Top 5 Reasons Why Space Exploration Is Important for the World. July 26. http://planetsave.com/2009/07/26/top-5-reasons-why-space-exploration-is-important-for-the-world/. Accessed 7 July 2016.

Holcombe, Randall. 1997. A Theory of the Theory of Public Goods. *Review of Austrian Economics* 10 (1): 1–10. http://www.mises.org/journals/rae/pdf/RAE10_1_1.pdf. Accessed 23 Apr 2016.

Holcombe, Randall G. 2014. President Obama's Investment Skills. March 12. https://mises.org/blog/president-obama%E2%80%99s-investment-skills.

Holdren, John P., and Eric Lander. 2012. Report to the President: Engage to Excel: Producing One Million Additional College Graduates with Degrees in Science, Technology, Engineering, and Mathematics. February. https://www.whitehouse.gov/sites/default/files/microsites/ostp/pcast-engage-to-excel-final_2-25-12.pdf. Accessed 23 May 2016.

Holler, Dan. 2015. Don't Believe the Hype: Boeing Will Be Just Fine Without the Export-Import Bank; The Sky Isn't Falling, and Companies Like Boeing Certainly Don't Need You to Guarantee Their Business Model. August 27. https://sanantonioteaparty.us/dont-believe-the-hype-boeing-will-be-just-fine-without-the-export-import-bank/. Accessed 29 June 2016.

Holodomor 1932-33. n.d. Holodomor Facts and History. http://www.holodomorct.org/history.html. Accessed 23 June 2015.

Hoover, Kent. 2015. IRS Seizes Millions from Law-Abiding Businesses; 3 Live to Tell House About It. *The Business Journals*. February 11. http://www.bizjournals.com/bizjournals/washingtonbureau/2015/02/irs-seizes-millions-from-law-abiding-businesses-3.html. Accessed 25 June 2015.

Hope, Bradley. 2015. Space Lawyers' Help Startups Navigate the Final Legal Frontier. *The Wall Street Journal*. March 20. http://www.wsj.com/articles/space-lawyers-help-startups-navigate-the-final-legal-frontier-1426813125. Accessed 24 June 2015.

Hoppe, Hans-Hermann. 1989a. Fallacies of the Public Goods Theory and the Production of Security. *The Journal of Libertarian Studies* IX (1): 27–46. http://www.mises.org/journals/jls/9_1/9_1_2.pdf. Accessed 23 Apr 2016.

———. 1989b. In Defense of Extreme Rationalism: Thoughts on Donald McClosky's *The Rhetoric of Economics*. *Review of Austrian Economics* 3: 179–214.

———. 1989c. *A Theory of Socialism and Capitalism. Economics, Politics, and Ethics*. Boston: Kluwer Academic Publishers. http://www.hanshoppe.com/publications/Soc&Cap.pdf.

———. 1990. Marxist and Austrian Class Analysis. *The Journal of Libertarian Studies* 9 (2): 79–94. http://mises.org/journals/jls/9_2/9_2_5.pdf.

———. 1991. Austrian Rationalism in the Age of the Decline of Positivism. *Journal des Economistes et des Etudes Humaines* 2 (2). Reprinted as Hoppe, Hans-Hermann. 1994. Austrian Rationalism in the Age of the Decline of Positivism. In *Austrian Economics: Perspectives on the Past and Prospects for the Future*, ed. Richard M. Ebeling, vol. 17, 59–96. Hillsdale, MI: Hillsdale College Press.

———. 1992. On Praxeology and the Praxeological Foundation of Epistemology and Ethics. In *The Meaning of Ludwig von Mises*, ed. J. Herbener. Boston: Dordrecht.

———. 1993. *The Economics and Thics of Private Property. Studies in Political Economy and Philosophy*. Boston: Kluwer Academic Publishers.

———. 1995. *Economic Science and the Austrian Method*. Auburn, AL: The Ludwig von Mises Institute.

———. 2001. *Democracy—The God That Failed: The Economics and Politics of Monarchy, Democracy, and Natural Order*. Rutgers University, NJ: Transaction Publishers.

———. 2006. Austrian Rationalism in the Age of the Decline of Positivism. In *The Economics and Ethics of Private Property: Studies in Political Economy and Philosophy*, 2nd ed., 347–379. Auburn, AL: The Mises Institute.

———. 2008. Reflections on the Origin and the Stability of the State. June 23. http://www.lewrockwell.com/hoppe/hoppe18.html. Accessed 23 Aug 2016.

———. 2011a. Of Private, Common, and Public Property and the Rationale for Total Privatization. *Libertarian Papers* 3 (1). http://libertarianpapers. org/2011/1-hoppe-private-common-and-public-property/. Accessed 23 Aug 2016.

———. 2011b. State or Private Law Society. April 10. http://www.lewrockwell. com/hoppe/hoppe26.1.html. Accessed 23 Aug 2016.

———. 2011c. Isn't It Time We Overthrew the State? May 6. http://www. lewrockwell.com/hoppe/hoppe26.1.html. Accessed 11 June 2016.

Howell, Elizabeth. 2013. Paul Allen: Billionaire Backer of Private Space Ventures. January 18. http://www.space.com/19333-paul-allen.html. Accessed 28 July 2016.

———. 2015. What Is a Geosynchronous Orbit? Space.com. April 24. http:// www.space.com/29222-geosynchronous-orbit.html. Accessed 18 Apr 2016.

Hudgins, Edward L. 2012. Time to Privatize NASA. http://www.cato.org/publications/commentary/time-privatize-nasa. Accessed 23 May 2016.

Huebert, Jacob. 2010. *Libertarianism Today*. Santa Barbara, CA: Praeger.

Huebert, J.H., and Walter E. Block. 2007a. Space Environmentalism, Property Rights, and the Law. *Memphis Law Review* 37 (2): 281–309. http://www. jhhuebert.com/articles/SpaceEnvironmentalism.pdf. Accessed 13 Dec 2015.

Huebert, J. H. and Walter E. Block. 2007b. In Defense of Advertising in Space. Proceedings of the 49th Colloquium on the Law of Outer Space: International Institute of Space Law, 479–489. http://adage.com/article?article_id=112401; http://www.jhhuebert.com/articles/In%20Defense%20of%20 Advertising%20in%20Space.pdf; http://www.commercialalert.org/issues/ culture/outer-space/an-ad-space-odyssey; http://thelede.blogs.nytimes. com/2006/11/22/space-marketing/. Accessed 13 Dec 2015.

———. 2008. Environmentalists in Outer Space. *The Freeman: Ideas on Liberty* 58 (2). http://fee.org/freeman/detail/environmentalists-in-outer-space. Accessed 13 Dec 2015.

Hughes, Jonathan R.T. 1977. *The Governmental Habit: Economic Controls from Colonial Times to the Present.* New York: Basic Books.

Hülsmann, Jörg Guido. 1999. "Economic Science and Neoclassicism." *Quarterly Journal of Austrian Economics,* Vol. 2 Num. 4, pp. 1–20.

Hummel, Jeffrey. 1990. National Goods vs. Public Goods: Defense, Disarmament and Free Riders. *The Review of Austrian Economics* IV: 88–122. http://www. mises.org/journals/rae/pdf/rae4_1_4.pdf. Accessed 23 Apr 2016.

IAU. n.d.. http://www.iau.org/; http://www.iau.org/. Accessed 22 June 2016.

IMDb. n.d. Jim Backus Biography. IMDb. http://www.imdb.com/name/ nm0000822/bio?ref_=nm_ov_bio_sm. Accessed 7 July 2016.

Impey, Chris. 2015. *Beyond: Our Future in Space.* W. W. Norton & Company.

Jankovic, Ivan, and Walter E. Block. 2016. Tragedy of the Partnership: A Critique of Elinor Ostrom. *American Journal of Economics and Sociology.* 75 (2): 289–318.

Jasentuliyana, N. 1995. A Survey of Space Law as Developed by the United Nations. In *Perspectives on International Law,* ed. N. Jasentuliyana. London, The Hague, and Boston: Kluwer Law International.

Jefferson, Thomas. 1801. Inaugural Address. March 4. http://avalon.law.yale. edu/19th_century/jefinau1.asp. Accessed 28 July 2016.

Jenkins, Holman W, Jr. 2016. Voters Should Be Mad at Electric Cars; If Trump and Sanders Fans Hate Absurd Handouts to Elites, the Tesla Economy Is the Place to Look. March 11. http://www.wsj.com/articles/voters-should-be- mad-at-electric-cars-1457737805. Accessed 23 May 2016.

Jessa, Tega. 2010. How Fast Is Mach 1. *Universe Today.* 10–31. http://www. universetoday.com/77077/how-fast-is-mach-1/. Accessed 17 Nov 2015.

Jet Propulsion Laboratory, California Institute of Technology. 2015. Finding Another Earth. http://planetquest.jpl.nasa.gov/news/207.

Jewkes, John, David Sawers, and Richard Stillerman. 1959. *The Sources of Invention.* St. Martin's Press.

Jones, Jimmy. 1960. Good Timin'. https://www.youtube.com/watch?v=modf q47onwU.

Jopson, Barney. 2014. Roosevelt-era Bank Faces Tea Party Assault. June 25. http://www.ft.com/cms/s/0/5f0dbe14-fc89-11e3-86dc-00144feab7de. html#axzz4D0nfgjVt. Accessed 29 June 2016.

Joyner, C.C. 1986. Legal Implications of the Concept of the Common Heritage of Mankind. *International and Comparative Law Quarterly* 35 (1): 190–199.

http://journals.cambridge.org/action/displayAbstract?fromPage=online&aid =1507532&fileId=S0020589300044201. Accessed 13 Dec 2015.

Juma, Calestous. 2016. *Innovation and Its Enemies, Why People Resist New Technologies*. New York: Oxford University Press.

Kaku, Michio. 2009. The Cost of Space Exploration. July 16. http://www. forbes.com/2009/07/16/apollo-moon-landing-anniversary-opinions-contributors-cost-money.html. Accessed 23 May 2016.

Karpoff, Jonathan M. 2001. Public Versus Private Initiative in Arctic Exploration: The Effects of Incentives and Organizational Structure. *The Journal of Political Economy* 109 (1): 38–78.

Katz, Joshua. n.d. Why Libertarians Should Reject Positive Rights. http://mises. org/journals/scholar/katz.pdf. Accessed 20 Apr 2016.

Kavli Foundation. n.d. Coming Soon—Earth-Like Planets in Other Solar Systems. http://www.kavlifoundation.org/science-spotlights/coming-soon-earth-planets-other-solar-systems#.VcbenbnbKic.

Kellard, Joseph. 1998. Reason vs Faith: Julian Simon vs Paul Ehrlich. April 26. http://capitalismmagazine.com/1998/04/reason-vs-faith-julian-simon-vs-paul-ehrlich/.

Kelly, Martha Hall. 2016. *Lilac Girls*. New York: Ballantine Books.

Kessels, Ursula, and Bettina Hannover. 2008. When Being a Girl Matters Less: Accessibility of Gender-Related Self-Knowledge in Single-Sex and Coeducational Classes and Its Impact on Students' Physics-Related Self-Concept of Ability. *British Journal of Educational Psychology*. http://www. ncbi.nlm.nih.gov/pubmed/17535522. Accessed 23 May 2016.

Keynes, John Maynard. 1920. *The Economic Consequences of the Peace*. New York: Harcourt Brace. http://www.gutenberg.org/ebooks/15776.

Kiel, Paul. 2012. Biggest Financial Crisis Bailout Fails. September 6. http:// www.huffingtonpost.com/2012/09/06/financial-bailout-wallstreet_n_ 1861853.html.

Kiely, Eugene. 2012. 'You Didn't Build That,' Uncut and Unedited. July 23. http://www.factcheck.org/2012/07/you-didnt-build-that-uncut-and-unedited/. Accessed 17 Aug 2015.

Kim, Kihoon. 2014. The Analysis of Government Financial Subsidies for the Electric Car Market. *The Korean Operations and Management Science Society* 39 (3): 41–49. http://www.koreascience.or.kr/article/ArticleFullRecord. jsp?cn=GOGGBB_2014_v39n3_41. Accessed 23 May 2016.

King, Seth. 2010. *Daily Anarchist* Interviews Walter E. Block. September 9. http://www.lewrockwell.com/block/block165.html. Accessed 23 Aug 2016.

Kinnucan, P. 1983. Push to Commercialize Space Runs into Budget Cutbacks, Boondoggle Charges, and Fear of High Risks. *High Technology* 3: 43–45.

Kinsella, Stephan. 1992. Estoppel: A New Justification for Individual Rights. *Reason Papers* 17 (Fall): 61.

———. 1995. Legislation and the Discovery of Law in a Free Society. *Journal of Libertarian Studies* 11 (Summer): 132.

———. 1996. Punishment and Proportionality: The Estoppel Approach. *The Journal of Libertarian Studies* 12 (1): 51–74. http://www.mises.org/journals/jls/12_1/12_1_3.pdf. Accessed 8 June 2016.

———. 1997. A Libertarian Theory of Punishment and Rights. 30 *Loy. L.A. L. Rev.* 607–645.

Kinsella, N. Stephan. 1998–1999. Inalienability and Punishment: A Reply to George Smith. *Journal of Libertarian Studies* 14 (1): 79–93. http://www.mises.org/journals/jls/14_1/14_1_4.pdf. Accessed 8 June 2016.

———. 2001. Against Intellectual Property. *Journal of Libertarian Studies* 15 (2): 1–53. http://www.mises.org/journals/jls/15_2/15_2_1.pdf.

Kinsella, Stephan N. 2003. A Libertarian Theory of Contract: Title Transfer, Binding Promises, and Inalienability. *Journal of Libertarian Studies* 17 (2): 11–37. http://www.mises.org/journals/jls/17_2/17_2_2.pdf. Accessed 23 Apr 2016.

———. 2006. How We Come to Own Ourselves. September 7. http://www.mises.org/story/2291. Accessed 23 Apr 2016.

———. 2009a. What Libertarianism Is. August 21. https://mises.org/library/what-libertarianism. Accessed 23 Apr 2016.

———. 2009b. Homesteading, Abandonment, and Unowned Land in the Civil Law. May 22. http://blog.mises.org/10004/homesteading-abandonment-and-unowned-land-in-the-civil-law/. Accessed 23 Apr 2016.

Kinsella, Stephan. 2009c. The Irrelevance of the Impossibility of Anarcho-Libertarianism. August 20. http://www.stephankinsella.com/2009/08/20/the-irrelevance-of-the-impossibility-of-anarcho-libertarianism/. Accessed 23 Aug 2016.

Kinsella, N. Stephan. 2012. Economic Freedom of the World Rankings and Intellectual Property: The United States' Bad Ranking Is Even Worse Than Reported. http://c4sif.org/2012/09/economic-freedom-of-the-world-indexes-and-intellectual-property-the-united-states-bad-ranking-is-even-worse-than-reported/.

Kitzinger, Jenny, Joan Haran, Mwenya Chimba, and Tammy Boyce. 2008. Role Models in the Media: An Exploration of the Views and Experiences of Women in Science, Engineering and Technology. UK Resource Centre for Women in Science, Engineering and Technology. https://www.researchgate.

net/publication/237553064_Role_Models_in_the_Media_An_ Exploration_of_the_Views_and_Experiences_of_Women_in_Science_ Engineering_and_Technology. Accessed 23 May 2016.

Klein, Natalie. 2004. *Dispute Settlement in the U.N. Convention on the Law of the Sea*. Cambridge Studies in International and Comparative Law. Cambridge University Press.

Klein, Peter G. 2013. Without the State, Who Would Invent Tang? *The Free Market* 31 (3): 1–3. https://mises.org/system/tdf/March2013_0.pdf?file=1; https://mises.org/library/without-state-who-would-invent-tang. Accessed 23 Apr 2016.

Klein, Peter J. 2014. Inequality and Envy. May 30. https://mises.org/blog/ inequality-and-envy. Accessed 13 Dec 2015.

Knapp, Alex. 2014. NASA Has Discovered the First Potentially Habitable Earth-Sized Planet. April 17. http://www.forbes.com/sites/alexknapp/2014/04/17/ nasa-has-discovered-the-first-potentially-habitable-earth-sized-planet/.

Koch, Charles. 2015. The Good Profit: How Creating Value for Others Built One of the World's Most Successful Companies. Crown Business. https:// www.amazon.com/Good-Profit-Creating-Successful-Companies-ebook/dp/ B00TWEMGE8

Kolko, Gabriel. 1963. *Triumph of Conservatism*. Chicago: Quadrangle Books.

Kopal, Vladimir. 1968. Treaty on Principles Governing the Activities of States in the Exploration and Use of Outer Space, Including the Moon and Other Celestial Bodies. In *Yearbook of Air and Space Law 1966* (Annuaire de droit aérien et spatial), ed. R.H. Mankiewicz. Montreal: McGill University Press.

———. 1996. United Nations and the Progressive Development of International Space Law. In *The Finnish Yearbook of International Law*, ed. M. Koskenniemi and K. Takamaa, vol. VII. The Hague, Boston, and London: Martinus Nijhoff Publishers and Kluwer Law International.

Kramer, Miriam. 2013. To Moonwalker Buzz Aldrin, 'Tang Sucks'. *Space.com*. June 12. http://www.space.com/21538-buzz-aldrin-tang-spaceflight.html. Accessed 30 June 2016.

———. 2015. Jupiter's Moon Ganymede Has a Salty Ocean with More Water than Earth. *Space.com*. March 12. http://www.space.com/28807-jupiter-moon-ganymede-salty-ocean.html. Accessed 19 Nov 2015.

Krasnozhon, Leo, Pedro Benitez, and Walter E. Block. 2015. The Privatization of Antarctica. *Washington and Lee Journal of Energy, Climate, and the Environment*. 6 (2): 397–401. http://scholarlycommons.law.wlu.edu/jece/.

Krauss, Lawrence. 2011. The Space Shuttle Programme Has Been a Multi-billion-dollar Failure. *The Guardian.* July 21. https://www.theguardian.com/science/2011/jul/21/space-shuttle-programme. Accessed 23 May 2016.

Krauthammer, Charles. 2016. Space Flight Goes Private. January 2. http://news.nationalpost.com/full-comment/charles-krauthammer-space-flight-goes-private. Accessed 2 Jan 16.

Kreuter, Urs P., and Linda E. Platts. 1996. Why the Ivory Ban Is Failing. *Christian Science Monitor.* March 20. http://perc.org/articles/why-ivory-ban-failing. Accessed 11 June 2016.

Krugman, Paul. 2015. Republicans' Climate Change Denial Denial. December 4. http://www.nytimes.com/2015/12/04/opinion/republicans-climate-change-denial-denial.html?_r=0. Accessed 5 Dec 2015.

Lachs, M. 1972. *The Law of Outer Space: An Experience in Contemporary Law-Making.* Leiden: Sijthoff.

Levin, Michael. 1996. Capitalism, Envy, and the Inner City. February 1. https://mises.org/library/capitalism-envy-and-inner-city. Accessed 13 Dec 2015.

Lewis, John S. 1997. *Mining the Sky: Untold Riches from the Asteroids, Comets and Planets.* New York: Basic Books.

Lewis, Rob. 2015. Should Climate Change Deniers Be Prosecuted? September 20. http://www.dailykos.com/story/2015/9/20/1423309/-Scientists-ask-for-prosecution-of-climate-deniers-under-RICO-law. Accessed 6 Dec 2015.

Light Sail. n.d. Solar Sailing—Flight by Light. The Planetary Society. http://sail.planetary.org/. Accessed 2 Dec 2015.

Lind, Michael. 2012. Thank You, Milton Friedman: How Conservatives' Economic Hero Helped Make the Case for Big Government. August 7. http://www.salon.com/2012/08/07/thank_you_milton_friedman/.

Lint, J. 2010. Statement on Behalf of the European Union, First Committee on Outer Space Cluster, 65th Session of the United Nations General Assembly. October 25. http://www.delusanyc.ec.europa.eu/articles/fr/article_10370_fr.htm.

Liptak, Adam. 2008. U.S. Prison Population Dwarfs that of Other Nations. April 23. http://www.nytimes.com/2008/04/23/world/americas/23iht-23prison.12253738.html?pagewanted=all. Accessed 21 Nov 2015.

Locke, John. 1690 [1955]. *Second Treatise on Government.* Chicago: Henry Regnery.

———. 1948. *An Essay Concerning the True Origin, Extent and End of Civil Government.* In *Social Contract,* ed. E. Barker, 17–19. New York: Oxford University Press.

Long, Roderick. 1995. The Libertarian Case Against Intellectual Property Rights. *Formulations* 3 (1). http://libertariannation.org/a/f3111.html.

Long, Roderick T. 1993. Abortion, Abandonment, and Positive Rights: The Limits of Compulsory Altruism. *Social Philosophy and Policy* 10 (1): 166–191. http://praxeology.net/RTL-Abortion.htm. Accessed 20 Apr 2016.

———. 2006. Realism and Abstraction in Economics: Aristotle and Mises Versus Friedman. *The Quarterly Journal of Austrian Economics* 9 (3): 3–23 http://www.mises.org/journals/qjae/pdf/qjae9_3_1.pdf.

———. 2004. Libertarian Anarchism: Responses to Ten Objections. http://www.lewrockwell.com/long/long11.html. Accessed 23 Aug 2016.

Lora, Manuel. 2006. What Happened to Katrina Aid? March 3. http://www.mises.org/story/2064.

———. 2007. If You Love Nature, Desocialize It. May 10. http://mises.org/daily/2539. Accessed 11 June 2016.

Maass, Harold. 2013. The Odds Are 11 Million to 1 that You'll Die in a Plane Crash [sic]. *The Week*. July 8. http://theweek.com/articles/462449/odds-are-11-million-1-that-youll-die-plane-crash. Accessed 6 July 2016.

Maltsev, Yuri N. 1993. *Requiem for Marx*. CreateSpace Independent Publishing Platform.

Marchis, F., et al. 2009. The Cybele Binary Asteroid 121 Hermione Revisited. 40th Lunar and Planetary Science Conference (2009). http://www.lpi.usra.edu/meetings/lpsc2009/pdf/1336.pdf. Accessed 29 July 2015.

Marder, Jenny, and Sculietti, Justin. 2015. Dawn over Ceres, a Mission of Humankind. *PBS Newshour* 6–24. http://www.pbs.org/newshour/updates/mission-humankind/. Accessed 27 July 2015.

Marshall Space Flight Center. n.d. Dr. Wernher von Braun First Center Director, July 1, 1960–Jan. 27, 1970. History Department. http://history.msfc.nasa.gov/vonbraun/bio.html. Accessed 5 Nov 2015.

Martin, Jonathan. 2010. Paul Allen gives $100,000 to Defeat Income-Tax Initiative. October 12. http://old.seattletimes.com/html/politicsnorthwest/2013139340_paul_allens_moment.html?syndication=rss. Accessed 11 June 2016.

Marx, Karl. 1906 [1867]. *Das Capital*. New York: Modern Library.

Mason, Betsy. 2010. The Tragic Race to Be First to the South Pole. *Science*. May 10. http://www.wired.com/2010/05/polar-race-gallery/.

Mathews, Don. 2002. The Price of Envy. April 11. https://mises.org/library/price-envy. Accessed 13 Dec 2015.

Maybury, Richard, and Jane A. Williams. 2003. *World War II: The Rest of the Story and How It Affects You Today* (Revised). October 1. Bluestocking Press.

Mazzucato, Mariana. 2013. *The Entrepreneurial State: Debunking Public vs. Private Sector Myths.* Anthem.

McChesney, Fred. 1991. Antitrust and Regulation: Chicago's Contradictory Views. *Cato Journal* 10 (3): 775–778.

McClintick, David, and Ross B. Emmett. 2005. Betting on the Wealth of Nature; The Simon-Ehrlich Wager. *PERC Report* 23 (3), September 29. http://www.perc.org/articles/betting-wealth-nature#sthash.M3R4F7jH.dpuf; http://www.perc.org/articles/betting-wealth-nature.

McConkey, Michael. 2013. Anarchy, Sovereignty, and the State of Exception: Schmitt's Challenge. *The Independent Review*, v. 17, n. 3, pp. 415–428. http://www.independent.org/pdf/tir/tir_17_03_05_mcconkey.pdf. Accessed 23 Aug 2016.

McCormack, Simon 2015. Ohio Cop Trying to Shoot Dog Shoots 4-Year-Old Girl Instead. *The Huffington Post* 6–22. http://www.huffingtonpost.com/2015/06/22/cop-shoots-girl-dog_n_7637456.html. Accessed 26 June 2015.

McCormick, Rich. 2016. Elon Musk Says the Falcon 9 Rocket SpaceX Successfully Landed Is 'Ready to Fire Again'. January 1. http://www.theverge.com/2016/1/1/10697914/elon-musk-says-falcon-9-rocket-spacex-ready-to-fire. Accessed 29 June 2016.

McGee, John S. 1958. Predatory Price Cutting: The Standard Oil (New Jersey) Case. *The Journal of Law and Economics*, October, 137–169.

McHale, Susan M., Ji-Yeon Kim, Aryn M. Dotterer, Ann C. Crouter, and Alan Booth. 2010. The Development of Gendered Interests and Personality Qualities from Middle Childhood Through Adolescence: A Bio-Social Analysis. Society for Research in Child Development. http://www.ncbi.nlm.nih.gov/pmc/articles/PMC3242364/. Accessed 23 May 2016.

McLaughlin, Elliot C. 2014. No Indictments for Georgia SWAT Team that Burned Baby with Stun Grenade. CNN. October 7. http://www.cnn.com/2014/10/07/us/georgia-toddler-stun-grenade-no-indictment/. Accessed 25 June 2015.

Megginson, W., and J. Netter. 2001. From State to Market: A Survey of Empirical Studies on Privatization. *Journal of Economic Literature* 39 (2): 321–389.

Melchoir, Jillian Kay. 2015. SolarCity Can't Shine Without Subsidies. January 14. http://www.iwf.org/news/2799084/SolarCity-Can't-Shine-Without-Subsidies. Accessed 17 June 2016.

Menell, Peter S. 2007a. Intellectual Property and the Property Rights Movement. *Regulation*, Fall. http://www.cato.org/pubs/regulation/regv30n3/v30n3-6. pdf.

———. 2007b. The Property Rights Movement's Embrace of Intellectual Property: True Love or Doomed Relationship? *Ecology Law Quarterly* 34.

Mercer, Ilana. 2001. Stealing Our Words. August 8. http://mises.org/story/750. Accessed 20 Apr 2016.

Meyer, Frank S. 1962. *In Defense of Freedom*. Chicago: Henry Regnery.

Milligan, T. 2011. Property Rights and the Duty to Extend Human Life. *Space Policy* 27 (4): 190–193.

Molyneux, Stefan. 2008. The Stateless Society: An Examination of Alternatives. http://www.mail-archive.com/libertarianenterprise@yahoogroups.com/ msg02056.html. Accessed 23 Aug 2016.

Moore, Stephen. 1987. Privatizing the U.S. Postal Service. In *Privatization*, ed. Stephen Moore and Stuart Butler. Washington, DC: Heritage Foundation.

Moore, Stephen, and Stuart Butler, eds. 1987. *Privatization*. Washington, DC: Heritage Foundation.

Mother Nature Network. 2015. 10 NASA Images of Planets Like Earth. http:// www.mnn.com/earth-matters/space/photos/10-nasa-images-of-planets-like- earth/a-new-earth.

Motichek, Amy, Walter E. Block, and Jay Johnson. 2008. Forget Ocean Front Property, We Want Ocean Real Estate! *Ethics, Place, and Environment* 11 (2): 147–155.

Mukherjee, Jay, and Walter E. Block. 2012. Libertarians and the Catholic Church on Intellectual Property Laws. *Journal of Political Philosophy Las Torres de Lucca* (1): 59–75. http://www.lastorresdelucca.org/index. php?option=com_k2&view=item&id=93:libertarios-y-la-iglesia-católica-en- las-leyes-de-propiedad-intelectual&Itemid=24&lang=en&Itemid=23.

Murphy, Robert P. 2002. *Chaos Theory: Two Essays on Market Anarchy*. New York: RJ Communications LLC. http://mises.org/books/chaostheory.pdf. Accessed 21 Mar 2016.

———. 2004. Profit, Loss, and Pluto. October 10. https://mises.org/library/ profit-loss-and-pluto. Accessed 11 July 2015.

———. 2005a. But Wouldn't Warlords Take Over? July 7. http://mises.org/ story/1855; http://mises.org/library/wouldnt-warlords-take-over. Accessed 23 Aug 2016.

———. 2005b. A Free Market in Space. *The Free Market* 53 (1), January.

———. 2005c. How the Market Might Have Handled Katrina. November 17. http://www.mises.org/story/1968.

———. 2006. The Labor Theory of Value: A Critique of Carson's Studies in Mutualist Political Economy. *The Journal of Libertarian Studies* 20 (1). http://mises.org/journals/jls/20_1/20_1_3.pdf. Accessed 29 June 2016.

———. 2011. Problems with the Cost Theory of Value. May 23. https://mises.org/library/problems-cost-theory-value. Accessed 29 June 2016.

Murray, Charles. 1984. *Losing Ground: American Social Policy from 1950 to 1980*. New York: Basic Books.

Napolitano, Andrew. 2013. Taxation Is Theft; The Constitution Doesn't Permit the Feds to Steal Your Money. But Steal, the Feds Do. April 18. http://reason.com/archives/2013/04/18/taxation-is-theft. Accessed 28 July 2016.

Narveson, Jan. 1988. *The Libertarian Idea*. Philadelphia: Temple University Press.

NASA. 2000. National Aeronautics and Space Administration. Liberty Bell 7 MR-4 (19). September 29. http://www.nasa.gov/externalflash/the_shuttle/. Accessed 1 July 2016.

———. 2009. National Aeronautics and Space Administration. Apollo 13. July 8. http://www.nasa.gov/externalflash/the_shuttle/. Accessed 1 July 2016.

———. 2015. National Aeronautics and Space Administration. https://www.nasa.gov/sites/default/files/files/FY15_Summary_Brief.pdf. Accessed 24 Apr 2016.

———, 2016a. National Space and Aeronautics Administration. Juno. February 11. https://www.nasa.gov/mission_pages/juno/main/index.html. Accessed 25 Mar 2016.

———, 2016b. National Space and Aeronautics Administration. Astronaut Scott Kelly Returns Safely to Earth After One-Year Mission. March 1. http://www.nasa.gov/press-release/nasa-astronaut-scott-kelly-returns-safely-to-earth-after-one-year-mission. Accessed 25 Mar 2016.

———. n.d.-a. National Space and Aeronautics Administration. The Nearest Star. https://heasarc.gsfc.nasa.gov/docs/cosmic/nearest_star_info.html. Accessed 8 July 2015.

———. n.d.-b. National Aeronautics and Space Administration. The Shuttle. http://www.nasa.gov/externalflash/the_shuttle/. Accessed 1 July 2016.

———. n.d.-c. National Space and Aeronautics Administration. STEM Lessons from Space. https://www.nasa.gov/audience/foreducators/stem-on-station/lessons. Accessed 7 July 2016.

Navabi, Ash. 2015. To Taylor, Love Freedom. June 23. https://mises.ca/posts/blog/to-taylor-love-freedom/. Accessed 4 Aug 2016.

Nelson, Peter Lothian. 2015. To Homestead a Nature Preserve. Liberty.me. July 14. https://peterlothiannelson.liberty.me/to-homestead-a-nature-preserve/. Accessed 29 Aug 2015.

Neu, Irene D., and George Rogers Taylor. 1956. *The American Railroad Network, 1861–1890*. Cambridge: Harvard University Press.

Nock, Albert Jay. 2011. *The Myth of a Guilty Nation*. Auburn, AL: The Mises Institute.

Nozick, Robert. 1974. *Anarchy, State and Utopia*. New York: Basic Books.

Ohashi, T.M. 1980. *Privatization, Theory and Practice: Distributing Shares in Private and Public Enterprise*. Vancouver, BC: The Fraser Institute.

Ohashi, T.M., T.P. Roth, Z.A. Spindler, M.L. McMillan, and K.H. Norrie. 1980. *Privation Theory & Practice*. Vancouver, BC: The Fraser Institute.

Olinga, Luc. 2015. New US Space Mining Law to Spark Interplanetary Gold Rush. December 8. http://phys.org/news/2015-12-space-law-interplanetary-gold.html. Accessed 13 Dec 2015.

Olson, Walter. 2015. Should Climate Change Deniers Be Prosecuted? October 1. http://www.newsweek.com/should-climate-change-deniers-be-prosecuted-378652. Accessed 6 Dec 2015.

Onion, Rebecca. 2014. 'Unclaimed Treasures of Science': Even During the Cold War, These Women Brought Feminism to STEM. July 13. http://www.slate.com/articles/health_and_science/science/2014/07/women_in_science_technology_engineering_math_history_of_advocacy_from_1940.html. Accessed 23 May 2016.

Oppenheimer, Franz. 1975 [1914]. *The State*. New York: Free Life Editions.

Orwell, George. 1949. *Nineteen Eighty-Four*. London: Harvill Secker.

Osborn, Andrew. 2002. Democratic Republic of the Congo, Belgium Confronts Its Colonial Demons. *The Guardian* (US Edition). July 18.

Osterfeld, David. 1989. Anarchism and the Public Goods Issue: Law, Courts and the Police. *The Journal of Libertarian Studies* 9 (1): 47–68. http://www.mises.org/journals/jls/9_1/9_1_3.pdf. Accessed 23 Apr 2016.

Ostrom, Elinor. 1990. *Governing the Commons*. Cambridge Press.

Palmer, Tom. 1989. Intellectual Property: A Non-Posnerian Law and Economics Approach. *Hamline Law Review* 12 (2): 261–304.

Palmer, Anna, and Jeremy Herb. 2015. Boeing, GE Cut Off Donations to Ex-Im Foes. August 5. http://www.politico.com/story/2015/08/boeing-ge-cut-off-donations-to-ex-im-opponents-121056. Accessed 29 June 2016.

Pasour, Jr., E.C., 1981, "The Free Rider as a Basis for Government Intervention," *The Journal of Libertarian Studies*, Vol. V, No. 4, pp. 453–464. http://www. mises.org/journals/jls/5_4/5_4_6.pdf. Accessed 23 Apr 2016.

Pasour, E.C., Jr. 1986. Rent Seeking: Some Conceptual Problems and Implications. *Review of Austrian Economics* 1: 123–143. http://mises.org/ journals/rae/pdf/RAE1_1_8.pdf; http://mises.org/sites/default/files/ rae1_1_8_5.pdf; http://mises.org/library/rent-seeking-some-conceptual-problems-and-implications. Accessed 11 June 2016.

Paul, Ellen Frankel. 1987. *Property Rights and Eminent Domain*. Livingston, NJ: Transaction Publishers.

Pearce, Rohan. 2012. What Went Wrong with the Hubble Space Telescope (and What Managers Can Learn from It). *CIO*. March 29. http://www.cio.com. au/article/420036/what_went_wrong_hubble_space_telescope_what_managers_can_learn_from_it_/?pp=3. Accessed 1 July 2016.

Pearson, Michael. 2015. Liquid Water Exists on Mars, Boosting Hopes for Life There, NASA Says. September 29. http://www.cnn.com/2015/09/28/us/mars-nasa-announcement/.

Peden, Joseph R. 1977. Property Rights in Celtic Irish Law. *The Journal of Libertarian Studies* 1 (2): 81–96.

Pegg, David. 2014. 25 Famous Predictions that Were Proven to Be Horribly Wrong. March 13. http://list25.com/25-famous-predictions-that-were-proven-to-be-horribly-wrong/. Accessed 25 Aug 2015.

Peters, Eric. 2016. Now Uncle Is 'Investing' in Tesla. Autos, Automobiles, Motorcycles, and Libertarian Politics. August 14. http://ericpetersautos. com/2016/08/14/now-uncle-investing-tesla/; https://www.lewrockwell. com/2016/08/eric-peters/champion-crony-capitalist/. Accessed 17 Aug 2016.

Physilicious. 2009. Conservation of Angular Momentum. *Geddes Physics*. February 22. https://www.youtube.com/watch?v=UZlW1a63KZs. Accessed 2 Sep 2016.

Pink, Roger. 2015. Understanding the Gravity of the Situation. *Roger's Equations*. March 10. http://cr4.globalspec.com/blogentry/25919/Understanding-the-Gravity-of-the-Situation. Accessed 19 Nov 2015.

Pinker, Steven. 2011. *The Better Angels of Our Nature: Why Violence Has Declined*. New York: Viking.

Pirie, Madson. 1986. *Privatization in Theory and Practice*. London: Adam Smith Institute.

Planetary Resources. 2015. President Obama Signs Bill Recognizing Asteroid Resource Property Rights into Law. November 25. http://www.planetaryresources.com/2015/11/president-obama-signs-bill-recognizing-asteroid-resource-property-rights-into-law/.

Planetary Resources, the Asteroid Mining Company. n.d. Asteroids: Composition. http://www.planetaryresources.com/asteroids/composition/. Accessed 29 July 2015.

Poeter, Damon. 2015. Check Out Paul Allen's Giant Rocket-Toting Monster Plane. February 26. http://www.pcmag.com/article2/0,2817,2477458,00. asp. Accessed 28 July 2016.

Polleit, Thorsten. 2008. Mises's Apriorism Against Relativism in Economics. April 25. http://blog.mises.org/archives/008051.asp. Accessed 9 Aug 2015.

———. 2011. True Knowledge from a Priori Theory. June 8. http://mises.org/daily/5349/True-Knowledge-from-A-Priori-Theory. Accessed 9 Aug 2015.

Pop, V. 2000. Appropriation in Outer Space: The Relationship Between Land Ownership and Sovereignty on Celestial Bodies. *Space Policy* 16 (4): 275–282.

Prado, Mark. 2013. Major Lunar Minerals. *Permanent.* http://www.permanent.com/lunar-geology-minerals.html. Accessed 1 Dec 2015.

Pufendorf, Samuel. 1673. Natural Law and the Law of Nations (De officio hominis et civis prout ipsi praescribuntur lege naturali).

Puffert, Douglas J. 2000. The Standardization of Track Gauge on North American Railways, 1830–1890. *The Journal of Economic History* 60 (4): 933–960.

Radosh, Ronald, and Murray N. Rothbard, eds. 1972. *A New History of Leviathan.* New York: E. P. Dutton.

Raico, Ralph. 1977. Classical Liberal Exploitation Theory: A Comment on Professor Liggio's Paper. *The Journal of Libertarian Studies* 1 (3): 179–184. http://mises.org/daily/4567/.

Rana, Harminderpal Singh. 1994. Common Heritage of Mankind & the Final Frontier: A Revaluation of Values Constituting the International Legal Regime for Outer Space Activities, The Note. *Rutgers Law Journal.* 26 (1): 225–250.

Rand, Ayn. 1943. *The Fountainhead.* New York: Signet.

———. 1957. *Atlas Shrugged.* New York: Random House.

———. 1969. Apollo 11. *The Objectivist* (September). https://ari.aynrand.org/issues/science-and-industrialization/scientific-and-technological-progress/Apollo-11.

———. n.d. http://books.google.ca/books?id=QV2OJqbt45oC&pg=PA387&lpg=PA387&dq=%22the+most+pernicious+thing+ever+issued+by+an+avowedly+conservative+organization%22&source=web&ots=DV4j_dhJA&sig=DZYoo1KjulTGviiR7kFGINFrbnY&hl=en&sa=X&oi=book_result&resnum=1&ct=result.

Rao, Joe. 2015. Planet Mercury: Some Surprising Facts for Skywatchers. *Space. com.* April 29. http://www.space.com/29265-mercury-planet-facts-for-sky-watchers.html. Accessed 18 Nov 2015.

Rapp, Donald. 2015. Why the NASA Approach Will Likely Fail to Send Humans to Mars for Many Decades to Come. October 30. http://link.springer.com/chapter/10.1007/978-3-319-22249-3_7. Accessed 23 May 2016.

Reagan, Ronald. 1981. [first] Inaugural Address. January 20. http://www.presidency.ucsb.edu/ws/?pid=43130. Accessed 16 Sep 2017.

Redd, Nola Taylor. 2012. What Is the Temperature of Uranus? *Space.com.* November 30. http://www.space.com/18707-uranus-temperature.html. Accessed 7 Dec 2015.

———. 2015. Titan: Facts About Saturn's Largest Moon. *Space.com.* February 4. http://www.space.com/15257-titan-saturn-largest-moon-facts-discovery-sdcmp.html. Accessed 20 Nov 2015.

Regis, ed. 2015. Let's Not Move to Mars. *New York Times.* September 21. http://www.nytimes.com/2015/09/21/opinion/lets-not-move-to-mars.html?_r=0.

Reisman, George. 2005. Envy Unleashed at the New York Times. June 6. https://mises.org/library/envy-unleashed-new-york-times. Accessed 13 Dec 2015.

———. 2006. Freedom Is Slavery: Laissez-Faire Capitalism Is Government Intervention: A Critique of Kevin Carson's Studies in Mutualist Political Economy. *The Journal of Libertarian Studies* 20 (1). http://mises.org/journals/jls/20_1/20_1_5.pdf. Accessed 29 June 2016.

Reynolds, Neil. 2012. Waiting for the Age of Abundance. April 16. http://www.theglobeandmail.com/report-on-business/rob-commentary/waiting-for-the-age-of-abundance/article4100664/. Accessed 29 June 2016.

Reynolds, Glenn Harlan. 2014. Mine Asteroids in Space to Help Us on Earth. *USA Today.* September 16. http://iucat-test.uits.iu.edu/iupui/articles/edsgsc/edsgcl.382537991/?resultId=4&highlight=%22Mines%20and%20mineral%20resources%20--%20Economic%20aspects%22. Accessed 15 Nov 2015.

Richards, Tori. 2015. Sunset of Solar Subsidies Shadows SolarCity. June 23. http://watchdog.org/225430/solarcity/. Accessed 17 June 2016.

Ridley, Matt. 2015. *The Evolution of Everything: How New Ideas Emerge.* New York: Harper.

Rizzo, Mario. 1979. Praxeology and Econometrics: A Critique of Positivist Economics. In *New Directions in Austrian Economics*, ed. Louis Spadaro, 40–56. Kansas City: Sheed Andrews and McMeel.

Robbins, Lionel. 1928. The Optimum Theory of Population. In *London Essays in Economics: In Honour of Edwin Cannan*, ed. T. Gregory and H. Dalton. Abingdon: Routledge.

———. 1966. *The Theory of Economic Development in the History of Economic Thought*. Lecture Two: Population and Returns, 22–33. London: Macmillan, St Martin's. http://library.mises.org/books/Lionel%20Robbins/The%20Theory%20of%20Economic%20Development.pdf. Accessed 10 Aug 2016.

Rockwell, Lew. 2013. What Would We Do Without the State? March 31. http://www.lewrockwell.com/blog/lewrw/archives/134782.html. Accessed 23 Aug 2016.

Rockwell, Jr., Llewellyn H. 2001. Liberty and the Common Good. December 31. http://www.mises.org/article.aspx?Id=860.

———. 2014. What Libertarianism Is, and Isn't. March 31. http://www.lewrockwell.com/2014/03/lew-rockwell/what-libertarianism-is-and-isnt/. Accessed 29 June 2016.

Rockwell, Llewellyn H., Jr., and Walter E. Block. 2010. The Economics and Ethics of Hurricane Katrina. *American Journal of Economics and Sociology* 69 (4): 1294–1320. http://www.walterblock.com/wp-content/uploads/V.335_The-Economics-and-Ethics-of-Hurricane-Katrina.pdf. Accessed 22 May 2016.

Roth, Veronica. 2011–2013. *Divergent* Series. New York: Katherine Tegen Books.

Rothbard, Murray N. 1951. Praxeology: Reply to Mr. Schuller. *American Economic Review* 41 (5): 943–946.

———. 1957. In Defense of Extreme Apriorism. *Southern Economic Journal* 23 (1): 314–320.

———. 1959 [2015]. *Science, Technology and Government*. Auburn, AL: The Mises Institute.

———. 1960. The Mantle of Science. Reprinted from *Scientism and Values*, ed. Helmut Schoeck and James W. Wiggins. Princeton, NJ: D. Van Nostrand; *The Logic of Action One: Method, Money, and the Austrian School*. Cheltenham: Edward Elgar, 1997, pp. 3–23.

———. 1963. *America's Great Depression*. Kansas City: Sheed Andrews. http://www.mises.org/rothbard/agd.pdf. Accessed 23 May 2016.

———. 1970. *Power and Market: Government and the Economy*. Menlo Park, CA: Institute for Humane Studies.

———. 1971a. Freedom, Inequality, Primitivism and the Division of Labor. Modern Age, Summer, 226–245. Reprinted in Kenneth S. Templeton, Jr.

(ed.), *The Politicization of Society*. Indianapolis: Liberty Press, 1979, pp. 83–126. Reprinted in *The Logic of Action Two: Applications and Criticism from the Austrian School.* Glos, UK: Edward Elgar Publishing Ltd., 1997, pp. 3–35. http://mises.org/fipandol.asp.

———. 1971b. Lange, Mises and Praxeology: The Retreat from Marxism. In *Toward Liberty*, vol. II, 307–321. Menlo Park, CA: Institute for Humane Studies. Reprinted in *The Logic of Action One: Method, Money, and the Austrian School.* Glos, UK: Edward Elgar Publishing Ltd., 1997, pp. 384–396.

———. 1972. War Collectivism in World War I. In *A New History of Leviathan*, ed. R. Radosh and M.N. Rothbard, 66–110. New York: E. P. Dutton.

———. 1973a. Praxeology and the Method of Economics. In *Phenomenology and the Social Sciences*, ed. M. Natanson, vol. 2, 311–342. Evanston, IL: Northwestern University Press. *Austrian Economics: A Reader* Vol. 18, Richard M. Ebeling, ed., Hillsdale, MI: Hillsdale College Press, 1991, pp. 55–91.

———. 1973b. Free Market, Police, Courts, and Law. *Reason*: 5–19.

———. 1973c. *For a New Liberty*. New York: Macmillan. http://mises.org/rothbard/newlibertywhole.asp. Accessed 23 Aug 2016.

———. 1975a. *Conceived in Liberty, Volumes I & II—A New Land, A New People, The American Colonies in the Seventeenth Century*. New Rochelle, NY: Arlington House Publishers. With the Assistance of Leonard P. Liggio.

———. 1975b. Society Without a State. *The Libertarian Forum* 7 (1), January. http://www.lewrockwell.com/rothbard/rothbard133.html. Accessed 23 Aug 2016.

———. 1977. Do You Hate the State? *The Libertarian Forum* 10 (7), July. http://www.lewrockwell.com/rothbard/rothbard75.html. Accessed 23 Aug 2016.

———. 1980. Review of *World War I and the Origins of Civil Liberties in the United States*, by P. Murphy. *Inquiry* 9: 22–24.

———. 1981. Frank S. Meyer: The Fusionist as Libertarian Manque. *Modern Age* 352–363. https://mises.org/library/frank-s-meyer-fusionist-libertarian-manqu%C3%A9. Accessed 28 July 2016.

———. 1982a. *The Ethics of Liberty*. Atlantic Highlands, NJ: Humanities Press.

———. 1982b. Law, Property Rights, and Air Pollution. *Cato Journal* 2 (1). Reprinted in *Economics and the Environment: A Reconciliation*, Walter E. Block, ed., Vancouver: The Fraser Institute, 1990, pp. 233–279. http://mises.org/story/2120; http://www.mises.org/rothbard/lawproperty.pdf. Accessed 20 Apr 2016.

———. 1985. Airport Congestion: A Case of Market Failure? The Free Market. Auburn, AL: The Ludwig von Mises Institute. http://www.mises.org/econsense/ch52.asp.

———. 1987. Adam Smith Reconsidered. In *Austrian Economics Newsletter*, 5–7. Auburn, AL: The Ludwig von Mises Institute. Reprinted in *Austrian Economics* (Vol. 1) by S. Littlechild. Brookfield, VT: Edward Elgar Publishing Company (1990), pp. 41–44. http://mises.org/daily/2012. Accessed 23 Aug 2016.

———. 1989. World War I as Fulfillment: Power and the Intellectuals. *The Journal of Libertarian Studies* 9 (1): 81–125. http://mises.org/journals/jls/9_1/9_1_5.pdf. Reprinted in *The Costs of War*, by J.V. Denson (ed.). New Brunswick, NJ: Transaction Publishers, 1998, pp. 203–254. Also Appears in 2nd Edition, 1999.

———. 1991. On Denationalizing the Courts. *Rothbard-Rockwell Report*, vol. 2, no. 10. Burlingame, CA: Center for Libertarian Studies.

———. 1995. *The Case Against the Fed*. Auburn, AL: Ludwig von Mises Institute.

———. 1997a. Toward a Reconstruction of Utility and Welfare Economics. Reprinted in *The Logic of Action One: Method, Money, and the Austrian School*, 211–254. Glos, UK: Edward Elgar Publishing Ltd.

———. 1997b. *The Logic of Action: Applications and Criticism from the Austrian School*. Vol. II. Cheltenham: Edward Elgar.

———. 1997c. Praxeology, Value Judgments, and Public Policy. In *The Logic of Action One*, ed. Murray N. Rothbard, 78–99. Glos, UK: Edward Elgar Publishing Limited.

———. 1997d. In Defense of 'Extreme Apriorism'. *Southern Economic Journal*, January 1957, 314–320. Reprinted in *The Logic of Action One*, ed. Murray N. Rothbard, 100–108. UK: Edward Elgar Publishing Limited.

———. 1998 [1982]. Isaiah Berlin on Negative Freedom. In *The Ethics of Liberty*, chapter 27, 215–218. New York: New York University Press. http://www.mises.org/rothbard/ethics/ethics.asp. Accessed 20 Apr 2016.

———. 2002. Milton Friedman Unraveled. *Journal of Libertarian Studies* 16 (4): 37–54 http://www.mises.org/journals/jls/16_4/16_4_3.pdf; https://www.lewrockwell.com/2016/02/murray-n-rothbard/totaldemolition-milton-friedman/.

———. 2004a [1962]. *Man, Economy and State*. Auburn, AL: Ludwig von Mises Institute, Scholar's Edition.

————. 2004b. The Case for Revisionism (and Against A Priori History). http://mises.org/library/case-revisionism-and-against-priori-history.

————. 2010. Jean Buridan and the Theory of Money. *Mises Daily Articles.* January 1. Auburn, AL.

————. 2011. Malthus and the Assault on Population. August 2. http://mises.org/daily/5501/. Accessed 10 Aug 2016.

Rothschild, Daniel Y., and Walet E. Block. 2016. Don't Steal; The Government Hates Competition: The Problem with Civil Asset Forfeiture. *The Journal of Private Enterprise* 31 (1): 45–56. http://journal.apee.org/index.php/2016_Journal_of_Private_Enterprise_vol_31_no_1_parte4.pdf. Accessed 10 Aug 2016.

Rozeff, Michael S. 2005. Original Appropriation and Its Critics. September 1. http://www.lewrockwell.com/rozeff/rozeff18.html. Accessed 23 Apr 2016.

Rummel, R.J. 1992. *Democide: Nazi Genocide and Mass Murder.* Rutgers, NJ: Transaction Publisher.

————. 1994. *Death by Government.* New Brunswick, NJ: Transaction.

————. 1997. *Statistics on Democide. Center on National Security and Law.* Charlottesville, VA: University of Virginia.

Runciman, David. 2014. The Stuntman. *London Review of Books* 36 (6): 21–25. http://www.lrb.co.uk/v36/n06/david-runciman/the-stuntman. Accessed 29 June 2016.

Rutan, Burt. n.d. Climate Change. http://www.liquisearch.com/burt_rutan/climate_change. Accessed 28 July 2016.

Salerno, Joseph T. 2010 [1998]. Beyond Calculational Chaos: Sound Money and the Quest for Economic Order in Ex-Communist Europe. In *Money: Sound and Unsound,* 467–496. Auburn, AL: Ludwig von Mises Institute.

————. 2015. How Reducing GDP Increases Economic Growth. Mises Daily. January 2. https://mises.org/library/how-reducing-gdp-increases-economic-growth. Accessed 17 Aug 2015.

Salter, Alexander W., and Peter T. Leeson. 2014. Celestial Anarchy: A Threat to Outer Space Commerce? *Cato Journal* 34 (3): 581–596. http://object.cato.org/sites/cato.org/files/serials/files/cato-journal/2014/9/cj34n3-8.pdf.

Sample, Ian. 2015. Nasa Scientists Find Evidence of Flowing Water on Mars. September 28. http://www.theguardian.com/science/2015/sep/28/nasa-scientists-find-evidence-flowing-water-mars. Accessed 25 Aug 2016.

Sanger, David E., and Rick Gladstone. 2015. Piling Sand in a Disputed Sea, China Literally Gains Ground. April 8. http://www.nytimes.com/2015/04/09/

world/asia/new-images-show-china-literally-gaining-ground-in-south-china-sea.html?_r=0. Accessed 11 Dec 2015.

Sato, Isao, et al. 2014. A 3-D Shape Model of (704) Interamnia from Its Occultations and Lightcurves. *Scientific Research—An Academic Publisher.* March. http://www.scirp.org/journal/PaperInformation.aspx?paperID=43533. Accessed 29 July 2015.

Savas, E.S. 1979. Refuse Collection: A Critical Review of the Evidence. *Journal of Urban Analysis.* 6: 1–13.

———. 1987. *Privatization.* Chatham, NJ: Chatham House Publishers.

Say, Jean-Baptiste. 1821. *Letters to Mr. Malthus.* https://mises.org/library/letters-mr-malthus.

Schirber, Michael. 2009. Hiding from Jupiter's Radiation. *Astrobiology Magazine.* January 19. http://www.astrobio.net/news-exclusive/hiding-from-jupiters-radiation/. Accessed 2 Dec 2015.

Schlenoff, Daniel C. 2011. Amundsen Becomes First to Reach South Pole, December 14, 1911. December 4. http://www.scientificamerican.com/article/south-pole-discovered-december-14-1911/.

Schmidtz, David. 1991. *The Limits of Government: An Essay on the Public Goods Argument.* Boulder, CO: Westview Press.

Schoeck, Helmut. 1966. *Envy: A Theory of Social Behavior.* New York: Harcourt Brace and World.

Schombert, James. 2015. Relativity. *Cosmology.* http://abyss.uoregon.edu/~js/cosmo/lectures/lec06.html. Accessed 8 July 2015.

Schumpeter, Joseph A. 1942. *Capitalism, Socialism and Democracy.* New York: Harper.

Sechrest, Larry. 2003. Privateering and National Defense: Naval Warfare for Private Profit. In *The Myth of National Defense: Essays on the Theory and History of Security Production,* ed. Hans-Hermann Hoppe, 239–274. Auburn, AL: The Ludwig von Mises Institute.

———. 2004a. Public Goods and Private Solutions in Maritime History. *The Quarterly Journal of Austrian Economics* 7 (2): 3–27. http://www.mises.org/journals/qjae/pdf/qjae7_2_1.pdf; https://dev.mises.org/journals/qjae/pdf/qjae7_2_1.pdf. Accessed 23 Apr 2016.

———. 2004b. Private Provision of Public Goods: Theoretical Issues and Some Examples from Maritime History. *ICFAI Journal of Public Finance* II (3): 45–73. http://www.mises.org/journals/scholar/Sechrest7.pdf. Accessed 23 Apr 2016.

———. 2007. Privately Funded and Built U.S. Warships in the Quasi-War of 1797–1801. *The Independent Review* 12 (1): 101–113.

Selgin, George A. 1988. Praxeology and Understanding: An Analysis of the Controversy in Austrian Economics. *Review of Austrian Economics* 2: 19–58; and Praxeology and Understanding, Auburn, AL: Ludwig von Mises Institute, 1990.

Selick, Karen. 2014. Housing Rights Case Illustrates Why Positive Rights Are Phony Rights. *National Post*. December 29. http://business.financialpost. com/2014/12/29/housing-rights-case-illustrates-why-positive-rights-are-phoney-rights/. Accessed 20 Apr 2016.

Seligman, Courtney. n.d. Planetary Magnetic Fields and Metallic Hydrogen. *Online Astronomy eText: The Planets*. http://cseligman.com/text/planets/ metallichydrogen.htm. Accessed 7 Dec 2015.

Sennholz, Hans F. 2001. The Envy Tax. August 1. https://mises.org/library/ envy-tax. Accessed 13 Dec 2015.

———. 2006. Milton Friedman, 1912–2006. December 16. http://mises.org/ story/2414.

Settlement of Claim Between Canada and the Union of Soviet Socialist Republics for Damage Caused by "Cosmos 954", 1981. April 2. http://www. jaxa.jp/library/space_law/chapter_3/3-2-2-1_e.html.

Sharp, Tim. 2014. SpaceShipOne: The First Private Spacecraft | The Most Amazing Flying Machines Ever. October 2. http://www.space.com/16769-spaceshipone-first-private-spacecraft.html. Accessed 28 July 2016.

Shaw, George Bernard. 1903. *Man and Superman*. "The Revolutionist's Handbook"—Maxims for Revolutionists—Idolatry.

Shugart, William F., II. 1987. Don't Revise the Clayton Act, Scrap It! *Cato Journal* 6: 925.

Simberg, R. 2012. Homesteading the Final Frontier: A Practical Proposal for Securing Property Rights in Space. *Competitive Enterprise Institute*, Issue Analysis No. 3.

Simmons, Randy, and Kreuter, Urs P. 1989. Herd Mentality: Banning Ivory Sales Is No Way to Save the Elephant. *Policy Review* (50): 46–49. http:// agrilifecdn.tamu.edu/kreuter/files/2013/01/Simmons-Kreuter-1989_3.pdf. Accessed 11 June 2016.

Simon, Julian. 1981. *The Ultimate Resource*. Princeton: Princeton University Press.

———, 1990. The Unreported Revolution in Population Economics. *The Public Interest* Fall: 89–100.

———. 1996. *The Ultimate Resource II*. Princeton University Press.

Simons, Robert. 2013. The Business of Business Schools: Restoring a Focus on Competing to Win. *Capitalism and Society* 8 (1): Art. 2. http://www.hbs.edu/faculty/publication%20files/cap%20and%20soc%20simons_054781c5-4cd0-4c99-bf9e-94cebf404a8d.pdf. Accessed 8 June 2016.

Skousen, Mark. 2001. *The Making of Modern Economics*. New York: M. E. Sharpe.

Smith, Adam. 1979 [1776]. *An Inquiry into the Nature and Causes of the Wealth of Nations*. Indianapolis, IN: Liberty Fund.

Smith, Jr., Fred L. 1983. Why Not Abolish Antitrust? *Regulation*, Jan–Feb, 2.

Solomon, L.D. 2012. *The Privatization of Space Exploration: Business, Technology, Law and Policy*. New Brunswick, NJ: Transaction Publishers.

Sowell, Thomas. 1983. *The Economics and Politics of Race: An International Perspective*. New York: Morrow.

———. 2000. Wake Up, Parents! *Jewish World Review*. August 18. http://www.jewishworldreview.com/cols/sowell081800.asp. Accessed 14 Dec 2015.

Space Safety. 2016. New Chart of Space Incidents and Close Calls. *Space Safety Magazine*. April 12. http://www.spacesafetymagazine.com/space-disasters/new-chart-space-incidents-close-calls/. Accessed 7 July 2016.

Spooner, Lysander. 1966 [1870]. *No Treason: The Constitution of No Authority and A Letter to Thomas F. Bayard*. Larkspur, CO: Rampart College. http://jim.com/treason.htm. Accessed 23 Aug 2016.

Sprague, Irving H. 2000. *Bailout: An Insider's Account of Bank Failures and Rescues*. Beard Books. http://www.amazon.com/Bailout-Insiders-Account-Failures-Rescues/dp/1587980177.

Statista. 2016. Countries with the Largest Number of Prisoners per 100,000 of the National Population, as of April 2016. http://www.statista.com/statistics/262962/countries-with-the-most-prisoners-per-100-000-inhabitants/. Accessed 10 Aug 2016.

Steele, David Ramsay. 1981. Posing the Problem: The Impossibility of Economic Calculation Under Socialism. *The Journal of Libertarian Studies* V (1): 7–22. http://www.mises.org/journals/jls/5_1/5_1_2.pdf. Accessed 29 June 2016.

———. 1992. *From Marx to Mises: Post Capitalist Society and the Challenge of Economic Calculation*. La Salle, IL: Open Court.

Steigerwald, Bill. 2015. NASA's LRO Discovers Lunar Hydrogen More Abundant on Moon's Pole-Facing Slopes. July 30. http://www.nasa.gov/content/goddard/lro-lunar-hydrogen. Accessed 26 Apr 2016.

Steinhart, Dan. 2014. How the Tea Party Caused a Plane Crash. June 13. https://www.caseyresearch.com/articles/how-the-tea-party-caused-a-plane-crash. Accessed 29 June 2016.

Stephens, Joe, and Carol D. Leonnig. 2011. Solyndra: Politics Infused Obama Energy Programs. December 25. http://www.washingtonpost.com/solyndra-politics-infused-obama-energy-programs/2011/12/14/gIQA4HllHP_story.html. Accessed 11 July 2015.

Stigler, George J. 1958. Ricardo and the 93 Per Cent Labor Theory of Value. *American Economic Review* 48 (June): 357–367.

Stimers, Paul. 2015. One Small Step for Man, One Giant Leap for Law. *Wall Street Journal*: A15. December 7. http://www.wsj.com/articles/one-small-step-for-man-one-giant-leap-for-law-1449444596. Accessed 13 Dec 2015.

Stinson, Liz. 2016. A Map of Mars That's Perfect for Everyday Earthlings. *Wired*. February 26. https://www.wired.com/2016/02/map-mars-thats-perfect-everyday-earthlings/. Accessed 2 Oct 2016.

Stockman, David, 2014. If the U.S. Had Stayed Out of WWI, There Would Have Been No Hitler or Stalin. July 13. http://libertycrier.com/u-s-stayed-wwi-hitler-stalin-david-stockman/#SgprliBV9jCVSFcb.99; http://libertycrier.com/u-s-stayed-wwi-hitler-stalin-david-stockman/?utm_source=feedburner&utm_medium=feed&utm_campaign=Feed%3A+LibertyCrier+%28Liberty+Crier%29.

Stockton, Nick. 2015. Congress Says Yes to Space Mining; No to Rocket Regulations. November 18. http://www.wired.com/2015/11/congress-says-yes-to-space-mining-no-to-rocket-regulations/. Accessed 13 Dec 2015.

Strauss, Mark L., and David Wegener. 2000. The Inclusive Language Debate, How Should The Bible Be Translated Today? Statement DI401. *Christian Research Journal* 22 (4).

Stringham, Edward. 1998–1999. Justice Without Government. *Journal of Libertarian Studies* 14 (1): 53–77.

———, ed. 2007. *Anarchy and the Law: The Political Economy of Choice.* Somerset, NJ: Transaction Publishers.

———. 2015. *Private Governance: Creating Order in Economic and Social Life.* New York: Oxford University Press.

Strow, Brian Kent, and Claudia Wood Strow. 2013. Gross Actual Product: Why GDP Fosters Increased Government Spending and Should Be Replaced. *The Journal of Private Enterprise* 29 (1): 53–71.

Tannehill, Morris, and Linda Tannehill. 1984 [1970]. *The Market for Liberty.* New York: Laissez Faire Books. http://www.lewrockwell.com/orig11/tannehill1.html. Accessed 23 Aug 2016.

Taylor, Allen. 2014. World War I in Photos: Technology. *The Atlantic.* http://www.theatlantic.com/static/infocus/wwi/wwitech/. Regarding Gas see Photos: 9, 13, 22, 28, 37, 38, and 39. Accessed 21 Oct 2015.

Terzian, Sevan G. 2006. 'Science World,' High School Girls, and the Prospect of Scientific Careers, 1957–1963. *History of Education Quarterly* 46 (1): 73–99. http://www.jstor.org/stable/20462031?seq=1#page_scan_tab_contents. Accessed 23 May 2016.

Thatcher, Margaret. 1976. Interview for *Thames TV*, February 5.

The Transcontinental Railroad. 2012. *A History of Railroad Technology*. Standardization of American Rail Gauge. http://railroad.lindahall.org/essays/rails-guage.html. Accessed 18 May 2017.

The Young Turks. 2016. Police Force Muslim Woman to Strip at Beach. August 24. https://www.youtube.com/watch?v=3kJcFYsxW4Y. Accessed 1 Sep 2016.

Thompson, David W. 2016. CEO's Welcome. https://www.orbitalatk.com/about/ceos-welcome. Accessed 11 June 2016.

Thoreau, Henry David. 1849. *Civil Disobedience*. https://en.wikisource.org/wiki/Aesthetic_Papers/Resistance_to_Civil_Government. Accessed 21 Oct 2015.

Thornton, Mark. 1999. The Government's Great Flood. September, 17 (9). http://www.mises.org/freemarket_detail.asp?control=8&sortorder=articled ate.

Tinsley, Patrick. 1998–1999. With Liberty and Justice for All: A Case for Private Police. *Journal of Libertarian Studies* 14 (1): 95–100. http://www.mises.org/journals/jls/14_1/14_1_5.pdf. Accessed 23 Aug 2016.

Tooley, T. Hunt. 2014. World War I in Our Minds: A Historical View. October 23. https://www.lewrockwell.com/2014/10/t-hunt-tooley/the-evil-of-wwi/.

Treaty on Principles Governing the Activities of States in the Exploration and Use of Outer Space, Including the Moon and Other Celestial Bodies. 1996. United Nations General Assembly Resolution 2222 (XXI), December 19.

Trefil, James. 2012. *Space Atlas*. Washington, DC: National Geographic Society.

Tucker, Jeffrey. 1998a. Controversy: Are Antitrust Laws Immoral? *Journal of Markets & Morality* 1 (1): 75–82.

———. 1998b. Controversy: Are Antitrust Laws Immoral? A Response to Kenneth G. Elzinga. *Journal of Markets & Morality* 1 (1): 90–94.

Tullock, Gordon. 1996. Comment on 'Roads, Bridges, Sunlight and Private Property', by Walter E. Block and Matthew Block. *Journal des Economistes et des Etudes Humaines* 7 (4): 589–592.

U.N. General Assembly. 1962a. *Declaration of Legal Principles Governing the Activities of States in the Exploration and Use of Outer Space*. http://www.unoosa.org/oosa/en/ourwork/spacelaw/treaties/introouterspacetreaty.html. Accessed 8 June 2016.

————. 1962b. Treaty on Principles Governing the Activities of States in the Exploration and Use of Outer Space, Including the Moon and Other Celestial Bodies. http://www.unoosa.org/oosa/en/ourwork/spacelaw/treaties/intro-outerspacetreaty.html. Accessed 8 June 2016.

U.S. Commercial Space Launch Competitiveness Act (USCSLCA). 2015. https://www.congress.gov/bill/114th-congress/house-bill/2262/text. H.R.2262. Accessed 13 Dec 2015.

United Nations. 2002. Treaties and Principles on Outer Space. United Nations Publication Sales No. E.02.I.20 ISBN 92-1-100900-6. http://www.unoosa.org/pdf/publications/STSPACE11E.pdf. Accessed 3 Aug 2015.

————. n.d. United Nations Convention on the Law of the Sea (UNCLOS). http://www.un.org/depts/los/convention_agreements/texts/unclos/unclos_e.pdf. Accessed 8 June 2016.

United Nations Office for Outer Space Affairs. 1979. Moon Agreement. http://www.unoosa.org/oosa/en/ourwork/spacelaw/treaties/intromoon-agreement.html.

United to End Genocide. 2015. Past Genocides and Mass Atrocities. http://endgenocide.org/learn/past-genocides/. Accessed 23 June 2015.

University of California Museum of Paleontology. 2007. *Asteroids and Dinosaurs: Unexpected Twists and an Unfinished Story*. Berkeley: Regents of the University of California. http://undsci.berkeley.edu/lessons/pdfs/alvarez_woflow.pdf. Accessed 16 Nov 2015.

Unreal. 2016. Field Trip to Mars: Framestore's Shared VR Experience Delivered with Unreal Engine 4. August. 15. https://www.youtube.com/watch?v=e0XNlsXnKp0. Accessed 1 Sep 2016.

UOH. 2002. University of Hawaii. Ham Club. Balloon Lift with Lighter than Air Gases. May. http://www.chem.hawaii.edu/uham/lift.html. Accessed 20 Apr 2016.

Valoy, Patricia. 2014. 6 Reasons Why STEM Outreach Is a Feminist Issue. April 18. http://everydayfeminism.com/2014/04/stem-outreach-feminist-issue/. Accessed 23 May 2016.

Vance, Laurence. 2005. The Curse of the Withholding Tax. April 21. http://www.mises.org/story/1797.

Vance, Laurence M. 1996. Friedman's Mistake. *The Free Market* 14 (11). http://www.mises.org/freemarket_detail.asp?control=158&sortorder=articledate.

————. 2010. Same Empire, Different Emperor. February 11. http://www.lewrockwell.com/vance/vance195.html. Accessed 28 July 2016.

Vaughan, Diane. 1996. *The Challenger Launch Decision: Risky Technology, Culture, and Deviance at NASA*. Chicago: University of Chicago Press.

Vaughn, Karen I. 1978. John Locke and the Labor Theory of Value. *The Journal of Libertarian Studies* 2 (4): 311–325.

Virgin Galactic. 2015. http://www.virgingalactic.com/. Accessed 9 Nov 2015.

Vlasic, Ivan A. 1967. The Space Treaty: A Preliminary Evaluation. *California Law Review* 55 (2): 507–519.

Von Braun, Wernher. 1961. Letter to Vice President Lyndon Baines Johnson. April 29. http://history.msfc.nasa.gov/vonbraun/documents/vp_ljohnson.pdf. Accessed 6 Nov 2015.

Von Mises, Ludwig. 1944. *Bureaucracy*. New Haven: Yale University Press.

———. 1947. *Planned Chaos*. Auburn: The Mises Institute. https://mises.org/library/planned-chaos. Accessed 21 Mar 2016.

———. 1969. *Theory and History: An Interpretation of Social and Economic Evolution*. New Rochelle, NY: Arlington House.

———. 1977. *A Critique of Interventionism*. New Rochelle, NY: Arlington House. http://www.mises.org/etexts/mises/interventionism/contents.asp.

———. 1978. *The Clash of Group Interests and Other Essays*. New York: Center for Libertarian Studies. http://www.mises.org/etexts/mises/clash/clash.asp.

———. 1981 [1922]. *Socialism: An Economic and Sociological Analysis*. Trans. J. Kahane. Indianapolis: Liberty Fund. http://mises.org/books/socialism/contents.aspx.

———. 1998 [1949]. *Human Action: The Scholar's Edition*. Auburn, AL: The Mises Institute. http://www.mises.org/humanaction.asp.

Vuk, Vedran. 2006a. Journalism and Underwater Basket Weaving. June 21. http://www.lewrockwell.com/orig6/vuk5.html.

———. 2006b. Socialist Man in the Big Easy. September 25. http://www.lewrockwell.com/vuk/socialist-man-no.html;   http://www.mises.org/story/2319.

Wapshott, Nicholas. 2012. A Lovefest Between Milton Friedman and J.M. Keynes. July 30. http://www.thedailybeast.com/articles/2012/07/30/nicholas-wapshott-a-lovefest-between-milton-friedman-and-j-mkeynes.html.

Walker, Michael A., ed. 1988. *Privatization: Tactics and Techniques*. Vancouver, Canada: The Fraser Institute.

Wall, Mike. 2013. Plastic Could Protect Astronauts from Deep-Space Radiation. *Space.com*. June 14. http://www.space.com/21561-space-exploration-radiation-protection-plastic.html. Accessed 23 Nov 2015.

————. 2014. NASA's Asteroid-Capture Mission May Test New Method to Defend Earth. *Space.com*. May 16. http://www.space.com/25897-asteroid-deflection-enhanced-gravity-tractor.html. Accessed 30 July 2015.

Walmsley, Roy. 2010. World Prison Population List. 9th ed. http://www.idcr.org.uk/wp-content/uploads/2010/09/WPPL-9-22.pdf. Accessed 21 Nov 2015.

Walter, Eugene. 1969. *Terror and Resistance, A Study of Political Violence*. New York: Oxford University Press.

Warhaft, Z. 1997. *The Engine and the Atmosphere: An Introduction to Engineering*. Cambridge and New York: Cambridge University Press.

Washington, George. 1796. Farewell Address. http://oll.libertyfund.org/quote/246. Accessed 28 July 2016.

Washington Animal Trafficking. 2015. https://ballotpedia.org/Washington_Animal_Trafficking,_Initiative_1401_(2015).

Watner, Carl. 1982. The Proprietary Theory of Justice in the Libertarian Tradition. *Journal of Libertarian Studies* 6 (3–4): 289–316. http://mises.org/journals/jls/6_3/6_3_6.pdf. Accessed 23 Apr 2016.

Weeden, B., and B. Baseley-Walker. 2010. Verification in Space: Theories, Realities, and Possibilities. *Disarmament Forum* 3: 39–50.

Weeden, B.C., and Tiffany Chow. 2012. Taking a Common-Pool Resources Approach to Space Sustainability: A Framework and Potential Policies. *Space Policy* 28 (3): 166–172. http://www.sciencedirect.com/science/article/pii/S0265964612000604.

Welch, Matt. 2011. Creation Myth: Governments Are Worse than No Good at 'Creating Jobs.' November. http://reason.com/archives/2011/10/10/creation-myth?utm_source=feedburner&utm_medium=feed&utm_campaign=Feed%3A+reason%2FArticles+%28Reason+Online+-+All+Articles+%28exce pt+Hit+%26+Run+blog%29%29. Accessed 11 July 2015.

Wenzel, Robert. 2012. How Milton Friedman Helped Make the Case for Big Government. August 9. http://www.economicpolicyjournal.com/2012/08/how-milton-friedman-helped-make-case.html.

————. 2013. Robert Ringer's Strawman Anarchist. February 2. http://archive.lewrockwell.com/wenzel/wenzel211.html. Accessed 23 Aug 2016.

————. 2016. Walter Block on the Intellectual War Path. April 25. http://www.economicpolicyjournal.com/2016/04/walter-block-on-intellectual-war-path.html?utm_source=feedburner&utm_medium=email&utm_campaign=Feed%3A+economicpolicyjournal%2FKpwH+%28EconomicPolicyJournal.com%29. Accessed 11 June 2016.

Wheeler, Joshua. 2014. Failure to Launch: How New Mexico Is Paying for Richard Branson's Space Tourism Fantasy. March 20. http://www.buzzfeed.com/jgwheel/failure-to-launch-how-new-mexico-is-paying-for-richard-brans#.sel3ryvP8. Accessed 29 June 2016.

White, Lawrence H. 1978. Privatization of Municipally-Provided Services. *The Journal of Libertarian Studies* 2 (2): 187–197.

White, W. N., Jr. 1997. Real Property Rights in Outer Space. *40th Colloquium on the Law of Outer Space*. www.spacesettlementinstitute.org/Articles/research_library/WayneWhite98-2.pdf.

———. 2000. Implications of a Proposal for Real Property Rights in Outer Space. *Proceedings of the 42nd Colloquium on the Law of Outer Space*. www.spacefuture.com/archive/implications_of_a_proposal_for_real_property_rights_in_ outer_space.shtml.

White, W.N., Jr. 2002. The Legal Regime for Private Activities in Outer Space. In *Space: The Free-Market Frontier*, ed. E.L. Hudgins, 83–111. Washington: Cato Institute.

White, W. N., Jr. 2003. Interpreting Article II of the Outer Space Treaty. Paper presented at the 54th International Astronautical Conference.

Whiteway, J.A., et al. 2009. Mars Water-Ice Clouds and Precipitation. *Science* 325 (5936): 68–70. http://www.sciencemag.org/content/325/5936/68.short.

Wilcke, Richard R. 1999. An Appropriate Ethical Model for Business, and a Critique of Milton Friedman. http://mises.org/journals/scholar/Ethics.PDF.

Williams, Walter E. 1999. Population Control Nonsense. *Jewish World Review*; February 24. http://www.jewishworldreview.com/cols/williams022499.asp. Accessed 10 Aug 2016.

Williams, Joan C. 2015a. The 5 Biases Pushing Women Out of STEM. *Harvard Business Review*. March 24. https://hbr.org/2015/03/the-5-biases-pushing-women-out-of-stem.

Williams, Matt. 2015b. Meet Eris, The Solar System's Largest Dwarf Planet. *Universe Today*. 5–30. http://io9.com/meet-eris-the-solar-systems-largest-dwarf-planet-1707948972. Accessed 27 July 2015.

Williams, David R. 2016a. NASA, Space Science Data Coordinated Archive. Planetary Fact Sheets. National Aeronautics and Space Administration. February 29. http://nssdc.gsfc.nasa.gov/planetary/factsheet/uranusfact.html; http://nssdc.gsfc.nasa.gov/planetary/factsheet/saturnfact.html. Accessed 18 Apr 2016.

Williams, Walter. 2016b. Rights Versus Wishes. April 20. https://www.lewrockwell.com/2016/04/walter-e-williams/rights-vs-wishes/. Accessed 20 Apr 2016.

Williams, Joan C., Katherine W. Phillips, and Erika V. Hall. 2014. Double Jeopardy? Gender Bias Against Women of Color in Science. http://www. uchastings.edu/news/articles/2015/01/double-jeopardy-report.pdf. Accessed 23 May 2016.

Winsor, Dorothy A. 1988. Communication Failures Contributing to the Challenger Accident: An Example of for Technical Communicators. *Professional Communication, IEEE Transactions on* 31 (3): 101–107.

Wintour, Patrick. 2015. UK Should Begin Decriminalising Drugs, Say Richard Branson and Nick Clegg. March 3. http://www.theguardian.com/politics/2015/mar/03/uk-should-begin-decriminalising-drugs-richard-branson-nick-clegg. Accessed 29 June 2016.

Wiśniewski, Jakub Bożydar. 2014. Defense as a Private Good in a Competitive Order. *Review of Social and Economic Issues* 1 (1): 2–35. http://rsei.rau.ro/images/V1N1/Jakub%20Bozydar%20Wisniewski.pdf. Accessed 27 Apr 2016.

Wittman, Donald. 2000. The Wealth and Size of Nations. *Journal of Conflict Resolution.* 44 (6): 868–884.

WND. 2014. IRS Seizes Life Savings for Deposits Under $10,000, Money Confiscated Even Though No Crime Committed. *WND Weekly.* 10/27. http://www.wnd.com/2014/10/irs-seizes-life-savings-for-deposits-under-10000/. Accessed 25 June 2015.

WNET. 2008. Marco Polo's Journey. October 30. http://www.wliw.org/marco-polo/2008/10/30/timeline-marco-polos-journey/. Accessed 25 Aug 2015.

Wollstein, Jarret B. 1969. Society Without Coercion. In *Society Without Government.* New York: Arno Press.

Woods, Tom. 2010. *Nullification: How to Resist Federal Tyranny in the 21st Century.* Washington, DC: Regnery Publishing.

———. 2013. The Question Libertarians Just Can't Answer. June 5. http://lewrockwell.com/woods/woods237.html. Accessed 29 June 2016.

———. 2014. Four Things the State Is Not. July 29. http://www.lewrockwell.com/2014/07/no_author/4-things-the-state-is-not/. Accessed 23 Aug 2016.

Woolridge, William C. 1970. *Uncle Sam the Monopoly Man.* New Rochelle, NY: Arlington House.

Worstall, Tim. 2013. But Why Did Julian Simon Win the Paul Ehrlich Bet? January 13. http://www.forbes.com/sites/timworstall/2013/01/13/but-why-did-julian-simon-win-the-paul-ehrlich-bet/.

Wu, Kane. 2015. South China Sea Work Dredges Up Questions, Delays Planned IPO. November 27. http://www.wsj.com/articles/chinese-dredger-delays-ipo-over-questions-about-island-building-1448623226. Accessed 11 Dec 2015.

Wynn, Todd and Steve Lafleur. 2009. A Free Market Perspective on Electric Vehicles. October. http://cascadepolicy.org/pdf/env/FMPonElecVehicles_100109a.pdf. Accessed 23 May 2016.

Ye He Lee, Michelle. 2015. Does the United States Really Have 5 Percent of the World's Population and One Quarter of the World's Prisoners? *Fact Checker, The Washington Post*. April 30. http://www.washingtonpost.com/blogs/fact-checker/wp/2015/04/30/does-the-united-states-really-have-five-percent-of-worlds-population-and-one-quarter-of-the-worlds-prisoners/. Accessed 24 June 2015.

Zak, Anatoly. 2007. People: Korolev. *RussianSpaceWeb.com*. January 12. http://www.russianspaceweb.com/korolev.html. Accessed 1 Dec 2015.

Zakaria, Fareed. 2015. Why America's Obsession with STEM Education Is Dangerous. March 26. https://www.washingtonpost.com/opinions/why-stem-wont-make-us-successful/2015/03/26/5f4604f2-d2a5-11e4-ab77-9646eea6a4c7_story.html. Accessed 23 May 2016.

Zeeberg, Amos. 2011. How to Avoid Repeating the Debacle That Was the Space Shuttle; It Promised the Moon but Delivered Low Earth Orbit at Exorbitant Cost. And It's Partly Your Fault. July 22. http://discovermagazine.com/2011/jul-aug/22-how-to-avoid-repeating-debacle-of-space-shuttle. Accessed 23 May 2016.

Zimmerman, Kim. 2012a. Callisto: Facts About Jupiter's Dead Moon. Space. *com*. February 13. http://www.space.com/16448-callisto-facts-about-jupi-ters-dead-moon.html. Accessed 19 Nov 2015.

———. 2012b. Io: Facts About Jupiter's Volcanic Moon. Space.*com*. July 3. http://www.space.com/16419-io-facts-about-jupiters-volcanic-moon.html. Accessed 20 Nov 2015.

———. 2014. Ganymede: Facts About Jupiter's Largest Moon. *Space.com*. February 13. http://www.space.com/16440-ganymede-facts-about-jupiters-largest-moon.html. Accessed 19 Nov 2015.

Zolfagharifard, Ellie. 2015. Two Earth-like Planets Could Be Hiding Close to Our Solar System—And Scientists Say There May Be Watery Worlds Nearby. March 27. http://www.dailymail.co.uk/sciencetech/article-3015308/Two-Earth-like-planets-hiding-close-solar-scientists-say-watery-worlds-nearby. html.

Zubrin, Robert. 2011. *The Case for Mars, The Plan to Settle the Red Planet and Why We Must*. New York: Free Press, Simon & Schuster.

Index[1]

---

[1] Note: Page numbers followed by 'n' refer to notes.

© The Author(s) 2018
P. L. Nelson, W. E. Block, *Space Capitalism*, Palgrave Studies in Classical Liberalism,
https://doi.org/10.1007/978-3-319-74651-7